Metaphor in European Philosophy after Nietzsche
An Intellectual History

LEGENDA

LEGENDA is the Modern Humanities Research Association's book imprint for new research in the Humanities. Founded in 1995 by Malcolm Bowie and others within the University of Oxford, Legenda has always been a collaborative publishing enterprise, directly governed by scholars. The Modern Humanities Research Association (MHRA) joined this collaboration in 1998, became half-owner in 2004, in partnership with Maney Publishing and then Routledge, and has since 2016 been sole owner. Titles range from medieval texts to contemporary cinema and form a widely comparative view of the modern humanities, including works on Arabic, Catalan, English, French, German, Greek, Italian, Portuguese, Russian, Spanish, and Yiddish literature. Editorial boards and committees of more than 60 leading academic specialists work in collaboration with bodies such as the Society for French Studies, the British Comparative Literature Association and the Association of Hispanists of Great Britain & Ireland.

The MHRA encourages and promotes advanced study and research in the field of the modern humanities, especially modern European languages and literature, including English, and also cinema. It aims to break down the barriers between scholars working in different disciplines and to maintain the unity of humanistic scholarship. The Association fulfils this purpose through the publication of journals, bibliographies, monographs, critical editions, and the MHRA Style Guide, and by making grants in support of research. Membership is open to all who work in the Humanities, whether independent or in a University post, and the participation of younger colleagues entering the field is especially welcomed.

ALSO PUBLISHED BY THE ASSOCIATION

Critical Texts
Tudor and Stuart Translations • *New Translations* • *European Translations*
MHRA Library of Medieval Welsh Literature

MHRA Bibliographies
Publications of the Modern Humanities Research Association

The Annual Bibliography of English Language & Literature
Austrian Studies
Modern Language Review
Portuguese Studies
The Slavonic and East European Review
Working Papers in the Humanities
The Yearbook of English Studies

www.mhra.org.uk
www.legendabooks.com

STUDIES IN COMPARATIVE LITERATURE

Editorial Committee
Chairs: Dr Emily Finer (University of St Andrews)
and Professor Wen-chin Ouyang (SOAS, London)

Dr Ross Forman (University of Warwick)
Professor Angus Nicholls (Queen Mary, University of London)
Dr Henriette Partzsch (University of Glasgow)
Dr Ranka Primorac (University of Southampton)

Studies in Comparative Literature are produced in close collaboration with the British Comparative Literature Association, and range widely across comparative and theoretical topics in literary and translation studies, accommodating research at the interface between different artistic media and between the humanities and the sciences.

ALSO PUBLISHED IN THIS SERIES

20. *Aestheticism and the Philosophy of Death: Walter Pater and Post-Hegelianism*, by Giles Whiteley
21. *Blake, Lavater and Physiognomy*, by Sibylle Erle
22. *Rethinking the Concept of the Grotesque: Crashaw, Baudelaire, Magritte*, by Shun-Liang Chao
23. *The Art of Comparison: How Novels and Critics Compare*, by Catherine Brown
24. *Borges and Joyce: An Infinite Conversation*, by Patricia Novillo-Corvalán
25. *Prometheus in the Nineteenth Century: From Myth to Symbol*, by Caroline Corbeau-Parsons
26. *Architecture, Travellers and Writers: Constructing Histories of Perception*, by Anne Hultzsch
27. *Comparative Literature in Britain: National Identities, Transnational Dynamics 1800-2000*, by Joep Leerssen
28. *The Realist Author and Sympathetic Imagination*, by Sotirios Paraschas
29. *Iris Murdoch and Elias Canetti: Intellectual Allies*, by Elaine Morley
30. *Likenesses: Translation, Illustration, Interpretation*, by Matthew Reynolds
31. *Exile and Nomadism in French and Hispanic Women's Writing*, by Kate Averis
32. *Samuel Butler against the Professionals: Rethinking Lamarckism 1860–1900*, by David Gillott
33. *Byron, Shelley, and Goethe's Faust: An Epic Connection*, by Ben Hewitt
34. *Leopardi and Shelley: Discovery, Translation and Reception*, by Daniela Cerimonia
35. *Oscar Wilde and the Simulacrum: The Truth of Masks*, by Giles Whiteley
36. *The Modern Culture of Reginald Farrer: Landscape, Literature and Buddhism*, by Michael Charlesworth
37. *Translating Myth*, edited by Ben Pestell, Pietra Palazzolo and Leon Burnett
38. *Encounters with Albion: Britain and the British in Texts by Jewish Refugees from Nazism*, by Anthony Grenville
39. *The Rhetoric of Exile: Duress and the Imagining of Force*, by Vladimir Zorić
40. *From Puppet to Cyborg: Pinocchio's Posthuman Journey*, by Georgia Panteli
41. *Utopian Identities: A Cognitive Approach to Literary Competitions*, by Clementina Osti
43. *Sublime Conclusions: Last Man Narratives from Apocalypse to Death of God*, by Robert K. Weninger
44. *Arthur Symons: Poet, Critic, Vagabond*, edited by Elisa Bizzotto and Stefano Evangelista
45. *Scenographies of Perception: Sensuousness in Hegel, Novalis, Rilke, and Proust*, by Christian Jany
46. *Reflections in the Library: Selected Literary Essays 1926–1944*, by Antal Szerb
47. *Depicting the Divine: Mikhail Bulgakov and Thomas Mann*, by Olga G. Voronina
48. *Samuel Butler and the Science of the Mind: Evolution, Heredity and Unconscious Memory*, by Cristiano Turbil
49. *Death Sentences: Literature and State Killing*, edited by Birte Christ and Ève Morisi
50. *Words Like Fire: Prophecy and Apocalypse in Apollinaire, Marinetti and Pound*, by James P. Leveque

Metaphor in European Philosophy after Nietzsche

An Intellectual History

Andrew Hines

LEGENDA
Studies in Comparative Literature 54
Modern Humanities Research Association
2020

Published by Legenda
an imprint of the Modern Humanities Research Association
Salisbury House, Station Road, Cambridge CB1 2LA

ISBN 978-1-78188-428-7 (HB)
ISBN 978-1-78188-431-7 (PB)

First published 2020

All rights reserved. No part of this publication may be reproduced or disseminated or transmitted in any form or by any means, electronic, mechanical, photocopying, recording or otherwise, or stored in any retrieval system, or otherwise used in any manner whatsoever without written permission of the copyright owner, except in accordance with the provisions of the Copyright, Designs and Patents Act 1988, or under the terms of a licence permitting restricted copying issued in the UK by the Copyright Licensing Agency Ltd, Saffron House, 6–10 Kirby Street, London EC1N 8TS, England, or in the USA by the Copyright Clearance Center, 222 Rosewood Drive, Danvers MA 01923. Application for the written permission of the copyright owner to reproduce any part of this publication must be made by email to legenda@mhra.org.uk.

Disclaimer: Statements of fact and opinion contained in this book are those of the author and not of the editors or the Modern Humanities Research Association. The publisher makes no representation, express or implied, in respect of the accuracy of the material in this book and cannot accept any legal responsibility or liability for any errors or omissions that may be made.

Trademark notice: Product or corporate names may be trademarks or registered trademarks, and are used only for identification and explanation without intent to infringe.

© Modern Humanities Research Association 2020

Copy-Editor: Dr Nigel Hope

CONTENTS

	Acknowledgements	ix
	Note	xi
	Introduction	1
1	The Aristotelian Paradigm of Metaphor and its Evolution	31
2	The Watershed Moment: Nietzsche and the Reversal of the Aristotelian Paradigm of Metaphor	59
3	Martin Heidegger, Paul Ricoeur and Metaphor as Poetic Revelation	87
4	Likeness as Consensus: Hans Blumenberg and the Riddle of Metaphor	123
5	Jacques Derrida and the Undecidability of Metaphoric Meaning	155
	Conclusion	183
	Bibliography	193
	Index	203

ACKNOWLEDGEMENTS

This book grew out of two places; my time as a PhD student at Queen Mary University of London, and the two years immediately following, which culminated in the Covid-19 pandemic. As the period 2013–2020 contains events of immense personal importance, such as getting married and finishing a PhD, but also events such as the Brexit referendum, the election of Donald Trump, the killing of George Floyd and subsequent Black Lives Matter protests, and the global Covid-19 pandemic, it is fitting to reflect on those individuals and institutions who helped this project be realised and provided a thread of stability to the seemingly timeworn garment of the world.

For continually challenging me, and for their support and guidance during my PhD, I would first like to thank my former supervisors Professor Angus Nicholls and Professor Galin Tihanov. This book would not be possible without you. Thank you especially to Angus for 'climbing the mountain' of chapter two with me as well as introducing me to Blumenberg's phlosophy. Thanks especially go to Galin for challenging my argumentation and pushing me to find my own voice in the project. I would also like to thank my PhD examiners Professor Clive Cazeaux and Professor Andreas Musolff for the comments, questions and advice that assisted me in moving this work from thesis to book.

A significant portion of the research in this book, particularly chapters two and four, was carried out in the summer of 2015 when Professor Benjamin Specht very kindly hosted me at the University of Stuttgart and, through our conversations, prompted me to critically engage with nineteenth-century German philology. During this summer I also had the opportunity to spend time at the Deutsches Literatur Archiv Marbach. I would like to thank their staff for their assistance with Hans Blumenberg's *Nachlass*. In particular, I would like to thank Professor Bettina Blumenberg for her permission to use her father's short text on Nietzsche and metaphor which is published in chapter 4 of this book.

Many of the ideas in this book have been shaped by fellow scholars. Special thanks go to all those who debated, challenged and questioned me at the 2016 RaAM conference in Berlin and the 2017 Blumenberg seminar in Leipzig. I am particularly grateful to Professor Petra Gehring for her deeply thought-provoking comments in our correspondence on the concept of truth in both Nietzsche and Blumenberg. Also, to Professor Anne Sheppard for helping me understand the context surrounding figurative language in the Graeco-Roman world. To Professor Joseph Cohen for, all those years ago, helping me see that there was more to Derrida than the anglophone reception of Derrida and for his injunction to 'remain rigorous' about my interest in metaphor. Finally, to my friend and fellow scholar Dr Bart Zantvoort for our endless discussions on all things philosophical and European.

Acknowledgements

The experience of bringing this book together would not be possibly without the support of my editors at Legenda, Dr Graham Nelson, Dr Emily Finer and Professor Wen-chin Ouyang. Thank you for your kindness, guidance and rigour. Thank you also to Dr Nigel Hope for his eye for detail and patient guidance in editing the final manuscript, and to Dr Amanda Wrigley for her expert editing of the index. Also, to the anonymous editors out there: thank you for thinking that there was something worth seeing the light of day in these pages.

The global circumstances of the last few years bring home, perhaps more than ever, the fact that intellectual work is deeply dependent on everyday life and friends and family. To those who proofread either sections or the entirety of this book, such as Laura, Charlie and Oliver, thank you. My copy-editor would have had an even more difficult job had it not been for you. Thank you also to my family in the USA for the variety of ways that you supported my decision to take a break from consultancy and take the time to turn my ideas into a book. Finally, and above all, thank you to Helen for more things than I could say. But particularly for putting up with more than the occasional conversation about Nietzsche before 9 a.m.

A.H., London, August 2020

NOTE

As this book deals with European philosophy, many of the works presented here are translated from the language in which they were originally written. However, as this is a book written in English, if an English translation exists, the work is referred to by its English language title. The date given for texts, however, refers to the publication of the text in its original language and not in English translation, as we are concerned with the ideas presented in their intellectual-historical context. So, for example, Paul Ricoeur's *La métaphore vive* is referred to by its English translation *The Rule of Metaphor*, the date cited is its original publication in French, 1975, and not its first English translation in 1977.

The standard English language translations of texts and titles are used consistently throughout, unless no translation exists. In this case the translations are the author's own. So, for example, in the case of passages from Gustav Gerber's *Die Sprache als Kunst*, no English language translation exists. Therefore, the German original is initially quoted, followed by the author's translation.

References to ancient works use the standard forms of citation (e.g. Bekker numbers for Aristotle, book and section numbers for Cicero), which are given in the Loeb translations cited.

INTRODUCTION

Metaphor is a concept with a distinct history. Upon reading these words we may already have an objection. After all, in the wake of the work of George Lakoff and Mark Johnson, when we think about the term metaphor, we might think of how metaphor conditions concepts and not the other way around. As Lakoff and Johnson write in *Metaphors We Live By* (1980), 'Our ordinary conceptual system, in terms of which we both think and act, is fundamentally metaphorical in nature.'[1] Similarly, when the German philosopher Hans Blumenberg was asked to provide an entry on metaphor to the journal *Archive for the History of Concepts*, he suggested that an entry on metaphor should be a supplement to a history of concepts because metaphor itself was foundational in the construction and understanding of concepts.[2] This view of metaphor is one that has gone through a significant transformation since the classical definition, found in Aristotle, which states: 'a metaphor is the application of a word that belongs to another thing: either from genus to species, species to genus, species to species, or by analogy'.[3]

The variety of connotations that metaphor can evoke today in academic discourse reinforces this transition from the classical view of metaphor. The second edition of the *Encyclopedia of Language and Linguistics* (2006), for example, has not one but seven entries on metaphor. These include 'Metaphor and Conceptual Blending', 'Metaphor: Philosophical Theories', 'Metaphor: Psychological Aspects', 'Metaphor: Stylistic Approaches', 'Metaphors in English, French, and Spanish Medical Written Discourse', 'Metaphors in Political Discourse' and 'Metaphor, Grammatical'.[4] The relevance of metaphor to fields as diverse as philosophy, medicine and grammar points to an understanding that metaphor is a more fundamental phenomenon, as Lakoff and Johnson suggest, rather than simply 'the application of a word that belongs to another thing'.[5] It also points to an understanding that the transference function of metaphor, as seen in Aristotle's definition, has a more fundamental role to play in thought and in discourse than that of a simple linguistic transference.

Liddell and Scott's *A Greek–English Lexicon* notes that the Greek term used in Aristotle's definition, μεταφορά, has a more general meaning in Greek as '*transport, haulage or change*'. This more general meaning was reflected in Greek rhetoric in thinkers such as Isocrates, Aristotle and Epicurus, who used the term μεταφορά to mean the '*transference* of a word *to a new sense*'.[6] So when Aristotle cites the poet Empedocles, calling old age 'the evening of life', the word evening has been transferred from its meaning as a time of day and given a new sense in referring to old age.[7] We will discuss the classical conception of metaphor in greater depth in chapter 1, but one thing to bear in mind is that in Aristotle's definition of metaphor all the hallmarks of the 'standard view' of metaphor are conveyed. We are reminded by the *Routledge Encyclopedia of Philosophy* that one of the basic presuppositions of such a standard view is that 'there is a difference between literal and nonliteral language; that figurative speech is nonliteral language and that a metaphor is an instance of figurative speech'.[8] What constitutes the possibility of transference between the literal and non-literal is what Aristotle calls similarities or likeness when he writes that 'to use metaphor well is to discern similarities'.[9] The two aspects of metaphor in Aristotle's definition, transference and likeness are what we will call the Aristotelian paradigm of metaphor. As a key methodology of this book is intellectual-historical, one of our concerns will be how the Aristotelian paradigm is transformed to reflect the view that the linguistic operation described by Aristotle is in fact a fundamental phenomenon in thought and discourse. One of the first things that we must grasp in this book is that the reversal of roles between a metaphor and a concept, which we have already seen in Lakoff and Johnson, does not simply view the *role* of metaphor differently from how it was viewed in Aristotle's day, but the *concept* of metaphor itself. While metaphor may condition our concepts, metaphor has its own history in terms of how it has been conceived. In order to consider this, it is useful to make a heuristic distinction between the history of the theorisation of metaphor in western thought and the phenomenon of the use of a variety of different types of metaphors that all seem to rely on a similar act of transference. For our purposes, we are looking at the history of the theorisation of metaphor as a history of metaphor as a concept in its own right.

This is our first essential theme and attentiveness to it will help us understand our second essential theme: the way that the history of the concept of metaphor develops in European philosophy in the nineteenth and twentieth century reflects the transition from the Aristotelian paradigm of metaphor. Observing this shift presents us with a case study of the hermeneutic challenge that faces us today. Simply put, the swiftly changing landscape of political ideology in the West demands a fresh account of semantic shifts. These two seemingly disparate questions, concerning the history of the concept of metaphor and a contemporary account of semantic shifts, are linked because the focus in both post-Kantian European philosophy and cognitive linguistics is how meaning is created through metaphor not how meaning shifts. And yet, despite their differences, both of these traditions are two of the most common ways that one interprets the meaning of a metaphor in the humanities and frequently provide both an academic and public point of analysis for political metaphors. Therefore, to lay the groundwork for providing an adequate account of the type of semantic shifts seen in contemporary political metaphor, one must address a few critical episodes in the history of the West's conceptualisation of metaphor.

However, as the history of European philosophy is vast and we are attempting to provide a brief intellectual history, one of the ways we can observe both how the concept of metaphor changes from the Aristotelian paradigm and the way that change affects our interpretation of semantic shifts, is to zoom in on a pivot point. That pivot point will act as a measure by which we can better understand some of the key preoccupations in the evolution of the concept of metaphor in European philosophy. Here, we find as our case study the philosophy of Friedrich Nietzsche. This introduction will seek to show why Nietzsche's philosophy is so relevant for understanding the distinct concept of metaphor we are concerned with in this book as well as the interpretive challenges that concept of metaphor brings with it.

Nietzsche and the History of the Concept of Metaphor

Nietzsche's philosophy of metaphor constitutes a watershed moment in the history of how the West has understood metaphor conceptually. However, far from being a pivotal moment in the history of the concept of metaphor, Nietzsche's philosophy is often understood as providing a critique of metaphysical propositions, like the concept of truth, via metaphor. For example, Sarah Kofman's work *Nietzsche and Metaphor* (1983) asserts that:

> right from *The Birth of Tragedy* we can find in Nietzsche a generalized 'theory' of metaphor, based on the loss of the 'proper' in two senses. On the one hand there is no metaphor without a stripping away of individuality, without masquerade and metamorphosis [...] on the other hand metaphor is linked to the loss of the 'proper' understood as the 'essence' of the world, which is indecipherable and of which man can have only have representations which are quite 'improper.'[10]

However, as this book will maintain, one can also read in Nietzsche's philosophy a critique of the concept of metaphor itself.

In Aristotle, the meaning of a metaphor is grounded in truthlikeness. When the poet Empedocles calls old age 'the evening of life' the transference of the word 'evening' to its metaphorical application of old age is grounded in the likeness between the two.[11] In the same way as one's eyes grow dim in old age, the body slows down and moves towards the metaphorical 'sleep of death', in the evening, the light grows dim, the pace of the day slows down, and the human being goes to sleep. In the study of rhetoric, the two parts of metaphor are referred to as tenor and vehicle, while in cognitive linguistics they are referred to as the target domain and source domain respectively.[12] It is the link between the tenor and a vehicle that produces the meaning of the metaphor 'old age is the evening of life' and this link is referred to by Aristotle as likeness or similarity.[13] As we shall see in chapter 1, Aristotle's view of likeness, as it is posited in his description of *mimesis*, is in turn grounded by a conception of truthlikeness.[14] Therefore, the type of likeness that grounds the meaning of Empedocles' metaphor 'the evening of life' is a truth-like match between the tenor and vehicle of the metaphor.

In the case of Nietzsche, because he critiques metaphysical propositions, such as truth and truthlikeness, with metaphor, one can also find in him a critique of the traditional conception of metaphor itself. Why? Because the traditional conception of the meaning of a metaphor is grounded in the metaphysical proposition of truthlikeness. Therefore, Nietzsche's philosophy presents us with a fundamentally different conceptualisation of metaphor from the classical conceptualisation. For Nietzsche, metaphor is like the Roman god Janus: on the one hand, looking back to the origins of meaning and relativising them, and on the other hand looking forward to the horizons of human experience and pragmatically orienting cognition through providing stable, if ultimately relative, meanings. As we shall see in chapter 2, when Nietzsche poses his famous question, 'What, then, is truth?', he is not simply critiquing truth when he answers that truth is

> A mobile army of metaphors, metonymies, anthropomorphisms, in short a sum of human relations which have been subjected to poetic and rhetorical intensification, translation, and decoration, and which after they have been in use for a long time, strike a people as firmly established, canonical and binding.[15]

Rather than placing the origin of metaphoric meaning in an Aristotelian notion of truthlikeness, Nietzsche relativises the origin of metaphoric meaning by placing it in 'a sum of human relations'. However, he also asserts that these 'human relations' can strike us as 'firmly established, canonical and binding' thus giving metaphor a function of orienting cognition.

A Hermeneutic Tension in Relation to the Post-Nietzschean Conception of Metaphor

This dual function in Nietzsche's conceptualisation of metaphor has oriented a particular hermeneutic tension in the interpretation of the meaning of metaphor. When we use the term 'hermeneutics' in this book, rather than specifically referencing the field of philosophical hermeneutics that issues forth from Wilhelm Dilthey, Martin Heidegger, Hans-Georg Gadamer and Paul Ricoeur, among others, we mean hermeneutics broadly as the art of interpretation, as any method employed to claim a semantic ground for the interpretation of metaphor. The particular hermeneutic tension that Nietzsche's conceptualisation of metaphor presents us with is the tension between the relativising function of metaphor and the pragmatic function of metaphor. When we refer to the pragmatic function of metaphor in this book, we are neither referring to the pragmatic philosophical tradition, found in thinkers such as William James, John Dewey and Richard Rorty, nor to the study of how context creates meaning in linguistic pragmatics. While both fields may have similarities to our approach in this book, when we use the phrase 'metaphor's pragmatic function', we are referring to metaphor's ability to provide a pragmatic service to cognition. While metaphor may relativise meaning, it nevertheless pragmatically functions in the face of this relativity and allows one to create provisional meanings for things and concepts.

One of the ways we can observe this hermeneutic tension in the trajectory of European philosophy is to use Nietzsche as a pivot point. On one side of the pivot point, we can observe the Aristotelian paradigm of metaphor and how that paradigm evolves up until the time of Kant. We can also observe the way that the term 'metaphor' was understood in studies of rhetoric and philology in Nietzsche's own time. This will be the focus of chapters 1 and 2 of this book. On the other side of the pivot point, chapters 3, 4 and 5 will observe how four representative

European philosophers respond to the questions that Nietzsche raises concerning metaphor. These thinkers are Martin Heidegger, Paul Ricoeur, Hans Blumenberg and Jacques Derrida. While their respective philosophies of metaphor do not always explicitly engage with Nietzsche, we can see them as implicit and representative responses to the philosophical problems with the modern European philosophical conception of metaphor.

In chapter 3, for example, we will observe how Heidegger, and following him Ricoeur, attempt to bypass the tension between the pragmatic and relativising functions of metaphor that Nietzsche's philosophy opened up and ground the problem of the meaning of metaphor in Heidegger's conception of Being. While Heidegger does not write extensively on metaphor, his distinct and divisive position, first in *Being and Time* (1927) and then at the 1929 Davos conference, on ontological and anthropological questions had a distinct impact on the post-Nietzschean conception of metaphor. If Nietzsche relates questions of anthropology and ontology to metaphor, Heidegger, in turn, makes these questions hermeneutic and existential. He outlines the case for an 'existential analytic' to answer the question of Being, and, within this framework, both ontological problems and anthropological problems become hermeneutic and existential problems. Ricoeur in *The Rule of Metaphor* (1975) then attempts to ground the problem of the meaning of metaphor in Heidegger's conception of Being.

Blumenberg and Derrida more clearly represent each side of the hermeneutic tension we see in Nietzsche's conception of metaphor. Blumenberg's theory of metaphor relates primarily to the pragmatic function of metaphor, while Derrida's writings on metaphor focus on metaphor's relativising function. We will argue that Blumenberg's most famous conception of metaphor — that of the absolute metaphor and of metaphorology as a supplement to conceptual history, outlined in his *Paradigms for a Metaphorology* (1960) — is a case study for a larger thesis on the production of meaning, primarily because of metaphor's ability to provide pragmatic orientation to cognition via rhetorical consensus.

In addition to offering a distinct contribution to the European philosophical landscape, the importance of Blumenberg in this book lies partly in the fact that the anglophone reception of his philosophy has been limited. In relation to metaphor, for example, there is no mention of him in Clive Cazeaux's *Metaphor and Continental Philosophy* (2007), the only English-language work on the continental theory of metaphor generally. This is partially because Blumenberg's main work on metaphor, *Paradigms for a Metaphorology*, was not translated into English until 2010, three years after the publication of *Metaphor and Continental Philosophy*. Therefore, this book will contribute to the anglophone reception of Blumenberg's philosophy, which is vital for a more nuanced understanding of a post-Nietzschean philosophy of metaphor. Derrida represents the opposite pole to Nietzsche's conception of metaphor. Derrida rejects our ability to achieve orientation through metaphor and instead considers the implications of all semantic gestures being metaphoric in 'White Mythology' (1971) and in 'The *Retrait* of Metaphor' (1978). We will consider both Blumenberg's and Derrida's philosophies of metaphor in more detail in chapters 4 and 5 respectively.

Guiding Question and a Symptom of its Necessity

This particular hermeneutic tension between the relativising and pragmatic functions of metaphor that we see first in Nietzsche and then more broadly played out in European philosophy poses a question which will be the guiding question of this book: *How do we interpret the meaning of metaphor if all semantic gestures are metaphoric?* A symptom of the necessity of this question is the historical reality, often seen in ideology, where metaphoric meaning swiftly takes hold and pragmatically orients cognition. We are calling this tension hermeneutic because, as we have seen in Aristotle, it is through likeness that we judge the meaning of a metaphor. How are we to reconcile likeness as both relative and pragmatic? How are we to affirm the fact that evening and old age have no necessary link between them, and yet similar metaphorical designations hold the ideas of entire cultures and epochs in history together, such as the metaphor of light for the divine or of light for truth? This is the hermeneutic tension at the heart of Nietzsche's conception of metaphor — a tension that characterises the concept of metaphor in post-Nietzschean European philosophy. As we shall see, although this tension is found at the origin of cognition, the effect of this is not often understood or fully realised in post-Nietzschean European philosophy.

We also see that our question is signalled to us, in part, by ideology. When we try to account for the historical reality, often seen in ideology, where metaphoric meaning swiftly takes hold and seems to orient cognition pragmatically, we are posing the question of the role of metaphor in the creation of ideology. By stating the question in this way, we are teasing out the underlining assumption, often unthought, that when we create a hermeneutics of metaphor, we are dealing either with poetic metaphors such as 'evening is the old age of life', or the type of metaphor that we use in everyday speech, such as, he *shed some light* on the subject. The much less innocent ideological metaphor goes hand in hand with the opposite side of Nietzsche's emphasis on relativism; that is, the ability of metaphor to orient cognition pragmatically and to inform action. What are we to do with metaphors involved in hate speech, propaganda, or those used to support divisive political ideologies?

If we think for a moment how, in 1979, Ayatollah Khomeini led the Iranian Revolution and the wave of anti-American sentiment that followed with his metaphorical description of the United States as 'the Great Satan', we can see how the ideological metaphor can generate meaning that holds entire linguistic and cultural communities in its sway. We could of course cite a similar example of the United States' metaphorical description of the Middle East when, in 2002, George Bush referred to Iran, Iraq and other countries as the 'Axis of Evil'. We will explore this question in more depth later in the introduction. It is important to note here that in this book, the relationship between metaphor and ideology is not our specific theme, but rather will be observed occasionally as a *symptom* of the hermeneutic tension in Nietzsche's conception of metaphor. Nietzsche's and Derrida's assertion of the relativising function of metaphor meets a hermeneutic limit when one considers how political metaphor builds ideology. While we may point to an ultimately relative ground of metaphoric meaning, we cannot pragmatically deny the social reality that metaphor seems to play in building ideologies. Therefore, we will occasionally return to examples relating to metaphor and ideology throughout this book to illustrate the symptom of the hermeneutic tension within Nietzsche's conception of metaphor.

But even if we can say ideology is a symptom of our question, how is it that our question explicitly ties into semantic shifts?

As we have seen, the widely accepted view, and also the view we are arguing, is that Nietzsche plays a significant role in introducing to our intellectual landscape the idea that metaphor has a fundamental role in cognition. Things that we would traditionally call concepts have a metaphoric basis and metaphors are essential for orienting thought. This change in metaphor's status arises from, to use Sarah Kofman's words, the 'loss of the proper'. Therefore, the question is, if everything is metaphoric, how does one determine the meaning of metaphor? Where do the grounds for such an interpretation come from?

This question makes the most sense when one reflects on the other consequence of the 'loss of the proper'. However relative concepts and structures of thought may be, metaphors orient cognition in the construction of those very concepts and structures of thought. The double bind comes when we reflect that this same 'loss of the proper' also relativises our traditional understanding of meaning in that all semantic gestures are metaphoric. There is no ground or concept that is not metaphoric and there is no meaning that is not metaphoric. Yet, metaphor is a phenomenon that seems not to need a separate ground to produce meaning. Despite its relative foundations it allows us cognitive orientation in its more pragmatic capacity. The point then is that metaphor seems to be the basis of all semantic gestures and concepts. But instead of making the world an unintelligible hall of mirrors, it in fact pragmatically orients cognition. One of the natural questions we are left with after Nietzsche is: how does metaphor do this? This question flows naturally within the post-Nietzschean European philosophical heritage, and even outside that heritage, within cognitive linguistics, the production of meaning ends up being the underlying philosophical focus. However, looking at the problem of interpreting the meaning of metaphor, if one affirms that all semantic gestures are metaphors, solely through the lens of the production of meaning, can lead to the unintended consequence that the phenomenon of semantic shifts often is overlooked.

Yet semantic shifts and semantic ubiquity are inextricably linked. When we think of the relativism produced by metaphor, realising the metaphoric basis of all thought and how radically different that is in different moments, our understanding of this phenomenon is often oriented by relativism between different cultures and different symbolics. Semantic change also involves looking at the ubiquity of metaphor. However, with semantic change we mean the phenomenon within one particular symbolic where the meaning of a metaphor or concepts shifts. This is most often seen in etymology and was fundamental in Nietzsche arriving at his view. But in post-Nietzschean European philosophy, a focus on original meaning, particularly in Derrida, is rejected. While, as we shall see, this rejection in Derrida's philosophy does profoundly deepen our understanding of the concept of metaphor, the loss of a diachronic focus, a focus on the history of a metaphor's meaning within the same symbolic, makes the question of semantic shift lopsided.

A very different tradition highlights the same problem in the form of cognitive linguistics. As we shall see, in its synchronic approach to language analysis, it looks at the production of meaning within one fixed language or historical period. When it does look at the change of meanings, it is between cultures as opposed to over time. It is not that either cognitive linguistics or post-Nietzschean European philosophy reject the reality of the historical development of meaning. Rather, the fear of a cultural or metaphysical 'origin' makes one treat the question of history at arm's length. But even though they may traditionally be linked they are by no means the same, as we shall see.

Therefore, when the creation of meaning through metaphor is considered, semantic shifts have often taken a back seat. However, as we have seen, our contemporary political moment highlights that new meanings can swiftly be created within the same symbolic. While we may reject the validity of new meanings, they still swiftly enter into use and orient a community, and this is why ideology is a symptom of the necessity of our question. As we shall see, while the twentieth century needed to speak urgently about the question of semantic relativity, the framework for how meaning was produced in light of, or as a reaction to, this, does not provide an adequate account of semantic shifts as we mean them here. So, to refine our question, why is Nietzsche's philosophy significant for providing a contemporary account of the ground or origin of swift meaning changes? Or, perhaps, we should ask what Nietzsche's philosophy tells us about whether the question of ground or origin is adequate when thinking about semantic change.

The Interpretation of Metaphor in Academic Discourse Today

The first thing we have to reflect on is: why Nietzsche? Why have we specifically chosen this hermeneutic tension, found in Nietzsche and in post-Nietzschean European philosophy, to address the conception of metaphor today, a conception that is so radically altered from the Aristotelian one? As we have seen, metaphor is considered a fundamental question in fields as diverse as philosophy, politics, medicine and grammar. Why do we focus on this particular hermeneutic tension found in Nietzsche? Is it the most suitable approach for our question and for a book that professes to say something about European philosophy more generally?

To answer the interpretive questions about metaphor that are at stake today, we must locate a change in the concept of metaphor itself. However, we find that most histories of the concept of metaphor are actually interested in its function. Western introductions to metaphor, for example, often cite several twentieth-century texts in linguistics and philosophy, such as Roman Jakobson's 'Two Aspects of Language and Two Types of Aphasic Disturbances' (1956), Max Black's *Models and Metaphors* (1962), and Donald Davidson's 'What Metaphors Mean' (1978). While all are significant in their respective fields, Black and Davidson in analytic philosophy,

Jakobson in structural linguistics, the perspectives of these contributions are often quite varied. Davidson, for example, making a semantic argument, states that 'metaphors mean what the words, in their most literal interpretation, mean, and nothing more'.[16] Jakobson, writing over twenty years before Davidson, creates a famous distinction between metaphor and metonymy and asserts that the respective figurative devices appear more frequently in different types of writing, metaphor in poetry, and literary movements such as romanticism and symbolism, and metonymy in prose. This is because while metaphor characterises substitution, metonymy characterises realism.[17] While both approaches are important contributions to the field of metaphor studies more broadly, we are interested in a particular intellectual-historical progression regarding the conception of metaphor itself.

As has already been stated, our theme is a conceptualisation of metaphor where metaphor is fundamental to cognition and concept formation and the hermeneutics that accompany such a conception. One representative perspective on metaphor in this vein that we could cite from structural anthropology is that offered by Claude Lévi-Strauss. In *The Savage Mind*, Lévi-Strauss made the case that what he called the 'savage mind' operated according to its own logic. While Lévi-Strauss himself did not critique the questionable term 'savage', he argued that what we would today call pre-industrial indigenous cultures had their own logic through which to understand the world that was highly sophisticated in its own right and not simply undeveloped as the term 'savage' might suggest.[18] This, of course, falls under Lévi-Strauss's famous use of the French term *bricolage* to describe the way in which mythical thought reuses the available content of one's world to solve new problems. Lévi-Strauss called this a 'science of the concrete' which arranges the world into mythical structures.[19]

A significant feature of the ability to arrange the world into mythical structures is what Lévi-Strauss called 'analogical thought'. In the *Savage Mind* he writes:

> The savage mind deepens its knowledge with the help of *imagines mundi* [world pictures]. It builds mental structures which facilitate an understanding of the world in as much as they resemble it. In this sense savage thought can be defined as analogical thought.[20]

When Lévi-Strauss locates a pre-industrial indigenous culture's ability to understand the world in analogical thinking, he is describing the fundamental function of metaphor in a cultural world far removed from our own. Not only does this gesture deepen our understanding of the sophisticated thinking at work in the mythology of a pre-industrial indigenous culture, it also shows that structural anthropology was a movement that elevated metaphor to a fundamental level in cognition. Structural anthropology, in the form of Lévi-Strauss, provides a hermeneutics of metaphor akin to what we are interested in, but however important Lévi-Strauss's position might be in the history of anthropology, it does not address the change in the concept of metaphor itself. It rather uses the traditional transference aspect of metaphor in a more fundamental way.

At this point, one could respond that we are off topic and that the examples given are not from thinkers working in the field of 'European Philosophy'. So far, we have referenced analytic philosophy, linguistics and Lévi-Strauss, though he has influenced European philosophy, technically hails from anthropology. Should we not we be asking ourselves, who else has posed our question within the field of European philosophy? However, the breadth of reference is intentional, to point out how widespread the neglect of our question is. Even for those scholars working within European philosophy, there is no consensus on this question. Rather, various scholars have dealt with various aspects of it.

Clive Cazeaux

In *Metaphor and Continental Philosophy* (2007), Clive Cazeaux does not specifically pose our question of the conflict between the relativising and pragmatic functions of metaphor. However, he does address an aspect of the relativising function of metaphor in the introduction to his study. Cazeaux suggests that his study of the role of metaphor in continental philosophy shows metaphor as 'being the structure of belonging and transposition which constitutes the possibility of experience *and the* world'.[21] What does Cazeaux mean by this? We will put his description of the word 'structure' aside for a moment and reflect on metaphor as being a structure 'which constitutes the possibility of experience *and the* world'. Cazeaux notes that he emphasises the 'and the' in between the words 'experience' and 'world' because

> epistemology conventionally distinguishes experience from the world, creating two distinct regions: the world, and our experience of it. In contrast, I present the two as conjoined within metaphor. This is not to say that they are seamlessly fused together or that experience is all there is. Rather, it is to assert the claim that metaphor can serve epistemology *as a structure* whose internal transpositions articulate the distinction between experience and the world that is normally, and problematically, expressed in terms of regions, domains, and other spatial metaphors.[22]

The key in this section seems to be Cazeaux's description of metaphor being a structure that has 'internal transpositions'. Therefore, he describes metaphor as 'being the structure of belonging and transposition'. We are all familiar with metaphor's function of 'transposition' from Aristotle's definition that a metaphor is 'the application of a word that belongs to another thing'.[23] Cazeaux is asserting here that the function of 'internal transpositions' within metaphor serves to join the traditional epistemological distinction between experience and world. But Cazeaux is also quick to remind us that to assert that metaphor joins the two together does not mean 'that they are seamlessly fused together or that experience is all there is'. This becomes relevant for our theme when he goes on to explain that, following the continental tradition, he will assign to metaphor an 'ontological value'.

About his stance on metaphor's 'ontological value', Cazeaux writes:

> assigning metaphor [an] ontological value means I take the view that *everything arises out of metaphor*, but this is not the same as saying 'everything is metaphor'. The latter locates everything within metaphor, has everything belong to metaphor, whereas the former, with its action of 'giving rise' to entities, grants us the room to question what belongs to metaphor.[24]

It seems that Cazeaux assigns metaphor an ontological value because it joins up both 'experience' and 'world'. This is relevant for us, because as we shall see in Nietzsche's conception of metaphor, all our designations of things in the world are metaphoric and this creates a hermeneutic tension by relativising the origin of the meaning of those designations. While Cazeaux doesn't articulate the conflict between metaphor's relativising and pragmatic functions, he does try to clarify that just because metaphor joins up the traditional epistemological categories of 'experience' and 'world', this need not mean that there is no ability to distinguish between metaphor and other entities. This is a helpful distinction that speaks to one of the problems that arises from Nietzsche's conception of metaphor and we will return to it in chapter 5.

Another significant aspect of Cazeaux's *Metaphor and Continental Philosophy* is that it is the only English-language book-length work to date to deal specifically with the theme of metaphor across several thinkers in the continental tradition. It arranges its chapters around themes, such as metaphor and metaphysics or metaphor and epistemology. In these chapters, he often looks at a combination of continental thinkers alongside thinkers from other traditions, such as Merleau-Ponty and Lakoff and Johnson, or Max Black and Paul Ricoeur. As the book seeks to provide an overview of a variety of continental thinkers, it often has several different arguments in its respective chapters on the relation between metaphor and problems within the continental tradition rather than one overarching argument about a single conception of metaphor in the continental tradition.

Finally, *Metaphor and Continental Philosophy* draws the reader's attention to the significance of Immanuel Kant for a continental theory of metaphor. Cazeaux makes the claim that 'the phenomenon of inventive metaphor is a concentration of the problem faced by Kant in the *Critique of Pure Reason*'.[25] This position will become quite important for us because we will both affirm Cazeaux's thesis on the relevance of Kant for the European philosophy of metaphor as well as depart from it. As we have already asserted, our problem is not simply post-Kantian, but also post-Nietzschean. We will return to an in-depth analysis of the relationship between Kant's philosophy and metaphor in chapter 1. For the moment, we can state that in *Metaphor and Continental Philosophy*, Cazeaux draws our attention to the relationship between the main problems in Kant's *Critique of Pure Reason* and the phenomenon of metaphor.[26] For Cazeaux, metaphor is a 'concentration of the problems' Kant identifies in the first *Critique*.[27] In a later chapter, Cazeaux builds on this initial analysis when he writes that:

> although Kant does not address metaphor directly, he does consider analogy, the kind of metaphor (following Aristotle's definition) which, instead of comparing one thing with another, compares one relationship with another in the form A is to B as C is to D [...] Analogy is vital to Kant's architectonic because, as a creator of relationships, it allows him to explain how the key terms in his system interact with one another...While Kant maintains the philosophical tradition (following Aristotle, Aquinas, and Descartes) of defining reason as the ability to think creatively and act according to principles which are independent of nature, he nevertheless departs from tradition with his claim that the objectivity

or validity of these supersensible principles lies not in themselves, in their own terms, but *in their application to sensible reality*. This is the relationship which has to be explained.[28]

While Cazeaux acknowledges that Kant does not discuss metaphor, he perhaps overstates the similarities between metaphor and Kant's thinking on cognition. This book will maintain that Kant's own thinking on the figurative, which we can deduce from his discussions of analogy and symbol in the *Critique of Judgement* (1790), is relegated to a more supplemental role in relation to reason rather than a substitute for reason.[29] We are in full agreement with Cazeaux that metaphor is a 'concentration of the problems' Kant identifies in the first *Critique*. But it is later thinkers, such as Hans Blumenberg or Jacques Derrida, who explicitly apply metaphor to Kant's understanding of cognition. The precondition for this later application of metaphor to Kant's philosophy is the collapse of the distinction between reason and metaphor. As we have seen in Sarah Kofman, a theory of metaphor based on the 'loss of the proper' is found in Nietzsche and it is for this reason that this book deals with metaphor after Nietzsche.[30] It is arguable that, without Nietzsche's philosophy, metaphor as an explicit philosophical theme would never have been read back into Kant's philosophy. As a result, a key distinction we will maintain in this book is that between Kant's view of metaphor and Nietzsche's view of metaphor.

Paul Ricoeur

The second thinker to have significantly dealt with our question in the European philosophical tradition is Paul Ricoeur. As mentioned early in this introduction, Ricoeur is one of the primary thinkers discussed in this book and will be dealt with in detail in chapter 3. However, we should briefly mark out how he relates to our question as a secondary source. Like Cazeaux, he does not explicitly address the tension between a relative and a pragmatic function of metaphor. However, Ricoeur is concerned with 'the creation of meaning in language'. This is the subtitle of *The Rule of Metaphor* (1975) in English.[31] One of the places where he sees a threat to the creation of meaning is in what he calls 'Jacques Derrida's unbounded "deconstruction" in "White Mythology"'.[32] As we have seen earlier, in this book Derrida will be treated as a post-Nietzschean thinker who takes up the relativising function of metaphor. We will maintain that Ricoeur bypasses metaphor's hermeneutic tension by grounding the meaning of metaphor in Heidegger's conception of Being and this will be discussed in detail in chapter 3.

There are two key differences here between our approach and that of Ricoeur. The first is that while this book will treat Heidegger's philosophy as indispensable to understanding the intellectual developments after Nietzsche that concern us in this book, we will not follow Ricoeur in grounding the meaning of language in a Heideggerian conception of Being. There are of course considerable differences between Ricoeur and Heidegger which we will explore in chapter 3, but this book will argue that, despite these differences, Ricoeur uses Heidegger's philosophy to create a semantic model that we deem unsuitable to answer our question. The second difference to note is that, even if this is done unintentionally, the types of metaphor present in Ricoeur's philosophy tend to be those of romantic or mystical poetry. As a result, the model through which he attempts to assess metaphor's role in the 'creation of meaning' does not address the semantic problems that political ideology or long historic change pose.

Dirk Mende

Another important work to mention is Dirk Mende's *Metapher — zwischen Metaphysik und Archäologie: Schelling, Heidegger, Derrida, Blumenberg* (Metaphor — Between Metaphysics and Archaeology: Schelling, Heidegger, Derrida, Blumenberg) (2013). Like the other works mentioned above, Mende's doesn't frame the problem of metaphor in terms of a conflict between metaphor's pragmatic function and its relativising function, but he does provide an explicit comparison, in the German language, between Blumenberg and Derrida. Methodologically, his approach is perhaps the most like ours in that, while he doesn't begin with Nietzsche, he is interested in shared conceptions of metaphor from Schelling to Derrida. In particular, Mende writes: 'Der späte Schelling und der späte Heidegger interessieren mich dabei insbesondere als Vorgeschichte des metaphorologisch-archäologischen Denkens Derridas und Blumenbergs' (The late Schelling and the late Heidegger interest me in particular as a prehistory of the metaphorological-archaeological thinking of Derrida and Blumenberg).[33] We see two things in this quotation. On the one hand, Mende finds in the thinking of both the late Schelling and the late Heidegger an earlier formation of the way in which Derrida and Blumenberg comprehend metaphor. On the other hand, he sees Derrida's and Blumenberg's conceptions of metaphor as linked.

We will return to the link between Derrida and Blumenberg in a moment. However, it is essential to point out that while Mende's methodological analysis may be similar to ours, his philosophical focus is fundamentally different from that of the present work. While Mende's methodology is to look at the relationship between shared conceptions of metaphor in Blumenberg and Derrida, he is not interested in a conception of metaphor as such. Rather he is interested in the *function* of metaphor in philosophical discourse. He makes this clear when he writes that, 'Mein Interesse der Funktion von Metaphern im philosophischen Diskurs, deren performative Verwendung ich exemplarisch in den Texten Schellings und Heideggers untersuche und abschließend mit Derrida und Blumenberg theoretisch beschreibe' (My interest is in the function of metaphors in philosophical discourse, whose performative use I illustrate in the texts of Schelling and Heidegger and then describe theoretically with Derrida and Blumenberg).[34] Therefore Mende's comparison of conceptions of metaphor is ultimately interested in the way metaphor functions in philosophical discourse. Here, Mende takes a conception of metaphor from Blumenberg and Derrida and then observes the ways in which metaphors are used in Schelling and Heidegger.

Mende's comparison of Blumenberg and Derrida is closer to the preoccupation of chapters 4 and 5 of this book. While the present work will draw a much clearer line between Blumenberg's and Derrida's respective philosophies than Mende, he does acknowledge that Blumenberg provides an alternative to the metaphysical conception of metaphor that Derrida critiques.

> Gegenüber Derridas umfassender Kritik an dem metaphysischen Ähnlichkeitsbegriff scheint Blumenbergs Vorgehen zunächst partieller: Er kritisiert nicht den metaphysischen Metaphernbegriff, sondern entwirft einen alternativen. Der zentrale Begriff seiner Metaphorologie, die absolute Metapher, ist als dezidiert nicht-aristotelischer Metaphernbegriff konzipiert.
>
> [In comparison to Derrida's more comprehensive criticism of the metaphysical concept of similitude, Blumenberg's approach initially seems to be more partial: he does not criticise the metaphysical concept of metaphors but creates an alternative. The central concept of his metaphorology, the absolute metaphor, is conceived as a decidedly non-Aristotelian concept of metaphors.][35]

However, we will clearly mark out a different trajectory from Mende's in terms of Derrida's relationship to the concept of a metaphorology. Mende frequently speaks of both Derrida and Blumenberg as having a metaphorology. For example, he writes that:

> Derridas und Blumenbergs Metaphorologien, so wie ich sie rekonstruiere, kommen darin überein, dass sie ihre Überlegungen zu einem nachmetaphysischen Metaphernbegriff zu einer Theorie diskursanalytischer Archäologie weiter entwickeln und damit den engeren Rahmen einer Theorie der Metapher übersteigen.
>
> [Derrida's and Blumenberg's metaphorologies, as I am reconstructing them, come to an understanding in that they develop their thinking on a post-metaphysical concept of metaphors into a theory of discourse-analytical archaeology, thus exceeding the narrower framework of a theory of metaphor.][36]

This is the crucial difference between Mende's analysis and our own. As we shall see in chapter 5, a metaphorology is impossible in Derrida's philosophy. In fact, the possibility of a 'discourse-analytical archaeology', as Mende puts it, is precisely what Derrida thinks we cannot do with metaphor. Because of this difference, it is even more important that we maintain a clearer division between the two thinkers than Mende's analysis does.

Sarah Kofman

The final work to mention on the theme of metaphor in post-Nietzschean philosophy is Sarah Kofman's *Nietzsche and Metaphor* (1983). Kofman does not deal with our question but she does raise a vital point that we will use as a first step towards identifying a new conception of metaphor in Nietzsche's philosophy. Though published in 1983, *Nietzsche and Metaphor* emerges from the era of the new Nietzsche in post-war France that brought about its own revolution in continental thinking.[37] Having moved to teach in Paris in 1963, Kofman herself was positioned right at the heart of the new Nietzsche in France. While popularly associated with Foucault's reading of Nietzsche in *The Order of Things* (1966), the new Nietzsche was brought about first by reactions to Heidegger's book on Nietzsche in 1961 and then Gilles Deleuze's *Nietzsche and Philosophy* (1962).[38] Jean Wahl called Deleuze's book the first major work on Nietzsche in French since the war.[39] Deleuze also was one of the key organisers of what Duncan Large calls 'the first of the major Nietzsche conferences of the period, the "Colloque de Royaumont" in July 1964'.[40] Kofman herself finished her doctorate under the supervision of Deleuze and references his work on Nietzsche frequently in *Nietzsche and Metaphor*. It was also in the early years of the 1960s that Nietzsche's most famous text on metaphor, 'On Truth and Lying in a Non-Moral Sense' (1873), was first translated into French.[41] Kofman's position on Nietzsche's philosophy of metaphor comes out of this context.

Kofman's overall project in *Nietzsche and Metaphor* is to perform a stylistic analysis of Nietzsche's own use of metaphor such as the beehive metaphor in *The Genealogy of Morality*, the pyramid in 'On Truth and Lying', or the spider and its web in *Untimely Meditations*. However, in her first three chapters, before moving on to an analysis of Nietzsche's own metaphors, she places the theme of metaphor at the heart of Nietzsche's philosophy. Kofman states that 'as early as *The Birth of Tragedy* Nietzsche judges the conceptual language of philosophy the most inappropriate to express the "truth of the world", since it is at three removes from it, simply a metaphor for a metaphor'.[42] She then goes on to give a reading of Nietzsche's position. For Nietzsche, Kofman maintains, 'we can have only representations of the essence of things, since we ourselves, and the universe along with us, are only images of this completely "indecipherable" innermost essence'.[43] She relates these representations to the symbolic spheres, such as music, found in Nietzsche's *The Birth of Tragedy*.

What Kofman attempts here in the opening of *Nietzsche and Metaphor* is to make the case that the problems of representation and metaphor are one and the same in Nietzsche's philosophy. Right from the beginning, she maintains, metaphor and representation are linked, and as themes in Nietzsche's thought, they relate to the 'indecipherable innermost essence' of both ourselves and the world. As we have seen earlier in this introduction, Kofman makes the case that from as early as *The Birth of Tragedy* Nietzsche presents us with a 'generalised theory of metaphor' based on the 'loss of the proper'. The loss of the proper is our inability to decipher the innermost essence of both ourselves and the world.[44]

This argument, which is outlined in the first three chapters of *Nietzsche and Metaphor*, puts metaphor into the heart of Nietzsche's philosophy. In fact, Kofman suggests that this 'generalized "theory" of metaphor' is an early draft of Nietzsche's later conception of the 'will to power'. Kofman writes that 'Nietzsche will substitute [metaphor for other] notions [like] "text" and "interpretation" [...] in light of these operative notions, [metaphor] is thought of as a metaphorical notion, symbolic of the artistic force of interpretation.' She then states that, 'this artistic force will be designated 'will to power"'.[45] Kofman's assertion that Nietzsche presents us with a generalised theory of metaphor, rather than simply a critique of propositional truth that utilises metaphor, is essential for our theme. Here, we find ourselves very much at home in Kofman's thought when we are asserting that Nietzsche presents a new conception of metaphor to Western thought. Another assertion of Kofman's that is relevant to our theme is that Nietzsche reverses the Aristotelian conception of the rational animal. Because Nietzsche's 'generalised theory of metaphor' is tied to the loss of the proper, the distinction between rationality and metaphor collapses and the rational animal becomes the metaphorical animal.[46]

However, for all Kofman's strengths in the first three chapters of *Nietzsche and Metaphor*, her overall project of a stylistic reading fails to highlight the conceptual change of metaphor itself. While she identifies for us that Nietzsche's philosophy presents a 'generalised theory of metaphor', she does not identify Nietzsche's role in contributing to the re-evaluation of the construction of the conception of metaphor itself. In connecting metaphor to *The Birth of Tragedy*, Kofman is perhaps too quick to put metaphor on the side of art, almost using metaphor as a catch-all for the opposite of reason, thus ignoring the profundity of the collapse between metaphor and reason which she herself highlights. Duncan Large calls this reading 'a Nietzsche in [Kofman's] own image [...] with its emphasis on rhetorical features, the expressive textual symptom'.[47] The Dionysian tone of the triumph of 'art' in her analysis too often ignores the nuance and profundity of what this triumph might mean for the conception of art, or of metaphor itself. As a result, she does not address the hermeneutic tension with which we are concerned.

The Prevalence of Cognitive Linguistics and its Response to the Hermeneutic Crisis of Metaphor

So finally, transitioning back out of European philosophical approaches to our question, we come to cognitive linguistics. We have already encountered one of the central tenets of cognitive linguistics, that 'our ordinary conceptual system, in terms of which we both think and act, is fundamentally metaphorical in nature' at the beginning of this introduction.[48] Through their perspective of 'embodied realism', cognitive linguistics attempts to respond to the hermeneutic tension we have identified.[49] But, as we shall see, this perspective does not necessarily respond to the vehicle of semantic change itself within metaphor. It is, however, the field that explicitly addresses the change in the concept of metaphor since Aristotle and one of the most dominant methods of interpreting the meaning of metaphor in academic discourse today. For this reason, it is essential to highlight how cognitive linguistics approaches the change in the concept of metaphor and why it is ultimately unsuitable to answer our question.

To show the breadth of the influence of cognitive linguistics, we can first turn to literary studies where George Lakoff and Mark Turner analyse poetic metaphors, from, among others, Milton, Shakespeare, Emily Dickinson, Rainer Maria Rilke, Robert Frost, T. S. Eliot and W. H. Auden. They conclude that:

> metaphor plays an enormous role in shaping one's everyday understanding of everyday events. That is an important part of the power of poetic metaphor: it calls upon our deepest modes of everyday understanding and forces us to use them in new ways.[50]

Building on Lakoff and Johnson's work, in his book *Understanding Metaphor in Literature: An Empirical Approach* (1994) Gerard Steen outlines an approach based in cognitive linguistics to understand how readers process metaphors in literary texts.[51] In the same year, Raymond W. Gibbs Jr. interpreted Emily Dickinson's metaphor of a 'liquor never brewed' for love as related to the larger conceptual metaphor category of 'love is a kind of nutrient', citing other examples such as '*I'm drunk with love*' and '*he's sustained by my love*' as all parts of the same cognitive theme.[52] Metaphorically to 'drink love' or to be 'sustained' by it suggests a metaphorical understanding of love in terms of nutrition. More recently Elena Semino opens her chapter on 'Metaphor in Literature' with a cognitive interpretation of a metaphor for a migraine in Ian McEwan's novel *Atonement*. She shows how a chain of metaphors in the relevant section of *Atonement* all link to the central conceptual metaphor of pain as a type of external presence. She then links up this metaphoric description with the empirical findings that people adopt metaphors referencing external threats to describe internal pain.[53] The cognitive linguistics approach to metaphor and literature is clearly a prominent form of analysis.

Moving on from literature to political discourse analysis we could cite, among others, George Lakoff, Andreas Musolff, René Dirven, Hans-Georg Wolf and Frank Polzenhagen as all contributing to the cognitive interpretation of metaphors in contemporary social and political discourse. In the examples we have listed here, the cognitive approach is used to help us to understand the mentalities of American political parties in the case of Lakoff, the role of metaphors in the 2014–15 'Brexit' debates in the case of Musolff, and the role of metaphor in economic discourse, in the cases of Dirven, Wolf and Polzenhagen.[54] Our intention is not to challenge these interpretations. Rather, we are simply trying to remind the reader of the prevalence of cognitive linguistics as a hermeneutic tool in contemporary academic discourse.

Because of this prevalence, it is an ideal contrast to help the reader understand why we have chosen an intellectual-historical approach to answer our question. When we state that we are interested in a conceptualisation of metaphor that views metaphor as fundamental to concept formation itself, cognitive linguistics is one of the fields to which we could naturally turn. However, the reason we have not chosen cognitive linguistics as our method of inquiry has to do with the relationship between our theme and our question. Our theme is the shift in the concept of metaphor since Aristotle. The concept of metaphor we are familiar with today, from cognitive linguistics among other fields, asserts that the transference function of metaphor, as seen in Aristotle's definition, has a more fundamental function to play in thought and in discourse than that of a simple linguistic transference. Our guiding question is, *how do we interpret the meaning of metaphor if all semantic gestures are metaphoric?* Cognitive linguistics does address the shift in the concept of metaphor since Aristotle. However, we are interested in the way in which the hermeneutic tension of metaphor, as stated in our question, arises from this new conception itself and what this can tell us about semantic shifts. As we shall see, cognitive linguistics can appear to dodge this dilemma by claiming that the problem of metaphoric relativism is grounded by embodied cognition. Lakoff and Johnson write:

> there is no poststructuralist person — no completely decentred subject for whom all meaning is arbitrary, totally relative, and purely historically contingent, unconstrained by body and brain. The mind is not merely embodied, but embodied in such a way that our conceptual systems draw largely upon the commonalities of our bodies and of the environments we live in. The result is that much of a person's conceptual system is either universal or widespread across languages and cultures. Our conceptual systems are not totally relative and not merely a matter of historical contingency, even though a degree of conceptual relativity does exist, and even though historical contingency does matter a great deal. The grounding of our conceptual systems in shared embodiment and bodily experience creates a largely centred self, but not a monolithic self.[55]

This 'grounding of our conceptual systems in shared embodiment and bodily experience' could be interpreted as resolving one aspect of the hermeneutic tensions of the concept of metaphor with which we are concerned. Our intention is not to challenge the empirical findings of cognitive linguistics but to ask about their hermeneutic limit.

In *Philosophy in the Flesh* (1999) Lakoff and Johnson claim that they provide the methodological and empirical basis that earlier thinkers lacked to ground their discoveries about the metaphoric nature of concepts. They write:

> Philosophical reflection, uninformed by cognitive science, did not discover, establish, and investigate the details of the fundamental aspects of mind we will be discussing. Some insightful philosophers did notice some of these phenomena but lacked the empirical methodology to establish the validity of these results and to study them in fine detail. Without empirical confirmation these facts about the mind did not find their way into the philosophical mainstream.[56]

In the 'Acknowledgments' of both *Metaphors We Live By* and *Philosophy in the Flesh* Lakoff and Johnson cite Claude Lévi-Strauss, Paul Ricoeur, Maurice Merleau-Ponty, and the continental tradition in philosophy as a whole as influences.[57] Presumably these are some of the 'insightful philosophers [who] did notice some of these phenomena, but lacked the empirical methodology to establish the validity of these results and to study them in fine detail'.[58] *Philosophy in the Flesh* was published to extraordinary critical and popular acclaim. It got a mention in the *New York Times* as well as in Stephen Pinker's popular science book *The Stuff of Thought* (2007) and quickly became a kind of textbook for what Lakoff and Johnson called, 'embodied realism'.[59] It is this perspective of 'embodied realism' that we can cite as one of the most prominent sources for a hermeneutics of metaphor today.

Clive Cazeaux's *Metaphor and Continental Philosophy* (2007) can be a useful starting point to understand the difference between cognitive linguistics and post-Nietzschean European philosophy. While discussing the relationship between Maurice Merleau-Ponty's view of embodiment and Lakoff and Johnson's, Cazeaux reminds us that the difference between the two is not simply methodological but epistemological. Merleau-Ponty's concern for example, is ontological and Lakoff and Johnson's is neurological.[60] These 'epistemic differences' as Cazeaux calls them, unearth deeper philosophical issues.[61] This point can be applied more generally, beyond Merleau-Ponty, in order to say that the difference between the two traditions — cognitive and continental — is generally epistemic.

We can see this epistemological difference quite clearly in *Philosophy in the Flesh* when Lakoff and Johnson lay out their reasons for why the findings of cognitive science suggest to us that the meaning of our conceptual system is grounded in a shared embodiment that creates a largely centred subject. This discovery, they claim, prompts a fundamental re-evaluation of the claims of Western philosophy in general. And they do this by proceeding through a list of philosophical perspectives and why these various perspectives must be abandoned because of the findings of cognitive science.[62]

Lakoff and Johnson's research suggests that the actual structure of our brain, our sensory organs, our ability to move and our everyday cultural experiences shape our concept formation and that the evidence of how our body shapes our concepts is found in metaphors.[63] Therefore, it is not, for Lakoff and Johnson, simply subjects perceiving objects and making empirical arguments but rather a case of embodied cognition. There is no subjectivity without the human body and its everyday experience in the world and this is what shapes our perceptions. The concepts we use often seem to match our world, they argue, because 'they have evolved from our sensorimotor systems which in turn evolved to allow us to function well in our physical environment'.[64] This is the answer provided by cognitive linguistics to the Nietzschean problem of likeness. This is also why likeness seems to act as truthlikeness, namely because concepts have evolved from our sensorimotor systems, which have in turn evolved from the physical environment within which the sensorimotor systems function.

An example of this would be the spatial origin of the metaphors we use to describe concepts that relate to values or relations, for example, 'HAPPY IS UP', 'INTIMACY IS CLOSENESS' or 'IMPORTANCE IS BIG'.[65] This equating of happy to up is what Lakoff and Johnson call a 'metaphorical concept' or a 'conceptual metaphor'.[66] The larger conceptual association is grounded in embodied cognition. There are several everyday metaphors that reflect these larger conceptual metaphors. A common phrase related to an important person might be, 'they are a real *bigshot*' or 'she's one of the biggest names in publishing at the moment'. Similarly, about happiness, we say, 'I'm feeling more *upbeat* today' or 'things are looking *up*'.[67]

For Lakoff and Johnson, it is not arbitrary that we use metaphors related to size to describe importance or directions to describe happiness; rather we use these metaphors because of the evolution of our sensorimotor systems and the way that concepts have evolved from them. The empirical work in cognitive science that supports this hypothesis, Lakoff and Johnson suggest, is that concept creation in the brain is a one-way system.[68] In the domain of the sensorimotor world, one's brain allows one's body to relate to the environment and much of this domain is shaped by the body's understanding of its environment in childhood, as is the case in Jean Piaget's now classic theory of cognitive development. Lakoff and Johnson write:

from a biological perspective, it is eminently plausible that reason has grown out of the sensory and motor systems and that it still uses those systems or structures developed from them. This explains why we have the kinds of concepts we have and why our concepts have the properties they have.[69]

There is of course also the domain in the brain where one's subjective experience forms abstract intangible concepts. According to Lakoff and Johnson, research suggests that there are neural connections between these two domains of the brain and that they are activated together when a concept is produced. The system of neural firing, they claim, is one-way, moving from the sensorimotor to the subjective, and they observe in this transference the same logic at work in metaphor. They write that:

> metaphor allows conventional mental imagery from sensorimotor domains to be used for domains of subjective experience. For example, we may form an image of something going by us or over our heads (sensorimotor experience) when we fail to understand (subjective experience).[70]

Therefore, on the one hand, in the same way that metaphor borrows a term from another domain to describe something, a more abstract, subjective concept borrows from the part of the brain where the sensorimotor experience takes place. On the other hand, this 'borrowing' is actually reflected in our use of metaphor itself, as we have seen in the descriptions of happiness in terms of 'up' or being important in terms of 'big'. Therefore, the meaning of the larger conceptual metaphor categories is grounded in embodiment. It is not simply that metaphors arise from our embodied experience, but so do their meanings.

While cognitive linguistics may significantly advance our insight into the role of metaphor in the mechanics of cognition, it presents a significant hermeneutic problem for those analysing metaphors, be they in political rhetoric or in the literary language of poetry and the novel. This problem lies in the inability of cognitive linguistics to account for the relative flux of metaphoric meaning, and the fact that meaning can swiftly change. There are two reasons for this. One the one hand, the analysis of cognitive linguistics is a *synchronic analysis* in that it limits its considerations of metaphor to one point in time rather than a *diachronic analysis* which would evaluate the historical evolution of a metaphor.[71] We might briefly note that, while cognitive linguistics is largely a synchronic approach to metaphor, some attempts have been made, such as in *Historical Cognitive Linguistics* (2010),[72] to look at the history of conceptual metaphors. However, despite several useful essays that put historical linguistics into conversation with a cognitive approach, the book does not address the fundamental problem that the thesis of embodiment poses to a diachronic analysis. This brings us to our second point.

The thesis of embodied meaning encounters problems in accounting for the relative flux of metaphoric meaning. Writing in the cognitive linguistics tradition, Zoltán Kövecses addresses an aspect of the tension between cognitive linguistics and the relative flux of metaphoric meaning in his book *Metaphor in Culture* (2005). The question Kövecses poses is: 'to what extent do people around the world share their understandings of aspects of the world in which they live?'[73] The question interests Kövecses because in the cognitive linguistics framework, as we have already seen, the meanings of metaphors are grounded in embodied experiences. Kövecses gives the example of how the metaphorical relationship between affection and warmth is generated in our formative years due to the embrace of our parents and the accompanying physical warmth.[74] Kövecses calls this a 'universal bodily experience' and asserts that 'universal primary experiences produce universal primary metaphors'. But what about cultural variations in understanding the world that do not reflect 'universal primary experience' like being held by one's parents?

This is precisely why Kövecses poses the question of metaphor in relation to the tension between cultural variation and universality. He writes,

> When we look at metaphors in the world's languages, we have the distinct impression that there is a large number of nonuniversal metaphors as well, and that they may be just as numerous as the universal ones [...] in other words, variation in metaphor appears to be just as important and common as universality [...] if variation in metaphor is so common, we need to be able to provide an explanation for it. So, we have a serious challenge: *How can we construct a comprehensive theory that can account for both the universality and variation in our use of metaphor?*[75]

Kövecses suggests there is 'a lot more that must be added to make the cognitive linguistic view of metaphor a more comprehensive and sophisticated account of both the universality and the variation of metaphor'.[76] He then gives a list of various issues about cultural variation that need to be considered in the cognitive linguistics model. Two of these concern us here, namely: 'bodily experience may be overridden by both culture and cognitive processes', and 'metaphors are not necessarily based on bodily experience — many are based on cultural considerations and cognitive processes of various kinds'.[77] In his concluding chapter, Kövecses picks up these two concerns and reminds us that 'the human body does not function in isolation; rather, it functions in a variety of contexts'.[78] The contexts that he lists which can shape the embodied meaning of metaphors are the environment, history and individual concerns. He groups these together under the heading, 'social-cultural experience' and while he does not resolve the conflict between cultural variation and universality, he does suggest that 'we can get cases in which social-cultural experiences override embodiment'.[79]

While this book is not concerned with the relationship between metaphor and embodiment, we can see Kövecses's thesis on metaphor and cultural variation going some way to fleshing out the objections we have raised to Lakoff and Johnson's attempt to ground metaphorical meaning in embodiment. Particularly salient is Kövecses's suggestion that there are 'cases in which social-cultural experiences override embodiment'. However, this book will approach the question of metaphor and relativism in different ways from those offered by Kövecses. The question he poses is based on inter-cultural relativism, not on historical relativism, although he does briefly mention that history is one of the contexts that can override embodiment. However, the overwhelming examples he uses come from a synchronic analysis and focus either on variations of metaphors between languages or intra-cultural variations such as those between ethnicities, regions and subcultures, rather than variations between historical periods.

We could briefly mention that this is not simply a problem encountered in the attempt of cognitive linguistics to grapple with semantic relativism. When European philosophy posed the question of relativism in the twentieth century, it also often looked to the variation between cultures. One example of this is Derrida's reference to Saussure in 'White Mythology' (1971). Speaking about the ultimate undecidability of a linguistic designation, Derrida references Saussure's ethno-linguistic finding that some groups of people living near the equator have no metaphoric description for sitting in the sun. Sitting in the sun is practically unfeasible in certain parts of the world and therefore what may seem to be a straightforward, truthlike metaphor in the West is in fact culturally and geographically relative.[80] So, in a similar way to Derrida in this example here, Kövecses poses the question of the change of the meaning of metaphor in terms of cultural relativism.

This leads us to our second point. Just because Kövecses poses the question of variation, this does not mean that he poses the question of change. In the same way that he gives no account of historical changes, he does not give any account of changes in meaning within a particular period. As we have previously stated, these changes can be seen in the form of political ideology, where an everyday word can suddenly take on an ideological dimension when used metaphorically. Kövecses's brief section on the cultural-ideological background of metaphors gives an excellent reading of the differences between metaphors relating to love in Hungarian and English, but conceives of ideology as the background mentalities of a particular language or culture rather than as political ideology.[81] Therefore the rich variation that Kövecses points out makes a compelling argument for the linguistic and cultural contingency of embodied meaning, but does not necessarily account for the vehicle of semantic change itself.

Ideology and Semantic Change

One example of the type of semantic change not accounted for by Kövecses's reading of cultural relativism is the way in which everyday metaphors can take on ideological dimensions. We have already seen examples of metaphor's role in the formation of ideological slogans such as the 'Great Satan' or the 'Axis of Evil' and the relationship between metaphor, and more broadly language, and ideology is a well-established field. One could cite classic examples from the European philosophical tradition, such as Theodor W. Adorno's *The Jargon of Authenticity* (1964) or Jürgen Habermas's *The Theory of Communicative Action* (1981), that have broad implications for the role of language in ideology. What concerns us here is the current state of the linguistic analysis of metaphor's role in the formation of ideology. While the linguistic analysis of ideology is a well-established field, we will limit ourselves to two examples in order to illustrate the underlying preoccupation in this field and ask how it relates to our question.

First, the linguist James W. Underhill examines the relationship between metaphor, ideology and world-view creation across multiple languages in his book *Creating Worldviews: Metaphor, Ideology and Language* (2011). For Underhill, ideology is a subset of world-view which he denotes by the term 'conceptual mindset'.[82] One example he cites to illustrate political ideology is Victor Klemperer's *The Language of the Third Reich* (1945). Klemperer was a professor of French Literature at Dresden University but in 1935 was removed from his post because he was Jewish. He survived the war due to his marriage.[83] *The Language of the Third Reich* arose from Klemperer's notebooks on the language of Nazism that he kept throughout the duration of the Nazis' rise to power and the Second World War.

Underhill's interest in Klemperer is the fact that Klemperer keeps a record of the role of metaphor in Nazi rhetoric. Underhill sees this record as a clash of world-views. He writes that Klemperer's 'personal world resisted the mindset of the Nazis, and resisted the transformation of the world-perceiving and world-conceiving of the German language which began to be eaten away by the Nazi mindset'.[84] Therefore, Underhill is interested in the clash between Klemperer's personal world-view and the ideological world-view of the Nazis and the way in which metaphor constructs these world-views. While Underhill's analysis is attentive to cultural variation between languages and the resistance of individuals to ideology, his abiding interest is in the *function* of metaphor within an ideological world-view rather than what ideology tells us about the Western *concept* of metaphor itself.

Another prominent analysis from the world of linguistics that is concerned with the relationship between ideology and metaphor comes in the work of Andreas Musolff. We have already cited Musolff as an example of a cognitive approach to political metaphor analysis. Musolff is generally of interest as a cognitive linguist who is aware of the interpretive limits of a purely cognitive approach to metaphor. This can be seen in his attentiveness to metaphor's role in persuasion in an article entitled, 'Metaphor and Persuasion in Politics' (2017),[85] in his appeal to consider diachronic perspectives in relation to cognitive models, and in his theorisation of how particular mental scenarios relate to particular discourse communities in *Political Metaphor Analysis: Discourse and Scenarios* (2016).[86] However, he has a particular relevance for our theme in his attentiveness to 'The Cognitive Import of Metaphor in Nazi Ideology' in his book *Metaphor, Nation and the Holocaust: The Concept of Body Politic* (2010).

For Musolff, part of the relevance of metaphor in ideology consists in providing a discourse scenario, such as National Socialist Germany, with an imagery. After looking at metaphors used in *Mein Kampf*, in particular, metaphors relating to body, nature and disease, Musolff looks at the role of the metaphorically embedded imagery of a 'body-parasite' and the role it played in the discourse scenario of National Socialist Germany.[87] Like Underhill, Musolff looks to Klemperer's *The Language of the Third Reich* as a source for metaphors in Nazi propaganda.[88] While Musolff is much more nuanced than Underhill, in that he does not simply view ideology as a subset of world-view, Musolff is also concerned with the *function* of metaphor in an ideological discourse. We see this when he writes about the *role* of body-related metaphors in Nazi propaganda.[89]

Although it is an incredibly fruitful area of research, considering the function of metaphor in ideology does not explicitly address the problem of the concept of metaphor as we are posing it here. We are maintaining that ideology shows its head as a symptom of a fundamental tension within the Western description of the concept of metaphor itself. The need to revaluate a particular concept of metaphor can be seen in the radical semantic change to metaphor that ideology can bring. Ideology not only creates world-views, or the imagery of discourse scenarios, but alters their semantic content. To put the question of ideology and metaphor in these terms brings us back to the conflict that is fundamental to the Nietzschean conception of metaphor: metaphor is infinitely malleable in its creation of truths and yet these truths appear 'firmly established, canonical and binding'.

One way to highlight this semantic problem is to draw another example from Victor Klemperer. As we have seen, both Underhill and Musolff use Klemperer to illustrate metaphor's function in ideology, but Klemperer also presents us with an interesting record of semantic change. Our question, in relation to Klemperer, will be: what role does the social reality of ideology play, not only in orienting cognition, but in shifting the meaning of metaphors used in that cognitive orientation?

One example of the language of Nazism that Klemperer points to is the way in which the seemingly innocent German word *aufziehen* was utilised by the Nazi party. As Klemperer notes, one of the most common meanings of *aufziehen* is 'to wind up' like one might do with a clock or mechanical toy.[90] However, the term also has a metaphorical connotation. He writes:

> The automaton, the humming top, the walking, nodding animal all point toward the metaphorical use of the term: I wind someone up (*aufziehen*). Which means that I tease him, I make a fool of him, I walk all over him [...] The term '*Aufziehen* (a wind-up)' is undoubtedly harmless in this context, but nevertheless a pejorative.[91]

Klemperer notes the further extension of the metaphorical connotations of *aufziehen* in the modern period when the term began to be used to describe advertising. He writes that:

> it was said of an advert that it had been impressively set up (*aufgezogen*). This constituted an acknowledgement of the commercial efficacy of the advertising campaign, but it also indicated that there was an element of excess, of sales patter which did not precisely match the real value of the thing on offer.[92]

What Klemperer points out here is that, as a metaphor, *aufziehen* had a harmless but nonetheless pejorative meaning, as shown in its use in advertising. It was an everyday metaphor used to comment on the creation of an excess value such as a well-marketed product. We are all familiar with how advertising can create an inflated sense of a product's value and it seems, in Klemperer's time, the metaphor *aufziehen* was used playfully to describe this.

The reason Klemperer includes this in a book about the language of Nazism is that the everyday meaning of the metaphor *aufziehen* goes through a semantic shift when used in Nazi propaganda. Klemperer records that on 30 June 1933,

> Goebbels stated in the University of Political Science that the NSDAP had 'set up (*aufgezogen*) a massive organization involving millions of people and bringing together all kinds of activities including folk theatre, popular games, tourism and sport, hiking, singing and all supported financially by the state'.[93]

Suddenly the meaning of *aufziehen* changes and any pejorative meaning of an excess of value is lost.[94] Klemperer notes that:

> here '*aufziehen* (to set up)' is nothing but honest, and when the government renders account for the success of the propaganda leading up to the vote in the Saarland it talks of 'an action set up (*aufgezogen*) on a grand scale'. It doesn't enter anyone's mind to associate the word with advertising.[95]

Klemperer notes that the final transformation seems to be when a German translator of the autobiography of the life of a publisher choses the word *aufziehen* to convey the meaning of setting up an organisation for the training of students.[96] Klemperer notes that the change in the metaphor's meaning is down to it being 'repeatedly uttered by an organisation'.[97] This change in a metaphor's meaning due to repeated utterance is something that features prominently in Nietzsche's conception of metaphor, which we will explore in chapter 2.

For the moment, we can reflect on this rapid semantic shift, in only two years from 1933 to 1935, as but one of countless examples of the semantic relativism of metaphor that is not reflected in cultural diversity, cannot be grounded in embodiment, and cannot solely be understood as a function in ideological discourse. The meaning of *aufziehen* moves from a playful but pejorative everyday metaphor to an altogether different meaning in the language of Nazism, and finally returns to being an everyday metaphor but with an altogether different meaning from its original one. These types of semantic shifts, of course, have resonances beyond the last century and with the types of changes we see in politics today. The possibility of such a flexible semantics is built into the very phenomenon of metaphor itself and is caught somewhere in between relativism and pragmatism.

This is why our analysis differs from those of Kövecses, Underhill and Musolff and why we cannot take the route of cognitive linguistics. We are concerned about the way in which the tension between the pragmatic and relativising function of metaphor is produced by the post-Nietzschean conceptualisation of metaphor itself. The general shared assumption between a post-Nietzschean framework and the cognitive linguistics framework is that metaphors are the foundations for concepts and not the other way around. We have also seen that Lakoff and Johnson view themselves as the heirs to the problems of metaphor that figures like Nietzsche articulated in the history of Western thought. We are interested in how the conflict between metaphor's pragmatic function and its relativising function is produced from this more general conception of metaphor that differs so dramatically from the classical, Aristotelian definition.

It is true that Lakoff and Johnson do assert the metaphoric basis of all concepts. However, they then seem to skirt the hermeneutic problems arising from this. We are not challenging the empirical findings of cognitive linguistics. Rather we are suggesting that they reach a hermeneutic limit and the reasons for this warrant further study. One way to approach this would be to look at cognitive linguistics in detail and in relation to a post-Nietzschean philosophy of metaphor. Another way to approach this, the route this book will take, is to examine in detail the intellectual-historical development of the West's new conception of metaphor, a development that cognitive linguistics claims to have found a methodology to explain. This approach will consider the hermeneutic challenges of both long diachronic changes in language and swift semantic changes within an ideological context, as we have seen in the Klemperer example. As the two faces of metaphor in Nietzsche, both relativising and pragmatic, represent a key moment in the theorisation of this type of semantic change in metaphor, they afford us an ideal point of departure for our analysis. We need to re-examine a conception of metaphor that accounts for diachronic and rapid semantic shifts, as this methodology is needed for certain types of texts and instances of metaphor, such as the ideological metaphor.

Our Approach

To re-examine a conception of metaphor that accounts for diachronic and rapid semantic shifts, part of the methodology of this book is intellectual-historical. Because of this, each chapter will include a section on the historical context in which the ideas presented in the chapter developed. Sometimes, as is the case with Blumenberg and Derrida, the historical context will also include biographical detail about a thinker because it is deemed to be inseparable from understanding the development of their philosophy. The historical section will then be followed by a close reading of the texts that develop the philosophical ideas at stake in that chapter which make up the trajectory in the change of the concept of metaphor. This method will allow us to observe how the hermeneutic tension between the relativistic and pragmatic function of metaphor first comes about in Nietzsche's thought. It will also allow us to observe how these tensions are at the heart of European philosophy more broadly and are fundamentally tied to a change in the conception of metaphor itself.

Observing how the Nietzschean conception of metaphor contributes to the change of the concept of metaphor itself, can clarify hermeneutic problems that stretch across a number of disciplines. It can also provide needed clarification of the genesis of the conception of metaphor as fundamental to cognition which is shared with cognitive linguistics. This book will base such a clarification on three key findings. First, Nietzsche's philosophy presents the West with a new conception of metaphor rather than just an observation of the function of metaphor. Second, the resulting conception of metaphor in European philosophy produces a fundamental hermeneutic tension that orients ways of interpreting metaphor in the humanities and social sciences. The tension between metaphoric meaning as pragmatic and metaphoric meaning as relativising, often seen within European philosophy, will be shown to come ultimately from the same conception of metaphor. Third, various attempts to ground this tension find their limit when they encounter the type of semantic change often seen in political ideology. This hermeneutic limit demands an acknowledgement of the difference between the theoretical undecidability of meaning (Derrida) and meaning used for social and historical orientation (Blumenberg). It also demands the need for a more robust semantics of metaphor; one that could account for how meaning shifts and not simply how meaning is created. Therefore, to address such challenges, the method this book will take is to look at the historical development of the concept of metaphor in order to clarify present philosophical presuppositions about metaphor. So, to begin, we will first turn to the origins of the conception of metaphor in Western thought.

Notes to the Introduction

1. George Lakoff and Mark Johnson, *Metaphors We Live By* (Chicago: University of Chicago Press, 1980), p. 3.
2. Hans Blumenberg, *Paradigms for a Metaphorology*, trans. by Robert Savage (Ithaca: Cornell University Press, 2010), pp. 3–4.
3. Aristotle, *Poetics*, 1457b.
4. Seana Coulson, 'Metaphor and Conceptual Blending'; Madeleine Arsenault, 'Metaphor: Philosophical Theories'; Raymond W. Gibbs, Jr., 'Metaphor: Psychological Aspects'; Gerard Steen, 'Metaphor: Stylistic Approaches'; Lourdes Divasson and Isabel K. Léon, 'Metaphors in English, French, and Spanish Medical Written Discourse'; Paul Chilton, 'Metaphors in Political Discourse'; and David Rose, 'Metaphor, Grammatical', in *Encyclopedia of Language and Linguistics*, ed. by Keith Brown, 2nd edn (Oxford: Elsevier, 2006), pp. 32 — 73.
5. Aristotle, *Poetics*, 1457b.
6. 'μεταφορά', in Henry George Liddell and Robert Scott, *A Greek–English Lexicon*. (Oxford: Clarendon Press, 1940), <http://www.perseus.tufts.edu/hopper/text?doc=Perseus%3Atext%3A1999.04.0057%3Aentry%3Dmetafora%2F> [accessed 13 May 2020].
7. Aristotle, *Poetics*, 1457b.
8. A. P. Martinich, 'Metaphor', in *Routledge Encyclopedia of Philosophy*, v, ed. by Edward Craig (London: Routledge, 1998), p. 6.
9. Aristotle, *Poetics*, 1459a.
10. Sarah Kofman, *Nietzsche and Metaphor*, trans. by Duncan Large (London: Athlone Press, 1993), p. 14.
11. Aristotle, *Poetics*, 1457b.
12. See Zoltán Kövecses, *Metaphor: A Practical Introduction* (Oxford: Oxford University Press, 2002), pp. 4–7, and I. A Richards, *The Philosophy of Rhetoric* (Oxford: Oxford University Press, 1936).
13. Aristotle, *Poetics*, 1459a.
14. Aristotle, *Rhetoric*, 1355a14, 1357a15–1357b16; Aristotle, *Poetics*, 1448b.
15. Friedrich Nietzsche, 'On Truth and Lying in a Non-Moral Sense', in *The Birth of Tragedy and Other Writings*, trans. by Ronald Speirs (Cambridge: Cambridge University Press, 2012), pp. 139–53 (p. 146).
16. Donald Davidson, 'What Metaphors Mean', *Critical Inquiry*, 5.1 (1978), 31–47.
17. Roman Jakobson, 'Two Aspects of Language and Two Types of Aphasic Disturbances', in *On Language*, ed. by Linda R. Waugh and Monique Monville-Burston (Cambridge, MA: Harvard University Press, 1995), pp. 115 — 33.
18. See Claude Lévi-Strauss, *The Savage Mind*, trans. by George Weidenfeld (London: University of Chicago Press, 1966), pp. 75–76, 252–63.
19. Ibid., p. 93.
20. Ibid., p. 263.
21. Clive Cazeaux, *Metaphor and Continental Philosophy* (New York: Routledge, 2007), p. 11.
22. Ibid.
23. Aristotle, *Poetics*, 1457b.
24. Cazeaux, *Metaphor*, p. 12.

25. Ibid., p. 13.
26. Henceforth 'the first *Critique*'.
27. Cazeaux, *Metaphor*, p. 13.
28. Ibid., p. 36.
29. Henceforth 'the third *Critique*'.
30. Kofman, *Nietzsche*, p. 14.
31. Paul Ricoeur, *The Rule of Metaphor*, trans. by Robert Czerny (London: Routledge, 2003).
32. Ibid., p. 336.
33. Dirk Mende, *Metapher — zwischen Metaphysik und Archäologie: Schelling, Heidegger, Derrida, Blumenberg* (Munich: Wilhelm Fink Verlag, 2013), p. 9.
34. Ibid.
35. Ibid., pp. 165 — 66.
36. Ibid., p. 166.
37. Duncan Large, 'Introduction', in Sarah Kofman, *Nietzsche and Metaphor*, trans. by Duncan Large (London: Athlone Press, 1993), p. x.
38. Ibid., p. x.
39. Ibid.
40. Ibid., p. xiii.
41. Ibid., pp. x–xv.
42. Kofman, *Nietzsche*, p. 6.
43. Ibid.
44. Ibid., p. 14.
45. Ibid., p. 17.
46. Ibid., p. 25.
47. Duncan Large, 'Kofman's Nietzsche', in *Interpreting Nietzsche: Reception and Influence*, ed. by Ashley Woodward (London: Continuum, 2011), pp. 116–30 (p. 125).
48. Lakoff and Johnson, *Metaphors*, p. 3.
49. George Lakoff and Mark Johnson, *Philosophy in the Flesh* (New York: Basic Books, 1999), p. 74.
50. George Lakoff and Mark Turner, *More than Cool Reason: A Field Guide to Poetic Metaphor* (London: The University of Chicago Press, 1989), p. 214.
51. Gerard Steen, *Understanding Metaphor in Literature: An Empirical Approach* (New York: Longman, 1994).
52. Raymond W. Gibbs Jr., *The Poetics of Mind: Figurative Thought, Language and Understanding* (Cambridge: Cambridge University Press, 1994), p. 6 (italics in the original).
53. Elena Semino, *Metaphor in Discourse* (Cambridge: Cambridge University Press, 2008), pp. 36–41.
54. See for example, George Lakoff, *Moral Politics: How Liberals and Conservatives Think* (Chicago: University of Chicago Press, 2002); Andreas Musolff, *Political Metaphor Analysis* (London: Bloomsbury Academic, 2016); René Dirven, Hans-Georg Wolf and Frank Polzenhagen, 'Cognitive Linguistics, Ideology, and Critical Discourse Analysis', in *The Oxford Handbook of Cognitive Linguistics*, ed. Dirk Geeraerts and Hubert Cuyckens (Oxford: Oxford University Press, 2007), pp. 1222–40.
55. Lakoff and Johnson, *Philosophy*, p. 6.
56. Ibid., p. 7.
57. See Lakoff and Johnson, *Metaphors*, pp. xi–xiii., Lakoff and Johnson, *Philosophy*, pp. ix–xi.
58. Lakoff and Johnson, *Philosophy*, p. 7.
59. Ibid., p. 74.
60. Cazeaux, *Metaphor*, p. 71.
61. Ibid.
62. Lakoff and Johnson, *Philosophy*, pp. 5–7.
63. Ibid., p. 93.
64. Ibid., pp. 43–44.
65. Lakoff and Johnson, *Metaphors*, pp. 14–21.
66. Ibid., p. 7; Lakoff and Johnson, *Philosophy*, p. 45.
67. Lakoff and Johnson, *Philosophy*, pp. 15–16.

68. Ibid., pp. 42–44.
69. Ibid., p. 43.
70. Ibid., p. 40.
71. Jean M. Aitchison ['J.M.A.'], 'Diachronic and Synchronic', in *Concise Oxford Companion to the English Language*, ed. by Tom McArthur (Oxford: Oxford University Press, Oxford Reference Online, 1998), p. 288, <https://www.oxfordreference.com/view/10.1093/acref/9780192800619.001.0001/acref-9780192800619-e-352?rskey=7iv70V&result=357> [accessed 19 June 2020].
72. *Historical Cognitive Linguistics*, ed. by Margaret E. Winters, Heli Tissari and Kathryn Allan (Berlin: De Gruyter, 2010).
73. Zoltán Kövecses, *Metaphor in Culture: Universality and Variation* (Cambridge: Cambridge University Press, 2007), pp. 2–3.
74. Ibid.
75. Ibid., p. 3.
76. Ibid.
77. Ibid.
78. Ibid., p. 285.
79. Ibid., p. 286, pp. 290–92.
80. Jacques Derrida, 'White Mythology', in *Margins of Philosophy*, trans. by Alan Bass (Chicago: University of Chicago Press, 1984), pp. 207–71 (pp. 218–19).
81. Kövecses, *Metaphor in Culture*, pp. 155–60.
82. James W. Underhill, *Creating Worldviews: Metaphor, Ideology and Language* (Edinburgh: Edinburgh University Press, 2011), p. 7.
83. 'Victor Klemperer: "I am German, the Others Are Un-German"', *Spiegel International*, Jan. 2005, <https://www.spiegel.de/international/victor-klemperer-i-am-german-the-others-are-un-german-a-341147.html> [accessed 19 June 2020].
84. Underhill, *Worldviews*, p. 136.
85. See Andreas Musolff, 'Metaphor and Persuasion in Politics', in *The Routledge Handbook of Metaphor and Language*, ed. by Elena Semino and Zsófia Demjén (London: Routledge, 2017), pp. 309–22.
86. See ibid., pp. 27–38, 133–40.
87. Andreas Musolff, *Metaphor, Nation and the Holocaust: The Concept of the Body Politic* (London: Routledge, 2010), pp. 43–68.
88. Ibid., p. 44.
89. Ibid., p. 43.
90. Klemperer, *Language*, p. 47.
91. Ibid.
92. Ibid.
93. Ibid., p. 48.
94. We could perhaps note here the dark irony of Goebbels's use of *aufziehen* with a straight face when it had previously been used with a smirk to point to the vapidity of that which it was describing. This seems to be a key feature of how ideology relates to metaphor: it demands that the metaphor speaks 'literally'; it demands it to speak in earnestness as if it is stating a fact.
95. Klemperer, *Language*, p. 48.
96. Ibid.
97. Ibid.

CHAPTER 1

The Aristotelian Paradigm of Metaphor and its Evolution

The earliest use of the word 'metaphor' in the English language, according to the *Oxford English Dictionary*, dates from 1477 in Thomas Norton's Middle English poem, *Ordinal of Alchemy*. Norton lists metaphor in its Middle English form of *methaphoris* alongside *poyses* (poetry), and *parabols* (parables), as literary devices which fill the books of scholars and 'causith peyne and wo' (cause pain and woe) due to their seemingly mysterious nature. Norton says that the scholars, with their use of poetry, parables and metaphor, 'made theire bokis to many men ful derk' (made their books dark and obscure to many men).[1] In being placed alongside poetry and parables, metaphor firmly emerges as a part of the figurative canon in its first appearance in the English language. However, this does not necessarily mean that it is distinguished from other elements of figurative language such as metonymy. Rather it is noted as a general poetic device. This is further emphasised in the *OED*'s next entry from 1533 when in a letter King Henry VIII places metaphor alongside allegory as one of the methods by which men can 'draw the word to the truth'.[2] While the emphasis on persuasion in Henry VIII's letter and the emphasis in Norton's poem on causing obscurity within language are clearly different, they both share the view that metaphor is a tool of language for human beings to use. They also share the view that metaphor is not what we would today call literal language; rather, it is figurative, as is reflected by Richard Sherry's 1550, *A Treatise of Schemes & Tropes*, where he defines metaphor as 'a worde [word] translated from the thynge [thing] that it properlye [properly] signifieth [signifies]'.[3] This view of metaphor as a tool of language for human beings to use comes from Aristotle's definition of metaphor and the philosophical paradigm that can be seen to surround it.

In this chapter, we will first seek to understand the Aristotelian paradigm of metaphor and then two key concepts from that paradigm which ground the meaning of metaphor, namely likeness and truthlikeness. Conceptions of likeness and truthlikeness underpin Aristotle's understanding of metaphor and, while both the philosophical conceptions of likeness and truthlikeness undergo a significant evolution in Western thought up until Nietzsche's time, metaphor's relation to these concepts remains unchallenged. Nietzsche's challenge to the idea that likeness and truthlikeness are the basis of metaphor changes metaphor from being understood as a tool of figurative language to the foundation of human cognition. Because this book argues that the conception of metaphor that we see in Nietzsche is a fundamental reversal of the Aristotelian paradigm, this first chapter will lay the intellectual-historical groundwork to assess this reversal from the proper vantage point. As we have seen in the introduction, the term metaphor is used in a very general way today and applied to a variety of fields. If we are claiming that Nietzsche reversed the Aristotelian paradigm of metaphor, then it is essential that we are clear on the development of the specific concept of metaphor that Nietzsche reversed, and that we do not simply speak of metaphor generally, because this general way of speaking was the result of very specific developments in the intellectual history of the West.

Therefore, the first task of this chapter is to understand the Aristotelian paradigm of metaphor. Its second task is to understand how the concept of metaphor as a tool of figurative language evolves. The final task will be to understand a key shift that takes place in the Western understanding of metaphysics, in the thought of Immanuel Kant. But why Kant? Kant sets the stage for Nietzsche's critique of the Aristotelian paradigm of metaphor because, as we shall see in Aristotle and then in Cicero, the semantics of metaphor function on a traditional metaphysical basis. That traditional metaphysical basis undergoes a significant revolution in Kant's philosophy. So, to understand the jump from Aristotle to Nietzsche, the final task of this chapter will be to look at the role which Kant's philosophy played in illuminating the contradiction in metaphysical reasoning that served as the grounds for metaphorical meaning in classical rhetoric. To begin, before turning to Aristotle, we will look at the role that metaphor may have played in the broader Greek and Roman world.

Metaphor in the Greek and Roman World

As we have seen in the introduction, the development of the Western concept of metaphor that led to Aristotle's now famous definition is, of course, Greek. The Greek word μεταφορά (metaphor) comes from μετά (after, with, across) and φέρειν (to bear or carry) and has the general sense of 'transfer'. In Latin, the term is translated as both *metaphora* and *translatio*.[4] Liddell and Scott's *A Greek–English Lexicon* notes that there is a more general meaning of μεταφορά in Greek as 'transport, haulage or change' and then defines the use of the term in Greek rhetoric specifically as a '*transference* of a word *to a new sense*', and attributes this particular meaning to a range of Greek thinkers including Isocrates, Aristotle and Epicurus.[5] However, while it is clear from Liddell and Scott that other Greek rhetoricians such as Isocrates provided definitions of metaphor similar to Aristotle's, as Paul Ricoeur reminds us in *The Rule of Metaphor*, the theories of figures of speech that were taught in rhetorical schools during Europe's age of Enlightenment were inherited primarily from Aristotle and his works the *Rhetoric* and the *Poetics*.[6] While dictionaries of linguistics and poetics may vary in how they define metaphor, all of the various definitions contain the basic vestiges of Aristotle's definition from the *Poetics* which states that 'a metaphor is the application of a word that belongs to another thing'.[7] The main idea in this definition that has continually been drawn upon in the Western tradition is the idea of *transference*. As we have seen, *metaphora* means transfer in Greek and is still used both in the world of economics and in the world of transport in modern-day Greek culture to refer to various kinds of transfer between locations.[8] Aristotle's definition of applying the meaning of one word to another moves *metaphora* from the sense of a transference in economics or transport and into the realm of a semantic transference. This classic Aristotelian definition is one with which the reader will be readily familiar.

The Princeton Encyclopedia of Poetry and Poetics echoes the Aristotelian emphasis on a semantic shift when it defines metaphor as 'a trope, or figurative expression, in which a word or phrase is shifted from its normal uses to a context where it evokes new meanings'.[9] However, when one looks at the larger Greek and Roman world, one is reminded that Aristotle's definition came from a much larger context. What we know about the Greek and Roman understanding of metaphor is largely inferred from the way it is defined and discussed in the Greek and Roman educational culture by the writers of treatises on rhetoric and poetics. While it was quite common by the Hellenistic period for someone to learn rhetoric prior to philosophy, both figures of speech and word order would have been regularly studied in one's education as far back as the Presocratics.[10] Thus our information on metaphor from the Greek and Roman world comes from a culture heavily educated in rhetoric, and from the treatises on rhetoric and poetics produced by that culture of study. From this, we can surmise the following four key aspects of metaphor in the Greek and Roman world.

First, we can see that not all uses of the term 'metaphor' suggest that the transfer or movement signified by the term reflect the Aristotelian definition. For example, in Longinus's treatise *On the Sublime*, he groups metaphor under the heading 'Noble Diction' and suggests it is one of the ways one can achieve sublimity with writing by 'transport[ing] us to the realm of the gods'. Metaphor retains its sense of movement here, but the emphasis is not placed on the mechanics of the word but rather on a somewhat mystical effect metaphor can have on the listener. Here the sense of movement is 'vertical' (transcendent) rather than 'horizontal' (syntactic, on the level of the sentence).[11]

Second, we can observe that brilliant uses of metaphor were noted for hundreds of years prior to Aristotle's definition. Even as far back as Homer and Hesiod we see the importance of the ability to use language well in Greek culture. Michael Gagarin writes:

> Whatever we might say about rhetoric or rhetorical theory, speech was clearly important in Greek culture from the beginning. We think of a Homeric hero like Achilles as the greatest of Greek fighters, but Achilles' tutor Phoenix was charged with teaching him about public speaking as well as about fighting.[12]

In regard to Hesiod's description of a king in the *Theogony*, Gagarin writes: 'the king's ability to use speech to persuade the disputants and others to accept his settlement is crucial to his success in judging'.[13] This suggests to us that using speech well was something valued in Greek culture from the beginning.

Third, we can infer from the prevalence of rhetorical schools that there were many definitions taught besides Aristotle's. The emphasis in these schools was on how to *use* metaphor rather than on what metaphor was.[14] One such pre-Aristotelian example noted by Liddell and Scott's *A Greek–English Lexicon* comes from Isocrates' fifth-century BC text *Evagoras*.[15] In a passage discussing how poetry describes the gods' association with men, Isocrates writes, 'they can treat of these subjects not only in conventional expressions, but in words now exotic, now newly coined, and now in figures of speech, neglecting none, but using every kind with which to embroider their poesy'.[16] The emphasis in this text is clearly on the new and exotic expressions that figures of speech can produce rather than on the mechanics of semantic transference that we see in the Aristotelian definition.

However, we also know that in Isocrates' time in the fifth century, speeches were typically divided up into four canonical parts: introduction, narrative, proof, and epilogue. Plato's *Phaedrus* from *c.* 370 BC reproduces this list.[17] However it is debateable whether the figures of speech themselves were divided up into a more technical classification by the fifth century. What we can say for certain, however, is that after Aristotle in the Hellenistic period, metaphor shows up in lists derived from earlier rhetorical handbooks that were used by Hellenistic scholars to analyse Greek lyric poetry.[18]

Even if the exact origins of an explicit rhetorical theory are debatable, what is evident is that, from as early as Homer's time, we can observe an awareness in Greek culture of how figures of speech and tropes were used, and this was then re-emphasised by the rhetorical schools, in particular by thinkers like Isocrates and Aristotle and then, finally, by Hellenistic scholars. Therefore, Aristotle's definition came from a much larger and older cultural context which viewed metaphor in a variety of ways. In conclusion then, we can say that the definition of metaphor that has shaped Western culture is strictly a definition inside a larger cultural milieu. Aristotle's definition of metaphor does not necessarily contradict other ancient uses of the term, but it is simply one definition from a world steeped in the discussion of the use of figures of speech in rhetoric and poetics.

The Aristotelian Definition

The Aristotelian definition of metaphor that we are familiar with comes from the *Poetics* in a larger section on the parts of speech called *Lexis*. In this section, Aristotle writes that,

> *A metaphor is the application of a word that belongs to another thing*: either from genus to species, species to genus, species to species, or by analogy. By 'from genus to species' I mean, e.g., 'my ship stands here': mooring is a kind of standing. Species to genus: 'ten thousand noble deeds has Odysseus accomplished'; ten thousand is many, and the poet has used it here instead of 'many.' Species to species: e.g. 'drawing off the life with bronze,' and 'cutting with slender-edged bronze'; here he has used 'drawing off' for 'cutting' and vice versa, as both are kinds of removing. Metaphor by analogy means this: when B is to A as D is to C, then instead of B the poet will say D and B instead of D. Sometimes people

add that to which the replaced term is related. I mean, e.g.; the wine bowl is to Dionysus as the shield to Ares: so one will call the wine bowl 'Dionysus' shield,' and the shield 'Ares' wine bowl.' Or old age is to life as evening to day: so one will call evening 'the day's old age' or like Empedocles, call old age 'the evening of life' or 'life's sunset.' In some cases of analogy no current term exists, but the same form of expression will still be used. For instance, to release seed is to 'sow' while the sun's release of fire lacks a name; but the latter stands to the sun as does sowing to the seed, hence the phrase 'sowing his divine fire.' This type of metaphor can further be used by predicating the borrowed term while denying one of its attributes: suppose one were to call the shield not 'Ares' wine bowl' but 'a wineless bowl.'[19]

The first thing to note about Aristotle's definition is that it is a *definition*. We have included this lengthy, technical section from the *Poetics* to emphasise this. Aristotle does not write a theoretical exploration of metaphor in the same way he does the subjects of poetics, rhetoric, physics, metaphysics, etc. If he had a more robust theory of metaphor or tropes in general, it has not survived into the collection of Aristotle's work that we have today. It is important to note this because when we say that Nietzsche reverses the Aristotelian paradigm of metaphor, it is implied that there is a distinction between the definition of metaphor and the accompanying philosophical presuppositions of that definition. The semantic ground of metaphor that Nietzsche critiques comes partially from the accompanying philosophical presuppositions of the Aristotelian definition. As we shall see, this is inferred from other works and, at times, the way these works have been interpreted. In the case of the Aristotelian definition itself, what we have in both the *Rhetoric* and *Poetics* is a larger section defining components of diction in which Aristotle defines various tropes including metaphor.[20] From the *Lexis* section of the *Poetics* we can see how metaphor, as a tool of the orator or the poet, can be used. This is seen in the variety of examples Aristotle gives such as when he cites Empedocles calling old age 'the evening of life'.

Aristotle writes in the *Poetics* that thoughts are the effects that need to be created by speech and that types of diction, including metaphor, help create these effects.[21] This is a reflection of what is traditionally cited as Aristotle's theory of language, which states that language is unique to human beings in that it is *logos* and is the external expression of internal ideas.[22] This forms the first part of the Aristotelian paradigm of metaphor: the human being is a rational animal that uses language to express his or her internal thoughts. Therefore, when we look at metaphor as a part of Aristotle's *Lexis*, we see that it is not a theoretical study of each part of speech, but a list of the parts of speech that one can use to either produce sentences or to produce the effect of poetry or persuasion. However, opinions differ and some scholars, such as Jonathan Barnes, hold the view that this is simply a technical breakdown and that Aristotle does not have the semantic concerns that occupy contemporary scholarship.[23] Barnes is correct in noting that the semantic interest in metaphor is particularly pronounced in contemporary scholarship. But we should also take Aristotle's technical definition of metaphor in view of the paradigm that surrounds it. While reading semantic concerns into Aristotle's thought is certainly a modern tendency, it is clear that the function of metaphor in Aristotle's thought is as a tool of *logos* with the purpose of persuasion. What, then, is the paradigm that surrounds this technical definition? There are two primary statements about the nature of metaphor that we can discern in Aristotle's thought. First, metaphor is a transfer of words, and second, metaphor is the recognition of similarity or likeness. We will look at each of these in turn.

The Two Parts of Aristotle's Definition

Transference

The first aspect of Aristotle's definition, the transfer of words, is its most readily recognisable aspect. The phrase 'a metaphor is the application of a word that belongs to another thing: either from genus to species, species to genus, species to species, or by analogy' appears frequently in the literature relating to metaphor.[24] A literal translation would read 'a *transference* is the application of a word that belongs to another thing'. This is because, as noted in the introduction to this chapter, metaphor means transfer. Presumably what is now a technical term to us, metaphor, was here in this definition a common description. But we can translate it literally like this for the moment to point out that this definition, for all its lack of beauty, is highly descriptive. It teaches us more about what Aristotle thought metaphor does than what metaphor is. As we have seen in the introduction, this book argues that Nietzsche's philosophy shifts the Western conception of what metaphor is and not simply what metaphor does.

This first aspect of transfer involves three parts that are reflected in every contemporary definition of metaphor. The first is the transfer itself. To cite Empedocles' 'old age is the evening of life' metaphor, suddenly the word evening is used when he is talking about old age. The second part of transference is the idea that the word belongs to something or somewhere. Evening does not belong to the associations we have with times of life such as youth or old age, but rather to a time of day. In cognitive linguistics, the 'somewhere else' is described as the source domain of a metaphor.[25] When Empedocles says, 'the evening of life', evening is a source domain for the metaphor. The figurative application of the word evening to describe old age is what transfers the literal meaning of evening into a figurative meaning when it is applied to the target domain, old age. This application of a word from a source domain to a target domain is the third part of Aristotle's conception of transference.[26] So, to sum up, the first part of Aristotle's definition of metaphor is transference and it consists of a word that belongs somewhere, the source domain, the application of that word to a target domain, and the overall transference of both word and meaning, *metaphora*. After the initial definition, at 1457b of the *Poetics*, Aristotle continues to unpack the various ways in which metaphoric transference can happen.

Likeness

The second aspect of Aristotle's definition, likeness, provides the reason for why transference has taken place. A likeness has been perceived and applied. While this is not an explicit theory that Aristotle develops, it is a theme that recurs in both the *Poetics* and the *Rhetoric*. In the *Poetics*, Aristotle writes that 'the greatest asset is a capacity for metaphor. This alone cannot be acquired from another, and is a sign of natural gifts: because to use metaphor well is to discern similarities.'[27] Similarly, in the *Rhetoric*, Aristotle writes: 'it is metaphor[s], therefore, that above all [make us learn something]; for when Homer calls old age stubble, he teaches and informs us through the genus; for both have lost their bloom'.[28] When Aristotle says that Homer draws on stubble's larger genus, Aristotle is referring to his definition of metaphor from the *Poetics*, where he writes that metaphor is the application of a word that belongs somewhere else by genus to species. Stubble can refer to the stalks of a plant that are left on the ground after harvest and therefore by pointing out the likeness between the loss of fresh bloom in plant stubble and a human's old age, Homer teaches us something about old age. About this section of the *Rhetoric*, Stephen Halliwell writes,

> The 'greatest attribute of all' in poetic style is the use of metaphor — it is unteachable and a sign of natural ability; and it consists in the capacity to *perceive likenesses*. Moreover, it particularly suits the style of the two most important genres, epic and tragedy. Although metaphor can be analytically examined and classified, as it is in both the *Poetics* and the *Rhetoric*, it *clearly remains resistant, in Aristotle's eyes, to a 'technical' understanding*. It is only in the case of metaphor that we sense a complete harmony of meaning and style in Aristotle's view of language. The reason for this is that metaphor, although it *can* be regarded as a stylistic ornament alongside other types, is valued by the philosopher as a unique means of expressing certain perceptions. As *Rhet*. 1410b 10ff explains, it is metaphor above all which communicates understanding and insight (whether serious or humorous) by indissoluble linguistic means.'[29]

Halliwell points out that in the *lexis* of both the *Poetics* and *Rhetoric*, Aristotle describes metaphor as a sign of genius because it is a marriage of transference and likeness.

When Empedocles calls old age 'the evening of life' the success of the metaphor relies on the likeness between evening and old age. Likeness, then, is what grounds the *metaphora*, the transference of both word and meaning, in Empedocles' metaphor. In the evening, the light is fading, and the pace of the day is slowing down and drawing to a close. We can easily see the comparison, in that, in old age, the eyesight begins to fade like the fading light of evening and the body begins to slow down like the slowing pace of the day. It is also the final stage of day before the new day begins, much like old age is the final stage of life before death, and in some religions, rebirth. Therefore, for the transference to work in Aristotle's definition, likeness must ground the transference between the source and target domains, or tenor and vehicle, of the metaphor. The final part of the Aristotelian paradigm is the metaphysical grounding of the likeness with the concept of truthlikeness.

Likeness and Truth

The role of likeness that we see in Aristotle's definition of metaphor also has a relationship with his idea of truth. In the *Rhetoric*, Aristotle describes the task of persuading the audience of the truth by showing the audience that which is probable.

> For, in fact, the true and that which resembles it come under the purview of [rhetorical argumentation], and at the same time men have a sufficient natural capacity for the truth [...] persuasion is produced by the speech itself, when we establish the true or apparently true from means of persuasion applicable to each individual subject [...] now that which is persuasive is persuasive [...] because it appears to be proved by propositions that are convincing [...] no art has the particular in view, medicine for instance what is good for Socrates or Callias, but what is good for this or that class of persons [...] similarly, therefore, Rhetoric will not consider what seems probable in each individual case [...] but that which seems probable to this or that class of persons.[30]

Here we see Aristotle outlining the goal of rhetoric as establishing and persuading of the truth through speech and doing this by showing what is universally probable. Often in rhetoric, Aristotle suggests, we must deductively prove the truth of this universal probability.[31] This is an example of the connection between rhetoric and enthymeme or a three-part syllogism such as all men are mortal, Socrates is a man, therefore Socrates is mortal. Thus, we see an early relationship here between the logic which will be employed in metaphysical thinking and the tools of rhetoric.

But there is also a more direct link between the goal of rhetoric and metaphysics and that of Aristotle's correspondence theory of truth. If the goal of rhetoric, as we have seen, is to persuade of the truth, then we must consider rhetoric, and its tools such as metaphor, in relation to Aristotle's correspondence theory of truth. The phrase, 'correspondence theory of truth' is typically associated with Thomas Aquinas's famous metaphysical version: 'A judgement is said to be true when it conforms to the external reality.'[32] However, as the *Routledge Encyclopaedia of Philosophy* notes, the basic premise of a correspondence theory is the 'oldest theory of truth in Western philosophy', and alongside Plato, can be traced to Aristotle in the *Metaphysics*.[33] In the *Metaphysics*, Aristotle writes, 'a statement is true if it says of what is that it is, and of what is not that it is not'.[34] As we have already seen, rhetoric helps the orator in the task of saying 'of what is that it is'. However, it could be said that this link is circumstantial, and it is certainly true that Aristotle does not define metaphor and the correspondence theory of truth in the same sentence.

There are two aspects of Aristotle's philosophy that help to flesh this out. The first is Aristotle's view of the human being as a rational animal who uses language and the second is Aristotle's theory of *mimesis*. In the *Nicomachean Ethics*, Aristotle writes that 'the soul consists of two parts, one irrational and the other capable of reason' and that while irrationality 'appears to be common to all animate things and not peculiar to man', rationality 'urges [the human being] in the right way and exhorts them to the best course'.[35] Aristotle posited that the soul has both a rational and an irrational part and the conflict between the two and the ability to choose between true and false, right and wrong, is one of the things that distinguishes the human being from other animals.

The second thing that makes the human being distinct is language. In fact, in Aristotle the rational animal and the ability to use language are linked. As Laurence Berns writes, 'the traditional definition of man as the rational animal, stemming from Aristotle, goes back to this statement, that man alone of the animals possesses *logos*, possesses thoughtful speech'.[36] Aristotle writes:

> Man alone of the animals possesses speech. The mere voice, it is true, can indicate pain and pleasure, and therefore is possessed by the other animals as well (for their nature has been developed so far as to have sensations of what is painful and pleasant and to indicate those sensations to one another, but speech is designed to indicate the advantageous and the harmful, and therefore also the right and the wrong; for it is the special property of man in distinction from the other animals that he alone has perception of good and bad and right and wrong and the other moral qualities, and it is partnership in these things that makes a household and a city-state.[37]

Here, Aristotle links the ability to use speech to rationality by suggesting that speech can indicate good and bad, right and wrong. This is precisely the way in which we saw Aristotle describe rationality above: the ability to wage war against the irrational part of the soul and choose what is right. Because of this ability to distinguish right from wrong, both speech and rationality also make the human being a political animal. This link between language and politics is one we shall return to later in the book. But for the moment, the ability to judge between things which are good and bad, true or false, and the way that this relates to both rationality and speech, suggests to us the first link between Aristotle's metaphysical paradigm and language.

The second link appears in Aristotle's theory of *mimesis* (imitation). Aristotle makes imitation that which is proper to the human being when he writes: 'from childhood man has an instinct for representation, and in this respect, differs from the other animals in that he is far more imitative and learns his first lessons by representing things'.[38] Not only is it proper to man because we use imitation to learn, we also gain pleasure from imitation. Aristotle writes: 'And then there is the enjoyment people always get from representations.' What links up the types of likeness that Aristotle discusses in his theory of *mimesis* with truthlikeness is that Aristotle describes them as 'accurate likenesses of things' that reflect the 'original'. Aristotle writes:

> What happens in actual experience proves this, for we enjoy looking at accurate likenesses of things which are themselves painful to see, obscene beasts, for instance, and corpses. The reason is this: Learning things gives great pleasure not only to philosophers but also in the same way to all other men, though they share this pleasure only to a small degree. The reason we enjoy seeing likenesses is that, as we look, we learn and infer what each is, for instance, 'that is so and so'. If we have never happened to see the original, our pleasure is not due to the representation as such but to the technique or the colour or some other such cause.[39]

This link between Aristotle's theory of metaphor and Aristotle's theory of *mimesis* is one made by Paul Ricoeur in the introduction to *Time and Narrative*. Here, Ricoeur writes of a semantic innovation that produces a 'meaning effect' which he sees at work in both narrative and metaphor. The meaning effect in both acts of language constitutes a single 'poetic sphere' and it is in this poetic sphere that a new meaning arrives in language.[40]

In this shared sense between both metaphor and *mimesis* of an 'actual likeness' that reflects the original, a shared sense that is re-emphasised by Ricoeur's reading, we see a theoretical link developing between metaphor and truthlikeness in the Western imagination. This link is cemented by a subsequent development in the thought of Cicero.

In his *On Invention*, Cicero adapts several of Aristotle's ideas into the context of Roman rhetoric. Cicero's *On Invention* was an early text and most likely written while he was still a student of rhetoric. He recalled later in life that *On Invention* was 'merely a rough draft, which escaped from my note-books between boyhood and youth'.[41] From this, Cicero's translator H. M. Hubbell infers that *On Invention* was probably based on the dictation of Cicero's teacher and his teacher in turn was teaching from a Greek textbook on rhetoric that was adapted for Roman students.[42] One of the most notable adaptations would have been the translation of Greek terms into the ever-evolving technical Latin terminology emanating from Rome.[43] Hans Blumenberg notes that *On Invention* itself contributed to the translation of terms from Greek to Latin in coining the Latin term *verisimile* (truthlikeness). The Latin *simile* (likeness) was the translation of the Greek term *homoion* which Aristotle uses for likeness, and which grounds the metaphoric transference. In coining the term *verisimile*, Cicero combines the Latin *veritas* (truth) with *simile* (likeness), which of course is what eventually finds its way into our English word verisimilitude, by drawing on another principle of likelihood from Aristotle's *Rhetoric*.[44]

As we have seen in the *Rhetoric*, one of the methods used to persuade the listener of the likelihood of the narrative is the syllogism. Cicero expands on this form of persuasion and then brings the terms truth and likeness quite literally together when he writes: 'The narrative will be probable if it seems to embody characteristics which are accustomed to appear in real life [...]; verisimilitude can be secured by following these principles.'[45] Thus, in a single stroke, Aristotle's theory of similarity, grounding the operation of a metaphor and Aristotle's theory of metaphysics, grounding the correspondence theory of truth, were brought together in the term *verisimile*.

Although *On Invention* was an early text that 'escaped from Cicero's notebooks', it is one of the classical rhetorical treatises that helped to define the subsequent tradition of rhetoric as it was taught in Europe during the Enlightenment.[46] Therefore, the rhetorical tradition that was passed down into European scholarship from Aristotle and then Cicero aimed to persuade the listener of the truth, using the tools of rhetoric, such as metaphor, in such a way that 'embody characteristics which are accustomed to appear in real life'.[47] Metaphor continued to carry out this task but, as Paul Ricoeur writes, it was 'relegated to the dead discipline [of rhetoric]'.[48] We know that metaphor was taught alongside other tropes in rhetorical schools and we could look at several examples of the extensive writing that went into clarifying just what a trope meant, such as in the Renaissance humanist Peter Ramus's *Rhetoricae distinctiones in Quintilianum* (1549). Here he famously classified tropes into four different types: metonymy, irony, metaphor and synecdoche. This classification was adopted widely in Renaissance university curriculum reform.[49] However metaphor's conceptualisation, as a trope, changed very little between the time of Aristotle and Cicero and the time of Immanuel Kant. As we shall see in the next section, with only a few exceptions, the very idea of what a trope was rested on the foundation of the idea of rhetorical device that functioned by likeness and comparison.

A Very Brief History of the Concept of Metaphor

Our next task will be to examine briefly a few key moments in the conceptualisation of metaphor from the Graeco-Roman world up until the time of Kant. It is, of course, impossible to recount accurately over a thousand years of philosophical history in a single section; moreover, the conceptual history of metaphor in the period between Aristotle and Kant warrants further study. However, in examining a few moments in the conceptualisation of metaphor, we might be able to see why such a jump is justified. Metaphor's conceptualisation, as a trope, as a device that functioned on the basis of likeness and comparison, changed very little from Aristotle and Cicero, up until the time of Immanuel Kant. It is these conceptual parameters of metaphor that we are particularly interested in understanding and we will focus specifically on examples from metaphor's conceptual history that highlight the evolution of these parameters.

To ask about the history of how metaphor has been conceptualised in the West since Aristotle is different from asking about its history in the study of rhetoric or poetics. There is certainly overlap, but, broadly speaking, to ask about the history of metaphor in the study of rhetoric or poetics is to ask about the history of what metaphor *does*, but to ask about the history of how metaphor has been conceptualised in the West is to ask about the history of what metaphor *is*. We note again the distinction that is vital for understanding why Nietzsche's critique of the Aristotelian paradigm was a key aspect of European philosophy that revolutionised the Western concept of metaphor, i.e. what metaphor *is*.

The Roman rhetorician Quintilian, who, above all, founded the rhetorical school tradition with his *Institutio Oratoria* in AD 95, provides us with examples of both approaches to metaphor.[50] On the subject of what metaphor and figurative language *does*, Quintilian is quoted as saying:

> [the subject of tropes] has given rise to interminable disputes among the teachers of literature, who have quarrelled no less violently with the philosophers than among themselves over the problem of the genera and species into which tropes may be divided, their number and their correct classification.[51]

Because of this dispute, Quintilian suggests a basic and general classification of tropes into three broad categories. He suggests that words are either, 'proper, newly coined or metaphorical'.[52] The correct classification of metaphor, as a trope as opposed to a proper or newly coined word, is a question that revolves around what metaphor does. To ask about what distinguishes a metaphorical use of language from a literal use of language, for example, conceptualises metaphor as a trope, and asks what it does in a sentence. Admittedly, asking what distinguishes metaphorical from literal language does raise the question of the identity of metaphor, but this question of identity is one of classification and not nature. The nature of metaphor stays the same in these debates. It is a phenomenon of figurative language, a trope. The shift that we are ultimately concerned with in this book, the shift from the nature of metaphor being that of figurative language to the nature of metaphor being the foundation of cognition, is a shift in how metaphor is conceptualised.

While this book argues that Nietzsche's philosophy plays a decisive role in the history of metaphor's conceptualisation, it is also interested in how such a decisive role fits into the European philosophy more generally. There are, therefore, a few essential examples to note before turning to Nietzsche. To begin, while Quintilian raises the question of classification, he also suggests a conceptualisation of metaphor that is an interesting permutation of Aristotle. *The Princeton Encyclopedia of Poetry and Poetics* points out that Quintilian's broad definition of metaphor, in which metaphor is simply contrasted to 'proper' or 'newly coined' words, can give rise to confusion.[53] Quintilian himself sensed this and to resolve the confusion suggested that 'metaphor is a substitution involving any permutation of the terms "animate" and "inanimate"'.[54] This gives us two conceptual characterisations. First, while related, the idea of substitution is slightly different from the semantic connotations of transfer that we see in Aristotle's definition. Second, the change between animate and inanimate is quite striking. Quintilian is suggesting a semantic metamorphosis between the domains of animate and inanimate. If we consider Aristotle's example of the metaphor *my ship stands here*, we can see this clearly. Not only can ships not stand, but standing is something that belongs to the domain of an animate creature whereas a ship is inanimate. In Quintilian's thought, at the birth of the rhetorical school tradition, metaphor here substitutes the animate for the inanimate. However, while a philosophically insightful definition, it is nonetheless a definition anchored in a contrast to literal language.[55]

The concept of metaphor continues to be constituted by a mixture of philosophical insight and linguistic classification in what is perhaps the most well-known treatment of figurative language in medieval philosophy, that of Thomas Aquinas. Aquinas seems initially to hold to the notion, quite common in the Middle Ages, that metaphoric substitution is based on a lack of equivalency between thing and object.[56] We see Aquinas voice this common view when in *Super Boethium De Trinitate*, a treatise on the philosopher Boethius, he writes: 'figurative speech doesn't contain any evidence or proof in itself'.[57] However, Aquinas also reinvents this notion because, for him, this lack of evidence is precisely what we need to speak about God.

In 'The Names of God' section in his *Summa Theologica*, Aquinas is discussing the application of names to the divine by human language. He begins by reminding the reader that, 'words relate to the meaning of things signified through the medium of the intellectual conception. It follows therefore that we can give a name to anything in as far as we can understand it.'[58] However, he is quick to remind the reader that 'the reason why God has no name, or is said to be above being named, is because His essence is above all that we understand about God and signify in word'.[59] We see that, for Aquinas, the essence of God is above being understood by the human being. We also see that the name of things has meaning only insofar as we can understand that thing. Therefore, it would seem to follow that, as we do not understand the essence of God, the names of God do not have a meaning for us. While Aquinas is quick to concede this point, he reminds the reader of the type of language used in the names of God and in doing so makes a distinction between literal and figurative language. As we saw in Quintilian, the philosophical insight seems to be mixed together with linguistic classification. Aquinas writes:

> It seems that no name is applied literally to God. For all names which we apply to God are taken from creatures; as was explained above. But the names of creatures are applied to God metaphorically, as when we say, God is a stone, or a lion, or the like. Therefore names are applied to God in a metaphorical sense.[60]

This metaphorical sense, for Aquinas, produces knowledge of God.

In the following section, in which Aquinas discusses whether a name can be applied to God in a literal sense, he writes that 'our knowledge of God is derived from the perfections which flow from Him to creatures [...] Now our intellect apprehends them as they are in creatures, and as it apprehends them it signifies them by names.'[61] It seems that while Aquinas shares the view that figurative language does not contain any truth in itself, he is quick to see its usefulness in producing knowledge. When one is speaking about God, an exact equivalence is impossible. Therefore, the metaphors that one uses to describe God, 'God is a stone, God is a lion', etc. give us knowledge of God indirectly. The very lack of equivalency between a metaphor and absolute truth, in Aquinas's case about God, nevertheless produces knowledge about God.

So, on the one hand Aquinas's understanding of metaphor diverges from Aristotle. We see that because of Aquinas's notion of a transcendent God, it is impossible for metaphors about God to have a truthlike match between the likeness in the metaphor and the thing it is describing. However, on the other hand, we can see the inheritance of the Aristotelian paradigm quite clearly: metaphor does not contain truth in itself, rather it is a useful tool to persuade the listener of the truth, and in the case of Aquinas, that truth is God. Either way, there is a clear line between metaphor and truth in Aquinas's thought and as in the case of Aristotle, a metaphor requires truthlikeness to verify the equivalence, or in Aquinas's case, lack of equivalence, between the tenor and the vehicle of the metaphor.

Moving forward in history, we have already seen that, in the Renaissance, metaphor was conceived of as a specific trope in contrast to other tropes in the wake of Ramus's *Rhetoricae distinctiones in Quintilianum*.[62] By the time of the Enlightenment, the contrast between reason and specific types of tropes, such as metaphor, becomes particularly pronounced. If in the Middle Ages we see the

Aristotelian paradigm of metaphor extended to theology, in the Enlightenment we see an inversion of the same paradigm. In the English Enlightenment, for example, metaphor was certainly a specific trope but for Thomas Hobbes and John Locke, it was also a dangerous deviation from the truth.[63] For example, in a section on the abuses of speech in *Leviathan*, Hobbes writes: 'when [human beings] use words metaphorically; that is, in [another] sense than that they are ordained for, [they] thereby deceive others'. At the end of the chapter, Hobbes connects metaphor with 'senseless words', writing, 'metaphors, and [senseless] and ambiguous words, are like *ignes fatui* [a delusion or false hope]; and reasoning upon them, is wandering amongst innumerable absurdities'.[64]

In his chapter 'Abuse of Words' in *An Essay Concerning Human Understanding*, John Locke expands on a similar sentiment. He includes metaphor under the heading of the 'wilful faults and neglects [of language], which men are guilty of'. Locke claims that 'wit and fancy finds easier entertainment in the world, than dry truth and real knowledge'.[65] Locke does write, however, that, 'in discourses, where we seek rather pleasure and delight, than information and improvement, such ornaments as are borrowed from them, can scarce pass for faults'.[66] But in regard to gaining knowledge and the use of judgement, Locke writes,

> all the artificial and figurative application of words eloquence hath invented, are for nothing else but to insinuate wrong ideas, move the passions, and thereby mislead the judgement, and so, are perfect cheats; and, therefore, however laudable or allowable oratory may render them in [...] popular addresses, they are certainly in all discourses that pretend to inform or instruct, wholly to be avoided; and where truth and knowledge are concerned, cannot but be thought a great fault, either of the language or person that makes use of them.[67]

In both Hobbes and Locke, we see Cicero's thesis that figurative language does not contain any truth in and of itself, pushed to the extreme. In Cicero, while a metaphor itself may not contain truth, it was a valuable tool to persuade the listener of the truth. Locke banishes that notion and puts the use of language in 'wit and fancy' on one side and 'dry truth and real knowledge' on the other, while Hobbes asserts that basing arguments on metaphors is to 'wander amongst innumerable absurdities'.

This sentiment is echoed in the French Enlightenment when Diderot contrasts rational argument with comparisons and similes. In a dialogue on philosophical language, Diderot writes, 'Je reviens au ton de la philosophie à qui il faut de raisons et non des comparaisons' (I return to the tone of philosophy in which we need arguments and reason and not comparisons).[68] In both the French and English Enlightenment, metaphor is clearly understood as a trope or a figurative device and the contrast between a figurative device and reason is also very clear. The Enlightenment solidifies for us not simply the contrast between the literal and the figurative, as we have seen in Quintilian, but both the contrast between truth and metaphor and the contrast between reason and metaphor.

While Jean-Jacques Rousseau echoes the contrast between reason and metaphor, he sees something positive in it. He even asserts a figurative origin to language and this is one of the places where we see the beginning of the conception that Nietzsche will eventually inherit. In *Essay on the Origin of Languages*,[69] Rousseau writes:

> as the first motives that made man speak were the passions, his first expressions were Tropes. Figurative language was the first to arise, proper meaning was found last. Things were not called by their true name until they were seen in their genuine form. At first, only poetry was spoken. Only long afterwards did anyone take it into his head to reason.[70]

In regard to a reader's objection that it would be impossible for a figurative meaning to come before any proper meaning, Rousseau writes that, 'words are transposed only because ideas are also transposed'. The explanation he gives us for ideas being transposed at the start of cognition is that because our first motives arise from emotion or 'passion', 'when passion fascinates our eyes [...] the first idea it offers us is not the true one'.[71] Thus, Rousseau suggests that figurative language corresponds to the 'passions' or emotions and that it is the emotions that present us with our first, instinctive, conceptions, even if these are illusory. As Paul De Man writes in his commentary on the *Essay*, '[for Rousseau], the metaphor [...] presents as certain what is, in fact, a mere possibility'.[72] This is why, for Rousseau, the initial impression is illusory. It is illusory because it is not fact, but the emotions and the corresponding language to the emotion, i.e. metaphor, present things to our cognition as certainties that are mere possibilities.

Rousseau then concludes by saying that this original language was only understood as metaphorical once the mind matured and recognised the error it had made, and that the original conception, which corresponded to the 'emotions', was not true. Rousseau writes: '[The first language] then became metaphorical when the enlightened mind, recognizing its first error, employed the expressions only with the same passions that had produced it.'[73] Rousseau belongs to a category of eighteenth- and nineteenth-century thinkers, such as Vico, Herder, Gerber, and Müller, who assert the figurative origin of language. Because of this, Rousseau's position is distinct from Diderot's. However, what links Rousseau and Diderot are their clear sense of reason being on one side and figurative language being on the other. Rousseau concludes this section of the *Essay* by stating that the only way we can recognise this original language as metaphoric is when a more 'enlightened mind' sees its initial error. The contrast of reason to metaphor, especially in thinkers like Locke or Diderot, begins to pull metaphor away from its Aristotelian province where it acts as a tool to persuade one of the truth. However, even in this stark contrast where metaphor is viewed as liable to cause errors in thought, it is still conceptualised as a figurative device that is distinct from either reason or truth.

Perhaps the most innovative characterisation of metaphor during the Enlightenment is found in Giambattista Vico's *New Science* (1725). In the *New Science*, metaphor becomes one of the four basic tropes through which Vico provided an analysis of the history of language and civilisation. Vico used Ramus's four categories of metonymy, irony, metaphor and synecdoche as interpretive tools for the history of Roman culture. In the age of the gods, for example, metonymy ruled, or in the age of heroes, synecdoche.[74] In the case of metaphor, Vico claimed, it belonged to the age of men. He writes that in 'the age of men',

> the most luminous and therefore the most necessary and frequent [trope] is metaphor. It is most praised when it gives sense and passion to insensate things [...] by which the first poets attributed to bodies the being of animate substances, with capacities measured by their own, namely sense and passion, and in this way made fables of them. Thus every metaphor so formed is a fable in brief. This gives a basis for judging the time when metaphors made their appearance in the languages. All the metaphors conveyed by likenesses taken from bodies to signify the operations of abstract minds must date from times when philosophies were taking shape. The proof of this is that in every language the terms needed for the refined arts and recondite sciences are of rustic origin.[75]

While Vico still makes a clear appeal towards philosophical reasoning as distinct from metaphor, the anthropomorphising of likeness creates striking parallels to Nietzsche's philosophy of metaphor that we will explore in depth in chapter 2; moreover, in chapter 4, we will also see the influence of Vico upon Hans Blumenberg's philosophy. Vico's concept of cognition is of course pre-Kantian. However, these connections with philosophers like Nietzsche and Blumenberg suggest a remarkably modern sensibility. As Wallace Martin suggests, Vico can be said to occupy the same position as modern discussions about 'metaphor's importance in the development of language', such as Max Müller's thesis that metaphoric language had a role to play in the development of mythology.[76]

Vico's thesis also foreshadows the collapse of the distinction between literal and figurative language. This is because Vico claimed that it was not sensible to speak of ancient language as either literal or metaphorical, since the distinction between the two did not exist in the period to which the modern theories point.[77] Vico's expansive proposal about the role of metaphor in the development of language, history and culture influenced various streams of romanticism, found, for example, in the ideas of Rousseau, Herder, Schelling or Shelley. It also influenced the nineteenth-century theses put forward by German philologists such as Max Müller or Gustav Gerber, to whom we shall turn in chapter 2.[78]

While Vico's *New Science* was published only eighteen years after the death of John Locke, his views are noticeably progressive. They bring us closer to an understanding of figurative language present in the 1781 publication of the *Critique of Pure Reason* by Immanuel Kant. Kant would have been aware of the rhetorical distinction between the types of tropes that Ramus helped to create, but was probably unaware of Vico's *New Science* as it was relatively unpopular in its day and was not translated into German until 1822.[79] Up to this point in this short history, with notable exceptions like Vico, we have seen metaphor understood as one classification within a wider set of tropes, as in Ramus; as a tool which indirectly produces knowledge of the divine, as in Aquinas; as a substitution of the inanimate for the animate, as in Quintilian; and, as the 'other' or opposite pole of reason, as in Diderot, Hobbes and Locke. However, in these conceptualisations, metaphor remains a device that functions on the basis of likeness and comparison, and whether viewed positively or negatively, it is distinct from truth or reason.

The common theme running through all these distinctions is still Aristotelian. In all of the examples we have seen, there is a commentary on metaphor's ability or inability to persuade of the truth much as we saw Henry VIII consider metaphor as one of the methods by which men can 'draw the word to the truth'.[80] We have also seen that the reasons for such a judgement on metaphor's ability to persuade relies on a presupposition of the ability to judge whether the likeness in the metaphoric comparison is truthlike. Metaphor requires truthlikeness to verify its equivalency or lack thereof. In Aquinas, for example, we saw that a metaphor could not provide an equivalence with the essence of God but was still helpful for producing knowledge about God. The ability to judge that the metaphor is inequivalent with God presupposes an absolute truthlikeness, i.e. God. A similar presupposition can be found in the cases of Hobbes and Locke. While the notion of a transcendent God does not appear, both are able to judge that metaphor misleads the reasonable mind because, in the Enlightenment, a notion of reason is paired with a notion of truth. The Enlightenment deems metaphor unreasonable and therefore unable to produce truthlikeness. While this is a different position from Aristotle's, it shares the presupposition of being able to judge the meaning of metaphor due to a match between likeness and truthlikeness. It is simply that, in the Enlightenment, this match is judged above all by reason and metaphor has been deemed unreasonable. However, when the foundations of the use of reason itself come into question in Immanuel Kant's philosophy, the scene was set for Nietzsche to question the foundations of metaphor itself and to reverse the Aristotelian paradigm.

Kant and Metaphor

In the preface to the second edition of the *Critique of Pure Reason*, Kant writes that logic since Aristotle, 'has not been able to advance even one step, so that, to all appearances, it may be considered as completed and perfect [...] that logic should in this respect have been so successful is due entirely to its limitations'.[81] While it is evident that Kant's critique of the idea of a pure form of reason is a response to the contradictions in metaphysical debates in his own day, such as in the Wolffian school, as we can see in this passage, Kant sees the assumptions that frame those very metaphysical debates as stretching back to Aristotle.[82] As Sebastian Gardner puts it, Kant 'takes Aristotle's logic to be definitive'.[83]

Of course, Kant's critique of metaphysics was not concerned with Aristotle specifically. It is often the case that when people look at relationships between Aristotle and Kant, they look at the relationship between Aristotle's virtue ethics and Kant's moral philosophy.[84] But even though Kant does not frame the critique of pure reason as a critique of Aristotle specifically, it is framed in several places as a critique of the assumptions of the entire metaphysical tradition, beginning with classical philosophers such as Plato and Aristotle. As we have seen in the example above, the problem of this limited, definitive, deductive logic extends back to Aristotle and has, in Kant's words, 'not been able to advance even one step' since him. When Kant creates his table of categories for certain concepts, he attributes the division of types of concepts into categories to Aristotle, although Aristotle, according to Kant, 'had no guiding principle, he merely picked them up as they occurred to him'.[85]

Finally, and perhaps definitively, in the final chapters of the first *Critique*, in a section entitled 'The History of Pure Reason', Kant points to three issues that represent key moments in the history of how reason has been conceived. Regarding 'the object of all knowledge of our reason, some philosophers were mere sensualists, others mere intellectualists'.[86] Here he cites these approaches to reason being founded in Epicurus and Plato respectively. Then, regarding how rational knowledge can be gained from experience, he cites Aristotle at the head of the empiricist school and Plato at the head of what he calls the noologist school, referencing the Greek word *nous* (intellect). While, on the one hand, these distinctions are basic and learned by all first-year philosophy students, the fact that Kant includes this information under his heading 'The History of Pure Reason' gives us some sense of how all-encompassing his critique is and how many of the problems to which he is directing his critique are founded in origins of Western philosophy. How is this all-encompassing critique relevant to metaphor?

In *Metaphor and Continental Philosophy*, Clive Cazeaux suggests that 'the phenomenon of inventive metaphor is a concentration of the problem faced by Kant in the *Critique of Pure Reason*'.[87] It is certainly true that Kant's philosophy provides the framework for key problems within which post-Nietzschean philosophers of metaphor, such as Hans Blumenberg or Jacques Derrida, situate metaphor, but Kant never explicitly engages with metaphor. A perusal of Howard Caygill's *A Kant Dictionary* shows us that while there are several issues pertaining to metaphor that we can read back into Kant, metaphor itself is not a key term in Kant's philosophy. Cazeaux notes this absence and suggests that we can instead look at the logic behind Kant's thinking on analogy. After all, Cazeaux argues, analogy is a subset of metaphor in the Aristotelian definition.[88] However, while Cazeaux is correct to draw our attention to Kant's view of analogy, as it is important for understanding the philosophical logic that post-Nietzschean thinkers like Derrida and Blumenberg draw on in their respective philosophies of metaphor, we should be careful not to attach later developments in philosophy to Kant's philosophy. Even in the attention Kant pays to analogy, he wants to confine it within clearly defined limits. Analogy never becomes a substitute for reason in Kant's philosophy, only a supplement to reason.

In the *Critique of Judgement* Kant calls analogy a 'mere rule of reflection'[89] and in the *Prolegomena to Any Future Metaphysics*, he makes clear that analogy 'does not signify [...] [a] similarity of two things'.[90] Rather, for Kant, analogy signifies 'a similarity of *relations* between two quite dissimilar things'.[91] Surely the logic of analogy has a marvellous capability for Kant, but it is clear that analogy does not perform a 1:1 identity match between perception and object but rather creates a rule of reflection that serves to find the similarity of the *relations* between the two things. This seems to imply that despite looking upon the category of the figurative in a much more positive light for cognition than earlier Enlightenment philosophers such as Hobbes, Locke or Diderot, Kant still maintains a distinction between the logic of the figurative and reason, in that it creates a rule of *reflection* rather than a rule of *identity*. Caygill's note in *A Kant Dictionary* confirms this, stating that, for Kant, analogy 'is an important supplement to logical identity, but must not surreptitiously be employed as a substitute for it'.[92] This is a critical reminder because what is so revolutionary about Nietzsche's thinking on metaphor is that it becomes a substitute for reason. It is not a supplemental tool of reason; rather, for Nietzsche there is no reason at all without metaphor. We will return to the relevance of Kant's philosophy for the mechanics of metaphor in a moment but, keeping in mind this initial provision, we will turn to the main issues in Kant's philosophy that foreshadow the problems that come to be significant in a post-Nietzschean theory of metaphor. Again, to remind the reader, the Western conception of metaphor will shift in Nietzsche's thought because the philosophical foundations that metaphor once rested upon are altered. It is in this way that Kant's philosophy plays a pivotal role in moving us one step closer to Nietzsche's revolution in the status of metaphor.

The Relationship between Epistemology and Metaphysics

The problem of the relationship between epistemology and metaphysics in Kant's thought is one of the main things that becomes particularly important for the context within which Nietzsche critiques truth via metaphor, thus reversing the Aristotelian paradigm of metaphor. A contradiction in the relationship between epistemology and metaphysics was the very impulse for writing *The Critique of Pure Reason* and as we have seen, Clive Cazeaux suggests that 'the phenomenon of inventive metaphor is a concentration of the problem faced by Kant in the *Critique of Pure Reason*'.[93] Thus, one of the views that can be taken on metaphor is that it poses a certain set of conceptual problems that are also encountered within the conceptual parameters and impetus of Kant's philosophical project.

What is the premise of Kant's philosophical project as it relates to the juncture of metaphysics and epistemology? Kant observed a contradiction within reason's ability to resolve metaphysical issues. In the 'Preface to the First Edition' of the *Critique of Pure Reason*, Kant reminds the reader that the basic use of reason begins with the initial conjecture of principles. Here he writes:

> with these principles [reason] rises, as required by the ways of its nature, higher and higher to more remote conditions. But when it becomes aware that in this manner its work would remain forever incomplete, because the questions never cease, it finds itself constrained to take refuge in principles which exceed every possible application in experience and nevertheless seem so little suspect that even ordinary human reason agrees with them. Thus, reason becomes involved in darkness and contradictions, from which [...] it may conclude that errors must be lurking somewhere; but it is unable to discover them because the principles which it follows transcend the limits of all experience [...][94]

In this contradiction, we could summarise the way in which Kant frames the problem as follows. We employ reason in empirical judgements and our empirical judgements are legitimate. The same faculty of reason that we use in our empirical judgements is also used in metaphysical judgement. Therefore, metaphysical judgements should be sound. But metaphysics results in contradictions and therefore reason as a whole contradicts itself.

Arising from this contradiction, Kant's most general project is to understand what reason can and cannot do. This was a logical progression for Kant from the Enlightenment theme *sapere aude!* (dare to use your own reason). In his now famous essay 'An Answer to the Question: What is Enlightenment?' Kant suggests that *sapere aude!* had come to mean that everything must be subjugated to critique by reason.[95] As Sebastian Gardner has pointed out, once Kant had observed the contradiction within the use of reason in metaphysics, it followed naturally in the spirit of the time for him in turn to subjugate reason itself to critique.[96] To remind the reader, the answer Kant posed to the contradiction he detected in metaphysical reasoning was a philosophical revolution in the style of Copernicus.

Hitherto it has been supposed that all our knowledge must conform to its objects. But all our attempts to establish something about them *a priori* by means of concepts, thus to expand our knowledge, have on this supposition come to nothing. We should therefore attempt to tackle the tasks of metaphysics more successfully by assuming that the objects must conform to our knowledge.[97]

The main thing to note regarding the theme of metaphor is that Kant observed that the human ability to process metaphysical questions was built into reason itself; yet even though reason could produce legitimate empirical judgements, it contradicted itself once it arrived at metaphysical judgements. For example, in the first *Critique*, Kant outlines contradictions that necessarily follow from speculation that our reason makes. These are Kant's 'antinomies'. Originally a word used to express a legal contradiction, after Kant the English term 'antinomy' evolved to refer to a logical contradiction or a paradox.[98] In the second book of 'the transcendental dialectic', Kant refers to four antinomies that result from cosmological speculation. The first example he gives comprises the contradictory theses that the world has a beginning in time and a limit in space and the opposing view that the world's space is limitless, and it has no temporal beginning.[99] The third example he gives is that of the idea of an original causality to freedom that exists separate from the laws of nature. This contradicts the hypothesis that there is no freedom, and everything occurs according to the laws of nature.[100]

The point of these antinomies for our purposes is that, on the one hand, for Kant, the ability to speculate about metaphysical questions like the temporal beginning of the world or the all-encompassing laws of nature is built into our cognitive processing and the very use of reason itself. As he wrote in the preface to the first *Critique,* 'with these principles [reason] rises, as required by the ways of its nature, higher and higher to more remote conditions'. On the other hand, a basic contradiction is built into our cognitive processing: '[reason] finds itself constrained to take refuge in principles which exceed every possible application in experience and nevertheless seem so little suspect that even ordinary human reason agrees with them. Thus, reason becomes involved in darkness and contradictions.'[101] So for example, reason necessarily leads us to posit a temporal origin to the universe but also leads us to posit that the universe is without a temporal origin.

As we have seen, Kant does not extend the logic of this flaw in metaphysical reasoning to metaphor but rather confines reflections on figurative language to a supplemental role. It is then all the more revolutionary that the basic contradiction Kant sees within metaphysical reasoning is shifted to metaphor in Nietzsche's thought, because the role of metaphor in relation to reason shifts. As we shall see, the main issue that Nietzsche perceives in metaphor is not only that it is built into the most basic aspects of our cognitive processing, but also that it reveals a flaw or contradiction within our cognitive processing.

The Schematism of Pure Understanding

Besides the basic framework of the first *Critique*, the other issues that become pertinent for metaphor in Kant's thought are the schematism, and the theories of analogy and symbol. Cazeaux has pointed to the importance of Martin Heidegger's interpretation of Kant's schematism for a theory of metaphor and we will return to the Heideggerian reading of Kant in chapter 3.[102] In this chapter we will look firstly at the schematism in its original context. In Kant's first *Critique*, on the section entitled 'The Transcendental Doctrine of the Power of Judgement', the schematism is introduced as an answer to the question 'how can intuitions be subsumed under concepts?'[103] For Kant, intuition is on the side of appearances and the disparity he sees arises from the riddle of how pure concepts of the understanding could be applied to appearances at all.[104]

One of Kant's well-known examples of this disparity between concept and appearance is that of the concept of dog as a four-legged creature and the image of a dog.[105] There must be something besides pure concepts and besides intuitions which allow us to synthesise concept and image. Therefore, Kant posits what he calls a schematism of the pure understanding: a procedure of judgement that mediates between concepts and intuition.[106] What is crucial about the schematism is that through this mediating operation between image and the concept, it allows judgement to take place. Kant states that the schematism is 'how a concept receives its image' and this 'is an art hidden in the depths of the human soul'.[107]

What is important for us here is that Kant sets out a procedure of judgement that holds the rules for how to synthesise concepts and images. The imagination then, takes a central role because Kant claims that this procedure of judgement is a product of the imagination.[108] As Mark Johnson puts it, the schematism is a 'procedure of the imagination for structuring images in accordance with concepts'.[109] However, the rules of synthesis that the schematism produces are not simply effects of the imagination. For Kant, they are a product of pure *a priori* imagination. In other words, the imagination is not working after experience, but like our intuitions of space and time in Kant's philosophy, it arises *a priori*.[110] This is an important distinction.

When we think of imagination in the everyday use of the word, one of the connotations may be the way a fantasy writer, for example, romanticises or re-imagines human experience in novel ways. For example, in reviewing the latest award-winning fantasy novel by British novelist China Mieville, *The Sunday Times* said that Mieville makes 'extraordinary use of the ordinary'.[111] But Kant's interest in the imagination, as it relates to the schematism, is not in this more colloquial sense where fantasy novelists may make ordinary things quite extraordinary, like a piece of wood becoming a magical wand or a wardrobe being a door to another world. When we speak of the imagination in this colloquial manner, we mean the novelist is using their power of imagination to make our mundane everyday human experience extraordinary. For Kant, as Howard Caygill writes, the imagination is a faculty of the original representation of the object (*exhibitio originaria*) rather than a faculty of derived representation (*exhibitio derivativa*) because Kant, according to Caygill, is most interested in the 'original representation of the object'.[112]

Analogy and Symbol

The representation of objects takes on a different dimension, however, when one is representing an abstract metaphysical concept, such as God for example, and not simply an empirically observed object, such as a dog. As we have seen earlier, this is where reason becomes involved in 'darkness and contradiction' because it is the very possibility of reason's contemplation of metaphysical conceptions that is the impetus for the first *Critique*. It could be argued then, that one of the decisive innovations for the concept of metaphor, but an innovation not yet seen by Kant, is the role he suggests that figurative language plays with the representation of such metaphysical concepts.

To return to Kant's theory of analogy, Kant is concerned with analogy in regard to the way in which it creates a relationship between two differing sets. A brief review of the history of the concept of analogy is helpful. The origins of the Western theory of analogy are situated within Pythagorean mathematics. The fourth-century BC thinker Eudoxus created a theory of analogy to attempt to resolve a conflict between incommensurable ratios that arose in the theories of followers of Pythagoras.[113] From this theory, a distinction between *logos* and *analogos* arose when Euclid defined the two terms in Book 5 of the *Elements*. Here, *analogos* was defined as a similar relationship between different ratios.[114] Aristotle extended this mathematical concept to a broader philosophical principle in his work on logic, the *Topics*, where he laid out his famous formula for analogy, $A:B = C:D$. Aristotle was concerned with the broader principle of the relationship between different genres, A and B being one genre and C and D being another.[115] Aristotle then went on in subsequent works to show how this form of reasoning worked in metaphysics, ethics, politics and poetics.[116] And it is to the application of analogy in the *Poetics*, under the broader theory of metaphor, that Cazeaux appeals when he links Kant's work on analogy to a theory of metaphor.[117]

This brief historical review serves to remind us that the concept of analogy had its origins in contrast to *logos*. *Analogos* literally means 'according to a due or proportionate logos'. As we have seen, in Kant's philosophy it takes the form of an operation that works in relation to reason, as a supplement to it. The second thing this historical review shows us is the origins of the term to denote similarity across seemingly incongruous or unbridgeable spheres. In §58 of *Prolegomena to*

Any Future Metaphysics, Kant writes that analogy is a 'perfect similarity of relations between two quite dissimilar things'.[118] Caygill draws our attention to the fact that this Kantian view of analogy often appeared in Kant's writing in the context of theological arguments. This may be one reason why, in the third *Critique*, Kant sees analogy as that which can bridge the gap between the realm of the sensible, the realm where we perceive nature, and the supersensible, the realm in which we conceptualise something like freedom or God.[119]

The gap between the sensible and supersensible is also the conceptual territory where Kant gives his definition of symbol in the third *Critique*, even putting the function of analogy and symbol together. Section 59 of the *Critique of Judgement* is entitled 'Beauty as the Symbol of Morality' and is the penultimate chapter of part I. Kant begins the section with a reminder that 'the call for a verification of the objective reality of rational concepts, i.e. of ideas, and what is more, on behalf of the theoretical cognition of such a reality, is to demand an impossibility, because absolutely no intuition adequate to them can be given'.[120] This is the problem that Kant addresses in the schematism and it also echoes the foundational problem of *The Critique of Pure Reason*: the contradiction between empirical and metaphysical judgements.[121] Therefore, Kant is beginning this section on symbolic judgement by reminding us that symbolic judgement is an operation of reason that is not empirically verifiable. This gives rise to the question, if our symbolic judgements cannot be verified empirically, how do they work?

Kant begins by explaining how the presentation of concepts to the understanding occurs. The term Kant uses is *hypotyposis* and while it is mainly described here in section 59, Howard Caygill reminds us in his *Kant Dictionary* that the concept of *hypotyposis* appears in different guises throughout Kant's philosophy, for example, in the section on *schematism* that was discussed in the last section.[122] As we saw in the last section, Kant makes a distinction between the two different ways in which our intuition can correspond with concepts, presenting them to the understanding. Kant writes that on the one hand, 'it is *schematic*, as where the intuition corresponding to a concept comprehended by the understanding is given *a priori*'. On the other hand, a *hypotyposis* can be characterised as *symbolic* 'where the concept is one which only reason can think, and to which no sensuous intuition can be adequate'.[123]

To understand the subtle distinction Kant is making between *schematic* and *symbol*, it is helpful to remember that the schematism is introduced as an answer to the question, 'how can intuitions be subsumed under concepts?'[124] The answer Kant provides is that the *schematic* is a procedure of judgement that holds the rules for how to synthesise concepts and images.[125] Like the *schematic*, the *symbol* is also a procedure of judgement that holds a synthesising power, but Kant writes in the *Critique of Judgement* that the *symbol* applies to a certain type of concept. This type of concept can only be thought by reason and cannot be intuited sensibly. The concept of God would be such a concept, for in Kant's view 'all our knowledge of God is merely symbolic'.[126] When one recalls that the example Kant uses to illustrate the *schematic* is the concept of a dog, one can clearly see the large gap separating the two concepts besides the fact that, in the English language, they consist of three identical letters simply arranged in a different order. We can thus conclude that, for Kant, a *symbol* is a type of *hypotyposis* that presents *ideas* to the understanding. To remind the reader, Kant defines an *idea* as 'a concept of reason whose object can be met nowhere in experience'.[127] So while I can readily meet a dog in my everyday empirical experience of the world, I do not encounter God in my empirical experience of the world. Even in the mysticism of a figure like St Teresa of Ávila to whom the adage 'God is in the pots and pans' is attributed, the Kantian sense of judgement still finds the God present in the pots and pans to be a symbolic judgement, even if the individual may have a numinous experience while immersed in the ordinary moments of daily life such as washing the pots and pans.

Kant calls this type of symbolic presentation indirect, because, as a presentation, it must make recourse to analogy or doubling of judgement. A concept is first applied to an object and then symbolically applied to another object.[128] Continuing Kant's example of the symbolic knowledge of God presented in religion, if we reflect on the symbol of light that represents the divine in Christianity, we can understand this principle more clearly. In the beginning of the Gospel of John, for example, Christ is described as a divine light that both animates being and overcomes dark forces:

> All things came into being through him [God], and without him not one thing came into being. What has come into being in him was life, and the life was the light of all people. The light shines in the darkness, and the darkness did not overcome it.[129]

Here the symbolic application begins with the concept of a life-giving force that overcomes evil. This concept is first applied to God and then symbolically applied to light. It is an indirect representation of the concept of a life-giving force that overcomes evil. This process of indirect representation is perhaps what later causes Kant to call the symbolic use of judgement 'schematism by analogy'.[130] If a symbol is a schematism by analogy and a schematism is also the rule for how the imagination synthesises, then it follows that a symbol synthesises indirectly, that is to say, by analogy.

Hans Blumenberg looks to Kant's definition of symbol to ground his understanding of metaphor, while Derrida extends the role of analogy in the third *Critique* to metaphor. So, while an understanding of the role of analogy and symbol in Kant's philosophy is essential for understanding the philosophical problems at stake in later philosophers of metaphor, it is also an example of the need not to push Kant's thinking on analogy too far in the direction of metaphor. When Kant writes that analogy is a 'perfect similarity of relations between two quite dissimilar things'[131] there is a distinction between Kant's view and the Aristotelian view of metaphor as a device which sees the similarities between things.[132] In the Aristotelian definition, metaphor calls out a similarity. The metaphor 'old age is the evening of life' works because we can see the similarities between the way the pace of life slows down in the evening and the way that the human body slows down before death, and between the way that the fading daylight is like the fading sight of ageing eyes. Analogy, while related, is distinct, and Kant's interest is in how it assists reason to bridge seemingly unbridgeable spheres, such as the sensible and supersensible. This relegates it to an altogether different realm from metaphor. It will not be until later, when thinkers extend this logic to the gap between language and concepts, that Kant's philosophy of analogy and symbol will have relevance for a conception of metaphor.

For the moment, we can say that the problems encountered in metaphysical reasoning suddenly became essential for the foundation of metaphor as it was understood in the traditional Aristotelian paradigm. While figurative language, like analogy, remains distinct in Kant's thought, he has unknowingly posed a question about the ability to judge the truthlikeness of a metaphor. It is these conditions that will be radicalised in Nietzsche's philosophy. The radicalisation of these conditions will, in turn, revolutionise the West's conception of metaphor.

Notes to Chapter 1

1. 'metaphor, n.', *OED Online*, June 2017, Oxford University Press. <http://www.oed.com/view/Entry/117328?redirectedFrom=metaphor> [accessed 13 May 2020].
2. Ibid.
3. Ibid.
4. Harald Weinrich, 'Metapher', in *Historisches Wörterbuch der Philosophie*, v, ed. by Joachim Ritter and Karlfried Gründer (Basel: Schwabe, 1980), pp. 1179–86.
5. 'μεταφορά', in Henry George Liddell and Robert Scott, *A Greek-English Lexicon* (Oxford: Clarendon Press, 1940), <http://www.perseus.tufts.edu/hopper/text?doc=Perseus%3Atext%3A1999.04.0057%3Aentry%3Dmetafora%2F> [accessed 13 May 2020].
6. Paul Ricoeur, *The Rule of Metaphor*, trans. by Robert Czerny (London: Routledge, 2003), p. 8.
7. Aristotle, *Poetics* 1457b.
8. Wallace Martin, 'Metaphor', in *The Princeton Encyclopedia of Poetry and Poetics*, 4th edn (Princeton: Princeton University Press, 2012), pp. 863–70.
9. Ibid.
10. Oleg V. Bychkov and Anne Sheppard, 'Introduction', in *Greek and Roman Aesthetics*, ed. Oleg V. Bychkov and Anne Sheppard (Cambridge: Cambridge University Press, 2010), pp. xx, xxvi.
11. Longinus, *On the Sublime*, pp. 150, 164.
12. Michael Gagarin, 'Background and Origins: Oratory and Rhetoric before the Sophists', in *A Companion to Greek Rhetoric*, ed. by Ian Worthington (Oxford: Blackwell Publishing, 2007), pp. 27–36 (p. 28).
13. Ibid.
14. Michael De Brauw, 'The Parts of the Speech', in *A Companion to Greek Rhetoric*, ed. by Ian Worthington (Oxford: Blackwell Publishing, 2007), pp. 187–202 (pp. 188–89).
15. 'μεταφορά', Liddell and Scott *Lexicon*.
16. Isocrates, *Evagoras*, 9.9.
17. De Brauw, 'The Parts of the Speech', pp. 188–89.
18. William H. Race, 'Rhetoric and Lyric Poetry', in *A Companion to Greek Rhetoric*, ed. by Ian Worthington (Oxford: Blackwell, 2007), pp. 509–25 (pp. 509–10).
19. Aristotle, *Poetics*, 1457b.
20. Ibid., 1456b–1457b.
21. Ibid., 1456b
22. Aristotle, *On the Soul*, 2.2 414b.
23. Jonathan Barnes, 'Rhetoric and Poetics', in *The Cambridge Companion to Aristotle*, ed. by Jonathan Barnes (Cambridge: Cambridge University Press, 1995), pp. 259–86.
24. Aristotle, *Poetics*, 1457b.
25. Zoltán Kövecses, *Metaphor: A Practical Introduction* (Oxford: Oxford University Press, 2002), pp. 4–7.

26. While cognitive linguistics speaks of the two parts of metaphor in terms of the target domain and source domain, the corresponding terms in the study of rhetoric are tenor and vehicle respectively. See I. A. Richards, *The Philosophy of Rhetoric* (Oxford: Oxford University Press, 1936).
27. Aristotle, *Poetics*, 1459a.
28. Aristotle, *Rhetoric*, 1410b.
29. Stephen Halliwell, *Aristotle's Poetics* (Chicago: University of Chicago Press, 1998), p. 349.
30. Aristotle *Rhetoric*, 1355a14, 1356b11–1357b16.
31. Ibid., 1356b10.
32. Thomas Aquinas, *Summa Theologiae*, trans. by The Dominican Council (Cambridge: Cambridge University Press, 2006), De Veritate, Q.1, A.1–3; Q.16.
33. Richard Kirkham, 'Truth, Correspondence Theory of', in *The Shorter Routledge Encyclopedia of Philosophy*, ed. by Edward Craig (London: Routledge, 2005), p. 1027.
34. Aristotle, *Metaphysics*, iv.1011.
35. Aristotle, *Nicomachean Ethics*, 1.13. 9–15.
36. Laurence Berns, 'Rational Animal — Political Animal: Nature and Convention in Human Speech and Politics', *The Review of Politics*, 38.2 (1976), 188–89 (p. 177).
37. Aristotle, *Politics*, 1253a9–18.
38. Ibid., 1448b.
39. Ibid.
40. Paul Ricoeur, *Time and Narrative*, 3 vols, trans. by Kathleen McLaughlin and David Pellauer (Chicago: The University of Chicago Press, 1984), I, pp. ix–xi.
41. H. M. Hubbell, 'Introduction', in Cicero, *On Invention; The Best Kind of Orator; Topics*, trans. by H. M. Hubbell, Loeb Classical Library (Cambridge, MA and London: Harvard University Press, 1949), pp. vii–xiv (p. vii).
42. Ibid., pp. vii–viii.
43. Ibid., p. ix.
44. Hans Blumenberg, *Paradigms for a Metaphorology*, trans. by Robert Savage (Ithaca: Cornell University Press, 2010), p. 82.
45. Cicero, *On Invention*, xxi.
46. Ricoeur, *Rule*, p. 9.
47. Cicero, *On Invention*, xxi.
48. Ricoeur, *Rule*, p. 9.
49. See Peter Ramus, *Arguments in Rhetoric against Quintilian: Translation and Text of Peter Ramus's 'Rhetoricae distinctiones in Quintilianum'*, trans. by Carole Newlands (Carbondale: Southern Illinois University Press, 1986). Also see Martin, 'Metaphor'.
50. 'Metaphor'.
51. Quintilian, *Institutio Oratio*, 8.3.24.
52. Ibid.
53. Martin, 'Metaphor'.
54. Quintilian, *Institutio Oratoria*, 8.3.24.
55. Ibid.
56. 'Metaphor', *Wörterbuch der Philosophie* (1980).
57. Thomas Aquinas, *Super Boethium De Trinitate*, trans. by Rose E. Brennan (London: B. Herder, 1946), prooem. q.2, a.3 ad 5.
58. Aquinas, *Summa Theologiae*, Prima Pars, Q.13., A1.
59. Ibid., A1.
60. Ibid., A3.
61. Ibid.
62. Ramus, *Arguments* and Martin, 'Metaphor'.
63. Martin, 'Metaphor'.
64. Thomas Hobbes, *Leviathan*, ed. by Richard Tuck (Cambridge: Cambridge University Press, 1996), pp. 26, 36. Also see Andreas Musolff's treatment of this passage in relation to cognitive linguistics and politics in Andreas Musolff, *Metaphor and Political Discourse: Analogical Reasoning in Debates about Europe* (New York: Palgrave Macmillan, 2004), pp. 1–7.

65. John Locke, *An Essay Concerning Human Understanding*, 27th edn (London: T. Tegg & Son, 1836), p. 372.
66. Ibid.
67. Ibid.
68. Denis Diderot, 'Lettre sur sourds et les muets I', *Œuvres complètes*, II (Paris: J. L. J. Brière, 1821), pp. 9–80 (p. 42).
69. Jean-Jacques Rousseau, *Essay on the Origin of Languages*, in *The Collected Writings of Rousseau*, VII, trans. and ed. by John T. Scott (Hanover, NH: University Press of New England, 1998), pp. 289–332. Henceforth *Essay*.
70. Ibid., p. 294.
71. Ibid.
72. Paul De Man, 'Theory of Metaphor in Rousseau's *Second Discourse*', *Studies in Romanticism*, 12.2 (1973), 475–98 (p. 490).
73. Rousseau, *Origin*, p. 295.
74. Martin, 'Metaphor'.
75. Giambattista Vico, *The New Science*, trans. by Thomas Goddard Bergin and Max Harold Fisch (London: Cornell University Press, 1984), p. 129, §404.
76. Martin, 'Metaphor'.
77. Ibid.
78. Ibid.
79. Timothy Costelloe, 'Giambattista Vico', in *The Stanford Encyclopedia of Philosophy*, ed. by Edward N. Zalta (Summer 2016 Edition), <https://plato.stanford.edu/archives/sum2016/entries/vico/>.
80. 'metaphor', OED (2017).
81. Immanuel Kant, *Critique of Pure Reason*, trans. by Marcus Weigelt (London: Penguin, 2007), p. 13, Bvii, viii.
82. Howard Caygill, *A Kant Dictionary* (Oxford: Blackwell, 1995), p. 291.
83. Sebastian Gardner, *Kant and the Critique of Pure Reason* (New York: Routledge, 1999), p. 131.
84. Ibid., p. 309.
85. Ibid., pp. 105–06, A80/B 106, A81, 82/B107, 108.
86. Ibid., p. 666, A854,855/B882, 883.
87. Clive Cazeaux, *Metaphor and Continental Philosophy* (New York: Routledge, 2007), p. 13.
88. Ibid.
89. Immanuel Kant, *Critique of Judgement*, trans. by James Creed Meredith (Oxford: Oxford University Press, 2008), p. 179, §59; p. 352, §248.
90. Immanuel Kant, *Prolegomena to Any Future Metaphysics that will be able to come forward as Science*, trans. by Gary Hatfield (Cambridge: Cambridge University Press, 2004), p. 108, §58.
91. Ibid. Emphasis added.
92. Caygill, *Kant*, p. 66.
93. Cazeaux, *Metaphor*, p. 13.
94. Kant, *Pure Reason*, p. 5, Avii, viii.
95. Immanuel Kant, *An Answer to the Question: What is Enlightenment?*, trans. by H. B. Nisbet (London: Penguin, 2009), pp. 1–3.
96. Gardner, *Kant and the Critique of Pure Reason*, p. 2.
97. Kant, *Pure Reason*, p. 18, Bxvi, xvii.
98. 'antinomy, n.', *OED Online*, June 2017, Oxford University Press. http://www.oed.com/view/Entry/8716?redirectedFrom=antinomy [accessed 28 September 2017].
99. Kant, *Pure Reason*, p. 391, A426–27/B454–55.
100. Ibid., p. 405, A444–45/B472–73.
101. Ibid., p. 5, Avii, viii.
102. See Cazeaux, *Metaphor*, pp. 4–5, 19–23.
103. Kant, *Pure Reason*, p. 176, A137, 138, B176, 177.
104. Ibid.
105. Ibid., p. 178, A141, B180.
106. Ibid., p. 176, A137, 138, B176, 177.
107. Ibid., pp. 178–79, A141, B180–A142, 143, B181, 182.

108. Ibid., p. 179, A142, 143, B181, 182.
109. Mark Johnson applies the notion of Kant's schematism to metaphor in 'The Philosophical Significance of Image Schemas', in *From Perception to Meaning: Image Schemas in Cognitive Linguistics*, ed. by Beate Hampe (Berlin: De Gruyter, 2005), pp. 15–33. This application is not done uncritically, however, for Johnson suggests there is a problem with Kant's account. Johnson claims it is based on a dichotomy between form and matter, because Kant believed in pure form. But, Johnson suggests, while Kant's metaphysics is laden with dichotomies that he has no interest in defending, what he thinks is worth salvaging from Kant's account of the schema is his 'recognition of imagination as the locus of human meaning, thought and judgement'. For Johnson, image schemas operate within conceptual metaphors that define basic concepts. Therefore, it bears noting that the relevance of Kant's schema for metaphor still has a contemporary relevance in the debate far beyond a purely historical significance. See Johnson, 'The Philosophical Significance of Image Schemas', p. 17.
110. Kant, *Pure Reason*, p. 179, A142, 143, B181, 182.
111. *The Sunday Times*, 4 May 2007.
112. Caygill, *Kant*, p. 247.
113. Ibid., p. 65.
114. Euclid, *Euclid's Elements*, trans. by Thomas L. Heath (Ann Arbor: Green Lion Press, 2007), pp. 99–122, V.Def 3–5, V.7.
115. Aristotle, *Topics* 108a, 7–8.
116. Caygill, *Kant*, p. 65.
117. Cazeaux, *Metaphor*, p. 35.
118. Kant, *Prolegomena*, p. 108.
119. Kant, *Judgement*, pp. 11–12, II, 176. It is interesting to note that this idea of figurative language bridging the gap between sensible and supersensible realms refreshes the horizontal sense of the word *metaphora* in its use by Longinus when he focused on the way that metaphor brought us 'into the realm of the gods'.
120. Kant, *Judgement*, pp. 178–79, §59, 352.
121. Kant, *Pure Reason*, p. 5, Avii, viii.
122. Caygill, *Kant*, p. 231.
123. Kant, *Judgement*, p. 179, §59, 352.
124. Kant, *Pure Reason*, p. 176, A137, 138, B176, 177.
125. Kant, *Judgement*, p. 179, §59, 352.
126. Ibid., p. 179–80, §59, 352–53.
127. Caygill, *Kant*, p. 236.
128. Kant, *Judgement*, p. 179, §59, 352.
129. John 1. 3–5 NRSV.
130. Caygill, *Kant*, p. 360.
131. Kant, *Prolegomena*, p. 108.
132. Aristotle, *Rhetoric*, 1410b10ff.

CHAPTER 2

The Watershed Moment: Nietzsche and the Reversal of the Aristotelian Paradigm of Metaphor

In this chapter we will outline the intellectual-historical background as well as the main argument of Friedrich Nietzsche's 'On Truth and Lying in a Non-Moral Sense' (1873) which leads him to his famous proclamation, 'What, then, is truth? A mobile army of metaphors [...]'.[1] We will see that this proclamation, often seen as a critique of the impossibility of propositional truth, is also a critique of the Aristotelian foundations of metaphor outlined in chapter 1. Thus, Nietzsche does not simply assert the metaphorical basis of truth claims but revolutionises the status of metaphor itself. This change in status is brought about firstly by the collapse of the distinction between reason and metaphor, and secondly, by all language becoming metaphoric, thus collapsing the distinction between the figurative and the literal. Finally, it is ultimately brought about by Nietzsche's unlinking of the concept of truthlikeness from the concept of likeness. As we have seen, the link between likeness and truthlikeness oriented the interpretation of the meaning of a metaphor in the Aristotelian paradigm. This chapter will argue that the severing of this hermeneutic capacity in Nietzsche's philosophy creates a crisis of metaphoric meaning. This crisis of metaphoric meaning creates a tension between, on the one hand, metaphor having a pragmatic function and, on the other hand, metaphor having a relativising function. This tension between the pragmatic and relativising functions of metaphor orients philosophical discourse about metaphor in European philosophy after Nietzsche.

After a review of the secondary literature on Nietzsche's philosophy of metaphor, we will see the influence of Nietzsche's philological reading and then his reading of post-Kantian philosophy, in particular Arthur Schopenhauer. The chapter will close by demonstrating why Nietzsche's critique of truth is in fact a critique of the concept of metaphor itself. It will also demonstrate how Nietzsche's new conception of metaphor is like the Roman god Janus, on the one hand pragmatic and on the other hand relative. These two faces of the same conception are often in conflict with each other.

Nietzsche on Metaphor in the Secondary Literature

To begin, we will consider three streams of the reception of Nietzsche's thinking on metaphor in the secondary literature. 'On Truth and Lying' is our first port of call. As Ernst Behler has suggested, 'out of all of Nietzsche's texts ['On Truth and Lying'] is the most explicit and clear on his philosophy of language'.[2] It provides an extended argument about the themes that feature frequently in Nietzsche's journals and lecture notes from the 1870s.[3] These themes include the relationship between language and truth as an epistemological problem, a relationship in which, for Nietzsche, metaphor plays a vital role. In a journal entry, the year before 'On Truth and Lying', Nietzsche wrote, 'Nun aber gibt es keine, eigentlichen Ausdrücken und kein "eigentliches" Erkennen ohne Metapher' (But now, there is no real expression and no 'real' knowing apart from metaphor).[4] However, these early writings on metaphor, language and rhetoric can appear at first glance to be, as Paul de Man reminds us, 'an eccentric and minor part of Nietzsche's enterprise'.[5] What Nietzsche writes about metaphor has generated quantitatively less interest than his writing on religion and morality, for example, or his most infamous concept, the *Übermensch*. The fact that the reception of Nietzsche is so heavily influenced by concepts like the will to power or a genealogy of morality can make this early, radical thesis on the nature of language and cognition seem foreign. Thus, De Man himself attempts to give a defence for why we might consider Nietzsche's writing on rhetoric as a window into his larger philosophy.[6] Admittedly, Nietzsche's explicit writing on metaphor takes up far less space than that of his more famous concepts. But De Man was writing in 1979. Over forty years on, the influence of 'On Truth and Lying' alone, not to mention the growing secondary literature on Nietzsche and metaphor, rhetoric and language, requires not a defence, as in De Man's case, but a reappraisal.

The following themes emerge in the secondary literature: (1) metaphor's role in the creation of a radical relativism; (2) metaphor as the provider of a radical cognitive pragmatism; and (3) the style and usage of Nietzsche's metaphors themselves as a window into Nietzsche's theory of metaphor. These themes are not announced by Nietzsche scholars as such. Rather, they can be detected as general interpretative trends within the secondary literature.

Metaphor and Radical Relativism

The reception of Nietzsche's ideas about metaphor has been overwhelmingly related to this first conceptual preoccupation. The observation of a type of radical relativism in Nietzsche's philosophy of metaphor has been emphasised in the French-speaking reception of Nietzsche, particularly in twentieth-century post-war French intellectual movements such as psychoanalysis, post-structuralism and deconstruction. De Man's writing on Nietzsche and metaphor fits into this intellectual preoccupation as do the writings of Sarah Kofman who, as we have seen in the introduction, is probably the best-known commentator on Nietzsche and metaphor.

In her 1972 book *Nietzsche and Metaphor*, which emerged in the era of the 'new Nietzsche' in post-war France, she usefully summarises the relationship between metaphor and a radical relativism when she writes, 'right from *The Birth of Tragedy* we can find in Nietzsche a generalized "theory" of metaphor, based on the loss of the "proper"'.[7] For Kofman, the proper is 'lost' because the distinction between the proper and the figurative, between rationality and invention and between truth and language, collapses in Nietzsche's philosophy. She goes as far as to suggest that this 'loss' constitutes an anthropological claim. The Aristotelian rational animal becomes the Nietzschean metaphorical animal in Kofman's view.[8] She also asserts that this 'loss' is carried through all of Nietzsche's philosophy and is at the heart of his thinking on metaphor. She suggests an implicit connection between metaphor and Nietzsche's more famous concept, the will to power. Nietzsche's conception of metaphor, she argues, is an early draft of his later conception of the will to power.[9]

This is the moment in Kofman's analysis of Nietzsche that is the most helpful for our theme. She discerns that Nietzsche does not simply use metaphor as a tool for a critique of propositional truth but develops a 'generalized "theory" of metaphor' in its own right. She also acknowledges that the loss of the proper and a 'generalized theory' necessarily implicate each other. However, after this initial analysis of Nietzsche's generalised theory of metaphor, Kofman moves onto a stylistic analysis of Nietzsche. As we shall see in a moment, while Kofman's position offers an important interpretation in its own right, it addresses neither the implications of a generalised theory of metaphor for the concept of metaphor itself, nor the hermeneutic tensions that arise from such a concept. This is perhaps because her stylistic reading is oriented too much by this first theme of interpretation, metaphor and radical relativism.

A few years after *Nietzsche and Metaphor*, David B. Allison, in the 1977 collection of essays, *The New Nietzsche*, re-emphasises Kofman's assertion of the link between metaphor and the will to power by pointing to the 'essentially active and relational quality' of both metaphor and the will to power. In the same way that words are only metaphors, the essence of the world is only the will to power.[10] In the will to power and in metaphor, Allison highlights a parallel rejection of transcendence. Language, from this perspective, 'makes sense because it can draw upon itself', rather than because of a transcendent ground of meaning.[11] It follows then that propositional truth, as a transcendent ground of meaning, 'becomes an impossibility [...] due to the primacy of metaphor'.[12]

The New Nietzsche was published in English for the first time two years before De Man's essay on Nietzsche and figurative language.[13] It was one of the first works to emphasise this reading in the anglophone reception of post-war continental thought. As De Man reminds us, figures such as Jacques Derrida, Michel Foucault, Philippe Lacoue-Labarthe and Jean-Luc Nancy had all written about Nietzsche and metaphor during this period.[14] Finally, later anglophone contributions such as Alan D. Schrift's *Nietzsche and the Question of Interpretation* (1990) continued and expanded this conceptual preoccupation.

Metaphor as the Provider of a Radical Pragmatism

The other side of the coin of the creation of a radical relativism is metaphor's role as the provider of a radical pragmatism for judgement and cognition. Though it is not the focus of his own reading of Nietzsche, Eugen Fink sums up this position in his overview of Nietzsche's early work, *Nietzsche's Philosophy* (1960). Fink writes: 'Nietzsche interprets the role of cognition pragmatically. Reason serves the will to live. It is based on a life-preserving illusion.'[15] This illusion, according to Fink, is created by metaphor. Fink writes that 'the concept is the empty shell of a metaphor once inspired by intuition'.[16] He points out that while the concept is an empty shell in this view, the artist knows the 'untruth of all concepts' and thus can relate 'creatively to reality'.[17] This 'creative relation' is the radical pragmatism that metaphor provides.

Fink's view is representative of the idea that with Nietzsche's philosophy we understand cognition to be pragmatically oriented by metaphors. This view was popularised in the anglophone world by, among others, Richard Rorty who, in May 1986, wrote in the *London Review of Books* that:

> Nietzsche did not abandon the idea of discovering the causes of our being what we are [...] He only rejected the idea that this tracking was a process of discovery. In his view, in achieving this sort of self-knowledge we are not coming to know a truth which was out there (or in here) all the time. Rather, he saw self-knowledge as self-creation. The process of coming to know oneself, confronting one's contingency, tracking one's causes home, is identical with the process of inventing a new language — that is, of thinking up some new metaphors.[18]

This view does not reject metaphor's role in the creation of a radical relativism. As Rorty says, 'in [Nietzsche's] view, in achieving this sort of self-knowledge we are not coming to know a truth which was out there [...] all the time'. Rather, it emphasises the role metaphor plays in pragmatically creating meaning in the face of the loss of the proper. In this vein, we could also cite Hans Blumenberg's 1960 *Paradigms for a Metaphorology*, which we will explore at length in chapter 4. *Paradigms* analyses the history of metaphors throughout Western thought and, while it does not mention Nietzsche, Blumenberg implicitly engages with this pragmatic preoccupation with a thoroughness not seen in many works that explicitly mention Nietzsche.

Stylistic Interpretation

The final of the three conceptual preoccupations is an interpretation of Nietzsche's style: that is, the use of metaphors themselves in Nietzsche's texts. Classic French commentators such as Jacques Derrida in 'The Question of Style' (1976) and Kofman in the second half of *Nietzsche and Metaphor* have approached Nietzsche's writing on metaphor in this way, as have more recent anglophone authors such as Gregory Moore in his 2002 *Nietzsche, Biology and Metaphor*.

Nietzsche uses metaphors to subvert, expand and attack ideas. By seeing how Nietzsche uses metaphors to subvert concepts, such as the beehive metaphor in *The Genealogy of Morality*, the pyramid in 'On Truth and Lying', or the spider and its web in *Untimely Meditations*, we can see the relationship between the metaphors used and the concepts Nietzsche attacks.[19] Therefore, Nietzsche's style makes a philosophical point. Because of this, Kofman devotes the second half of *Nietzsche and Metaphor* to looking at several of Nietzsche's recurring metaphors. As Kofman's translator Duncan Large notes, Kofman focuses on Nietzsche's method as much as she does on the conceptual content of his writing. One of her overriding interests is the 'textuality of Nietzsche's writing'.[20] Kofman's conclusion is that Nietzsche is not particularly interested in inventing new metaphors but rather in subverting traditional metaphors.[21]

A more recent example of this approach is Gregory Moore's *Nietzsche, Biology and Metaphor*. While Moore is writing in a completely different intellectual context from Kofman, he acknowledges Kofman, among other twentieth-century theorists, for providing a helpful methodological approach to Nietzsche's work.[22] For Moore, the language of biology and the biological metaphors in Nietzsche's text are a window into Nietzsche's own convictions. These convictions, Moore argues, were in part determined by the prominence of biological rhetoric in Nietzsche's time.[23] Moore goes on to say that the rhetorical nature of Nietzsche's writing 'may be interpreted as the expression of one of Nietzsche's most basic philosophical convictions: that all language is intrinsically rhetorical [...] all linguistic functions [...] are fundamentally, inescapably metaphorical'.[24]

This conviction that, for Nietzsche, 'all linguistic functions are inescapably metaphorical', is a widely accepted interpretation of Nietzsche that stretches across all three conceptual preoccupations. Yet the emphasis of these preoccupations has been overwhelmingly on what Nietzsche's philosophy says about truth claims and concepts, rather than on what Nietzsche's philosophy says about the status of metaphor itself and the philosophical problems that may arise from this change in status. The emphasis on the loss of a ground for metaphoric transference is brilliantly observed in a thinker like Kofman. But there is a problem created for metaphor itself when the perception of likeness between word and truth vanishes. In Nietzsche's philosophy, the referent of metaphor becomes the human being who uses the metaphor. As we have seen in the introduction, while Kofman brilliantly observes the relationship between metaphor and the loss of the proper, her stylistic reading fails to highlight the conceptual change of metaphor itself and as a result fails to highlight hermeneutic and semantic problems arising from this new conception. Therefore, to understand this new conception of metaphor better, we will move away from the stylistic reading of Nietzsche and not limit ourselves to either the relativistic or pragmatic reading. We need to assess why Nietzsche's critique of truth produces a new conception of metaphor and to do this, an intellectual-historical reading of Nietzsche's philological education is needed.

Nietzsche and Nineteenth-Century German Philology

The influence of philology in Nietzsche's early period also has a philosophical significance for our theme, because while the metaphorical root of human culture and thought was something Nietzsche inherited from German philology, Nietzsche also collapses the distinction between reason and metaphor and between the figurative and the literal. This distinctly changes the notion of metaphor with which Nietzsche is working. It is also in this subversive reading of German philology that the conflict between a pragmatic function of metaphor and a relativistic function of metaphor first shows its head. When Nietzsche wrote 'On Truth and Lying' in the 1870s while still a professor of philology at Basel, both his library records and his lecture notes show that he was reading works by, among others, Gustav Gerber and Max Müller.[25] Therefore, we can begin by looking at the philological root of Nietzsche's preoccupation with metaphor.

The 1870s were a particularly conflicted period for Nietzsche intellectually. On the one hand, he was hiding lectures from his colleagues out of fear that his ideas would seem too radical.[26] On the other hand, within the same year, he was writing quite traditional introductions to handbooks for Latin grammar.[27] It was a time marked by a dialectical relationship between his philosophical reading and his philological university reading. From this dialectic, Nietzsche takes the nineteenth-century German tradition of philology and comparative linguistics and uses key concepts within it to wage a war against the correspondence theory of truth by inverting the role of metaphor's relation to truth.

Nietzsche was trained as a philologist in Leipzig and it is commonly acknowledged that this training had a significant impact on the hermeneutic tendency of his philosophy.[28] Nietzsche came from a family that included generations of Lutheran clergy and Nietzsche himself began a theological education before turning to philology.[29] The German biographer Rüdiger Safranski points out that this created some tension in the Nietzsche family, among his mother and sister particularly.[30] The break with theology and the vocation of his family is helpful to note because it provides a backdrop to the Nietzsche we see emerging in the letters from his years of philological training. As a student he was at odds with his tutors and often concentrated on his own reading and interests.[31] This is suggestive of the beginnings of a deeply personal intellectual journey that Nietzsche undertook during this period, against the backdrop of a break from the tradition of his family and the paradigm of Western Christianity.

During this period, Nietzsche was tutored by two of the most respected philologists of his day, F. W. Ritschl and Georg Curtius. The nineteenth century was a period of philological flourishing in German intellectual life. Perhaps in the same way that significant developments in cognitive science have influenced a vast range of fields today, the culture surrounding Nietzsche's philological education was also new and ground-breaking. One example of this is Hermann von Helmholtz's innovative research on acoustic phonetics, which was informed by advances in comparative linguistics.[32] In the broader cultural context, 1872 was the year of the publication of some of the great realist and naturalist novels of the late nineteenth century: Tolstoy began his serialisation of *Anna Karenina*; Emile Zola, George Eliot and Thomas Hardy had all published major works in either the same or the following year; and, in 1874 the German Periodical *Deutsche Rundschau* was founded. Politically and culturally, the 1870s was largely viewed as a 'liberal high point in 19th-century Germany'.³³ This also coincided with a high point of German nationalism with the victory of Prussia in the Franco-Prussian War (1870–71), in which Nietzsche was an ambulance driver, if only for two weeks.³⁴ When Nietzsche wrote 'On Truth and Lying' in 1873, it was in an altogether different orbit than the prevailing tendencies of realism, nationalism and liberalism, and sometimes it was in outright opposition to them. It is a text deeply rooted in its age and in Nietzsche's own educational background and yet it is a text at war with both. This foundational text on metaphor is a text that wrests metaphor out of the prevailing *Weltanschauung* of the day.

As has already been stated, in this period, Nietzsche's library records and lecture notes show that he was reading works by Müller and Gerber. What links Müller and Gerber, as Benedetta Zavatta has argued, is their fascination with anthropology, that is to say: they study language 'in relation to the man who speaks it'.³⁵ As Max Müller famously said in his *Lectures on the Science of Language*, 'the one great barrier between the brute and man is *Language*. Man speaks, and no brute has ever uttered a word. Language is our Rubicon, and no brute will dare to pass it.'³⁶ This quote shows an anthropological interest in language in that Müller clearly holds on to language as a demarcation of what it means to be a human being. We will see how Nietzsche departs from this notion later in the chapter. However, Nietzsche also draws heavily from Müller and Gerber. There are two ideas in particular that concern us here. First, there is the idea that human forgetfulness and error play a part in the creation of abstract notions like the concept of truth or an idea of divinity. Second, there is the idea that metaphor is an unconscious cognitive pattern that is relative to human perception. We will treat each of these in turn to see how Nietzsche subverts their philological conceptions to change the status of metaphor.

Max Müller became Chair of Comparative Philology at Oxford University shortly after he began his famous *Lectures on the Science of Language* in 1860. This text was frequently cited by Ritschl and Curtius in the lectures Nietzsche would have attended in Leipzig. It was also a text that Nietzsche frequently borrowed from the Basel University library from 1869 to 1874, alongside Müller's *Comparative Mythology*. Nietzsche's lecture notes from the 1870s were full of references to both texts by Müller.³⁷

Metaphor occupies a strategic place in Müller's famous notion of mythology as a 'disease of language'. The phrase 'disease of language' refers to Müller's suggestion that key features in a myth, such as the name of a god, are metaphorical descriptions of natural phenomena. However, these metaphors are imbued with anthropomorphism and over time become more substantial. As Lourens P. van den Bosch puts it in his biography of Müller, the 'disease of language comes down to human beings misunderstanding fundamental and anthropomorphic metaphors and turning them into myths'.³⁸ One example of this can be seen in Müller's long essay *Comparative Mythology* when he writes about the gendered nouns in Greek or Sanskrit. Because of these gendered nouns, he says, it was 'simply impossible to speak of morning or evening, of spring and winter, without giving to these conceptions something of an individual, active, sexual and at last personal character'.³⁹ Gendered nouns inevitably anthropomorphise because they project a human characteristic — gender — onto natural phenomena like morning or spring.

In his *Lectures on the Science of Language*, Müller generalises this idea to show the process of how names imbued with human characteristics, such as a gendered noun, assume a substantial existence over time. In the *Science of Language*, he writes:

> Mythology, which was the bane of the ancient world, is in truth a disease of language. A myth means a word, but a word which, from being a name or an attribute, has been allowed to assume a more substantial existence. Most Greek, Roman, Indian and other heathen gods are nothing but poetical names, which were gradually allowed to assume a divine personality never contemplated by their original inventors. *Eos* was a name of the dawn before she became a goddess, the wife of *Tithonos*, or the dying day.[40]

So, on the one hand, metaphor is radical for Müller. It has the power to shape beliefs over time. Eos, the name for the natural phenomenon of the dawn, becomes a goddess. However, as Andreas Musolff reminds us, for Müller, this aspect of metaphor is liable to create fictitious elements and fundamental misunderstandings in thought.[41] In an article specifically on Müller and metaphor, Musolff draws our attention to the fact that Müller's critical view of mythology as 'diseased language' was 'denounced in the next generation of philosophical anthropology by Ernst Cassirer and Susanne K. Langer, who caricatured his position as alleging that mythology was a mere "by-product of language", a "monstrosity", and the result of "verbal errors"'.[42] However, while Müller's ideas about mythology may be open to criticism, the role metaphor played in Müller's thought was central to Nietzsche's development as a student.

Whatever else we may say about Müller's ideas on metaphor, a core principle remains of paramount importance: namely that, in Müller's *Lectures*, metaphor is accorded the role of the thing that drives conceptual change.[43] This core principle of conceptual change was what had such an influence on Nietzsche. According to Musolff,

> Today, Müller's influence on philosophy after the 'linguistic turn' (Rorty) has started to be acknowledged, especially as a source for Nietzsche's denunciation of 'truth' as a 'sea' of archaic, forgotten metaphors in *Über Wahrheit und Lüge im außermoralischen Sinne* (On Truth and Lying in an Extra-Moral Sense). Via Nietzsche, one can pursue further influences on Hans Blumenberg's, Paul Ricoeur's and Jacques Derrida's concepts of metaphor and myth as central problems of epistemology.[44]

In Nietzsche's 'denunciation of "truth" as a "sea" of archaic, forgotten metaphors', an extrapolation takes place. From Müller's assertion that metaphor is a central feature of our forgetfulness of the natural origin of myths comes Nietzsche's view of the role of metaphor in the production of abstract concepts more generally, such as truth. As Zavatta notes, one thing Nietzsche took from Müller was the idea that language simplifies impressions, such as when a gendered noun is created for an entire array of stimuli. This process of simplification 'produces the illusion that these concepts have corresponding metaphysical entities'.[45] This can be seen in 'On

Truth and Lying' where Nietzsche writes:

> no leaf is ever exactly the same as any other leaf [...] the concept leaf is formed by dropping these individual differences arbitrarily, by forgetting those features which differentiate one thing from another, so that the concept then gives rise to the notion that something other than leaves exists in nature, something which would be 'leaf', a primal form [...] from which all leaves were woven, drawn, delineated.[46]

While in quotes like this we can see a clear inheritance of the idea of metaphor as a disease of language, Nietzsche's thought also displays a clear reversal concerning the role of metaphor in relation to reason. As Musolff has pointed out, for Müller, metaphor creates a 'fundamental misunderstanding' in thought. That Müller calls it a misunderstanding at all comes down to his view of reason. Müller believed that language was a unique human phenomenon and indicative of an underlying rational mind. This can be reflected in Müller's debate with Darwin.[47] As we have seen earlier in this chapter, Müller calls language 'the one great barrier between the brute and man', and 'our Rubicon' that 'no brute will dare to pass'.[48] This quotation shows that Müller has a clear line in his thinking between rational language and irrational language. When a human being uses language, from Müller's perspective, he or she is using language as a rational being.

Therefore, it follows that, for Müller, 'the disease of language' is apparent because, within his notion of rationality, there is a clear line between the natural phenomenon, the metaphor used to describe it, and the mythological personality. It is true that this clearly influences Nietzsche's concept of the anthropomorphism involved in various truth claims. However, Nietzsche takes the concept of 'the disease of language', or forgetfulness, a step further when he writes:

> The intellect shows its greatest strengths in dissimulation, since this is the means to preserve those weaker, less robust individuals who, by nature, are denied horns or the sharp fangs of a beast of prey with which to wage the struggle for existence.[49]

This 'disease of language' as Müller would call it, is the greatest strength of the intellect according to Nietzsche.

In other words, what Müller is calling an aberration of rationality is what Nietzsche uncompromisingly asserts to be an unconscious drive for deception employed for our preservation. It is the rule and law of cognition. As he writes a few lines below the above quotation,

> keeping up appearances, living in borrowed finery, wearing masks, the drapery of convention, play-acting for the benefit of others and oneself — in short, the constant fluttering of human beings around the one flame of vanity is so much the rule and law that there is virtually nothing which defies understanding so much as the fact that an honest and pure drive towards truth should ever have emerged in them.[50]

With Nietzsche's subversive reading of Müller, he collapses the gap between metaphor and reason and transforms the Aristotelian rational animal, which Müller holds up as the clear distinction between ourselves and animals, into the metaphorical animal emphasised by Sarah Kofman.⁵¹ Nietzsche makes this case quite plainly when he calls the drive to form metaphors 'that fundamental human drive which cannot be left out of consideration for even a second without also leaving out human beings themselves'.⁵² As we saw in chapter 1, Aristotle paired the notion of rationality with language. While Müller's adaptation of this notion can seem quite noble, Nietzsche turns this nobility on its head.

This collapse of the distinction between metaphor and reason is also what separates Nietzsche's philosophy of metaphor from the relevance of Kant's philosophy for metaphor.⁵³ It is why we can talk of a specifically post-Nietzschean philosophy of metaphor. As we have seen in chapter 1, Kant does not specifically address metaphor but rather analogy. But even here Kant wants to maintain a clear separation between analogy and reason, such as in the *Critique of Judgement* where Kant calls analogy a 'mere rule of reflection' or in the *Prolegomena to Any Future Metaphysics*, where he makes it clear that analogy 'does not signify [...] [a] similarity of two things'.⁵⁴ Rather, for Kant, analogy signifies 'a similarity of *relations* between two quite dissimilar things'.⁵⁵ To be sure, the logic of analogy has a marvellous capability for Kant, but it is clear that analogy does not perform a one-on-one identity match between perception and object but rather creates a rule of reflection that serves to find the *relations* between the two things. As we have seen in chapter 1, this seems to imply that despite looking upon the category of the figurative in a much more positive light than earlier Enlightenment philosophers such as Hobbes, Locke or Diderot, Kant still maintains a distinction between the logic of the figurative and reason in that it creates a rule of *reflection* rather than a rule of *identity*.

When Nietzsche ties the greatest strength of the intellect to dissimulation and, in turn, dissimulation to metaphor, he collapses the distinction in cognition that Kant seems to maintain as well as subverting the anthropological role that metaphor plays in Max Müller's thought. We have said that in Nietzsche's thought we can see metaphor as having a pragmatic function and this is one of the origins of that approach. It is pragmatic in the sense that we can observe the usefulness of metaphor within the formation of concepts in history. The final philological influence on Nietzsche on whom we will focus is Gustav Gerber. It is in Gerber that we can see one of the origins of metaphor's relativising function, due to the collapse of the distinction between figurative and literal language.

Nietzsche began reading Gerber's *Die Sprache als Kunst* (Language as Art) in 1872 and quoted from him frequently in his *Darstellung der antiken Rhetorik* (Lecture on Ancient Rhetoric), which he taught between 1872 and 1874. 'On Truth and Lying' is also taken from the lecture notes in this period.⁵⁶ If Müller's influence on Nietzsche revolved around the role of tropes, like metaphor, in the formation of mythology, then Gerber's influence revolved around the role of tropes in the formation of language itself. However, Gerber's *Die Sprache als Kunst* is hardly a treatise on relativism. If anything, it is an important, and possibly overlooked, early contribution to cognitive linguistics.

Ernst Behler contended that Gerber's thought constituted 'the most important aspect' of 'On Truth and Lying' and was the 'main source for Nietzsche's theory of tropes'.[57] Behler bases his claim on Anthonie Meijers and Martin Stingelin's highly significant 1988 concordance of Nietzsche's citations of Gerber's *Die Sprache als Kunst*, which was published alongside an article by Meijers on the intellectual-historical background to Nietzsche's early period.[58] Meijers asserts that Nietzsche's new outlook on metaphor, particularly 'der Trieb zur Metaphernbildung, die sozialen Konventionen, welche die Bedeutung der Wörter fixieren, und das Vergessen der Rolle dieses Triebes zur Metaphernbildung' (the drive to formulate metaphors, the social conventions which fix the meaning of words, and the forgetting of the role of this drive for the formation of metaphors), has its equivalent ideas in Gustav Gerber's *Die Sprache als Kunst*.[59]

We can certainly affirm with both Meijers and Behler that Nietzsche's conception of what a trope is would be inconceivable without Gerber. The concordance shows that in both the *Darstellung der antiken Rhetorik* and in 'On Truth and Lying', Nietzsche cites Gerber over sixty times, frequently in direct quotation. These citations occur in several key passages of 'On Truth and Lying', which we will discuss in a moment.

This influence of Gerber on Nietzsche is one of the things that shifts Nietzsche's philosophy of metaphor in a decisively cognitive direction. However, we must depart from Behler when he claims that Gerber's thought constituted 'the most important aspect' of 'On Truth and Lying'. In this book, we will contend that metaphor becomes so philosophically radical in 'On Truth and Lying' because of the way in which Nietzsche combines Gerber's thought with Müller to throw likeness as the ground of metaphoric meaning into question. The way Nietzsche does that is with the implication he draws from Gerber's theory of tropes. Therefore, we can claim that Gerber influences the relative function of metaphor in Nietzsche's philosophy. It is not an implication of historical or cultural relativism that Nietzsche takes from Gerber, but rather a 'cognitive relativism'. So, while Gerber is certainly 'the main source' for Nietzsche's 'definition' of a trope, Nietzsche takes Gerber's definition that all language is metaphoric a step further. The implication that all language is metaphoric collapses the distinction between literal and figurative language for Nietzsche and he asserts that metaphor is relative to human perception alone rather than to some kind of literal or true match with the object that the metaphor is describing.

One of the key terms that Nietzsche took from Gerber's *Die Sprache als Kunst* was the German term *Lautbild* (a phonetic or articulated image). Gerber used the term in quite a different fashion from his predecessors, to refer to a phonetic image produced by words. In a very early foray into cognitive science, Gerber suggested that when a nerve was stimulated in the perception of an object, the articulation of a word happened simultaneously. This accounts for the word's construction: the term *Laut*, meaning loud, aloud, sound or tone, and the term *Bild* meaning picture or image. This of course is a slightly different usage from that of today when the related term *Lautbildung* can mean articulation or the production of speech sounds in phonetics. Because of Gerber's distinct understanding of *Lautbild*, he believed that the image we experience is transferred immediately to the word and therefore that all words, as *Lautbilder*, find the beginning of their meaning as tropes. Therefore, the beginning of language, for Gerber, was rooted in a basic operation of transference. In a section on tropes in language Gerber writes: 'Alle Wörter sind Lautbilder und sind in Bezug auf ihre Bedeutung an sich und von Anfang an Tropen' (All words are *Lautbilder* (phonetic images) and are, from the beginning, tropes with respect to their meaning).[60] If all words, as *Lautbilder*, are rooted in this basic operation of transference, then the meaning of words emerges from this transference.

As we have seen above, the evidence of Meijers and Stingelin's concordance shows that Nietzsche made use of this section of *Die Sprache als Kunst* extensively in his *Darstellung der antiken Rhetorik*.[61] From this notion of all words being *Lautbilder*, Nietzsche infers that it is meaningless to distinguish between literal and figurative meanings. However, this inference is as important for us as Meijers's, Stingelin's and Behler's assertion that Gerber's theory of tropes informed Nietzsche's own. Far beyond a philologically informed understanding of the category trope, Nietzsche sees Gerber's proclamation that 'All words are *Lautbilder*' and that all words are 'from the beginning, tropes with respect to their meaning' as having philosophically radical implications.[62] These philosophically radical implications have to do with *where* language becomes figurative.

As we have seen in chapter 1, the notion of a figurative origin to language dates back to thinkers like Rousseau and Vico. Rousseau claims, for example, that 'the enlightened mind, recogniz[ed] its first error' in the use of metaphors at the historical origin of language.[63] We of course can see the echo of this view in Müller's view of metaphor's involvement in the production of mythology. Gerber himself even argues that in the roots of words, language is figurative because it is an act of transference at the moment of our perception of an object, an object that we simultaneously have given a name. This act of transference then evolves, and the habits of metaphorical description become centuries old. This leads Gerber to call language a process of 'unceasing translation and of unending displacements'.[64] But what is key for Gerber is the pervasiveness of these unending displacements. All language is an act of transference. For Nietzsche, the implication of Gerber's ideas was that the metaphorical origin of language was not historic but rather cognitive. It is not something that the 'enlightened mind, recogniz[ed] [as] its first error' as Rousseau claims.[65] Rather, it is something that occurs when the mind perceives an object and comprehends the meaning of a word.

This can be seen explicitly in the first section of 'On Truth and Lying' where Nietzsche writes:

> The 'thing-in-itself' (which would be, precisely, pure truth, truth without consequences) is impossible for even the creator of language to grasp, and indeed this is not at all desirable. He designates only the relations of things to human beings, and in order to express them he avails himself of the boldest metaphors. The stimulation of a nerve is first translated into an image: first metaphor! The image is then imitated by a sound: second metaphor! And each time there is a complete leap from one sphere into the heart of another, new sphere [...] We believe that when we speak of trees, colours, snow and flowers, we have knowledge of the things themselves, and yet we possess only

metaphors of things which in no way correspond to the original entities. Just as the musical sound appears as a figure in the sand, so the mysterious 'X' of the thing-in-itself appears first as a nervous stimulus, then as an image, and finally as an articulated sound.[66]

In this passage, dense with images, we can see the influence of Gerber immediately when Nietzsche writes of the 'boldest metaphors' through which humans express their relation to things and the complete leap from sphere to sphere undertaken through these metaphors. The Meijers and Stingelin concordance cites this passage in 'On Truth and Lying' as being drawn from a section in *Die Sprache als Kunst* where Gerber asserts that an image is the most accurate reproduction of the material world that cognition encounters, sound being one step removed. Gerber writes: 'Da es nun aber ein fremdes ist, — der Laut — wie kann da Genaueres herauskommen, als ein Bild?' (But since it is something foreign — the sound — how could something more accurate than an image emerge?).[67]

The movement from image to sound, which Nietzsche calls the leaping from sphere to sphere, takes place, Nietzsche claims, on the very basic level of nerve stimulation. Nietzsche even expands this notion to the creation of words. He discusses the word 'snake', or *Schlange* in German, and writes: 'when we speak of a snake, the designation captures only its twisting movements and thus could equally well apply to a worm'.[68] When one looks at an edition of Grimm's *Deutsches Wörterbuch* from 1899, one sees that by Goethe's time *Schlange* was a commonplace comparison for any kind of twisting, whether the literal twisting of an object or a more figurative twisting.[69] One reading of this is that Nietzsche could be referring to the sound of the word and the association it musters, much as in Gerber's notion of *Lautbilder*. However, Meijers and Stingelin's concordance also links up this passage with a section in *Die Sprache als Kunst* where Gerber is listing the very close relationship in the Hebrew language between a variety of words, including snake, whale, viper, and compensate/redress. These in fact only represent an etymological association with either a literal twisting motion, such as in a snake or viper, or a figurative malleability such as compensate/redress, rather than the object associated with it.[70] While an argument can be made that Nietzsche also had in mind Gerber's notion of *Lautbilder*, the influence of Gerber's sensitivity to similar associations of a twisting movement is seen in a variety of words. This suggests that the match between a word and thing it describes is relative in nature.

Therefore, like Gerber, Nietzsche is expanding the word metaphor to mean an unconscious 'cognitive pattern' responsible for the creation of language rather than a figure of discourse standing separate from our cognitive patterns.[71] As Nietzsche says later in 'On Truth and Lying', metaphors are 'century-old habits' that are unconscious.[72] If this is the case, then the implication is that, as we see in Nietzsche's reading of Müller, the origin of cognition is figurative and there is no room for a distinct faculty of reason unaffected by tropes. This lack of separation that we see here in Gerber's influence on Nietzsche is not simply historic, as in Müller, but also cognitive.

With Nietzsche's appropriation of Gerber, we get a view of an ever-present metaphoricity that pervades moments outside the Aristotelian *lexis* and we see that the lack of separation between metaphor and reason takes place on the everyday level of perception. As radical as this is, the mere collapse of the distinction between metaphor and rationality is only half of the reversal of the Aristotelian paradigm of metaphor. It does not fully relativise metaphor. We see that the metaphorical origin of language is cognitive and not historic, and we also see that this cognitive origin is simply rooted in human perception rather than the thing the metaphor references. The final step in the reversal of the status of metaphor is Nietzsche's severing of the link between likeness and truthlikeness which is the ground for metaphoric meaning in the Aristotelian paradigm. Nietzsche finds the fuel for the critique of this final piece of the Aristotelian paradigm of metaphor in the post-Kantian philosophy of Schopenhauer, where issues regarding the relationship between perception and truth abound.

The Influence of Schopenhauer on Nietzsche's Conception of Metaphor

Arthur Schopenhauer's philosophy is essential for us to understand why Nietzsche severs the link between likeness and truthlikeness that traditionally holds the meaning of metaphor together. In the opening lines in the original German of *The World as Will and Representation* (1818/19) Schopenhauer writes: 'Die Welt ist meine Vorstellung' (The world is my representation).[73] Then a few pages later he writes, 'Die Welt ist mein Wille' (The world is my will).[74] When one reads the book's German title, *Die Welt als Wille und Vorstellung*, and then reads the opening lines of 'Die Welt ist meine Vorstellung' and 'Die Welt ist mein Wille', one can see how, for Schopenhauer, *mein* is the mediator between the subject and the world. It is the subject that is representing and the subject that is willing and in 'On Truth and Lying', and Nietzsche writes that '*truth* is a sum of human relations'.[75]

Schopenhauer's profound influence on Nietzsche is well documented. Safranski, for example, recounts how Nietzsche discovered Schopenhauer's *The World as Will and Representation* in a second-hand bookshop in October 1866 and while reading it experienced what Safranski describes as 'almost a conversion'.[76] In the period between 1866 and 1869, the most pronounced years of Nietzsche's Schopenhauer phase, he even went so far as to try to create a quasi-ascetic regime for himself in order to devote himself to self-denial so that he could more fully find redemption through the means that Schopenhauer's book suggested.[77] During this period, Nietzsche was also reading Friedrich Albert Lange's *History of Materialism and Criticisms of its Present Importance*, which Nietzsche called a 'treasure house'.[78] However, the influence of Schopenhauer's philosophy is more important for the development of Nietzsche's metaphysical critique and therefore we will focus almost exclusively on the influence of Schopenhauer's philosophy upon 'On Truth and Lying'.

This 'almost conversion' could lead one to view this period as a complete break from philology. In 1866, Nietzsche himself wrote: 'Kant, Schopenhauer, this book by Lange — I don't need anything else.'[79] However, there was more nuance to this period than this quote may initially suggest. The year before he penned this total reliance on Kant, Schopenhauer and Lange, Nietzsche wrote that the scholarly approach to philology offered him 'peace of mind and an uplifting feeling'.[80] Then in 1869, when Nietzsche learned of his appointment to an academic post in Basel and he was musing on what drove him into the field of philology, he wrote: 'The feeling of not getting to the basis of universality drove me to the arms of exacting scholarship. Then the longing to escape from the abrupt mood swings of artistic inclinations into the harbour of objectivity.'[81] This book will thus maintain that in order to understand the significance of Nietzsche's revolution of the concept of metaphor, it is essential not to view the period in which 'On Truth and Lying' was written as either exclusively philosophical or philological, but rather as a period of an ongoing dialectical tension between the two. As we have seen, certain philological conceptions prompted Nietzsche to re-evaluate the relationship between metaphor and reason and metaphor and representation. However, Nietzsche also seems to be deeply influenced by questions regarding the nature of representation itself and the relationship between representation and the nature of truth.

The influence of Schopenhauer's thought on Nietzsche's view of representation and the nature of truth, of course, comes from Schopenhauer's departure from Kant. Schopenhauer, like Kant, held the view that our forms of cognition constitute the representations of our perception. To remind the reader, when Schopenhauer gives his book the title *The World as Will and Representation*, he is borrowing the term 'representation' (*Vorstellung*) from Kant's first *Critique*. Here Kant writes: 'representations are always only representations, that is, inner determinations of our mind in this or that relation of time'.[82] For Kant, these 'inner determinations of our mind' are our forms of cognition and are 'always only representations' in relation to the objects we experience in time. As we saw in chapter 1, the building blocks of cognition as well as the problem between epistemology and metaphysics form the impetus for the first *Critique*.

For example, in the preface to the second edition of the first *Critique*, Kant observes that 'hitherto it has been supposed that all our knowledge must conform to its objects'. But then Kant goes on to write that:

> all attempts to establish something about them *a priori* by means of concepts, and thus to expand our knowledge, have on this supposition come to nothing. We should therefore attempt to tackle the tasks of metaphysics more successfully by assuming that the objects must conform to our knowledge.[83]

As we have seen in chapter 1, this is Kant's 'Copernican revolution' and in it is the implicit view that representations as the inner determinations of our mind are one of the fundamental building blocks of the view that objects conform to our knowledge. However, for Schopenhauer, because the true core of the human personality is the will, we cannot understand the world through objective, Kantian causal laws. While Schopenhauer agrees with Kant that our knowledge is rooted in the representation of objects, this representation of the world in our perception is filtered through the unconscious, where the will rages, and this is the original and natural condition of things.[84]

The title page of *The World as Will and Representation* bears a Goethe quotation: 'I wonder whether, in the end, Nature will fathom itself.'[85] Schopenhauer compares this search in the history of philosophy to the attempt to enter a castle by going round and round the outside perimeter without ever actually going in.[86] The entrance to the castle, for Schopenhauer, is found in the will and it is the will itself that is the *Ding-an-sich*.[87] In *The World as Will and Representation*, Schopenhauer writes:

> Kant bases the assumption of the thing-in-itself, although concealed under many different turns of expression, on a conclusion according to the law of causality, namely that empirical perception, or more correctly *sensation* in our organs of sense from which it proceeds, must have an external cause. Now, according to his own correct discovery, the law of causality is known to us a *priori*, and consequently is a function of our intellect, and so is of *subjective* origin. Moreover, sensation itself, to which we here apply the law of causality, is undeniably *subjective*; and finally, even space, in which, by means of this application, we place the cause of the sensation as object, is a form of our intellect given a *priori*, and is consequently *subjective*. Therefore the whole of empirical perception remains throughout on a subjective foundation, as a mere occurrence in us, and nothing entirely different from and independent of it can be brought in as *thing-in-itself*, or shown to be a necessary assumption. Empirical perception actually is and remains our mere representation; it is the world as representation.[88]

Therefore, because the empirical perception that Kant outlines is nothing more for Schopenhauer than a representation that emerges from the unconscious will, the concept of the *Ding-an-sich* refers ultimately to the will itself. How might the concept of will and the concept of representation relate to metaphor? Representation is easy to understand in relation to metaphor. When one reflects upon the multitude of meanings within the meaning of the German word *Vorstellung*, which both Kant and Schopenhauer use for representation, we can see a host of meanings contained within two semantic poles, many of which are lost in the English translation, 'representation'. Alongside the more common form of the representation of an object, *Vorstellung* can also mean 'idea'. If we remember for a moment that Kant defines an 'idea' as 'a concept of reason whose object can be met nowhere in experience', and that therefore a type of symbolic presentation is needed, we can begin to see the link.[89] This begins to reflect Nietzsche's view that an idea, such as truth, is merely the other side of the same coin of metaphor. However, in Kant's philosophy, there is of course a clear distinction between an idea (*Idee*) and a representation (*Vorstellung*). But for Schopenhauer the representation of the world in our perception is filtered through the unconscious where the will rages. Therefore, the ideas that representation produces are filtered through the will. For Schopenhauer, it is only in the will, expressing itself through human representations, where one could understand the true inner nature of the world because it is the will that is the *Ding-an-sich*.[90]

While this critique of Kant was hugely influential for Nietzsche, there was an aspect of it that remained unconvincing. As we see in the second half of *The World as Will and Representation*, philosophers, including Kant, have been searching for an entry point to the truth of the world but have been bogged down in representation. For Schopenhauer the entrance to the castle is found in the will. But Nietzsche cannot agree to a single solution or a single point of entry to gain access to the truth of the world. In fact, it is here that Nietzsche provides a philological critique of Schopenhauer.

Metaphor

To remind the reader, the aim of this chapter is to see the way in which Nietzsche's critique of truth alters the grounds of the conception of metaphor itself. With Nietzsche's philological critique of Schopenhauer, we begin to see a fundamentally new concept of metaphor emerging. Nietzsche's 'philological answer' to Schopenhauer can be seen in the passage we quoted above to demonstrate the influence of Gerber's theory of tropes. Nietzsche writes:

> the 'thing-in-itself' (which would be, precisely, pure truth, truth without consequences) is impossible for even the creator of language to grasp, and indeed this is not at all desirable. He designates only the relations of things to human beings, and in order to express them he avails himself of the boldest metaphors.[91]

This passage, rather than simply showing the philological influence of Gerber's theory of tropes, as Behler might suggest, uses Gerber to critique both Kant and Schopenhauer.

At first, Nietzsche affirms Schopenhauer's critique of Kant when he speaks of our linguistic designations being only the 'relations of things to human beings'. As we have seen, for Schopenhauer, our representations are filtered through the unconscious, where the primal will rages. But Nietzsche goes a step further and announces that Schopenhauer's metaphorical entrance to the castle is 'impossible to grasp'.[92] Reaffirming this, in the opening of 'On Truth and Lying' when Nietzsche describes the arrogance of human beings ever to think that they will discover the truth of nature, he writes: 'Nature has thrown away the key.'[93] It is almost as if Nietzsche has answered the Goethe quotation from the beginning of *The World as Will and Representation*, 'I wonder whether, in the end, Nature will fathom itself.'[94] For Nietzsche, to assign any title to objects in the world or to the *Ding-an-sich*, as Schopenhauer does with the will, is to assign an answer to something that is unanswerable. It is a popular prejudice that we could assign an answer to this question. Nietzsche reaffirms this sentiment later in *Beyond Good and Evil* where he writes:

> Philosophers are given to speaking of the will as if it were the best-known thing in the world; Schopenhauer, indeed, would have us understand that the will alone is truly known to us, known completely, known without deduction or addition. But it seems to me that in this case too Schopenhauer has done only what philosophers in general are given to doing: that he has taken up a *popular prejudice* and exaggerated it. Willing seems to me to be above all something complicated, something that is a unity only as a word — and it is precisely in this one word that the popular prejudice resides [...][95]

On the one hand, this does reflect the Kantian distinction of immanent and transcendental metaphysics. Immanent metaphysics of course concerns those things close at hand that we can understand through empirical knowledge, such as a table or chair, or the example Kant gives, the concept of a dog. Transcendental Metaphysics is, of course, knowledge of things like the idea of God and it is here that Kant also places knowledge of the *Ding-an-sich*. Here the will is seen by Schopenhauer to mediate between the immanent and the transcendental.

However, Nietzsche does not simply reject the will as the identity of the *Ding-an-sich* only to return to a Kantian understanding of the *Ding-an-sich*. Rather, for Nietzsche, even our descriptions of the *Ding-an-sich* are inflected with metaphor. As Nietzsche writes,

> We believe that when we speak of trees, colours, snow and flowers, we have knowledge of the things themselves, and yet we possess only metaphors of things which in no way correspond to the original entities. Just as the musical sound appears as a figure in the sand, so the mysterious 'X' of the thing-in-itself appears first as a nervous stimulus, then as an image, and finally as an articulated sound.[96]

Thus, it is on this basis that Nietzsche affirms the fundamentally unconscious nature of the will, through which our perceptions are filtered. But he also is so deeply influenced by Gerber's thesis of metaphor being an unconscious cognitive pattern that the very idea of the *Ding-an-sich* appears first as a metaphor. For this reason, to name the origin of the will, as Schopenhauer does, is impossible because metaphor is at the origin of both perception and cognition.

Metaphor and Truth

We have seen that both the distinction between metaphor and reason, and the distinction between figurative and literal language, collapse in Nietzsche's theory of metaphor. Now we must turn to Nietzsche's famous critique of truth. This is of course well known and as we have seen in the introduction it is a theme that stretches into his later philosophy, most pronouncedly in *Beyond Good and Evil*. But let us see how this critique of truth is also a critique of the Aristotelian conception of metaphor.

As we have seen, Nietzsche understands representation in a similar way to Schopenhauer in that it is not a reflection of what a thing is but rather how humans relate to it. As we saw in Nietzsche's example of the snake, the likeness perceived only expresses the associations with a twisting movement that the word can express, rather than telling us anything about the truth of the snake itself. This is the beginning of the Nietzschean inversion of the relationship between likeness and truthlikeness. Before we go further, we will briefly remind the reader of the Aristotelian formulation of a correspondence theory of truth, upon which the notion of truthlikeness was based. As we have seen in chapter 1, the concept of likeness, *homoion* in ancient Greek, was as central to Aristotle's understanding of rhetoric as the link between likeness and truthlikeness.[97] In classical rhetoric, the truthlikeness of metaphor was related to Aristotle's correspondence model of truth. The phrase 'correspondence theory of truth' is typically associated with Thomas

Aquinas's famous metaphysical version: 'A judgement is said to be true when it conforms to the external reality.'[98] However, as the *Routledge Encyclopaedia of Philosophy* notes, the basic premise of a correspondence theory is the 'oldest theory of truth in Western philosophy', and alongside Plato, can be traced to Aristotle in the *Metaphysics*.[99]

In the *Metaphysics*, Aristotle writes, 'a statement is true if it says of what is that it is, and of what is not that it is not'.[100] What grounds the 'is' or 'is not'? This is where the term 'truthlikeness' that was coined by Aristotle in the *Rhetoric* comes into play.[101] As we saw in chapter 1, with the translation of Aristotle's *Rhetoric* into Latin, and the popularisation of the term *verisimile*, from which we derive the English term verisimilitude, Cicero put metaphor in the service of this model of truthlikeness. This puts Nietzsche's war with truth as correspondence on the footing of an attack against the very foundations of Western thought. As Fink suggests, Nietzsche's philosophy presents 'a great crossroads of European man'.[102]

Here it is useful to look at Aristotle's formulation and consider it in relation to Nietzsche: 'To say that which is not is, is a falsehood; and to say that which is, is, is true.' What does Aristotle mean by 'that which is'? He always connects 'that which is' with 'is' or 'is not'. This 'is', the existing status of something, is the verb 'to be', and it can either be affirmed or denied and from this affirmation or denial we determine truth or falsehood.

For example, let us state something that is the case. If someone were to say that the British Library sits next to St Pancras International in London, a glance at Google Maps would prove them correct. However, if instead of this someone said, the British Library sits next to Gare du Nord in Paris, they have stated something that is not the case and according to Aristotle it is a falsehood. This reaffirms Aquinas's later statement that 'a judgment is said to be true when it conforms to the external reality'. In this case, the external reality is the location of the British Library as verified by Google Maps. However, when Nietzsche is evaluating metaphor in 'On Truth and Lying', he uses this Aristotelian formulation of something which is or is not to explain the origin of the truth itself.

Nietzsche writes:

> The liar uses the valid tokens of designation — words — to make the unreal appear to be real; he says, for example, 'I am rich', whereas the correct designation for this condition would be precisely, 'poor'. He misuses the established conventions by arbitrarily switching or even inverting the names for things.[103]

Note the way in which the liar in this passage states a falsehood: words! Words, Nietzsche writes, are the 'valid tokens of designation'. Thus, that which is either affirmed or denied as a truth or a falsehood is, for Nietzsche, dependent on the words which designate the state of things. In English, when we say that something 'sits next to something' it is an accepted designation of nearness and proximity in geographical space. This alone is what keeps the phrase 'The British Library sits next to Gare du Nord in Paris' from being a true statement. But if the accepted designation of the phrase 'sits next to' meant 'the nearest point accessible by an international train', then, remembering the Eurostar link between St Pancras and Gare du Nord, we could affirm that the British Library does indeed sit next to the Gare du Nord.

This arbitrariness is too much for Nietzsche and in the next few lines he asks ironically, 'Is there a perfect match between things and their designations? Is language the full and adequate expression of all realities?'[104] We can see the revolutionary implications of 'On Truth and Lying' more clearly in this light. It is because Nietzsche adheres to Gerber's unique understanding of *Lautbilder*, the understanding that all words have their beginnings as transference, that he thinks basic designations like rich and poor and 'sits next to' are fundamentally metaphoric. When Nietzsche moves from this notion of metaphor as an unconscious cognitive pattern that extends to all language to considering the role of language in the basic correspondence theory of truth, this is when the Aristotelian status is reversed. In this light, Nietzsche's famous formulation follows naturally:

> What, then, is truth? A mobile army of metaphors, metonymies, anthropomorphisms, in short a sum of human relations which have been subjected to poetic and rhetorical intensification, translation, and decoration, and which after they have been in use for a long time, strike a people as firmly established, canonical, and binding; truths are illusions of which we have forgotten that they are illusions, metaphors which have become worn by frequent use and have lost all sensuous vigour, coins which, having lost their stamp, are now regarded as metal and no longer as coins.[105]

Here Nietzsche decouples metaphor's likeness from truthlikeness by designating it as a sum of human relations, thereby redefining truth. In chapter 1, we saw that the poet Empedocles metaphorically named evening old age. Yet in Nietzsche's view there is no true resemblance or likeness of evening to old age beyond our human relation. So, if we reflect on the experience of staying out late as a student in one's twenties, we could say that evening is the youth of life. What, then, is metaphor in this view? Like truth, it is 'a sum of human relations'.[106]

The Crisis of Metaphoric Meaning

This unlinking of truth from truthlikeness lets metaphor reign supreme, not on a lesser throne in the service of rhetoric employed in a brilliant fashion to persuade, but rather on the highest throne as the origin and progenitor of the very concepts that conditioned it in classical rhetoric. The status of metaphor is revolutionised. However, this revolution creates a great crisis in the concept of metaphor itself. How are we to judge the meaning of the metaphoric transference? Like the Samsa family when they are confronted with their son's transformation into a giant cockroach in Kafka's *The Metamorphosis*, how are we to judge this transference that does not resemble what it should? How are we to reconcile the fact that we could equally say 'evening is the old age of life' and 'evening is the youth of life' with the fact that this very arbitrariness of metaphoric meaning is the same thing that allows the meaning of concepts to be conditioned by metaphors? To ask this question is to ask about a change in the Western conception of metaphor itself, not simply how metaphor alters our conception of truth. What the figurative is, by definition, has gone through a fundamental alteration.

This is our first main point in this book and it brings us to the crux of our hermeneutic problem: how can we interpret the meaning of a metaphor? This change in the status of the figurative produces two possible functions of metaphor. We have already seen the function of metaphor in cognition as that which relativises meaning. We could equally say 'evening is the old age of life' or 'evening is the youth of life'. This relative function of metaphor is built into Nietzsche's critique of the correspondence theory of truth itself. However, metaphor also adopts a pragmatic function in cognition once the figurative undergoes this fundamental change in status. Because in the same moment when Nietzsche announces that truth is simply a 'mobile army of metaphors', which is nothing more than a 'sum of human relations', he also announces that 'after [the metaphors] have been in use for a long time, [they] strike a people as firmly established, canonical, and binding'.[107] It is this pragmatic function of metaphor to create established, canonical and binding concepts, portrayed by Nietzsche as a drive for deception, that we also employ for our preservation. As we shall see, this pragmatic function of metaphor comes into a fundamental conflict with metaphor's relativising function. Because, once the reversal of the status of metaphor takes place, we see that likeness, for Nietzsche, is torn between, on the one hand, a never-ending echo chamber of human relations and on the other hand, an unconscious drive for deception that is pragmatically employed for our preservation.

Likeness as an Unconscious Drive for Deception

Nietzsche writes that humans are masters of 'keeping up appearances' (*repräsentieren*).[108] In the same passage where we saw Nietzsche develop Müller's idea of 'the disease of language', he also addresses the impossibility of the human intellect corresponding to truth. In a slew of accusations Nietzsche writes:

> As a means for the preservation of the individual, the intellect shows its greatest strengths in dissimulation, since this is the means to preserve those weaker, less robust individuals who, by nature, are denied horns or the sharp fangs of a beast of prey with which to wage the struggle for existence. This art of dissimulation reaches its peak in humankind, where deception, flattery, lying and cheating, speaking behind the backs of others, keeping up appearances, living in borrowed finery, wearing masks, the drapery of convention, play-acting for the benefit of others and oneself — in short, the constant fluttering of human beings around the one flame of vanity is so much the rule and the law that there is virtually nothing which defies understanding so much as the fact that an honest and pure drive towards truth should ever have emerged in them. They are deeply immersed in illusions and dream-images; their eyes merely glide across the surface of things and see 'forms'; nowhere does their perception lead into truth; instead it is content to receive stimuli and, as it were, to play with its fingers on the back of things.[109]

Here, Nietzsche states in no uncertain terms that keeping up appearances, *repräsentieren* in German, is both a rule and a law of cognition.[110] The subversive spin that Nietzsche puts on *repräsentieren* is that it is a sophisticated art of deception. The English translation in this passage of the German *repräsentieren* is keeping up appearances. As the translator notes, *repräsentieren* can mean to keep up a public show or 'represent one's family, country, or social group before the eyes of the world'.[111]

In order to clarify Nietzsche's point, let us imagine Agatha Christie's Miss Marple. Miss Marple is a character who is able to perceive the deception of the people in her little English village and the various funny ways in which they keep up appearances. But Miss Marple is a master detective because she recognises that the appearance of the good people of her little English village is a mask over the drama going on within their homes. This of course is a trope in English literature and in particular English detective fiction. But Marple can pierce through the appearance and find out what is truly going on precisely because she is able to recognise that the 'good people of the village' are only keeping up an appearance. Her spinsterhood is disarming because she appears at first as a gentle old lady, a simple fixture of English village life. But in the role of simple old lady who observes the comings and goings of the village she is aware of the pretext of appearance and the fact that appearance is inherently deceptive. In the same way, metaphors describing the natural world can mask over the fact that what is truly going on is the chaos and the movement of the primal will. However, what is distinctive with Nietzsche is that he does not believe a Marple-like character is possible within the world of our cognition. There is no ability to pierce through the cycle of keeping up appearances, which is the work of *repräsentieren*, and to understand the truth of the *Ding-an-sich*. We may critique one of the many metaphors that masquerade as truth claims, but rather than breaking out of the cycle of 'keeping up appearances', we only arrive at another metaphor.

As we have seen earlier, this is reflected in Nietzsche's subversion of Max Müller's conception of the role of metaphor in mythology as a 'disease of language'. For Müller, the human being, as the rational animal, can correct his or her error. For Nietzsche, the human being as the metaphorical animal cannot pierce through the work of *repräsentieren*. However, there is another aspect of the work that metaphor does in cognition that Müller's conception of metaphor is particularly helpful in highlighting.

While Nietzsche portrays likeness as, in fact, a drive for deception, this drive also generates stable concepts. To remind the reader, Müller says that the poetic names or metaphors were 'gradually allowed to assume a divine personality'.[112] Harnessing this idea, Nietzsche writes:

> For that which is to count as 'truth' from this point onwards now becomes fixed, i.e. a way of designating things is invented which has the same validity and force everywhere, and the legislation of language also produces the first laws of truth, for the contrast between truth and lying comes into existence here for the first time: the liar uses the valid tokens of designation — words — to make the unreal appear to be real; he says, for example, 'I am rich', whereas the correct designation for this condition would be, precisely, 'poor'. He misuses the established conventions by arbitrarily switching or even inverting the names for things. If he does this in a manner that is selfish and otherwise harmful, society will no longer trust him and therefore exclude him from its

ranks [...] what is the status of those conventions of language? Are they perhaps products of knowledge, of the sense of truth? [...] only through forgetfulness could human beings ever entertain the illusion that they possess truth to the degree described above.[113]

While Nietzsche is discussing the established and conventional names for things that become fixed through the various interactions of society, and Müller is describing the way metaphors assume divine personalities over time, the connection is clear: both thinkers are suggesting the meaning of language develops through the use of language reinforcing the established conventions. We can see this in the famous 'what, then, is truth?' passage where Nietzsche writes of 'metaphors which have become worn by frequent use and have lost all sensuous vigour, coins which, having lost their stamp, are now regarded as metal and no longer as coins'.[114] Here the analogy is between the frequent use of the coin and the frequent use of the metaphor. The stamp on the coin that bears the image of the monarch has been worn away, but does it matter as far as the established conventions are concerned? A packet of crisps, 99p, a bottle of beer, £2.50, a postcard, 50p, and all the while we pass the coin along. The cashier glances to make sure the change is correct, before dumping it into the register and yelling, 'next please!' The convention of commerce *works*. It is established and reinforced *without* having to look down at the monarch's face and check and say, 'yes, it is Queen Elisabeth, you can have your packet of crisps'.

Therefore, there is a social dimension to this deceptive drive that Nietzsche asserts that we have. While likeness is suddenly decoupled from truthlikeness and is labelled by Nietzsche as a drive for deception, he sees a pragmatic function in this drive for deception. He does not simply say, 'only through forgetfulness could human beings ever entertain the illusion that they possess truth'.[115] Nietzsche also carries on to write:

> The intellect shows its greatest strengths in dissimulation, since this is the means to preserve those weaker, less robust individuals who, by nature, are denied horns or the sharp fangs of a beast of prey with which to wage the struggle for existence.[116]

This social dimension of the pragmatic function of metaphor is pronounced clearly when Nietzsche highlights the role of language in creating 'peace treaties' so that human beings can live together in society rather than have a perpetual Hobbesian 'war of all against all'.[117]

It does not simply end with the prevention of a 'war of all against all', however. On the contrary, Nietzsche writes that:

> Originally, as we have seen, it is language which works on building the edifice of concepts; later it is science. Just as the bee simultaneously builds the cells of its comb and fills them with honey, so science works unceasingly at the great columbarium of concepts, the burial site of perceptions, builds ever-new, ever-higher tiers, supports, cleans, renews the old cells, and strives above all to fill that framework which towers up to vast heights, and to fit into it in an orderly way the whole empirical world, i.e. the anthropomorphic world.[118]

Once language creates a peace treaty and, using this established convention, reinforces a concept, science itself can, like a bee building its comb, 'work unceasingly [...] to fill that framework which towers up to vast heights'.

In *Nietzsche and Metaphor*, Sarah Kofman reminds us that Nietzsche is using the beehive metaphor subversively here. She points out that the beehive metaphor is traditionally used when 'instinctive work is opposed to the intelligent but defective work of man'.[119] However, Kofman points out that Nietzsche subverts this traditional contrast between instinctive work and intelligent work. Kofman writes that:

> [Nietzsche] intends [the beehive metaphor] to inscribe scientific work directly in life, to delete the opposition between the speculative and the practical, mind and instinct: concepts are the product of an instinctive metaphorical activity as is the construction of honey cells by the bee. The beehive, as a geometrical architectural ensemble, is the symbol for the systematic ordering of concepts.[120]

This reinforces the subversion of Müller's adherence to the Aristotelian rational animal. Kofman is insightful in her attentiveness to the way in which the style of the beehive metaphor tells us something about the instinctive nature of science, which, of course, is held up by the Enlightenment to be a departure from instinct.

However, as we have seen earlier in this chapter, Kofman links Nietzsche's philosophy of metaphor to the 'loss of the proper'.[121] In her haste to do so and relegate science to the side of instinct, the side traditionally reserved for the animal and not the human, she rushes past the startling realisation that science works, and that the established conventions of language do, in fact, create peace treaties. Nietzsche seems more attentive to this dual function of metaphor. The bee *needs* to make its beehive. It is not only out of instinct but also for survival. On the one hand Nietzsche speaks of concepts as 'the burial site of perceptions' and bemoans the arrogance of the human intellect, writing that, 'only through forgetfulness could human beings ever entertain the illusion that they possess truth'.[122] On the other hand we see that from metaphor's ability to produce concepts, science is born. It is perhaps here that we should add a caution to our claim that Nietzsche does not think we can pierce through the cycle of representation. While the unmasking of one metaphor would simply be followed by another, this does not mean that no knowledge is gained. In fact, Kofman would have done well to remember that in *Human, All Too Human*, Nietzsche distinguishes metaphysics from science and, while he continues his war against metaphysics, praises science for 'esteeming humble truths [and that this] is the sign of a higher culture'.[123] So while it is the case that Nietzsche characterises the drive to produce metaphors as a drive for deception, this same drive is also 'a means for the preservation of the individual, [where] the intellect shows its greatest strengths in dissimulation'.[124]

This is where the hermeneutic tension in Nietzsche's conception of metaphor is born. It is a hermeneutic tension because, traditionally, it is through the interpretation of likeness that we judge the meaning of a metaphor. We have seen that Nietzsche unlinks the likeness by which we can judge the meaning of a metaphor from truthlikeness. In turn he seems to map the likeness in metaphor onto both a relativising function and a pragmatic function. But how are we to reconcile likeness as both relative and pragmatic? How are we to affirm the fact that evening and old age have no necessary link between them and yet similar metaphorical designations hold the ideas of entire cultures and epochs in history together, such as the metaphor of light for the divine or the metaphor of light for truth?

It would be an easy solution if we could simply say that Nietzsche is describing two aspects of figurative language. But in Nietzsche's account, figurative language as a distinct category has collapsed, as has the separation between the figurative and reason. Thus, for Nietzsche, the pragmatic function and the relativising function of metaphor come from the same cognitive root. The 'great columbarium of concepts' is also 'the burial site of perceptions'. The 'coins which have lost their stamps' are the same ones that are frequently used. Nietzsche's new conception of metaphor is this very dissonance. The only suggestion he gives as to its resolution is not cognitive but social. When Nietzsche speaks of a 'mobile *army* of metaphors' or how 'the man of reason and the man of intuition stand side by side [... and] both desire to rule over life'[125] he is suggesting that it is in power that we see a social resolution to cognitive dissonance. Therefore, one of the key themes we will come back to in subsequent chapters is the way in which the hermeneutic problems that come from Nietzsche's conception of metaphor must be accounted for in terms of, on the one hand, the way in which metaphor creates mutual understanding and, on the other hand, the way in which it is a cornerstone of the semantics of ideology.

However, Nietzsche himself does not resolve the cognitive dissonance to which he points. It is this dissonance that makes us pose the question, *how can we interpret the meaning of metaphor if all semantic gestures are metaphoric?* A hermeneutic question born out of cognitive dissonance cannot be interpreted solely by means of power. We have seen several examples in the twentieth century and beyond of where purely political interpretations of Nietzsche may lead. But while Nietzsche certainly observes that power is often employed to provide a social resolution to cognitive dissonance, the resolution is superficial. This is precisely why Nietzsche calls it an illusion and why he bemoans our forgetfulness. Therefore, this cognitive dissonance remains in Nietzsche's new conception of metaphor and it is this dissonance that orients the concept of metaphor in post-Nietzschean European philosophy. We will explore this dissonance in the remainder of this book.

Notes to Chapter 2

1. Friedrich Nietzsche, 'On Truth and Lying in a Non-Moral Sense', in *The Birth of Tragedy and Other Writings*, trans. by Ronald Speirs (Cambridge: Cambridge University Press, 2012), pp. 139–53 (p. 146). Henceforth 'On Truth and Lying'.
2. Ernst Behler, 'Nietzsche's Conception of Irony', in *Nietzsche, Philosophy and the Arts*, ed. by Salim Kemal, Ivan Gaskell and Daniel W. Conway (Cambridge: Cambridge University Press, 2002), pp. 13–35 (p. 24).
3. Benedetta Zavatta, 'Nietzsche and Linguistics', in *Nietzsche on Consciousness and the Embodied Mind*, ed. Manuel Dries (Berlin: De Gruyter, 2016), pp. 265–89 (p. 267).
4. Friedrich Nietzsche, *Kritische Gesamtausgabe*, ed. by Giorgio Colli and Mazzino Montinari, 9 vols (Berlin and New York: De Gruyter, 1967), VII, 491.
5. Paul de Man, *Allegories of Reading* (New Haven: Yale University Press, 1979), p. 103.
6. Ibid., pp. 103–04.

7. Sarah Kofman, *Nietzsche and Metaphor*, trans. by Duncan Large (London: Athlone Press, 1993), p. 14.
8. Ibid., p. 25.
9. Ibid., pp. 6–17.
10. David B. Allison, *The New Nietzsche: Contemporary Styles of Interpretation* (London: MIT Press, 1985), pp. xiv–xv.
11. Ibid., p. xvi.
12. Ibid.
13. Duncan Large, 'Kofman's Nietzsche', in *Interpreting Nietzsche: Reception and Influence*, ed. by Ashley Woodward (London: Continuum, 2011), pp. 116–30 (p. 119).
14. De Man, *Allegories*, pp. 103–04.
15. Eugen Fink, *Nietzsche's Philosophy*, trans. by Goetz Richter (London: Bloomsbury, 2013), p. 25.
16. Ibid.
17. Ibid., p. 26.
18. Richard Rorty, 'The Contingency of Selfhood', *London Review of Books*, 8 (1986), 11–15.
19. Kofman, *Nietzsche*, pp. 59–80.
20. Large, 'Kofman', p. 118.
21. Ibid., p. 119.
22. Gregory Moore, *Nietzsche, Biology and Metaphor* (Cambridge: Cambridge University Press, 2002), p. 10.
23. Ibid., pp. 1–3.
24. Ibid., p. 10.
25. See Zavatta, 'Nietzsche', p. 267. We could also note that Nietzsche was reading Heymann Steinthal's *Einleitung in die Psychologie und Sprachwissenschaft* in this period. However, Max Müller and Gustav Gerber are the most relevant philological thinkers for the aspect of Nietzsche's argument on which this book focuses.
26. Rüdiger Safranski, *Nietzsche: A Philosophical Biography*, trans. by Shelley Frisch (London: Granta Books, 2002), p. 63.
27. Zavatta 'Nietzsche', p. 268.
28. Keith J. Ansell-Pearson, *How to Read Nietzsche* (London: Granta Books, 2005), pp. 2–3.
29. Safranski, *Nietzsche*, p. 47.
30. Ibid.
31. Zavatta, 'Nietzsche', p. 266.
32. Ibid., p. 265.
33. David Blackbourn, *History of Germany 1780–1918: The Long Nineteenth Century* (Oxford: Blackwell, 2003), p. 201.
34. Ibid., p. 185, Safranski, *Nietzsche*, p. 67.
35. Zavatta, 'Nietzsche', p. 285.
36. Friedrich Max Müller, *Lectures on the Science of Language*, 2 vols (London: Longmans, Green, & Co., 1880), I, 403.
37. Zavatta, 'Nietzsche', pp. 273–74.
38. Lourens P. Van den Bosch, *Friedrich Max Mueller: A Life Devoted to the Humanities* (Leiden: Brill, 2002), p. 163.
39. Friedrich Max Müller, *Comparative Mythology: An Essay* (London: Routledge, 1909), pp. 72–73.
40. Müller, *Science*, p. 12.
41. Andreas Musolff, 'Friedrich Max Müller's Cultural Concept of Metaphor', *Publications of the English Goethe Society*, 85.2-3 (2016), 125–43 (pp. 128 — 30).
42. Musolff, 'Müller', pp. 129–30.
43. Ibid., p. 131.
44. Ibid.
45. Zavatta, 'Nietzsche', p. 274.
46. Nietzsche, 'On Truth and Lying', p. 145.
47. Bosch, *Müller*, p. 186.
48. Müller, *Science*, p. 403.
49. Nietzsche, 'On Truth and Lying', p. 142.

50. Ibid.
51. Kofman, *Nietzsche and Metaphor*, p. 25.
52. Nietzsche, 'On Truth and Lying', pp. 150–51.
53. It is noteworthy that Max Müller produced one of the classic translations of Kant's *Critique of Pure Reason* into English. Müller was influenced by the 'back to Kant' emphasis in neo-Kantianism, as we can see from his correspondence in 1886 where he urges his interlocutor to go back to both Kant and Goethe. See *The Life and Letters of The Right Honourable Friedrich Max Müller*, ed. by Georgina Adelaide (London: Longmans, Green, & Co., 1903), p. 195.
54. Immanuel Kant, *Critique of Judgement*, trans. by James Creed Meredith (Oxford: Oxford University Press, 2008), p. 179, §59; Immanuel Kant, *Prolegomena to Any Future Metaphysics that will be able to come forward as Science*, trans. by Gary Hatfield (Cambridge: Cambridge University Press, 2004), p. 108, §58.
55. Kant, *Prolegomena*, p. 108. My emphasis.
56. Zavatta, 'Nietzsche', p. 280.
57. Ernst Behler, 'Nietzsche's Study of Greek Rhetoric', *Research in Phenomenology*, 25 (1995), 3–26.
58. See Anthonie Meijers and Martin Stingelin, 'Konkordanz zu den wörtlichen Abschriften und Übernahmen von Beispielen und Zitaten aus Gustav Gerber: Die Sprache als Kunst (Bromberg 1871) in Nietzsches Rhetorik-Vorlesung und in "Über Wahrheit und Lüge im aussermoralischen Sinne"', *Nietzsche-Studien*, 17 (1988), 350–68, and Anthonie Meijers, 'Gustav Gerber und Friedrich Nietzsche: Zum historischen Hintergrund der sprachphilosophischen Auffassungen des frühen Nietzsche', *Nietzsche-Studien*, 17 (1988), 369–90.
59. Meijers, 'Gustav Gerber und Friedrich Nietzsche', p. 385.
60. Gustav Gerber, *Die Sprache als Kunst*, 2 vols (Bromberg: Mittler'sche Buchhandlung H. Heyfelder, 1871), I, 333.
61. Zavatta, 'Nietzsche', p. 280.
62. Gerber, *Sprache*, p. 333.
63. Jean-Jacques Rousseau, *Essay on the Origin of Languages*, in *The Collected Writings of Rousseau*, VII, trans. and ed. by John T. Scott (Hanover, NH: University Press of New England, 1998), p. 295.
64. Gerber, *Sprache*, p. 362. Gerber uses the Latin for metaphor, *translatio*, in place of a German variant for the word translation.
65. Rousseau, *Origin*, p. 295.
66. Nietzsche, 'On Truth and Lying', pp. 144–45.
67. Gerber, *Sprache*, p. 159.
68. Nietzsche, 'On Truth and Lying', p. 144.
69. Jacob Grimm und Wilhelm Grimm, 'Schlange', *Deutsches Wörterbuch*, IX (Leipzig: Hirzel, 1899).
70. Meijers and Stingelin, 'Konkordanz', p. 367.
71. Zavatta, 'Nietzsche', p. 281.
72. Nietzsche, 'On Truth and Lying', p. 146.
73. Arthur Schopenhauer, *Die Welt als Wille und Vorstellung*, Schopenhauer Sämtliche Werke (Stuttgart and Frankfurt am Main: J. G. Cotta'sche Buchhandlung Nachfolger, 1960), p. 31.
74. Ibid., p. 33.
75. Nietzsche, 'On Truth and Lying', p. 146. My emphasis.
76. Safranski, *Nietzsche*, p. 45.
77. Ibid.
78. George Stack, *Lange and Nietzsche* (Berlin: De Gruyter, 1983), p. 22. It is prudent to note that the extent to which Lange influenced Nietzsche is more disputed than Schopenhauer's influence. While some influence is universally acknowledged, the evidence of a direct borrowing of ideas is thought by some to be less evident than with Schopenhauer. See for example, Keith J. Ansell-Pearson, 'The Question of F. A. Lange's Influence on Nietzsche: A Critique of Recent Research from the Standpoint of the Dionysian', *Nietzsche-Studien*, 17 (1988), 539–54.
79. Friedrich Nietzsche, *Nietzsche Briefwechsel*, in *Kritische Gesamtausgabe*, ed. G. Colli and M. Montinari, 9 vols (Berlin; New York: Walter de Gruyter, 1975), I.2, 184.
80. Safranski, *Nietzsche*, p. 44.
81. Ibid., p. 43.

82. Immanuel Kant, *Critique of Pure Reason*, trans. by Marcus Weigelt (London: Penguin, 2007), p. 218, B242/A197.
83. Kant, *Pure Reason*, p. 18, Bxvi–xvii.
84. Christopher Janaway, 'The Real Essence of Human Beings: Schopenhauer and the Unconscious Will', in *Thinking the Unconscious: Nineteenth Century German Thought*, ed. by Angus Nicholls and Martin Liebscher (Cambridge: Cambridge University Press, Cambridge Books Online, 2010), <http://dx.doi.org/10.1017/CBO9780511712272>, pp. 144–45.
85. Schopenhauer, *Die Welt*, p. 1.
86. Ibid., p. 156.
87. Safranski, *Nietzsche*, p. 45.
88. Arthur Schopenhauer, *The World as Will and Representation*, trans. by R. B. Haldane and J. Kemp (London: Kegan Paul, Trench, Trübner & Co., 1909), p. 436.
89. Howard Caygill, *A Kant Dictionary* (Oxford: Blackwell, 1995), p. 236.
90. Schopenhauer, *Die Welt*, p. 156.
91. Nietzsche, 'On Truth and Lying', pp. 144–45.
92. Ibid., p. 144.
93. Ibid., p. 142.
94. Schopenhauer, *Die Welt*, p. 1.
95. Friedrich Nietzsche, *Beyond Good and Evil*, trans. by R. J. Hollingdale (London: Penguin, 2003), pp. 47–48.
96. Nietzsche, 'On Truth and Lying', pp. 144–45.
97. Aristotle, *Rhetoric*, 1355a14, 1357a15–1357b16.
98. Thomas Aquinas, *Summa Theologiae*, trans. by The Dominican Council (Cambridge: Cambridge University Press, 2006), De Veritate, Q.1, A.1–3; Q.16.
99. Richard Kirkham, 'Truth, Correspondence Theory of', In *The Shorter Routledge Encyclopedia of Philosophy*, ed. by Edward Craig (London: Routledge, 2005), p. 1027.
100. Aristotle, *Metaphysics*, iv. 1011.
101. Aristotle, *Rhetoric*, 1355a14.
102. Fink, *Nietzsche*, p. 3.
103. Nietzsche, 'On Truth and Lying', p. 143.
104. Ibid.
105. Ibid., p. 146.
106. Ibid.
107. Ibid.
108. Ibid., p. 142.
109. Ibid.
110. Friedrich Nietzsche, *Über Wahrheit und Lüge im aussermoralischen Sinne* (Stuttgart: Reclams Universal Bibliothek, 2015).
111. Nietzsche, 'On Truth and Lying', p. 142 n. 2..
112. Müller, *Science*, p. 12.
113. Nietzsche, 'On Truth and Lying', p. 143.
114. Ibid., p. 146.
115. Ibid.
116. Ibid., p. 142.
117. Ibid., p. 143.
118. Ibid., p. 150.
119. Kofman, *Nietzsche*, pp. 61–62.
120. Ibid., p. 62.
121. Ibid., p. 14.
122. Nietzsche, 'On Truth and Lying', pp. 150, 143.
123. Friedrich Nietzsche, *Human, All Too Human*, trans. by Marion Faber and Stephen Lehmann (London: Penguin, 2004), p. 15.
124. Nietzsche, 'On Truth and Lying', p. 142.
125. Ibid., p. 152.

CHAPTER 3

Martin Heidegger, Paul Ricoeur and Metaphor as Poetic Revelation

This lengthy chapter may seem like a detour. While chronologically correct, it examines aspects of both Martin Heidegger's and Paul Ricoeur's philosophy not explicitly related to metaphor in detail and often takes a polemical tone. However, in doing so, our hope is to achieve three aims. First, to decentre the European philosophical reception of metaphor away from Heidegger and Ricoeur. For reasons this chapter will make clear, both Heidegger and Ricoeur certainly are one essential voice in any study of a European philosophy of metaphor. However, there is a difference between being one essential voice among a collection of other essential voices on a topic and having a paradigmatic place as 'The Voice' about that topic. At times, Heidegger and Ricoeur have been taken as 'The Voice' on the question of metaphor in European philosophy. As a result, the range of philosophical questions at stake has been too heavily demarcated by their thought and this demarcation presents a lopsided view of the concept of metaphor.[1] For reasons both intellectual-historical and philosophical, this chapter will seek to see Heidegger and Ricoeur as one part of a larger set of key reactions to the development of the post-Nietzschean concept of metaphor.

The second aim of the chapter is to remind the reader of the development of early twentieth-century European thought seen through the lens of the 1929 Davos disputation between Martin Heidegger and Ernst Cassirer. Finally, the overriding philosophical aim of the chapter is to highlight the difference between an articulation of the creation of meaning, a theme essential to Ricoeur's deployment of Heidegger's philosophy in his own philosophy of metaphor, and an articulation of the creation of mutual understanding.

In chapter 2, we saw how Nietzsche's subversion of the Aristotelian paradigm of truthlikeness created a fundamentally new concept of metaphor. For Nietzsche, metaphor is like the Roman god Janus: on the one hand, looking back to the origins of meaning and relativising them, and on the other hand, looking forward to the horizons of human experience and pragmatically orienting cognition through asserting stable, if ultimately relative, meanings. These two sides of the same cognitive root create a hermeneutic tension for judging the meaning of a metaphor.

In this chapter, to continue our critical analysis of the trajectory of this hermeneutic tension in post-Nietzschean European philosophy, we will observe how Heidegger's philosophy sidesteps this hermeneutic tension. This may initially seem like a strange claim to make of Heidegger's philosophy. The twentieth-century philosophers most readily associated with the term 'hermeneutics', Hans-Georg Gadamer and Paul Ricoeur, drew heavily on Heidegger. In *Truth and Method*, one of the seminal works of a philosophical approach to hermeneutic questions in twentieth-century European philosophy, Gadamer went so far as to suggest that 'in *Being and Time* [Heidegger] gave the general hermeneutical problem a concrete form in the question of being'.[2]

From another perspective, the reader may rightly point out that Heidegger's philosophy is not explicitly a philosophy of metaphor. As we shall see, what he writes about metaphor is always brief and usually an aside on the way to a larger point. However, while there are certainly other significant developments in early twentieth-century European thought, we are ultimately interested in the conflict between the pragmatic and relativising functions of metaphor, and Heidegger dramatically shapes the philosophical parameters of this post-Nietzschean question. If Nietzsche's revolt against the Aristotelian foundations of metaphor was one of the key developments in the concept of metaphor in European philosophy, then Heidegger's thought was another. We will argue that implicit in his philosophy is one attempt to 'ground' the hermeneutic conflict that Nietzsche opened up. In this chapter, we will consider this 'ground' as a 'manifesto of poetic revelation' as Anselm Haverkamp puts it.[3] This philosophical position orients a number of post-war philosophical discussions about metaphor, including those of Hans Blumenberg and Jacques Derrida, whom we will consider in subsequent chapters.

Finally, it is worth reminding the reader that Heidegger was a devoted reader of Nietzsche. In the years immediately following the Davos disputation, and then through the Second World War, he delivered one of the first set of lectures devoted to Nietzsche not simply as a *Lebensphilosoph* (life philosopher) or as an essayist with philosophical themes, but as a philosopher making an explicit philosophical contribution to the Western canon.[4] In fact, Heidegger called Nietzsche 'the last great metaphysician'.[5] Therefore, this chapter will consider the Davos disputation between Ernst Cassirer and Heidegger in order to provide a context for a key aspect of European philosophy in the early twentieth century and the decisive turn that it took with Heidegger's philosophy. We will then consider why it is the case that when Heidegger redirects so-called 'regional' questions such as 'what is the human being?' (the theme of the Davos disputation) to the more fundamental question of Being, he deepens the hermeneutic tensions within the Nietzschean concept of metaphor.[6] From this context, we will consider the two passages in which Heidegger mentions metaphor and finally, despite his criticisms and distinct differences with Heidegger, we will consider how Paul Ricoeur's philosophy of metaphor ultimately appropriates Heidegger's philosophy.

As we will see in this chapter, both philosophers ultimately attempt to ground the meaning of metaphor in a type of poetic revelation. This answer fails to resolve the hermeneutic tension in Nietzsche's conception of metaphor and places the focus on how meaning is created rather than how mutual understanding is created. This conflates meaning and judgement. While it is indispensable for judging a certain type of metaphor in a certain context, such a conflation is ultimately unable to speak to the cognitive dissonance between the pragmatic and relativistic functions of metaphor which we find at the heart of the question of mutual understanding. This limit exists partially because the type of metaphors implicit in both Heidegger's and Ricoeur's philosophies are themselves limiting. The metaphors employed by both thinkers are quite epic and noble, often calling to mind romantic poetry and sacred texts. While this model may be appropriate for some things, it leaves us at a loss when we are considering the dynamic dissonance between the relativising and pragmatic functions of metaphor and often does not account for the variety of metaphors we encounter, particularly destructive or oppressive ones. This creates an unintentionally static view of metaphor when it would like to present metaphor to us as being alive. But in order to understand why this is the case, we will first set the stage by looking at the 1929 Davos disputation as a window into philosophy in Europe at the time.

The Relevance of Davos for a Post-Nietzschean Concept of Metaphor

There is no direct intellectual-historical line from Nietzsche's 1873 essay 'On Truth and Lying in a Non-Moral Sense' and the disputation between Martin Heidegger and Ernst Cassirer at the second annual meeting in 1929 of the International Davos Conference (Internationale Davoser Hochschulkurse). Heidegger's *Being and Time* (1927), for example, does not reference 'On Truth and Lying' and even Heidegger's lecture series on Nietzsche in the 1930s does not explicitly cite the text. Rather, the connection is thematic, and Davos represents for us an early twentieth-century turning point in many of the issues Nietzsche raised over fifty years earlier. One of the ways we can understand the revolution that Nietzsche's philosophy brings to the concept of metaphor is that, after Nietzsche, metaphor no longer stands as a device of figurative language separate from reason, or truth claims. Rather, when Nietzsche collapses the distinction between reason and metaphor, and between metaphor and the truth claims reason produces, metaphor becomes a foundational question in both metaphysics and anthropology. In his philosophy generally, Heidegger redirects questions from both the fields of metaphysics and anthropology to the conditions that allow us to pose anthropological or metaphysical questions in the first place. This is, of course, famously, the existential analytic that seeks out a more fundamental ontology than the one traditionally posed by the metaphysical tradition.[7]

At Davos, the central question addressed by both Heidegger and Cassirer was 'Was ist der Mensch?' (What is the Human Being?).[8] This echoes Kant's fourth question from his *Logic* (1800). Kant laid out four questions in the introduction to the *Logic*, each of which corresponded to a different discipline respectively: 'What can I know?' in relation to metaphysics, 'what should I do?' in relation to ethics, 'what can I hope for?' in relation to religion and, ultimately, 'what is the human being?', to which all three previous questions are related.[9] Kant's fourth question was also one of the key questions which occupied German thought in the early twentieth century. Philosophical anthropology, for example, in the form of Scheler, was an attempt to put Kant's fourth question in the context of modern science and it is an attempt that, as we shall see, Heidegger explicitly rejects at Davos.[10]

But with regard to metaphor, we can see that both Heidegger's and Cassirer's positions on Kant's fourth question have relevance to related issues beyond purely anthropological questions. This is the case, for example, for myth. Angus Nicholls points out in *Myth and Human Sciences: Hans Blumenberg's Theory of Myth* that at Davos, Heidegger related myth to the concept of *thrownness*, which Heidegger asserted was one of *Dasein*'s key components.[11] We can also assert here that, like myth, Davos has a significance for the concept of metaphor. When we consider Kofman's assertion that in Nietzsche's philosophy, the human being becomes the metaphorical animal, Kant's anthropological question takes on a particular significance for us. When Nietzsche claims in 'On Truth and Lying' that the human being shows its greatest strength in 'dissimulation, the wearing of masks and living in borrowed finery' he arguably gives a definition of the human being grounded in 'dissimulation', which, as we know for Nietzsche, is metaphor.[12] Thus, the development of the conception of the human being at Davos is directly relevant to the post-Nietzschean conception of metaphor.

One of the key ideas that emerges in Heidegger's philosophy at Davos is that the manner in which a human being generates an ontological concept is relevant for an understanding of the nature of the human being itself. From this position, Heidegger makes his famous distinction between himself and Cassirer. Heidegger asserts that his philosophy is concerned with the *terminus a quo* (from where) of a philosophical question, and that Cassirer's is concerned with the *terminus ad quem* (to where) of a philosophical question.[13] As we have seen, one of the themes at Davos in 1929 was 'Was ist der Mensch?' (What is the Human Being?).[14] Regarding this question, Heidegger asserts that anthropological questions are merely regional questions and should be redirected and related to more fundamental questions such as what is the Being of beings.[15] This is because, for Heidegger, the question of the Being of beings is what allows for an anthropological question to be posed in the first place. This would mean that, if Nietzsche asserts that the human being is a metaphorical animal, this too must ultimately be related to a more fundamental question. We will see later how Heidegger asserts precisely this in his brief treatment of metaphor.

The Context of Davos

The geopolitical and intellectual-historical context within which the 1929 Davos disputation took place was ripe for such a dramatic philosophical redirection. The International Davos Conference was a yearly colloquium for intellectuals from across Europe that had four meetings in total.[16] To understand the context of the 1929 conference specifically, we will rely heavily on Peter Gordon's book *Continental Divide* (2010), as it is the most recent standard work on Davos. In *Continental Divide*, Gordon reminds us that Thomas Mann had set another fictional debate in Davos in his 1924 novel *The Magic Mountain*. The debate in the novel amounts to an allegorical philosophical conflict whose themes reflect the cultural crises that were already commonplace in mid-1920s Weimar Germany.[17]

Weimar Germany was in a period of 'relative stabilisation from 1924 to 1929'[18] and the Davos disputation took place at the end of March 1929, just over six months before the October Wall Street Crash. This triggered the withdrawal of American loans that had been in place in Germany since its defeat in the First World War and had underpinned the country's subsequent attempt to build a republic. When Hermann Müller's coalition government could not find a suitable strategy to handle the unemployment and bankruptcy that had been exacerbated by the withdrawal of American loans, the German economic crisis of the early 1930s ultimately led to the National Socialist victory in 1933.[19] But prior to all of this, up until 1929 in Weimar's relative stability, the golden twenties 'saw an explosion of creativity across a wide range of scientific and artistic fields'.[20] However, the key for us is the reminder that the cultural creativity of this time was not a homogeneous entity. The historian Mary Fulbrook describes it as 'a deeply divided phenomenon' and writes that 'the one element that united the widely differing aspects of this culture within Germany, on both the Right and the Left, was the problematic relationship with "modernity" in general as well as the Weimar Republic'.[21] It is important to put all this into context because like the debate played out in Mann's *Magic Mountain*, as Peter Gordon reminds us, the problematic relationship with modernity is played out in the Davos disputation and part of the shift was the departure from any kind of objective starting point to philosophical questioning.[22]

If we can say that Nietzsche's 'On Truth and Lying' is the definitive, if perhaps little known at the time, philosophical text within which a new conception of metaphor raises its head, then Davos is the definitive historical event where the philosophical implications for related issues, such as metaphor, gained widespread attention and in which a departure from an objective starting point to philosophical questioning is deeply felt. The French philosopher Emmanuel Levinas was a young student attending Davos in 1929. Levinas recalled that it was only after attending Davos that he understood why a fellow student referred to going see Heidegger speak as 'going to see the greatest philosopher in the world'. Levinas adds that he himself 'knew right away that this was one of the greatest philosophers in history'.[23]

However, we need to be careful not to treat Davos as some kind of Heideggerian victory. Rather we want to acknowledge the public impact that Heidegger's thought had at Davos on the philosophical dispute about objective place from where one can begin philosophical questioning. We want to show why his thought charts a distinctive reinterpretation of both anthropological and metaphysical questions that in turn have a bearing on the concept of metaphor. So rather than following Levinas in proclaiming that after Davos it is evident that Heidegger was one 'of the greatest philosophers in history' we want to view it, more broadly, as a significant development in the transformation of European philosophy. This is especially the case because, despite their differences, both Heidegger and Cassirer shared 'a deeply historical awareness that modern European philosophy was embarking on a phase of radical transformation'.[24] Philosophical movements, such as philosophical anthropology for example, were an attempt to put Kant's fourth question in the context of modern science and both Heidegger and Cassirer were trained in schools of thought that were attempting to come to terms with philosophy's relationship to science, a hallmark of the modern intellectual and cultural crisis.

Heidegger was trained by Edmund Husserl, the founder of phenomenology, and Husserlian phenomenology attempted to reconceive philosophy as a form of transcendental science rather than a form of science based on the natural sciences as Husserl famously outlined in his essay 'Philosophy as Rigorous Science' (1910–11).[25] Cassirer, on the other hand, was trained by one of the most prominent neo-Kantians of the day, Hermann Cohen. The neo-Kantian paradigm saw philosophy as a transcendental groundwork for science.[26] From their engagement with and transformation of their respective philosophical foundations, both thinkers arrived at differing normative images of humanity during philosophy's 'radical phase of transformation'.[27] Therefore, when these two normative images collided in late March 1929, one of the guiding questions concerning metaphor after Nietzsche, 'what is the human being?', was set on a course for a radical reorientation. To understand the context of this reorientation, we will acquaint ourselves with Cassirer's position first.

Cassirer's Position

In his final statement to Heidegger at Davos, Cassirer said:

> each of us speaks his own language, and it is unthinkable that the language of one of us is carried over into the language of the other. And yet, we understand ourselves through the medium of language. Hence there is something like *the* language. And hence there is something like a unity which is higher than the infinitude of the various ways of speaking. Therein lies what is for me the decisive point. And it is for that reason that I start from the Objectivity of the symbolic form, because here the inconceivable has been done.[28]

It is important to understand this position for two reasons. One is to understand clearly the type of objectivity that Heidegger rejects when he reorients regional questions to more fundamental ones. For Heidegger, any claim that thinks it is objective is oriented by our finitude from the beginning.[29] In contrast, for Cassirer, language, as we shall see, is considered to be one of the symbolic forms, such as art or myth, and therefore he views it as a pure, symbolic synthesis of the imagination that creates conceptions without any pre-conditioning.[30] Cassirer maintains this position throughout the Davos disputation in his responses to Heidegger and this is a key difference between the two thinkers.[31] Like Nietzsche, Heidegger maintains that ontological claims are conditioned by our finitude, and because of this, he rejects such an objectivity. Therefore, it is implied that the use of Heidegger's philosophy for an analysis of metaphor includes such a rejection.

The second reason that it is important to understand Cassirer's position is that even though, as Heidegger does, we will depart from Cassirer's view of language as a part of a pure, symbolic synthesis, Cassirer does raise a vital question about the nature of communication. At Davos, Cassirer maintains that in language's ability to create understanding, 'the inconceivable has been done'.[32] For Cassirer, this suggests that 'there is something like a unity which is higher than the infinitude of the various ways of speaking' and this unity is the objectivity of the symbolic forms such as language.[33] Like Heidegger, we will depart from the view that because understanding is produced, there must be something like an objective unity that transcends the subjective 'various ways of speaking'. But Cassirer's willingness to be in awe of the 'inconceivable' creation of understanding via language poses an important question that is too easily swept aside by Heidegger. Implicit in Cassirer's statement is the question 'how is understanding achieved?'

To a certain extent, Cassirer's point is pragmatic, because, despite philosophical objections against the concept of objectivity, we still understand each other, and this is quite remarkable. Therefore, we can see that Cassirer's reply to Heidegger brings us back to the hermeneutic tension seen in Nietzsche's conception of metaphor. While metaphor relativises meaning, it also seems to create mutual understanding. Heidegger's philosophy, particularly with regard to metaphor, does not address this. It is certainly the case that, as Clive Cazeaux points out in *Metaphor and Continental Philosophy*, Heidegger's attention to the anticipatory structures of understanding in his reading of Kant does indeed provide a helpful framework to understand the creation of a new metaphor.[34] However, as we have maintained since the introduction, the creation of new meaning does not necessarily account for the creation of mutual understanding, which is one of the essential hermeneutic tensions that Nietzsche's conception of metaphor brings up. So, with these two points in mind, let us turn to a deeper understanding of Cassirer's position.

In the early twentieth century, Cassirer emerged from a group of thinkers who supported the philosophical tradition of Kantianism and often saw an intellectual defence of Kant as a defence of European civilisation itself. For Cassirer, in his day the modern crisis in philosophy 'was only a local symptom of the larger crisis of European civilization'.[35] As we saw earlier in this chapter, philosophical anthropology was one movement that responded to this perceived crisis via a particular interpretation of Kant's fourth question. For our purposes, another major influence that also put Kant's thought into the centre of the Davos debate was the Marburg neo-Kantian school. This is the movement in which Cassirer was trained, and it saw philosophy as a transcendental groundwork for science.

This neo-Kantian paradigm was characterised by the nineteenth-century slogan that the German philosopher Otto Liebmann made famous, 'back to Kant'; in both France and Germany this slogan 'inspired more rigorous methodologies in logic, philosophy of science, philosophy of value and even the growing field of sociology'.[36] Cassirer's teacher, Hermann Cohen, contributed to this renewed rigour by arguing that Kant's aim was to develop 'a theory of scientific discovery' where Kant's famous thing-in-itself (*Ding an sich*) was not something to be thought of in the realm of metaphysics, as it traditionally had been, but rather should be a 'label for the "as-yet-unexplained" thing that scientific knowledge sets out to explain'.[37]

What does this mean? It means that the thing-in-itself is merely a thought object for Cohen. The origins of the thing-in-itself are simply in thought alone. However, this does not mean that Cohen regarded the idea of the thing-in-itself as a lesser idea because it was simply in thought alone. On the contrary, the fact that the origins of the thing-in-itself were in thought alone re-emphasised, for Cohen, the profound nature of Kant's project for scientific knowledge. It allowed Cohen to stress the 'essentially epistemological purpose of Kant's enquiry' and the fact that Kant's philosophy draws our attention to 'the conditions for knowledge' of objects in the world.[38] In other words, for Cohen, the fact that an idea like the thing-in-itself occurs simply in the mind alone draws our attention to the conditions that make knowledge possible. This is what helps us to develop a theory of scientific discovery in light of Kant.[39]

So, for Cohen, the empiricist model of truth as correspondence to an independent object, which we have already seen rejected by Nietzsche, was replaced by an 'intellectualistic model' of *truth as the systematic coherence among concepts*. This view of truth made the thing-in-itself lose its metaphysical status and it was 'transformed into a regulative concept for scientific discovery'.[40] This is neither the Nietzschean 'truth is a metaphor' thesis, nor is it the Aristotelian/Aquinian 'truth is correspondence' thesis. Rather, it is truth as conceptual coherence and is thus a tool of science. While admittedly a generalisation, the model of truth as coherence in the service of science was what gave Cohen and the neo-Kantian Marburg group, of which Cohen was a founder, one of their most well-known features.[41]

Cassirer's thought emerged from this, but by the time he debated with Heidegger in Davos in 1929, Cassirer had, of course, already transformed Cohen's thought and the neo-Kantians in his own way. The first volume of Cassirer's *Philosophy of Symbolic Forms* had been published in 1923 and had developed a distinct relationship to the neo-Kantian viewpoint.[42] In 1914, before the publication of *Symbolic Forms*, as Cassirer was finding his own way out of the Marburg neo-Kantian school, he published an article on Kant in an issue of *Die Geisteswissenschaften* where he focused a large amount of attention not on the thing-in-itself as a regulative concept for science, but rather on the significance of Kant's schema and the role of judgement as a unifying feature of Kant's system.[43] This was a theme he explored in detail in the 1916 volume of his multi-volume work *Kants Leben und Lehre*.[44]

Cassirer built upon this reinterpretation of Kant in volume 1 of 1923's *Philosophy of Symbolic Forms*. The emphasis of this work is a movement from Kant's focus on a critique of reason and judgement to a critique of culture itself. In the same way that Kant was concerned with logical forms in his exploration of judgement, Cassirer was concerned with cultural forms. While in the natural sciences our judgements revolve around the facts of science, Cassirer was concerned with 'the fact of culture' and ultimately with the human being as a symbolic animal.[45] Although Cassirer thought the role of judgement in Kant's thought was central to his entire philosophy, he felt that Kant neglected fields of 'common experience' like language, myth and art and the way that that these functioned as 'synthesising activities of human reason'.[46] It is imagination then, for Cassirer, shown in language, myth and art that is one of the synthesising powers of reason.[47] In *The Philosophy of Symbolic Forms* Cassirer concludes that, 'in all its achievements and in every particular phase of its progress, language shows itself to be at once a sensuous and an intellectual form of expression'.[48] This is why Cassirer appeals to the creation of 'mutual understanding' in his final reply to Heidegger and here we have arrived at the first relevance of Cassirer for our understanding of Heidegger's contribution to a philosophy of metaphor. Which aspects of Cassirer's reading of Kant's thought, understood as a critique of culture, does Heidegger reject?

As stated above, imagination was central to Cassirer's appropriation of Kant's philosophy and it also was a dividing line between Heidegger and Cassirer. As we shall see, the way that imagination works ultimately affects the *terminus a quo* or *terminus ad quem* of a philosophical question. The reference point for both Cassirer and Heidegger on the question of imagination was Kant's schematism first introduced in *The Critique of Pure Reason*.[49] In the section on the 'transcendental doctrine of the power of judgement', the schematism is introduced as an answer to the question, 'how can intuitions be subsumed under concepts?'[50] For Kant, intuition is on the side of appearances and the disparity he sees arises from the riddle of how pure concepts of the understanding could be applied to appearances at all.[51]

As we saw in chapter 1, one of Kant's well-known examples of this disparity between concept and appearance is that of the concept of dog as a four-legged creature and the image of a dog.[52] There must be something besides pure concepts and besides intuitions which allow us to synthesise concept and image. Therefore, Kant posits what he calls a schematism: a procedure of judgement that mediates between concepts and intuition.[53] This is the role of the imagination in Kant's philosophy, as we saw in chapter 1. Here the imagination is a faculty of the original representation of the object (*exhibitio originaria*) rather than a faculty of derived representation (*exhibitio derivativa*).[54] The interpretation of this issue in Kant's thought would be a dividing line for Heidegger and Cassirer and can be seen as a key to why Heidegger rejects Cassirer's notion of objectivity. It is also a window onto why Heidegger thinks all conceptions are conditioned by finitude from the outset; he uses Kant's anthropological question as a case study for this issue.

Divergent Positions at Davos

Like Heidegger, Cassirer agreed that in Kant, the imagination allows the synthesis of concept and image, as outlined above, for the symbolic grasping of concepts. However, unlike Heidegger, Cassirer argued that the imagination synthesised concepts and images purely spontaneously, i.e. without any conditioning. This is how Cassirer interpreted Kant's interest in the imagination as pure *a priori* imagination.[55] As we have seen, for Cassirer, this pure spontaneity that synthesised concept and image or the senses and ideas, could be seen in language, because 'language shows itself to be at once a sensuous and an intellectual form of expression'.[56] Therefore, for Cassirer, the pure spontaneity of language is an example of this pure and symbolic synthesis that Kant suggests we need so that we can pair images and concepts. As a pure and symbolic synthesis, it implies an objectivity and it is because of this objectivity that Cassirer marvels at language's ability to create mutual understanding.[57] But this appeal to objectivity is why Heidegger characterises Cassirer's manner of philosophical questioning as taking place from the position of the *terminus ad quem*.[58]

As we have already seen, Heidegger characterised his own philosophical interest as the *terminus a quo* (from where) of a philosophical question and Cassirer's as the *terminus ad quem* (to where) of a philosophical question. Cassirer accepted this distinction but thought that it was a tension that could not be resolved.[59] This distinction has been pointed to as a clear dividing line between Cassirer's and Heidegger's philosophical projects and one of the major dividing lines of Davos.[60] But what exactly does this distinction mean and why does it have a bearing on metaphor?

Heidegger explains this dispute with Cassirer by characterising the two positions in terms of Kant's question 'what is the human being?'. Heidegger states that Kant's question 'is questionable'.[61] How exactly is the question questionable? It is questionable in two senses. On the one hand, it is 'questionable' meaning dubious. Heidegger casts doubt on our ability to ask the question 'what is the human being?'. But the doubt arises for Heidegger for a very specific reason, which in turn relates to the second sense of the meaning of the word 'questionable'. We can ask a question about a question itself. In other words, the question is questionable because we can ask what it means to ask such a question, how a question is constructed, for example, and the perspective from which a question is asked.[62] The doubt, the questionability of such a question arises for Heidegger not because the question is futile, but because the way the answer has been presented, in Cassirer's case for example, does not ask about the perspective from which the question has been asked.

The perspective from which a question has been asked, and the position which Heidegger has associated with his philosophy, is the *terminus a quo* (starting point or point of departure). To not consider the starting point of a question, the *terminus a quo*, is to view the imagination as producing concepts without any conditioning. Heidegger claims that Cassirer is concerned with the *terminus ad quem* (finishing point, aim or goal) because Cassirer believes the imagination produces conceptions without conditioning.[63] As we have seen, Cassirer was ultimately concerned with the fact that the pure spontaneity of language can create something like common experience.

However, to begin with this objectivity is to philosophise from the perspective of the *terminus ad quem* in Heidegger's view. Therefore, in rejecting the pure spontaneity of the imagination and its capacity to create something like an objectivity of symbolic forms, Heidegger also rejects the question of the creation of understanding. It is possible that Heidegger is too focused on rejecting Cassirer's appeal to objectivity to appreciate Cassirer's observation that the 'inconceivable has been done' in the creation of the understanding.[64] Instead, at Davos, Heidegger focuses on the conditioning of the understanding by our finitude.

What does this mean? When Heidegger says the question 'what is the human being?' is questionable, he means that any answer to the question does not consider the conditions from which the question can be posed. Therefore, it does not give us any kind of fundamental understanding of the nature of the human being. What allowed Kant to pose such a question in the first place? This is Heidegger's interest, and for him the answer provided by philosophical anthropology is only a regional description in that it is 'much too narrow, much too preliminary'.[65] For Heidegger, anthropology is only a secondary question. We might then call anthropology a mere 'regional hermeneutics'. An analogy we could draw would be with biblical hermeneutics, which historically sought to create a science of interpretation for the Bible. While both anthropology and biblical hermeneutics might create regional sciences of interpretation, anthropology for the description of the human species as described by science, and biblical hermeneutics for the description of the Bible, both of these regional hermeneutics, in Heidegger's view, would rely on a more fundamental description, an ontological hermeneutics.

A quote from the 'Introduction' of *Being and Time* can help us here. In discussing how various philosophers, including Kant in the *Critique of Pure Reason*, have laid the foundation for science but have not necessarily posed the question of Being, Heidegger writes:

> basically, all ontology, no matter how rich and firmly compacted a system of categories it has at its disposal, remains blind and perverted from its ownmost aim, if it has not first adequately clarified the meaning of Being, and conceived this clarification as its fundamental task.[66]

What harsh and yet very clear words from Heidegger!

Heidegger does not criticise Kant here but rather argues that a system of science based solely on Kantian categories would not produce an understanding of nature in the way it hopes to, because it has not first clarified the meaning of Being. What we can infer from this quote is that, for Heidegger, if we consider anthropology as a science, unless it first clarifies the meaning of Being it 'remains blind and perverted'.[67] The question 'what is the human being' presupposes knowledge of Being, or an ontology, and therefore answering the question would presumably give us knowledge about the world. It would create a world-view. But as Heidegger puts it in his debate with Cassirer, 'philosophy does not have the task of giving a world-view [...] world-view is the presupposition of philosophizing'.[68] While biblical hermeneutics or anthropology may think they are providing us with a world-view through their descriptions of the phenomenon in question, Heidegger would argue that their regional descriptions presuppose a more fundamental world-view. Therefore, if one wants to gain knowledge of a regional question like 'what is the human being', one must first proceed through an ontological hermeneutics that would give one more fundamental and general knowledge of Being itself.

Therefore, with regard to Kant's fourth question, the primary question that we should be asking, in Heidegger's view, concerns *Dasein*, the Being of beings. For it is here that we find the conditions for a question like Kant's fourth question in the first place. In the same way, Cassirer's attempt to start with the objectivity of symbolic forms, the *terminus ad quem*, arises out of finitude and is only possible based on what Heidegger calls a metaphysics of *Dasein*.[69]

At one point, Cassirer attempted to clarify Heidegger's position and asked if he maintained that there are no eternal or necessary truths for a human being. He then posed this question to Heidegger: 'does Heidegger want to renounce the entire objectivity that Kant advocated and withdraw completely to the realm of the finite creature?'[70] With Nietzsche, we have seen the answer to the question clearly already: there is no objectivity. Any attempt at objectivity is a metaphoric creation of the metaphoric creature. Though Cassirer does not mention Nietzsche, his question could be read as creating a straw man argument that asks Heidegger whether he holds to such a Nietzschean-like radical finitude. However, rather than answering directly, Heidegger reorients the question.[71] In the same way that in *Being and Time* Heidegger reorients the question of gaining knowledge of Being to a question about the structure of existence itself, which is where the question about Being arises from in the first place, he reorients the question about the relation between objectivity and finitude to a question about how finitude produces objective concepts.

After a few provisos, Heidegger claims that the concept of an eternal truth or a universal maxim arises in the finite sphere. He claims that our universal claims and laws, such as the kind that may arise in Kant's categorical imperative, both constitute human existence while simultaneously emerging from it.[72] About the concept of a universal law, Heidegger says that instead of asking if there are universal laws, the question we should ask is 'what does the law mean? And how is lawfulness constitutive for *Dasein* and personality?'[73] What does it mean for a universal principle, like a universal law in the categorical imperative, to constitute our experience of existence? For Heidegger, a universal principle arises in our imagination; that is, it arises from finitude. We see this clearly when Heidegger writes that 'ontology requires only a finite creature'.[74]

Thus, like the Nietzschean metaphorical animal, any anthropological conception or conception about symbolic forms would be generated in the finite sphere, the sphere of human relations. Yet, for Heidegger, even this is not fundamental enough to answer the question of the Being of beings. This deeper inquiry into a more fundamental ontology, which Heidegger calls the existential analytic, and which will allow us to carry out a metaphysics of *Dasein*, is what gives the post-Nietzschean conception of metaphor a unique twist.[75] The relationship of metaphor to the existential analytic carries with it a certain set of assumptions in Heidegger's thought. One of these is the unspoken assumption of Being grounding the hermeneutic tension found in a Nietzschean conception of metaphor. As we have stated, this assumption does not account for the creation of mutual understanding or the effect of ideology. Therefore, while we could focus on other areas of Heidegger's thought in relation to metaphor, we will focus on the problem of the relationship between the existential analytic and metaphor, rather than on other areas such as the creation of new meaning. In order to do this, we must remind ourselves of the existential analytic and the metaphysics of *Dasein* to see how metaphor relates to it. If, on the one hand, we have seen that, like Nietzsche, Heidegger asserts that there are conditions for the question 'what is the human being?' even being posed, we will also see, on the other hand, that Heidegger's answer is neither purely Nietzschean nor does it allow room for the Nietzschean conception of metaphor.

The Existential Analytic and a Metaphysics of Dasein

In *Being and Time*, Heidegger writes that '*fundamental ontology*, from which alone all other ontologies can take their rise, must be sought in the *existential analytic of Dasein*'.[76] How can we understand the concept of a fundamental ontology which gives rise to other ontologies? One way we could approach this question is to draw an analogy from the Nobel prize winner Haldor Laxness's 1957 novel, *The Fish Can Sing*. The novel is a coming-of-age story of an orphaned boy, Alfgrimur, who is raised by his grandparents on the outskirts of early twentieth-century Reykjavik. The first quarter of the novel revolves around Alfgrimur's childhood and the role of his adopted grandparents in it. As Alfgrimur's character narrates the novel, he describes his grandfather and grandmother as always being there in the background even if he does not know exactly where they are some days, even if he doesn't even hear them or see them. Alfgrimur narrates that even if he isn't thinking about his grandparents, the sounds of their activity filter in and out of his consciousness and form the structure of his world; sounds such as the creak of the door of his Grandfather's shed or his Grandmother's humming. He describes this background activity as something he was born into and has always known.[77] This analogy of a background that, while it may not be in the front of the mind nevertheless forms the conditions for the experiential structure of our world, is precisely the more fundamental ontology that Heidegger is investigating.[78]

Laxness also beautifully illustrates the rift that metaphysical knowledge causes to the 'background structure' of our world when he describes how Alfgrimur is out fishing one day and learns that he must begin his education in Latin. For Alfgrimur, the word 'Latin' becomes a symbolic fissure in the horizon of his boyhood world.[79] Whether Heidegger attempts to maintain this boyhood illusion is something we will have to ask ourselves in later sections. But what Heidegger seeks with the existential analytic is that background structure which forms the horizon of our world, like the presence of Alfgrimur's grandparents before he suddenly has to go off to become educated and learn Latin. In the same way that Alfgrimur's grandparents provide food, shelter a sense of place, identity and a sense of care, Heidegger is after a description of the very Being of beings. To just give a description of a character in the story, such as Alfgrimur or his grandparents, would be like undertaking a study of anthropology or biblical hermeneutics and would imply the type of objectivity that Heidegger rejects in Cassirer. Rather, Heidegger seeks what allows for that particular character, that particular being in the first place. Alfgrimur's grandparents are the conditions for his existence so when Alfgrimur's grandfather announces that he is to be educated in Latin, Alfgrimur is only able to recognise Latin as a fissure to his existence because, in his boyhood world, his grandparents acted as the fundamental conditions for his existence. This is why he describes them in the novel as always there in the background even if he does not know where they are. When Heidegger uses the term *Dasein* instead of 'human being', he is seeking the conditions for the existence of the human being, the Being of beings, much as Alfgrimur's grandparents are the conditions for Alfgrimur's existence.

The term *Dasein*, so used and abused in Heidegger scholarship, when typed into any German dictionary, simply means existence, being or life. The first English translators of Heidegger's *Being and Time*, John Macquarrie and Edward Robinson, note in their footnotes that the term *Dasein* plays such an important role in *Being and Time* and yet will be so familiar to any English-speaking reader who has read about Heidegger that it is simpler to leave it untranslated. They then go on to note that, while *Dasein* was a technical term in German philosophy before Heidegger, it is used very widely to denote the existence of a variety of everyday things. The everyday usage of the word in German reflects the kind of existence or being that also belongs to persons, and Heidegger follows suit with this everyday usage. However, Macquarrie and Robinson also note that while following the everyday usage of the type of being that belongs to persons or tables or chairs, Heidegger also gives the term a meaning of its own in his philosophy.[80]

What is important for us in relation to this distinct meaning is why Heidegger so frequently uses *Dasein* instead of another term, such as 'human existence' or 'human reality'.[81] While it is clear from the everyday use of the term *Dasein* that it relates to the existence of a person rather than existence generally, Heidegger's use of the term focuses on the structure of existence itself. For Heidegger, *Dasein* refers to the Being of beings as we see in *Being and Time* where he writes:

> Thus, to work out the question of Being adequately, we must make an entity — the inquirer — transparent in his own Being [...] This entity which each of us is himself and which includes inquiring as one of the possibilities of its Being, we shall denote by the term '*Dasein*.' If we are to formulate our question explicitly and transparently, we must first give a proper explication of an entity (*Dasein*), with regard to its Being.[82]

The last phrase is key. For Heidegger, we must not merely give an explication of an entity, but rather explain the relation between that entity and its Being as we have seen in the allegory of Alfgrimur and his grandparents. What then would a metaphysics of *Dasein* be? For surely, this is the *terminus a quo*, the place from which the question 'what is the human being?' comes. For Heidegger, a metaphysics of *Dasein* is what allows there to be any kind of starting point or supply of building blocks for metaphysical questions in the first place and, as we have seen, Cassirer's attempt to start with objectivity of the cultural forms, the *terminus ad quem*, is only possible based on a metaphysics of *Dasein*.[83]

When Heidegger writes that, 'ontology requires only a finite creature', we see clearly the two sides of the phrase 'metaphysics of *Dasein*'.[84] On the one hand, Heidegger clearly states that the type of being, or existence, that concerns him is that of a finite creature. But on the other hand, this is where we are to seek knowledge because ontology arises from historical finitude, from our position in history, not from a temporal objectivity in the way that Cassirer claims. For Heidegger, this means two things that we see in the last section of the debate: first, in order to answer a question like 'what is the human being', you cannot use an anthropological system such as Cassirer's objective symbolic forms; second, you must clarify the perspective from which the question is posed. If you understand the perspective or vantage point from which you pose the question, it helps you to answer it.⁸⁵ Why? Because any ontological question or claim only emerges from *Dasein*. This means that, for Heidegger, the imagination synthesises images and concepts in posing questions and making claims only after experience conditions it, rather than purely spontaneously as Cassirer has claimed.

In this way, the originary perspective, the *terminus a quo*, does not simply give context to the question, 'what is the human being?'; it is not, for example, like the historical context we are considering at the start of each chapter in this book. Rather it gives you a clue, a reminder of the structure of ontology itself. Questions like 'what is the human being?' are ultimately conditioned by this more fundamental ontological structure and arise solely in the finite sphere. As Heidegger puts it, they are regional questions.⁸⁶ Therefore, Heidegger believes the *terminus a quo* must be made into a fundamental philosophical problem because philosophy itself, in its questions like 'what is the human being?', starts from *Dasein*.⁸⁷ That is why a metaphysics of *Dasein* is the condition for any other type of question. Starting with the analysis of *Dasein* to gain knowledge about any other type of metaphysical questioning, Cassirer's objectivity of cultural forms, for example, is what Heidegger refers to as the existential analytic.⁸⁸ Therefore, Heidegger rejects traditional metaphysics or an objectivity of cultural forms that would come after the immediacy of existence, and appeals instead to an analysis of the structure of existence itself. Where does such an appeal leave metaphor?

Heidegger and Metaphor

Heidegger's pursuit of the structure of existence itself, in the form of the existential analytic, frames the philosophical context within which later thinkers, such as Paul Ricoeur, deploy their philosophy of metaphor. As we have seen, there are other aspects of Heidegger's philosophy, such as his position on Kant's schematism, that are also relevant to a philosophy of metaphor, and one way we could explain Heidegger's relationship to metaphor would be to look at the implications of issues in Heidegger's philosophy for a theorisation of metaphor. Clive Cazeaux's treatment of Heidegger in *Metaphor and Continental Philosophy*⁸⁹ could be said to be in this vein. Heidegger is a key figure in Cazeaux's *Metaphor*, and in the first chapter Cazeaux focuses on what he calls 'Heidegger's retrieval of the schematism' and the way in which the anticipatory structures of the understanding in Heidegger's philosophy explain how a metaphor can generate multiple new meanings.⁹⁰ While Cazeaux's analysis is certainly a rich and active reading of Heidegger's thought, this book will take a different path. Our theme is the post-Nietzschean conception of metaphor and one part of our method is intellectual-historical. Therefore, we will focus specifically on the places in which Heidegger mentions metaphor and how these relate to his philosophy generally as well as how they influence Paul Ricoeur's philosophy of metaphor.

While it may be the case that Heidegger's thought generally, such as his work on Kant and the 'retrieval of the schematism', provides a framework for understanding aspects of theorisation of metaphor, we will make an assertion about Heidegger that follows a different line of inquiry. We will assert that when Heidegger speaks about metaphor specifically, he condemns its ability to reveal the truth of Being if it is understood through a traditional metaphysical framework. The implication is that, for Heidegger, metaphor must be understood through the existential analytic to provide meaningful statements about Being. Heidegger's inability to read the concept of metaphor as anything other than part of the metaphysical tradition stops him from adequately addressing the hermeneutic tension seen in Nietzsche's conception of metaphor. It is also essential for us to note that Nietzsche's proclamation 'what, then, is truth? A mobile army of metaphors'[91] does not equate to the same thing as when Heidegger writes, 'the metaphorical exists only within metaphysics'.[92] These are different statements and we must make clear why. So, while Heidegger's notion of finitude that we can see in the Davos disputation may be heavily influenced by Nietzsche, his notion of metaphor is not. Nietzsche reads metaphor as something foundational to and yet distinct from the metaphysical tradition. Heidegger, by contrast, with his reading of Nietzsche as the 'last great metaphysician', relegates even metaphor to the metaphysical tradition, hence the need for Heidegger to read it through the existential analytic.[93]

These encounters with metaphor are brief in Heidegger. He does not explicitly write on metaphor as a part of his larger philosophical project. In 'the *Retrait* of Metaphor' (1978), Derrida points out that only two places are frequently cited where Heidegger seems to have any position on metaphor at all. Firstly, the collection of Heidegger's lectures on reason, *The Principle of Reason* (1957) and second, the collection of Heidegger's writings and lectures on language, *On the Way to Language* (1959).[94] As we shall see, the section from *The Principle of Reason* has traditionally been the most widely discussed, in part because both Ricoeur and Derrida discuss it in their seminal works on metaphor while at the same time discussing each other's interpretation of it.

In *The Principle of Reason*, Heidegger writes, 'the metaphorical exists only within metaphysics'.[95] The quote comes from Heidegger's sixth lecture in the collection on the grounds of cognition and refers to the idea of cognitive transposition in a discussion on the distinction between the sensible and non-sensible. It stresses the necessity of this traditional metaphysical distinction for the concept of metaphor to exist. This is because a transposition, one of the meanings of the Latin *metaphora*, can only occur between two distinct spheres. We will return to this statement in a moment, but for now, we want to look at it in connection with Heidegger's other well-known statement on metaphor from *On the Way to Language*. Heidegger's statement on metaphor in *On the Way to Language* has also had a favourable reception, specifically in late twentieth-century France. It takes a prominent place in Jean Greisch's essay entitled 'Les mots et les roses: la métaphore chez Martin Heidegger' [Words and Roses: Metaphor in the World of Martin Heidegger] (1973) and, as we shall see, Ricoeur also writes about it in *The Rule of Metaphor* (1975).[96] Derrida himself devotes a large portion of 'The *Retrait* of Metaphor' to discussing it.

The passage in *On the Way to Language* comes out of a discussion of Hölderlin's poem 'Brot und Wein' [Bread and Wine].[97] Here, Heidegger writes, 'Wir blieben in der Metaphysik hängen, wollten wir dieses Nennen Hölderlins in der Wendung "Worte, wie Blumen" für eine Metapher halten' (We would stay bogged in metaphysics if we wanted to regard this naming of Hölderlin, in the phrase 'words, like flowers', as a metaphor).[98] This almost appears as an aside. This aside is more about Heidegger's desire to destroy metaphysical thinking and redirect our understanding of rhetorical devices, such as Hölderlin's comparison of words with the blooming of flowers, to an analysis of the existential situation rather than an analysis of the distinction between the literal and the figurative. As we have seen in the introduction to this chapter, Anselm Haverkamp writes that Heidegger interprets this line of Hölderlin's to be a 'manifesto of poetic revelation'.[99] We can certainly read Heidegger's comment here to mean that if we think about 'Worte, wie Blumen' as a figurative device, we are still caught up in metaphysical thinking.

But what do Heidegger's two small references to metaphor taken together mean? How can we read a figurative device as being anything but figurative? Does Heidegger mean that metaphor is something beyond the classic distinction between the literal and the figurative? Is he announcing, with Nietzsche, that metaphor is now an unconscious cognitive pattern of the kind we see in Gerber?

Hardly. In these passages where Heidegger explicitly mentions metaphor, he doesn't present a philosophy of metaphor but rather a commentary on the way that figurative concepts, like that of metaphor, function because of metaphysical distinctions. What we are emphasising here is that in the same way that Heidegger rejects an anthropological definition of the human being at Davos and turns towards the existential analytic, we can see a rejection of a traditional description of metaphor and a reorientation of metaphor as a device for poetic revelation. Because Heidegger views the concept of metaphor as allowed for by a metaphysical distinction, any new notion of metaphor that follows, like that inherited from Nietzsche, will be oriented by this suspicion of metaphysics. Therefore, for those who would follow Heidegger and seek a more fundamental description of metaphor, they would need to approach the question of metaphor through the existential analytic in order to gain access to the Being of beings and thus the Being of metaphor.

What does it mean to approach the question of metaphor through an existential analytic? The question of the creation of metaphor by a finite creature, as we have already seen in Nietzsche, suggests that the human being is a truth creator with his or her metaphors. The creation of metaphor by a finite creature becomes an existential question in light of Heidegger's philosophy. Nietzsche has defined the human being for us as a metaphorical animal. When we see the question, 'what is the human being' in Heidegger's thought becoming a question, not just about a biological creature but about Being itself, it puts the question of metaphor after Nietzsche into the middle of Heidegger's existential analytic. The question of metaphor suddenly becomes framed as an existential question and we could almost claim that Heidegger wants language to speak 'literally', that is without any substitution between the truth of Being and the creation of meaning.

One way we could read Heidegger's comment on Hölderlin is to see Heidegger as suggesting that viewing a poetic statement such as Hölderlin's through the logic of metaphorical substitution is to see it through a metaphysical logic. Because of this, the 'truth of poetry' would not shine through. While he does not make an explicit case for metaphor as a device of poetic revelation, he does suggest that without poetic revelation, metaphor holds no power to reveal the truth of Being. We can recall here Heidegger's lines from the 'Letter on Humanism' (1947) where he writes:

> Language is the house of Being. In its home man dwells. Those who think and those who create with words are the guardians of this home. Their guardianship accomplishes the manifestation of Being insofar as they bring the manifestation to language and maintain it in language through their speech.[100]

Therefore, by implication, metaphor must be existential or nothing in Heidegger's thought.

This argument is reinforced if we reflect on Heidegger's claim about Nietzsche's philosophy. In the opening sections of his Nietzsche lecture, Heidegger asserts that Nietzsche's answer to the question, 'what is the Being of beings?' is to say that 'all Being ultimately is will to power'.[101] By putting this in the context of Sarah Kofman's claim that, for Nietzsche, metaphor was an early draft of the conception of the will to power, we can see yet another way in which metaphor in Heidegger's thought could be viewed as ultimately existential.[102]

So, to sum up, Heidegger's view at Davos, that the imagination in Kant's schematism is not ultimately related to objective cultural forms but instead arises in finitude, serves to shift the imagination, and, by implication, metaphor, from being a noble synthesising part of reason, as in Cassirer, to becoming a part of the very fabric of finitude. This is a shift we are very familiar with from Nietzsche. We have seen this means that our ontological reality is both created by the metaphors we use and creates the metaphors we use as well. For both Heidegger and Nietzsche, metaphor does not simply build conceptual systems but rather allows for judgements in the first place. We are reminded of Nietzsche's brutal 'first metaphor!, second metaphor!' section in 'On Truth and Lying'.[103] Every moment of judgement is a metaphor. However, what is distinct from Nietzsche in Heidegger is the way in which Heidegger transforms what he considers to be regional questions into existential questions. While, in Nietzsche, the 'first metaphor!, second metaphor!' section in 'On Truth and Lying' reminds us of the pervasiveness of metaphor in cognition, unlike Nietzsche, Heidegger attempts to ground the pervasiveness of metaphor in a notion of Being. While the phrase 'the metaphorical exists only within metaphysics' certainly acknowledges the metaphorical foundation of metaphysics, taken in conjunction with Heidegger's assertion that '[w]e would stay bogged in metaphysics if we wanted to regard this naming of Hölderlin, in the phrase "words, like flowers," as a metaphor', we see that, unlike Nietzsche, Heidegger reorients the ground of metaphoric meaning and makes metaphor a device for 'poetic revelation'.[104] In a moment, we will look at how the philosopher Paul Ricoeur can be seen to appropriate this aspect of Heidegger's philosophy for an explicit philosophy of metaphor. However, before proceeding, it would be prudent to demarcate clearly Ricoeur's differences with Heidegger generally.

Heidegger and Ricoeur

So far in this chapter, we have looked primarily at early twentieth-century German philosophy. As we now turn to the French philosopher Paul Ricoeur, we come to a philosophy firmly rooted in the post-war European philosophical landscape. While Ricoeur's thinking displays an attempt to find a path through the divergent philosophical positions of his time, his own life experience particularly roots him to this period. In the early 1940s, Ricoeur was held in a German prisoner-of-war camp where he began a translation of Edmund Husserl's *Ideas*.[105] This translation was completed after the war with an accompanying commentary and published in 1950. The commentary was not uncritical, and aspects of it look at how Heidegger's philosophy can be seen to resolve certain tensions in Husserl's model of how consciousness interprets the world.[106] This is one of the ways in which Ricoeur inherits Heidegger's philosophy. However, he does not inherit this philosophy uncritically and the relevance of this criticism for us is that part of his critique of Heidegger informs how he approaches subjects such as metaphor.

One of the clearest places we see this critique articulated is in an article titled 'The Task of Hermeneutics' (1973), published in *Philosophy Today* just two years before the French publication of Ricoeur's main text on metaphor, *La métaphore vive* (*The Rule of Metaphor*) (1975). In the article, Ricoeur's call for a return path from fundamental ontology that would allow a theoretical and methodological space for philosophy to engage with the human sciences such as literary criticism, linguistics or anthropology. Ricoeur writes,

> With Heidegger's philosophy, we are always engaged in going back to the foundations, but we are left incapable of beginning the movement of return that would lead from the fundamental ontology to the properly epistemological question of the status of the human sciences. Now a philosophy that breaks the dialogue with the sciences is no longer addressed to anything but itself. Moreover, it is only along the return route that we could substantiate the claim that questions of exegesis and, in general, of historical critique are *derivative*. So long as this derivation has not been undertaken, the very movement of transcendence towards questions of foundation remains problematic [...] For me, the question that remains unresolved in Heidegger's work is this: *how can a question of* critique *in general be accounted for within the framework of a fundamental hermeneutics?* It is, nevertheless, along this return path that we can witness and demonstrate the claim that the hermeneutic circle in the sense exegetes is *grounded* in the fore-structure belonging to understanding on the plane of fundamental ontology. But ontological hermeneutics seems incapable, for structural reasons, of developing the problematic of this return path.[107]

As the quote above shows, part of the reason that Ricoeur is critical of focusing exclusively on Heidegger's ontological hermeneutics has to do with a theoretical space for critique. Is there space in ontological hermeneutics for the question of critique, which is so fundamental to the interpretive questions of the human sciences? For Ricoeur, the unanswered question of critique is one of the primary things that calls for the development of a return route. We will take an in-depth look at the question of critique and its relation to the hermeneutic circle later in the chapter. However, our first task is to clarify what Ricoeur means by a return route from fundamental ontology.

Ricoeur seem to be writing explicitly here about the limitations, both methodological and philosophical, of Heidegger's call for an ontological hermeneutics that would render all other aspects of the human sciences as mere regional hermeneutics. This can be seen when Ricoeur writes that ontological hermeneutics is 'incapable, for structural reasons, of developing the problematic of this return path'.[108] What are these structural reasons that create such a limitation?

As we have seen in the Davos disputation, for Heidegger, an anthropological question such as 'what is the human being', is merely regional in that it does not concern itself with the starting point, the *terminus a quo*, of one's ability to pose such a question. This would be found in the existential analytic, the analysis of one's relation to Being, which would provide a more fundamental knowledge. As we have seen, for Heidegger, if a field like anthropology does not position its question within the existential analytic, it would provide an interpretation of the human being at what Heidegger would call a merely regional level. To ask interpretive questions on a fundamental level would be an ontological hermeneutics. Such a hermeneutics would not simply ask 'what is the human being?', but what it means for the human being to relate to Being itself.

In the 'The Task of Hermeneutics', we see Ricoeur calling into question whether this tendency constantly to go back to an ontological hermeneutics has a limit for, not simply a field like anthropology, but all of the exegetical and interpretive questions posed by the human sciences. The limit that Ricoeur observes is that Heidegger is unable to achieve his own aim by only focusing on a more fundamental questioning. Heidegger seeks to show us that the interpretive questions of the sciences have a fundamental dependency on ontological hermeneutics. Yet because the focus of his philosophy is going back to or uncovering the foundations of an ontological hermeneutics, sticking too closely to such an approach can blind one from seeing one of the very aims of his philosophy: the way in which the interpretive questions of the sciences are in fact derived from the more fundamental question of Being. Ricoeur seems to be suggesting here that we must find a return route from Heidegger's fundamental questions. This would mean finding a way of engaging with the interpretive and exegetical questions of the human sciences if we want to see any kind of meaningful relationship between them and the question of Being. To put it in the words of Richard Kearney, Ricoeur argued that 'the meaning of Being is always mediated through an endless process of interpretations — cultural, religious, political, historical and scientific'.[109]

Ricoeur showcases such a return route in which the meaning of Being might be mediated in his treatment of metaphor. While this engagement with a wider set of interpretive questions certainly goes some way to calling into question the limit of Heidegger's ontological hermeneutics, it does not call into question the foundations of such an approach. In fact, as we shall see, Ricoeur uses ontological hermeneutics to ground the meaning of metaphor. He may indeed break from Heidegger in accusing his philosophy of 'no longer [being] addressed to anything but itself', but we will pose the question in the next section whether Ricoeur himself, in his treatment of metaphor, escapes from this trap.[110]

Ricoeur and Metaphor

An entire book could be written on Paul Ricoeur and metaphor. *The Rule of Metaphor* (1975) is a masterpiece of comparative study.[111] It could very well be viewed as an example of the return route from Heidegger's fundamental ontology that Ricoeur advocates above. The book considers the subject of metaphor in relation to rhetoric, poetics, linguistics, intellectual history, philosophy and other disciplines. Therefore, *Rule* is an ever-present touchstone in studies of metaphor. It takes a prominent place in Cazeaux's *Metaphor and Continental Philosophy* and is frequently cited in dictionaries and encyclopaedias such as *The Princeton Encyclopedia of Poetry and Poetics*.[112] In this section we will limit ourselves to the relationship between Ricoeur's theory of metaphor and Heidegger's philosophy. We will conclude two things: first that both he and Heidegger do not account for the diversity of metaphors used in discourse, and second, that the model of the existential analytic cannot be used to give an adequate account of the hermeneutic tension that Nietzsche presents us with in his new conception of metaphor. For all the richness of Ricoeur's philosophy and despite his attempt to create a return route from Heidegger's philosophy, the way in which he does appropriate aspects of Heidegger's thought limits the type of metaphors that can be discussed within his model. As a result, Ricoeur's thought does not fully address metaphor's ability to create mutual understanding.

However, this is not to say that, in *Rule*, Ricoeur is not attentive to the type of sentiment Cassirer expressed about the role of language in the creation of understanding. The subtitle given to *Rule* in the English translation is 'the creation of meaning in language'. Ricoeur reinforces this sentiment in the first volume of *Time and Narrative* (1983) where he writes of the meaning effect of both metaphor and narrative sharing a single 'poetic sphere'.[113] Therefore, his focus in relation to both narrative and metaphor is on their ability to generate meaning. The comparison of metaphor to narrative brings to mind Giambattista Vico when he writes in the *New Science* that 'the first poets attributed to bodies the being of animate substances, with capacities measured by their own, namely sense and passion, and in this way made fables of them. Thus, every metaphor so formed is a fable in brief'.[114] Ricoeur does not discuss Vico, but the sentiment of metaphor as a 'fable in brief' that creates meaning is common. However, what we will need to ask in the next section is whether the creation of meaning is the same as the creation of mutual understanding. To do this, we will first look at how Ricoeur attempts to ground the meaning of metaphor using concepts from Heidegger's philosophy.

Right from the beginning, Ricoeur places the capacity of metaphor to create meaning in language in the context of Heidegger's thought when he writes that metaphor has an 'ontological function in discourse' and is that which 'expresses existence as alive'.[115] Ricoeur's aim in *Rule* is to show that the project of 'resurrecting rhetoric from its ashes' is not in vain. Ricoeur reminds us that the paradox of assessing metaphor philosophically is that the understanding of metaphor in the West comes from the dead discipline of rhetoric. Therefore, Ricoeur wants to show metaphor as alive (the French title of the book is *La métaphore vive* (literally *The Lively Metaphor*)) and he employs Heidegger's philosophy to do so.[116] To show how Ricoeur does this, we will limit ourselves to the first chapter of *Rule*, where Ricoeur lays out his overall thesis, and to the final chapter, where he explicitly engages with Heidegger's philosophy.

At the end of the first chapter, Ricoeur is discussing the role of metaphor in the imitation of nature as outlined in Aristotle's thought. As we have seen in chapter 1 of this book, for Aristotle, the human being imitates nature to learn, and this learning can be produced both in our use of language and in our production of narrative. Here, in this passage, Ricoeur discusses the relationship between imitation and nature.[117]

> We believe that we understand *phusis* when we translate it by *nature*. But is not the word *nature* as far off the mark with respect to *phusis* as is the word *imitation* concerning *mimesis*? Certainly Greek man was far less quick than we are to identify *phusis* with some inert 'given.' Perhaps it is because, for him, nature is itself living that *mimesis* can be not enslaving and that compositional and creative imitation of nature can be possible. Is this not what the most enigmatic passage of the *Rhetoric* suggests? Metaphor, it relates, makes one *see things* because it 'represents things as in a state of activity' (1411b 24–25). The *Poetics* echoes that one may 'speak in narrative' or present 'personages as acting [*hos prattontas*] and doing [*energountas*]' 1448a 22, 28). Might there not be an underlying relationship between 'signifying active reality' and speaking out *phusis*? [...] All *mimesis*, even creative — nay, *especially creative* — *mimesis*, takes place within the horizons of a being-in-the-world which it makes present to the precise extent that the *mimesis* raises it to the level of *muthos*. The truth of imagination, poetry's power to make contact with being as such — this is what I personally see in Aristotle's *mimesis*. *Lexis* is rooted in *mimesis*, and through *mimesis* metaphor's deviations from normal *lexis* belong to the great enterprise of 'saying what is.' But *mimesis* does not signify only that all discourse is of the world; it does not embody just the referential function of poetic discourse. Being *mimesis phuseos*, it connects this referential function to the revelation of the Real as Act. This is the function of the concept of *phusis* in the expression *mimesis phuseos*, to serve as an index for that dimension of reality that does not receive due account in the simple description of that-thing-over-there. To present men '*as acting*' and all things '*as in act*' — such could well be the *ontological* function of metaphorical discourse, in which every dormant potentiality of existence appears *as* blossoming forth, every latent capacity for action *as* actualized. *Lively* expression is that which expresses existence as *alive*.[118]

At the end of this passage, Ricoeur adds an endnote which states that the present interpretation will be taken up again in the final chapter. And so, before unpacking the above quotation, we will quote from the relevant section of the final chapter so as to discuss both sections together. In the final chapter, there is a discussion of the tension separating poetry and philosophy and an initial criticism of Heidegger for a 'laziness in thinking, [that] lump[s] the whole of Western thought together under a single word, metaphysics'.[119] Then, Ricoeur states that despite this, in Heidegger's philosophy he finds something that appropriately brings together poetry and philosophy. It is here that we see our first quotation from the first chapter echoed. Ricoeur writes:

> In concluding, I should like to retain only this excellent statement from the later works of Heidegger: 'Between these two [thinking and poetry] there exists a secret kinship because in the service of language both intercede on behalf of language and give lavishly of themselves. Between both there is, however, at the same time an abyss for they "dwell on the most widely separated mountains."' What is described here is the very dialectic between the modes of discourse in their proximity and in their difference. On the one hand, poetry, in itself and by itself, sketches a 'tensional' conception of truth for thought [...] poetry, in combination with other modes of discourse, articulates and preserves the experience of belonging that places man in discourse and discourse in being. Speculative thought, on the other hand, bases its work upon the dynamism of metaphorical utterance, which it construes according to its own sphere of meaning. Speculative discourse can respond in this way only because the *distanciation*, which constitutes the critical moment, is contemporaneous with the experience of belonging that is opened or recovered by poetic discourse, and because poetic discourse, as text and as work, prefigures the distanciation that speculative thought carries to its highest point of reflection [...] What is given to thought in this way by the 'tensional' truth of poetry is the most primordial, most hidden dialectic — the dialectic that reigns between the experience of belonging as a whole and the power of distanciation that opens up the space of speculative thought.[120]

There is enormous richness in both of these quotations and much that we can agree with, but we do not have the time to explore them. What is important for us is that, although Ricoeur criticises Heidegger's generalising rejection of metaphysics, if we look closely at Ricoeur's language, we can see that he himself is still stuck in a different kind of generalising, that of fundamental ontology as a ground to metaphoric meaning. Despite, as we have seen, Ricoeur's attempt to create a return route from fundamental ontology, grounding the meaning of metaphor in a Heideggerian concept of Being generalises the creation of meaning. This is betrayed by Ricoeur's language. In phrases such as '[w]hat is given to thought in this way by the "tensional" truth of poetry is the most primordial, most hidden dialectic' and 'by this turn of expression, poetry, in combination with other modes of discourse, articulates and preserves the experience of belonging that places man in discourse and discourse in being', Ricoeur is relying on the Heideggerian framework of a metaphysics of *Dasein* for the generation of metaphoric meaning. He is also relying on the thesis of the poetic revelation of Being via language. This is reinforced in our quote from the first chapter of *Rule of Metaphor* where Ricoeur writes: 'The truth of imagination, poetry's power to make contact with being as such — this is what I personally see in Aristotle's *mimesis*.' The implied Heideggerian perspective that 'the truth of imagination [can] make contact with being as such' is explicitly brought into contact with a view of metaphor as revelation, when he distinguishes between the *referential* function of metaphor and the *revelatory* function of metaphor.

He clearly privileges the *revelatory* function, placing metaphor, like Heidegger in his analysis of 'Brot und Wein', within the framework of actualising the potentialities of existence. As we saw in relation to Heidegger's interpretation of 'Brot und Wein', if we understand the metaphor 'Worte, wie Blumen' as a figurative device, we are still caught up in metaphysical thinking. When Ricoeur privileges the *revelatory* function of metaphor over the *referential* function of metaphor, he seems to provide a much more explicit answer to the problem of the metaphysically tinged figurative/literal distinction that Heidegger articulates and criticises.

As we saw in the quotation above, Ricoeur writes: '*mimesis* does not signify only that all discourse is of the world; it does not embody just the referential function of poetic discourse'. When he writes this, our understanding of *mimesis* is widened and enriched. The reminder that the Greek concept of *mimesis* could well be different from the referential function that it takes on in the subsequent tradition of Western rhetoric and poetics is a poignant reminder. However, Ricoeur goes on to write of the ontological function of metaphor actualising the potentialities of existence. This places Ricoeur's initial reclaiming of *mimesis* within a Heideggerian frame.

Mimesis actualising the potentialities of existence is also what we have seen in the quote above from the last chapter of *Rule* where Ricoeur writes that, 'What is given to thought in this way by the "tensional" truth of poetry is the most primordial, most hidden dialectic.'[121] Ricoeur is reminding us that, for Heidegger, poetry gives or reveals to thought the truth of a 'primordial' and 'hidden' nature. This type of truth refers to the more fundamental ontology, which, for Heidegger, metaphysics obscures. We have seen Heidegger himself write, more generally, that 'those who create with words accomplish the manifestation of Being' in the 'Letter on Humanism'.[122] It would seem that Ricoeur relies on this paradigm as a ground for metaphoric meaning. We will now try to articulate why metaphor as a device for 'poetic revelation' does not allow space for the hermeneutic tensions of metaphor that we see in Nietzsche's thought.

While it is Ricoeur's attempt to show metaphor as lively, placing it within the Heideggerian framework as a device for poetic revelation, his explanation actually presupposes a static view of metaphor. While Ricoeur gives a lively defence of metaphor's ability to aid cognition in the creation of meaning, he does not account for the historical evolution of the meanings of metaphors, nor the conflict over their interpretations. Yet in Nietzsche, we have seen these very things are what point towards the foundational role of metaphor in cognition in the first place. The metaphors chosen by Ricoeur may be lively, but they are only one type. If we look at a smattering of the representative metaphors that Ricoeur uses as his case studies in *Rule*, we see types of metaphor that reinforce the thesis of poetic revelation: the metaphors of romantic poetry and mysticism. In chapter 6, 'The Work of Resemblance', Ricoeur references a line from Keats's poem 'To Hope': 'When by my solitary hearth I sit, | And hateful thoughts enwrap my soul in gloom'.[123] Of this Ricoeur writes, 'the metaphorical expression *enwrap* consists in presenting sorrow as if enveloping the soul in a cloak'.[124] The point of this section is to widen our understanding of what Ricoeur calls 'the iconic moment of metaphor' and suggests that the metaphor *enwrap* displays such a moment of iconicity in its presentation of the feeling of sorrow.

If we consider the experience of sorrow, we can easily see the resemblance between how sorrow makes us feel surrounded or enveloped, and the way a cloak wraps around us. The metaphor rings true. To this effect, we can also say that the Keats metaphor falls into the same type of sentiment expressed in 'old age is the evening of life' that we have returned to throughout the book. Keats speaks to our experience of what it means to exist when he writes: 'hateful thoughts enwrap[ping] the soul in gloom'. In its romanticism, the metaphor poetically reveals a truth of the experience of sorrow.

Continuing in this vein we could cite a section of the seventh chapter , entitled, 'Towards the Concept of 'Metaphorical Truth', where Ricoeur appeals to Coleridge. In a figurative expression for the concept of figurative language itself, Coleridge writes that a symbol 'abides itself as a living part of that unity of which it is the representative'.[125] About this Ricoeur writes that Coleridge appeals to:

> the *quasi-vegetal* power of imagination, concentrated in the symbol, to draw us to the growth of things [...] thus, metaphor accomplishes an exchange between poet and world, thanks to which individual life and universal life grow together. In this way, the growth of plants becomes the metaphor for metaphorical truth.[126]

Again, Ricoeur's analysis of Coleridge is very apt and surely there is much to be gained from contemplating the kind of truth metaphor gives us as a living, growing thing such as a plant. The point is that Ricoeur's selection of metaphor is still within the same orbit as the Keats example. Here, however, Ricoeur even goes a step further. In Keats, Ricoeur references a metaphor that rings true about our experience of sorrow. With the reference to Coleridge, Ricoeur not only references a metaphor where the truthlikeness between the two parts of a metaphor, the tenor and vehicle, is easily seen, but he references a metaphor that provides a thesis on the type of truth that metaphor provides. Ricoeur's appropriation of Coleridge's metaphor of the life of a plant reinforces the quasi-mystical overtone to the quote we looked at earlier where he writes of the ontological function of metaphor as making actualities out of potentialities and presenting existence as alive.

Finally, in the last chapter, entitled 'Metaphor and Philosophical Discourse', Ricoeur employs the German Catholic poet Angelus Silesius, followed by Heidegger's reference to the Hölderlin passage discussed earlier in this chapter. The Silesius poem referenced is perhaps his most famous: 'the rose has no why; it flowers because it flowers'.[127] Ricoeur then links this poem to Hölderlin's figurative description of language as 'words, like flowers'.[128] Ricoeur links Silesius's mystical musings on the hidden primordial power of flowers blooming with Heidegger's thesis on the flowering of language manifesting the hidden primordial power of language to reveal Being. From here, Ricoeur provides the definitive link for us between metaphor and poetic revelation when he rhetorically asks 'is this not what living metaphor does?'[129]

Our point here is not to judge the mystical profundity of Silesius's poem or the philosophical poignancy of Hölderlin's metaphor. Indeed, a theologian reading this passage would find much richness in seeing a philosophy of language linked with Silesius's mysticism. However, it does show us that the metaphors Ricoeur has in mind seem to be those which 'give to thinking, the truth of a primordial and hidden dialectic'.[130] When the concept of metaphor is only assessed in terms of those metaphors that reveal 'primordial' and 'hidden' truths, then the hermeneutic tension between the pragmatic and relative function of metaphor that Nietzsche identifies is stopped dead in its tracks.

Despite the fact that he calls metaphor 'lively' with the function of bringing forth the 'dormant potentiality of existence', his view of metaphor can at times feel static.[131] This is because, as we have seen, only a singular type of metaphor is considered. So, while a particular metaphor may be very lively, metaphor as a whole in Ricoeur's conception is limited and confined to those metaphors which have the potential to reveal an existential truth. Being may be alive in this model, but the life of metaphor, in all its pragmatic and relative variety, is constrained. Why? Because Ricoeur's model based on poetic revelation does not consider the historic evolution or cultural conflict over the meaning of metaphors. And what of destructive metaphors used in hate speech and ideology? Can we really say that these poetically reveal the truth of Being? Answering the crisis of likeness that Nietzsche's concept of metaphor initiates with a thesis of poetic revelation, as Ricoeur does in his appropriation of Heidegger, may be very useful in the realm of romantic poetry or theology, but it does not address the variety of metaphors used that are so often, as Nietzsche points out, a product of power or the process of historic evolution. Therefore, in the end, Ricoeur's thesis on the creation of meaning does not equate to the creation of mutual understanding.

The position we are adopting is similar to the position that the French philosopher Alain Badiou takes on Heidegger in his essay 'Philosophy and Art' (1992). The beginning of the essay revolves around a critique of what Badiou calls the 'indistinction' in Heidegger's thought between 'the poem and philosophical discursivity'.[132] On the one hand, as we have seen, when Heidegger writes of 'those who think and create with words' as the guardians of Being, he sets up a thesis on the revelation of Being through language. We have also seen this thesis applied specifically to poetry earlier on in the chapter when we looked at Heidegger's interpretation of Hölderlin's poem 'Brot und Wein'. On the other hand, we have also seen that Heidegger's turn to the existential analytic is his attempt to address what is, for him, the fundamental question of philosophy, that of *Dasein*, the Being of beings. When Badiou claims that in Heidegger's philosophy there is an 'indistinction between the poem and philosophical discursivity', he is linking up Heidegger's position on these two fields of knowledge. Badiou's critique relies on his position of the clear distinction between the two fields. He writes, 'every truth that accepts its dependence in regard to narrative and revelation is still detained in mystery; philosophy exists solely through its desire to tear the latter's veil'.[133]

This book will not go as far as to determine the limits of philosophy as fundamentally separate from 'narrative and revelation' as Badiou does here. We are taking as our starting point the revolution that occurs in Nietzsche's philosophy when the very truth claims that philosophers have used to build metaphysical systems turn out to be inseparable from metaphor. However, Badiou does something slightly different in his critique of Heidegger that we will apply to Ricoeur as well. Badiou does not try to distinguish the *concepts* of philosophy from those of 'narrative and revelation'. Rather he is interested in what we might call the *gesture* of the philosophical enterprise itself. Here, Badiou writes: 'philosophy exists solely through its desire to tear the latter's veil'.[134] This is philosophy as a critical gesture.

One could make the link between Badiou's thesis, expressed here as a division between philosophy and art,[135] and Marx's famous proclamation from the 'Theses on Feuerbach' where he writes: 'The philosophers have only interpreted the world, in various ways; the point is to change it.'[136] We must ask whether a philosophy of interpretation, such as Ricoeur's, has room for a critical gesture. For the critical gesture is essential for disentangling the way metaphor creates mutual understanding.

This is because, time and again, we see ideology showing its head as a symptom of the hermeneutic tension that Nietzsche identified. Therefore, we can concede Badiou's point that when philosophy is reduced to poetic revelation, it finds its hermeneutic limit when it attempts to make a critical philosophical gesture. Because of this, Ricoeur's philosophy of metaphor finds its hermeneutic limit when his model of metaphor finds itself confronted with the question of ideology. The Heideggerian-Ricoeurian thesis of poetic revelation as the answer to the crisis of truthlikeness after Nietzsche fails to resolve the hermeneutic tension in Nietzsche's conception of metaphor when it is confronted with the symptom of that tension, in the form of ideology. However, Ricoeur himself recognised the tension between his own position and a critique of ideology several years after *Rule* was written and poses this very question himself. So before closing this chapter we will consider Ricoeur's attempt to resolve this conflict.

Ricoeur on Hermeneutics and Ideology

The relationship between a hermeneutics of metaphor and a critique of ideology warrants further study. In this book we are, from time to time, considering ideology as one of the symptoms of the hermeneutic tension between a pragmatic and relative account of metaphor. We have, for example, seen, in the introduction, Victor Klemperer's account of the semantic change that the word *aufziehen* went through when used in Nazi rhetoric. In the case of Ricoeur, he himself seems to be aware of the problems that a hermeneutics rooted in Heidegger's philosophy poses to the critique of ideology and he dedicates the last section of *From Text to Action: Essays in Hermeneutics II* to this problem.

In an essay entitled, 'Hermeneutics and the Critique of Ideology' (1986), Ricoeur poses the question, 'is the "gesture of philosophy" either 1. hermeneutics, which avows the reign of finitude over human understanding or 2. an act of defiance, a critical gesture'.[137] While Ricoeur acknowledges that the critique of ideology marks the limit of hermeneutics, he is sceptical of viewing the philosophical gesture as an either/or alternative. Instead, he asks: is it not the case that 'the alternative itself must be challenged?'[138]

Therefore, to attempt to resolve the conflict, he places his question about the 'gesture of philosophy' in the context of the Gadamer–Habermas debate that took place in a series of published articles between 1967 and 1968, in which Gadamer defended philosophy as an interpretive gesture and Habermas defended it as a critical gesture.[139] Ricoeur begins by admitting that both hermeneutics and the critique of ideology speak from different places. However, he wants to show that 'each can recognise the other's claim to universality in a way that marks the place of one in the structure of the other'.[140] When Ricoeur writes of the 'claim to universality', he is drawing our attention to the distinctness of the philosophical gesture in each tradition. For example, Ricoeur says that hermeneutics 'avows the reign of finitude over human understanding'. This 'avowal of the reign of finitude' is a claim to universality because it asserts what consciousness is capable of when it engages in philosophical questioning. Therefore, Ricoeur wants to show that in these two seemingly universal claims of what consciousness can achieve, both can find an aspect of each other's claim.

Ricoeur begins by reminding the reader of Gadamer's rehabilitation of prejudice, authority and tradition, and 'historical-effective consciousness'.[141] This is the Gadamer of chapter 4 of *Truth and Method* (1960) in which he writes that:

> the prejudices of the individual, far more than his judgments, constitute the historical reality of his being [...] If we want to do justice to man's finite, historical mode of being, it is necessary to fundamentally rehabilitate the concept of prejudice and acknowledge the fact there are legitimate prejudices.[142]

To remind the reader, Gadamer explicitly places his philosophical hermeneutics within the framework of the general hermeneutical problem of Heidegger's *Being and Time*. Gadamer writes:

> In *Being and Time* [Heidegger] gave the general hermeneutical problem a concrete form in the question of being. In order to explain the hermeneutical situation of the question of being in terms of fore-having, fore-sight, and fore-conception, he critically tested his question, directed at metaphysics, on important turning points in the history of metaphysics. *Here he was only doing what historical-hermeneutical consciousness requires in every case.* Methodologically conscious understanding will be concerned not merely to form anticipatory ideas, but to make them conscious, so as to check them and thus acquire right understanding from the things themselves.[143]

Earlier in this section, we saw how Heidegger makes the ontological problem a hermeneutic problem. In turn, Gadamer then 'ontologised hermeneutics'.[144] The phrase is Ricoeur's and he asserts that this is what Habermas saw as the principal flaw of Gadamer's work.[145] For Habermas, Gadamer ultimately 'regards *Sprachlichkeit* [linguisticality] as an ontological constitution [... and] he anchors the hermeneutics of understanding in an ontology of finitude'.[146]

Ricoeur interprets Habermas to mean that hermeneutics is something that insists that understanding or consensus precedes us and is 'something constitutive, something given in being'.[147] By making understanding ontological, Gadamer has 'hypostatised a rare experience'.[148] What is this 'rare experience'? Habermas seems to be suggesting that it is in fact rare that understanding is pre-given. He asserts that Gadamer canonises these rare moments of understanding and makes them the paradigm for all communication. We might read a metaphor like Keats's 'thoughts enwrapping the soul' as such a rare moment. Keats's metaphor of 'enwrapping' brilliantly reveals a truth that seems to provide a truthlike match with many people's experience of sorrow. However, such a moment cannot be the paradigm for all communication. Ricoeur concedes this point to Habermas and writes that 'what prevents us from [making these rare moments a paradigm for all communication] is precisely the ideological phenomenon'.[149] We may view this in terms of the criticism we have levelled against Ricoeur himself. Does he overcome this criticism here?

Ricoeur lays out his view on the relationship between hermeneutics and ideology when he writes:

> a critique of ideology must think in terms of anticipation where the hermeneutics of tradition thinks in terms of assumed tradition. In other words, the critique of ideology must posit as a regulative idea, in front of us, what the hermeneutics of tradition conceives as existing at the origin of understanding.[150]

We should note that, to a certain extent, these are the two sides to Nietzsche's conception of metaphor, on the one hand, looking forward to the horizon, and on the other hand, back to the origin. Does Ricoeur's philosophy of metaphor resolve this tension?

His claim that 'the hermeneutics of tradition conceives [of a regulative idea] as existing at the origin of understanding' is what we see in section 32 of *Being and Time*, in which Heidegger discusses the hermeneutic circle. The section is entitled, 'Understanding and Interpretation'. Here, Heidegger asserts that 'interpretation is grounded in something we *have* in advance [...] something we *see* in advance [...] and something we *grasp* in advance' and these three correspond to fore-having, fore-sight and fore-conception respectively, which is what Gadamer cites as his grounds for the rehabilitation of prejudice.[151] Having, seeing and grasping are all metaphors related to understanding. Heidegger makes it extremely clear that they occur at the very origin of consciousness, with Being, when he writes that 'as understanding, *Dasein* projects its Being upon possibilities [...] the projecting of the understanding has its own possibility — that of developing itself. This development of the understanding we call "interpretation."'[152] For Heidegger, understanding is a mode of *Dasein*. So, as a mode of *Dasein*, the Being of beings, understanding occurs at the very beginning of consciousness and it projects itself out. Heidegger asserts that the development of this initial projection is what we call interpretation.[153]

When Ricoeur places metaphor within a 'hermeneutics of tradition (that) conceives [of a regulative idea] as existing at the origin of understanding' he is explicitly linking metaphor with understanding as happening in advance of critical interpretation. Therefore, the problem of ideology rears its head and 'a critique of ideology must think in terms of anticipation'.[154] Ricoeur's reply to this is to ask: can hermeneutics find a 'return route' from this regulative idea it conceives as existing at the origin of understanding, to the anticipatory, critical gesture of the critique of ideology?[155] He sees one point in Heidegger's thought as a possibility. In section 32 of *Being and Time* Heidegger seems to abandon this possibility in the very the moment in which he proposes it. After the discussion above concerning fore-having, fore-sight and fore-conception, Heidegger makes a brief nod to a positive possibility of the understanding hidden within the hermeneutic circle. Heidegger writes:

> In the circle [of understanding] is hidden a *positive possibility* of the most primordial kind of knowing. To be sure, we genuinely take hold of this possibility only when, in our interpretation, we have understood that our first, last, and constant task is never to allow our fore-having, fore-sight, and fore-conception to be presented to us by fancies [*Einfälle*] and popular conceptions [*Volksbegriffe*], but rather to make the scientific theme secure by working out these fore-structures in terms of *the things themselves*.[156]

Heidegger's phrase 'In the circle [of understanding] is hidden a *positive possibility* of the most primordial kind of knowing' jumps out at us. This 'primordial kind of knowing' is precisely what Ricoeur pointed to in *Rule* when he reminded us that, for Heidegger, poetry reveals truth of a 'primordial' and 'hidden' nature. Looking for a positive possibility in this, Ricoeur reads Heidegger as saying that this positive possibility for a critique of ideology lies in the distinction between the anticipation of things in themselves and the anticipation of fancies.[157] However, Ricoeur maintains, this positive possibility cannot be actualised in Heidegger's thought because Heidegger has an 'obsessive concern with radicality [that] blocks the return route from general hermeneutics toward regional hermeneutics: toward philology, history, depth psychology, and so on'.[158] Why? Because, for Heidegger, ontology is hermeneutical and the confrontation with the history of metaphysics takes precedence over the critique of prejudice and by implication of ideology, which he only briefly raises as we have seen here, in fore-having, fore-sight and fore-conception. Therefore, Heidegger's concern 'to anchor the hermeneutic circle more deeply than any epistemology, prevents the epistemological question from being raised on ontological grounds'.[159] Therefore, Ricoeur suggests that in order to find a positive possibility within hermeneutics for a critique of ideology one must proceed indirectly rather than directly from a primordial knowing.[160]

But what would proceeding 'indirectly' mean? Here Ricoeur suggests the concept, borrowed from biblical hermeneutics, of *distanciation*, the distancing of the observer from the object, such as the distance between myself and a historic text like the Bible or the *Odyssey*.[161] This type of *distanciation*, acknowledged throughout the biblical hermeneutic tradition, raises a host of problems such as the contemporary significance of the text not coinciding with the authors' intention, the difference between verbal transmission and written transmission, and so on. Ricoeur seems to be suggesting that the tension between poetic revelation and ideology can be resolved by applying the principles of *distanciation*, because he argues that the precondition for hermeneutics is the conflict of interpretations that arises in these traditional problems associated with *distanciation*. Ricoeur writes:

> would it not be appropriate to shift the initial locus of the hermeneutical question, to reformulate the question in such a way that a certain dialectic

between the experience of belonging [presupposed by Heidegger and Gadamer's view of the understanding] and alienating *distanciation* becomes the mainspring, the key to the inner life, of hermeneutics?[162]

With this position, we are one step closer to a semantics of metaphor that does not simply focus on the creation of meaning but on the creation of mutual understanding. Ricoeur calls this conflict of interpretations suggested by *distanciation* an 'ontological fall from grace'.[163] Here, Ricoeur is magisterial in recognising the conditions of the possibility for hermeneutics being found in conflict, and in this way, he goes much further than Gadamer's appropriation of Heidegger.[164]

However, when we reflect on where Ricoeur locates that conflict, we must depart from him. As we have seen in Nietzsche, metaphor relativises the meaning of the concepts it creates at the origin; that is to say, from the very moment of perception. This is because, for Nietzsche, the reference of metaphoric meaning, rather than being truthlikeness or Being, is simply, 'a sum of human relations'.[165] Ricoeur locates the relativising of meaning in a different place. He follows the biblical hermeneutic tradition somewhat too closely and places the origin of the conflict in the 'ontological fall from grace' that provides the condition for hermeneutics *after the origin of ontology*. While he attempts to find a space within hermeneutics for a critique of ideology, he unwittingly remains in the language of revelation and falls into the same trap as Gadamer while trying to escape it.

We have deduced this from the fact that Ricoeur looks to *distanciation* as a model for understanding. About *distanciation* he writes:

> the moment of *distanciation* is implied by fixation in writing and by all comparable phenomena in the sphere of the transmission of discourse [...] what the text signifies no longer coincides with what the author meant; verbal meaning and mental meaning have different destinies.[166]

Here it is apparent that the presupposition underlining an 'ontological fall from grace' is *after* the origin of meaning rather than at the very moment of perception that Nietzsche asserts in 'On Truth and Lying'. The problem of the text no longer signifying what the author meant is indeed a hermeneutical problem. However, in this case, it implies a state of innocence, an Eden-like state, whether in truthlikeness or Being, that existed at the origin of meaning. This implies that Ricoeur is still relying on some notion of a 'hidden, primordial knowing' that can reveal the truth of metaphor at the origin and it also unintentionally creates a very static view of metaphor. It is the metaphor of romantic or mystical poetry or the biblical text. But to account for the problem of mutual understanding found in historical and ideological change, we need to stick with the problem Nietzsche presents us with: the radical semantic relativism that we see, via metaphor, at the origin of our understanding of the object itself. This includes our ability to judge all metaphors.

When Heidegger asserts in *Being and Time* that we are 'always already' in Being, then we must reply that if this is the case, we are too close to Being to stabilise the meaning of a metaphor by relying on Being.[167] In the end, while he does attempt to find a return route from Heidegger's fundamental ontology and adds incredible value to aspects of the interpretive methods of the human sciences, Ricoeur fails to resolve the tension that ideology poses to a hermeneutics of metaphor. It is not that Ricoeur's model is wrong. It is indispensable for judging a certain type of metaphor in a certain context. But it is ultimately inadequate to speak to the cognitive dissonance between the pragmatic and relativistic functions of metaphor.

Notes to Chapter 3

1. See for example Clive Cazeaux, *Metaphor and Continental Philosophy* (New York: Routledge, 2007). One excellent aspect of Cazeaux's study is the relevance he sees in Heidegger's thought for an articulation of how the meaning of metaphor is created. Cazeaux's book is indispensable in this regard. However, we will argue that we must see this dimension of the European philosophy of metaphor in a wider intellectual-historical and philosophical context.
2. Hans-Georg Gadamer, *Truth and Method*, trans. by Joel Weinsheimer and Donald G. Marshall (London: Continuum, 2004), p. 272.
3. Anselm Haverkamp, *Leaves of Mourning: Hölderlin's Late Work: With an Essay on Keats and Melancholy*, trans. by Vernon Chadwick (Albany: State University of New York Press, 1996), p. 4.
4. Sean Ryan, 'Heidegger's Nietzsche', in *Interpreting Nietzsche*, ed. by Ashley Woodward (London: Continuum, 2011), p. 5.
5. Martin Heidegger, *Nietzsche*, trans. by David Farrell Krell, 2 vols (New York: Harper Collins, 1991), I, 4.
6. Martin Heidegger, *Being and Time*, trans. by John Macquarrie and Edward Robinson (New York: Harper Collins, 2008), p. 34; Martin Heidegger, *Kant and the Problem of Metaphysics*, trans. by Richard Taft (Bloomington: Indiana University Press, 1997), p. 199.
7. Heidegger, *Being and Time*, p. 34.
8. Peter Eli Gordon, *Continental Divide* (Cambridge, MA: Harvard University Press, 2010), p. 92.
9. Immanuel Kant, *Werke in sechs Bänden: Schriften zur Metaphysik und Logik*, 6 vols (Darmstadt: Wissenschaftliche Buchgesellschaft, 1998), III, A 25–26.
10. Angus Nicholls, *Myth and the Human Sciences* (London: Routledge, 2015), pp. 3–4.
11. Ibid., p. 93.
12. Friedrich Nietzsche, 'On Truth and Lying in a Non-Moral Sense', in *The Birth of Tragedy and Other Writings*, trans. by Ronald Speirs (Cambridge: Cambridge University Press, 2012), pp. 139–53 (p. 142).
13. Heidegger, *Kant*, pp. 202–03.
14. Gordon, *Continental Divide*, p. 92.
15. Heidegger, *Kant*, p. 199.
16. Gordon, *Continental Divide*, p. 92.
17. Ibid., p. 89.
18. Mary Fulbrook, *A History of Germany 1918–2014: The Divided Nation* (Chichester: Wiley, 2014), p. 36.
19. Ibid., p. 47.
20. Ibid., p. 33.
21. Ibid., p. 36.
22. Gordon, *Continental*, p. 89.
23. Dominique Janicaud, *Heidegger in France*, trans. by François Raffoul and David Pettigrew (Indianapolis: Indiana University Press, 2015), p. 19.
24. Gordon, *Continental*, p. 11.
25. Ibid., pp. 7–9.
26. Ibid.
27. Ibid.
28. Heidegger, *Kant*, p. 205.
29. Ibid., p. 197. However, Heidegger's characterisation of Cassirer has not gone unchallenged. Jürgen Habermas, for example, suggests that Cassirer is far more in tune to the inescapability of

historical and cultural situations than Heidegger claims. See Jürgen Habermas, 'The Liberating Power of Symbols', in *The Liberating Power of Symbols: Philosophical Essays*, trans. by Peter Dews (Cambridge: Polity Press, 2001), pp. 1–29.
30. Ernst Cassirer, *The Philosophy of Symbolic Forms*, trans. by Ralph Manheim (London: Yale University Press, 1953), I, 319.
31. Heidegger, *Kant*, pp. 201, 204–06.
32. Ibid., p. 205.
33. Ibid.
34. Cazeaux, *Metaphor*, pp. 4–5, 19–23.
35. Gordon, *Continental*, p. 45.
36. Ibid., p. 52.
37. Ibid.
38. Frederick C. Beiser, *The Genesis of Neo-Kantianism 1796–1880* (Oxford: Oxford University Press, 2014), p. 466.
39. Gordon, *Continental Divide*, p. 52.
40. Beiser, *Genesis*, p. 466.
41. Ibid., p. 53.
42. David R. Lipton, *Ernst Cassirer: The Dilemma of a Liberal Intellectual in Germany, 1914–1933* (London: University of Toronto Press, 1978), p. 37.
43. Ibid.
44. Ibid., pp. 37–39. With the declaration of war in August 1914 a wave of nationalism swept across Germany embracing multiple tiers of society, including academia, leading one commentator to call the 'ideas of 1914' a remembrance of when a 'new spirit was born [...] the new German state!' Cassirer, however, was reluctant. Instead he spoke of the 'depressing atmosphere in Berlin during mobilisation'. In his intellectual history of Cassirer, David Lipton makes the case that the First World War tended to politicise the German academic community in one way or another. In the case of Cassirer, he remained aloof from the sweeping nationalism, sceptical that a nationalist passion might distort the actual situation of Germany. However, Cassirer was also pragmatic and realised that his existence as an academic was partially tied to the Imperial political system. At the time, intellectual positions were considered a reflection of political outlook, thus Cassirer, as Lipton tells us, put other projects on hold and devoted his time to this new understanding of Kant, seen in the 1914 article, in a partial attempt, as David Lipton put it, to 'offer his own vision of the German spirit'.
45. Ibid., p. 111.
46. Cassirer, *Symbolic Forms*, p. 319.
47. Lipton, *Ernst Cassirer*, p. 111.
48. Cassirer, *Symbolic Forms*, p. 319.
49. Heidegger, *Kant*, p. 194.
50. Immanuel Kant, *Critique of Pure Reason*, trans. by Marcus Weigelt (London: Penguin, 2007), p. 176.
51. Ibid., p. 176.
52. Ibid., p. 178.
53. Ibid., p. 176.
54. Howard Caygill, *A Kant Dictionary* (Oxford: Blackwell, 1995), p. 247.
55. Gordon, *Continental*, p. 147.
56. Cassirer, *Symbolic Forms*, p. 319.
57. Heidegger, *Kant*, p. 205.
58. Ibid., p. 194.
59. Ibid., pp. 202–05.
60. Gordon, *Continental*, pp. 193–209; Nicholls, *Myth*, p. 98.
61. Heidegger, *Kant*, p. 202.
62. Ibid.
63. Ibid., pp. 202–03.
64. Ibid..

65. Heidegger, *Kant*, p. 199.
66. Heidegger, *Being and Time*, p. 31 (italics in the original).
67. Ibid.
68. Heidegger, *Kant*, p. 200.
69. Ibid., p. 202.
70. Ibid., p. 195.
71. The reorientation of Cassirer's question at Davos is similar to what Heidegger frequently does in his early work, beginning with *Being and Time* (1927). Reorientation of key philosophical questions becomes a trope in Heidegger's early period, first in *Being and Time*, then in his work on Kant completed immediately after Davos, then in his war-year lectures on Nietzsche as well as in most of his early lectures, essays and books.
72. Heidegger, *Kant*, p. 196.
73. Ibid., pp. 196–97.
74. Ibid., p. 197.
75. Heidegger, *Being and Time*, p. 34.
76. Ibid.
77. Haldor Laxness, *The Fish Can Sing*, trans. by Magnus Magnusson (London: Harvill Press, 2000), p. 108.
78. Heidegger, *Being and Time*, pp. 21–31. See especially p. 31 where Heidegger writes: 'the question of Being aims therefore at ascertaining the *a priori* conditions not only for the possibility of the sciences [...] but also for the possibility of those ontologies themselves which are prior to the ontical sciences and which provide their foundations.'
79. Laxness, *Fish*, p. 108.
80. Translator's footnote, Heidegger, *Being and Time*, p. 27.
81. In *Being and Nothingness* Jean-Paul Sartre translated *Dasein* as 'réalité-humaine' (human-reality) which gave a distinctly humanist interpretation to Heidegger's philosophy. As we shall see in chapter 5, much post-war French thought was occupied with re-reading Heidegger and moving away from the Sartrean interpretation of *Dasein* as 'human-reality'. See Jacques Derrida, 'Les fins de l'homme', in *Marges De La Philosophie* (Paris: Minuit, 1972), p. 136.
82. Heidegger, *Being and Time*, p. 27.
83. Heidegger, *Kant*, p. 202.
84. Ibid., p. 197.
85. Ibid.
86. Ibid., p. 199.
87. Ibid., p. 204.
88. Heidegger, *Being and Time*, p. 34.
89. Henceforth *Metaphor*.
90. Cazeaux, *Metaphor*, pp. 4–5, 19–23.
91. Nietzsche, 'On Truth and Lying', p. 146.
92. Martin Heidegger, *The Principle of Reason*, trans. by Reginald Lilly (Indianapolis: Indiana University Press, 1996), p. 48.
93. Heidegger, *Nietzsche*, I, 4.
94. Jacques Derrida, 'The *Retrait* of Metaphor', in *Psyche: Inventions of the Other*, trans. by Peggy Kamuf (Stanford: Stanford University Press, 2007), pp. 48–80 (p. 52).
95. Heidegger, *Reason*, p. 48.
96. Jean Greisch, 'Les mots et les roses: la métaphore chez Martin Heidegger', *Revue des sciences théologiques et philosophiques*, 57.3 (1973), 443–56.
97. The lines Heidegger quotes are often mistakenly attributed to Hölderlin's 'Germanien' because Heidegger moves swiftly from an analysis of 'Germanien' to an analysis of 'Brot und Wein' without telling the reader he has switched poems. However, 'Germanien' does not feature the line, but it can be found in the last line of the fifth section of 'Brot und Wein'.
98. Martin Heidegger, *Unterwegs zur Sprache* (Tübingen: Neske, 1979), p. 207.
99. Haverkamp, *Leaves*, p. 4.
100. Martin Heidegger, 'Letter on Humanism', in *Basic Writings*, trans. by Frank A. Capuzzi and J. Glenn Gray (London: Routledge, 2010), pp. 214–65 (p. 217).

101. Heidegger, *Nietzsche*, p. 4.
102. Sarah Kofman, *Nietzsche and Metaphor*, trans. by Duncan Large (London: Athlone Press, 1993), pp. 6–17.
103. Nietzsche, 'On Truth and Lying', pp. 144–45.
104. Heidegger, *Principle of Reason*, p. 48; Heidegger, *Unterwegs*, p. 207.
105. Richard Kearney, *On Paul Ricoeur: The Owl of Minerva* (London: Routledge, 2004), p. 2.
106. Ibid., pp. 2, 17, 19.
107. Paul Ricoeur, 'The Task of Hermeneutics', in *From Text to Action: Essays in Hermeneutics*, II, trans. by John B. Thompson (London: Continuum, 2008), pp. 51–71 (p. 670.
108. Ricoeur, 'The Task', p. 67.
109. Kearney, *On Paul Ricoeur*, p. 1.
110. Ricoeur, 'The Task', p. 67.
111. Henceforth *Rule*.
112. For Cazeaux's discussion of Ricoeur, see *Metaphor and Continental Philosophy*, chs 1 and 8.
113. Paul Ricoeur, *Time and Narrative*, trans. by Kathleen McLaughlin and David Pellauer, 3 vols (Chicago: The University of Chicago Press, 1984), I, pp. ix–xi.
114. Giambattista Vico, *The New Science*, trans. by Thomas Goddard Bergin and Max Harold Fisch (London: Cornell University Press, 1984), p. 129, §404.
115. Paul Ricoeur, *The Rule of Metaphor*, trans. by Robert Czerny (London: Routledge, 2003), p. 48.
116. Ibid..
117. The use of italics is reproduced from the original text.
118. Ricoeur, *Rule*, p. 48.
119. Ibid., p. 368.
120. Ibid., pp. 370–71.
121. Ibid.
122. Heidegger, 'Letter', p. 217. As the reader will recall, 1947's 'Letter on Humanism' is a response to Sartre's 1946's 'Existentialism is a Humanism'. Heidegger's thesis on language here in the 'Letter' is but one way he attempts to distinguish his own position from that of Sartre.
123. Keats, 'To Hope', 1815.
124. Ricoeur, *Rule*, p. 223.
125. Coleridge, 'Appendix C to *The Statesman's Manual*', quoted in I. A. Richards, *The Philosophy of Rhetoric* (London: Routledge, 2001), p. 109.
126. Ricoeur, *Rule*, p. 294.
127. Angelus Silesius, *Cherubinischer Wandersmann*, in *Sämtliche poetische Werke*, I, ed. by Hans Ludwig Held (Munich: Hanser, 1952), pp. 7–218 (p. 289). Ricoeur does not cite his translation. I have provided the original German reference here.
128. Ricoeur, *Rule*, p. 335.
129. Ibid., p. 336.
130. Ibid., pp. 370–71.
131. Ibid., p. 48.
132. Alain Badiou, 'Philosophy and Art', in *Infinite Thought: Truth and the Return of Philosophy*, trans. by Oliver Feltham and Justin Clemens (London: Bloomsbury, 2014), pp. 75–89 (p. 76).
133. Ibid.
134. Ibid.
135. Although one could certainly pose the question to Badiou, 'is it not possible that art itself could be a critical gesture?'
136. Karl Marx, 'Theses on Feuerbach', in *Marx/Engels Selected Works*, I, trans. by W. Lough (Moscow: Progress Publishers, 1969), p. 15. <https://www.marxists.org/archive/marx/works/1845/theses/theses.pdf> [accessed 13 May 2020].
137. Paul Ricoeur, 'Hermeneutics and the Critique of Ideology', in *From Text to Action: Essays in Hermeneutics*, II, trans. by John B. Thompson (London: Continuum, 2008), pp. 263–99 (p. 263).
138. Ibid.
139. Ibid. Also see textual note 1 on p. 335 where Ricoeur gives a detailed recounting of the publication history of the articles involved in the debate.

140. Ibid., p. 264.
141. Ibid.
142. Gadamer, *Truth and Method*, p. 278.
143. Ibid., p. 272. Emphasis added.
144. Ricoeur, 'Hermeneutics', p. 285.
145. Ibid.
146. Jürgen Habermas, *Hermeneutik und Ideologiekritik*, ed. by Karl-Otto Apel and Jürgen Habermas (Frankfurt: Suhrkamp, 1971), p. 149. The English translation I have used here is taken from Ricoeur, 'Hermeneutics', p. 285.
147. Ricoeur, 'Hermeneutics', p. 285.
148. Ibid.
149. Ibid., p. 286.
150. Ibid.
151. Heidegger, *Being and Time*, p. 191; Gadamer, *Truth and Method*, p. 272.
152. Heidegger, *Being and Time*, p. 188.
153. Ibid.
154. Ricoeur, 'Hermeneutics', p. 286.
155. Ibid., pp. 287–89.
156. Heidegger, *Being and Time*, p. 195. Emphasis added.
157. Ricoeur, 'Hermeneutics', p. 288.
158. Ibid., p. 289.
159. Ibid., p. 288.
160. Ibid.
161. Ibid., p. 290.
162. Ibid., p. 289.
163. Ibid.
164. Ricoeur deals at length with the theme of the origin of hermeneutics arising in conflict in *The Conflict of Interpretations: Essays in Hermeneutics* (1969).
165. Nietzsche, 'On Truth and Lying', p. 146.
166. Ricoeur, 'Hermeneutics', p. 290.
167. Heidegger, *Being and Time*, pp. 24–28.

CHAPTER 4

Likeness as Consensus: Hans Blumenberg and the Riddle of Metaphor

At the conclusion of chapter 2 we arrived at the heart of the philosophical conflict with which this book is concerned. In Nietzsche's philosophy, the same cognitive root produces both a pragmatic and a relativising function of metaphor and thus leads us to our overarching hermeneutic question, 'from where can we judge the meaning of metaphor?' Then, in chapter 3 we observed how the development of Heidegger's philosophy in early twentieth-century European thought might be viewed as one response to the hermeneutic tension in Nietzsche's conception of metaphor. We asserted that for both Heidegger and Ricoeur, Being must ground the meaning of metaphor rather than a metaphysical opposition like truthlikeness. As a result, metaphor acts as a device for poetic revelation. However, we have also seen that the 'existential meaning of metaphor' brings with it a set of problems, particularly in relation to ideology. In this chapter, we return to one of the directions in which the hermeneutic tension of a post-Nietzschean conception of metaphor faces. Like one side of the Roman god Janus, Hans Blumenberg's philosophy of metaphor looks forward to the horizon of the Life-world and makes a case for metaphor's role in orienting the human being by providing pragmatic, historical truths.[1] When metaphor is viewed as grounding pragmatic historical truths, rhetorical consensus can be seen to ground metaphoric meaning. This perspective also presents a picture of metaphor that is reducible neither to a traditional metaphysical description nor to the existential description found in Heidegger and Ricoeur.

As Blumenberg's main work on metaphor, *Paradigms for a Metaphorology* (1960)[2] is a study of the metaphorical basis of key concepts in Western intellectual history, and one could easily focus solely on this relationship between metaphorical and conceptual thinking. However, this book will maintain that metaphor, for Blumenberg, is not simply an archaeology of conceptual history, but rather an essential ground for the production of rhetorical meaning. Metaphors, as a supplement to conceptual history, are but one case study for this more general principle. As we saw in the introduction, the importance of Blumenberg's inclusion in this book lies partly in the fact that the anglophone reception of his philosophy has been limited. Seeing Blumenberg's philosophy of metaphor not simply as a reflection on metaphor's relation to conceptual history, but as a distinct contribution to a theory of the production of rhetorical meaning itself, contributes to the need for a wider anglophone reception of Blumenberg.

In his text of 1979, 'Prospect for a Theory of Nonconceptuality',[3] Blumenberg calls metaphor a *riddle*, when he writes: 'The riddle of metaphor cannot be understood solely in relation to difficulties in the formation of the concept. What is enigmatic is precisely why metaphors are "tolerated" at all.'[4] The emphasis on 'toleration' is pragmatic. Regardless of whether the nature of metaphor is metaphysical, understood as a figurative/literal split, or existential, understood as speaking literally about Being, we see repeatedly that metaphors are 'tolerated' throughout history. They are tolerated to such an extent that they, in Blumenberg's view, are '*foundational elements* of philosophical language, "translations" that resist being converted back into authenticity and logicality'.[5] This reminds us of Nietzsche's understanding of metaphors in 'On Truth and Lying in a Non-Moral Sense' where Nietzsche writes, 'an edifice of concepts [is] constituted [...] from the metaphors themselves [...] language [...] works on building the edifice of concepts'.[6]

To view metaphor in this way does not mean simply selecting a different focus for metaphorical analysis, i.e. to leave philosophical questions aside and instead assess the instances of metaphorical usage in philosophical language. This would be to look at the function of metaphor rather than the concept of metaphor. Rather, to understand metaphor's pragmatic and historical relevance produces a deeper philosophical understanding of the nature of metaphor itself, in that it reveals the way in which human beings orient themselves in the world through metaphors. Blumenberg's most prominent work on metaphor, *Paradigms*, is a case study of this very principle. We will see that Blumenberg's view of the pragmatic, historical truths of metaphor provides an answer to the problem that arises in Nietzsche's thought when he critiques truthlikeness as a ground of metaphoric meaning. It is precisely because of the pragmatic and historical view that Blumenberg takes that we can understand rhetorical consensus as a ground for metaphoric meaning.

Hans Blumenberg and Post-War German Thought

In his *Myth and the Human Sciences*, the first book-length critical analysis of Blumenberg's theory of myth in English, Angus Nicholls writes:

> today [Hans Blumenberg] counts among the most renowned philosophers in Germany, is the subject of a critically acclaimed novel, and features regularly in German newspapers [...] yet outside of Germany and especially in the Anglophone world, his profile does not begin to approach that of his immediate forbears and contemporaries like Theodor W. Adorno, Hans-Georg Gadamer or Jürgen Habermas.[7]

It could also be argued that Blumenberg is one of the most significant post-war European thinkers on metaphor and therefore it makes it all the more important, in light of his limited anglophone reception, to include him as a representative thinker in an intellectual history of metaphor after Nietzsche. As Nicholls's book is one of the only English-language works available on Blumenberg, it will be referred to frequently, particularly regarding biographical detail. And it is the biographical detail, we will argue, that in our case is relevant to understanding Blumenberg's position on metaphor. Because of this, we will take a moment to familiarise ourselves with a sketch of relevant sections of Blumenberg's life.

Hans Blumenberg (1920–96) was born in 1920 in Lübeck and attended the same secondary school (*Gymnasium*) as Thomas Mann. His mother had Jewish ancestry and converted to Protestantism, and his father was baptised as a Catholic. Upon leaving *Gymnasium*, Blumenberg expressed interest in studying Catholic theology, possibly because the anti-Semitic political climate at the time barred him from normal university study. But eventually, because of political pressure, even the Catholic philosophical-theological colleges that he attended cut him off from further education in the summer of 1940. Unable to continue his studies, Blumenberg was assigned compulsory work by the National Socialist regime. Blumenberg only avoided being sent to a concentration camp because of the intervention of Dr Heinrich Dräger. Dräger initially employed Blumenberg in his company Drägerwerk AG. but in February 1945 Blumenberg was eventually sent to a National Socialist work camp at Zerbst. Sometime later, before the end of the war, Dräger intervened again and enabled Blumenberg and other former employees of Drägerwerk to be released. Blumenberg remained hidden for the rest of the war in the family home of his future wife Ursula in Lübeck. After the war, Dräger gave Blumenberg 6,000 Reichsmarks, which financed Blumenberg's doctoral dissertation.[8]

Blumenberg wrote his dissertation on medieval scholastic philosophy in Kiel. His *Habilitation* on Edmund Husserl's phenomenology led to a professorship in Hamburg and then to a succession of full professorial appointments in Giessen, Bochum and finally Münster.[9] Only two public photos exist from Blumenberg's time as an academic, and from what we know of his working methods throughout these years, he seemed to work systematically and in solitude.[10] From at least the 1940s, Blumenberg's working method consisted of transcribing quotations from primary sources and pasting newspaper articles and images from magazines onto index-cards, assembling them thematically, and then working through them while writing. From the 1960s this process was complemented by speaking into a tape recorder or Dictaphone with the transcriptions later typed up by his secretary. Blumenberg would then edit the transcripts.[11] According to his close interlocutor Henning Ritter, in Blumenberg's later life, he increasingly retreated to his home in Altenberge and worked through his index-cards late into the night, drawing Ritter to compare Blumenberg to Proust, 'insulated from the external world'.[12] Owing to this working method, Nicholls calls Blumenberg a 'materialist', not in the philosophical sense but rather in the sense that 'his arguments seem to have been built from the ground up, based on his astonishingly wide reading of primary sources from all periods of Western culture'.[13]

This 'astonishingly wide reading' is something seen throughout Blumenberg's academic career, which should be understood in the context of the post-war

Federal Republic of Germany. He can be distinguished from several other German philosophers of the period with Jewish backgrounds, such as Max Horkheimer, Karl Löwith and Theodor Adorno, in that he never 'undertook an explicit and extended examination of National Socialism and the Holocaust in his published works'. Nicholls points to the fact that while Horkheimer, Löwith and Adorno left Germany during the National Socialist period, it was not a matter as simple as choosing to leave in Blumenberg's case and he stayed behind.[14]

Post-war Germany had a varied intellectual landscape. Blumenberg gave his first lecture on what was to become the concept of a metaphorology at the Senatskommission für Begriffsgeschichte (Senate Commission for the History of Concepts), an early post-war attempt to form a large interdisciplinary research project in the humanities. In the early 1960s Blumenberg was also a part of the Poetics and Hermeneutics research group, which he co-founded together with Hans Robert Jauss and Clemens Heselhaus.[15] In addition to attempts such as these to form interdisciplinary research projects, the philosophy of post-war Germany also had constructive and deep engagements with the recent past. As Nicholls has noted, Horkheimer, Löwith and Adorno all were explicitly engaging with the question of National Socialism and the Holocaust.[16] However, the post-war period also brought more divisive philosophical currents.

We have already seen in chapter 3 that Heidegger had a significant role to play in shaping the landscape of late Weimar Germany. After the Second World War, he remained an extremely influential figure, but if his thinking was not already provocative enough, his National Socialist membership in the 1930s made him divisive.[17] Criticisms of Heidegger abounded after the war, one particularly poignant example being Adorno's book of 1964, *The Jargon of Authenticity*. The question of the political overtones of Heidegger's writings or the degree of his anti-Semitism has always been a contentious issue. It has been made even more so with the 2014 publication of Heidegger's *Black Notebooks*. However, as Nicholls has noted, Blumenberg did not undertake an extended examination of National Socialism and while the question of Heidegger and National Socialism is indispensable, it is not inside the explicit scope of Blumenberg's relationship to Heidegger's thought. Nevertheless, although there are many things we may not be able to say with certainty about Blumenberg's relationship to Heidegger, and while interpretations of Blumenberg's thought as a response to Heidegger, as in Anselm Haverkamp's work, remain controversial, we can at least say that Heidegger's philosophy was a significant and divisive part of the post-war intellectual landscape in which Blumenberg began his professional career.[18]

One of the earliest academic projects of Blumenberg's career in this post-war period was on metaphor. In 1958, he gave a lecture entitled 'Theses Towards a Metaphorology' at the first conference of the Senatskommission, in which he asserted that absolute metaphors might precede and underlie concepts in the process of formulating theories. To show this he outlined major Western philosophical concepts and their corresponding metaphors, elaborating his famous notion of a metaphorology. The Senatskommission led to Erich Rothacker's journal *Archive for the History of Concepts* as a means of researching key concepts in the history of philosophy.[19] While the journal did not go on to use this rather novel approach to conceptual history, one of the things that emerged from it was Blumenberg's *Paradigms for a Metaphorology*.[20]

Paradigms for Metaphorology and Heidegger

Here we can end our biography of Blumenberg and address the claim that *Paradigms* is an implicit critique of Heidegger's philosophy. Robert Savage, the English-language translator of *Paradigms*, brings this interpretation to anglophone scholarship when he suggests that 'Blumenberg grasped metaphorology as a rival conception to [Heidegger's] fundamental ontology.' For Blumenberg, 'the price paid by fundamental ontology for its "perfection" and "comprehensiveness" is vacuousness and vapidity'.[21] In the 'Translator's Afterword', Savage creates a hypothetical critique that Blumenberg might level against Heidegger, based on a section of *Paradigms*. In chapter 2, Blumenberg gives a brief case study of voyage metaphors in the *Odyssey*. He then writes that this case study is only a 'semifinished product [*Halbzeug*], and the perfection and comprehensiveness with which one can deal with "Being" is quite unattainable in this field'.[22] Robert Savage suggests the use of *Halbzeug* is a critique of 'the jargon of authenticity' cultivated by Heidegger and his followers, invoking Heidegger's use of the word *Zeug* in *Being and Time*. The German word *das Zeug* can translate as 'stuff', 'instrument' or 'tool'. One common English translation for Heidegger's use of *das Zeug* is 'equipment', because Heidegger uses the term often as a collective noun designating the variety of 'stuff' used for something.[23] For Heidegger this 'equipment' designates the things in the world whose function is 'ready-to-hand'. To remind the reader, ready-to-hand, in Heidegger's thought, means that we accept something automatically without thinking of it in our practical interactions with the immediate world around us. Heidegger gives the example of things in a room:

> Equipment (*das Zeug*) [...] always is *in terms of* its belonging to other equipment: ink-stand, pen, ink, paper, blotting pad, table, lamp, furniture, windows, doors, room. These 'Things' never show themselves proximally as they are for themselves, so as to add up to a sum of *realia* and fill up a room. What we encounter as closest to us [...] is the room; and we encounter it not as something 'between four walls' in a geometrical spatial sense, but as equipment for residing [...] before [an individual item of equipment shows itself], a totality of equipment has already been discovered.[24]

The key thing for us to take from this passage is that Heidegger's use of the term *Zeug* characterises everyday things, such as pens, papers, lamps, and tables, as something we encounter automatically and accept their function without thinking about them. When we pick up a specific piece of paper, for example, we have already accepted it automatically as a finished part of the totality of the room.

Savage creates a hypothetical critique of the Heideggerian *Zeug* based on Anselm Haverkamp's own reading of Blumenberg. Haverkamp has argued that it was 'Heidegger's Kant-interpretation [at Davos] that triggered Blumenberg's own *Paradigms for a Metaphorology*' and he has also suggested that metaphor itself could be understood as a 'semi-finished product' in that it is half intuitive — that is, situated in the 'Life-world', a term that we will address later in this chapter — and half conceptual.[25] However, Haverkamp's own reading takes the idea of 'semi-finished product' even further. He suggests that unlike other major works by German thinkers published around the same time, such as Gadamer's *Truth and Method* or Adorno's *Negative Dialectics*, the ideas in *Paradigms* itself outlined a research programme that was left in draft form, abandoned in an experimental or half-finished state.[26]

Therefore, in this light, for both Haverkamp and Savage, this early, experimental thesis seems all the more radical. If metaphor can be viewed as a *Halbzeug* in Blumenberg's thought, then we could view it as a critique of Heidegger's idea of *Zeug*. 'The Heideggerian *Zeug*', Savage writes, 'will never break down [...] because it can never meet with any resistance from "the everyday" world of beings.'[27] The 'everyday' world of beings, is of course, the intuitive Life-world, in which metaphor always has a foothold. We will explore this concept later in the chapter. But the Heideggerian *Zeug* is a concept which, in its abstraction, Heidegger has removed too far from the 'everyday world' even though it is, ironically, meant to describe it. The study of metaphor, on the other hand, may only deliver to us a *Halbzeug*, but it does provide a more direct description of the 'everyday world' of beings than Heidegger's fundamental ontology does.

It is possible that both Savage and Haverkamp, in this hypothetical critique of Heidegger, have made too much out of Blumenberg's phrase *Halbzeug*. It is clear that the quote surrounding it is a passing jab at Heidegger, but whether Blumenberg intended *Halbzeug* as a metaphor for the nature of metaphors is debatable. We could also read Blumenberg here in a more straightforward manner. Perhaps he intended to convey something like this:

> the voyage metaphor is quite an enticing project of study. However, I'm afraid I don't have time to go into it now. I'm just creating a few semi-finished sketches to get my main point across: not everyone can write with such sweeping perfection and comprehensiveness about their subject matter as Heidegger does about 'Being'.[28]

While the joke directed at Heidegger is apparent in this reading, it remains a joke and does not imbue Blumenberg's words with a deeper meaning about how the nature of metaphor might critique Heidegger.

Whatever the case may be, there is something helpful about Haverkamp's and Savage's contrast of *Halbzeug* and *Zeug*. Blumenberg clearly thought more insight was to be gained about the human being's 'ground of existence' (*Daseingrund*) by looking at the particularity and the facticity of that existence arising from the world of everyday life. For Blumenberg, metaphor was one such form of particularity and facticity. As Blumenberg wrote to Erich Rothacker, 'Expositions in the history of concepts quite simply demand the spreading out of "material", otherwise everything becomes as unreal as if one were talking about Being.'[29]

To achieve this 'spreading out of "material"', Blumenberg laid out a metaphorology in *Paradigms*. Tracing key metaphors in the history of Western thought, Blumenberg initially felt a metaphoric history could act as a supplement to a conceptual history.[30] For Heidegger, a conceptual history was a 'history of Being's concealment' and though his thinking became more nuanced over the years, conceptual history remained at a distance from any true access to the meaning of Being, precisely because concepts are trapped in metaphysics.[31] We will look at a more direct response to Heidegger by Blumenberg later in this chapter, but the essential difference we can highlight at the moment is that, for Blumenberg, looking at the metaphorical history of concept formation was essential. Particularly in Blumenberg's thesis in *Paradigms*, we see that metaphors give us insight into our 'ground of existence' (*Daseingrund*) because metaphors form the substructure of thought and this substructure, as Savage implies, always has one foot in the Life-world. Nicholls clarifies the way in which Blumenberg sees this principle at work.

> When Descartes compares nature with a machine, or a natural organism such as a tree with a clock, he suggests that the inner workings of nature are mechanistic, even if [...] we are unable [...] to take nature to pieces and perceive all of its intricate cause-and-effect relations. In other words, the metaphor provides one with a basic frame of theoretical expectations.[32]

Metaphor and Concepts

It could be said that the thesis 'metaphor provides one with a basic frame of theoretical expectations' is reflective of the core of one of the most common interpretations of *Paradigms*. Here Savage is quite good in pointing out that a metaphorology does not do away with conceptual history but rather 'radicalizes conceptual history, in the literal sense that it directs its attention to the roots of concept formation'.[33] In *Blumenberg lesen: Ein Glossar*, Petra Gehring provides the helpful characterisation of this method of using metaphors to understand concept formation as a 'working relationship' (*Arbeitsverhältnis*) and one that finds a middle ground between the extremes of an empirical methodology or a theoretical study of metaphor.[34] In 1971, Blumenberg himself refers to this middle ground as an 'auxiliary service'.

> Metaphorology performs in conceptual history the auxiliary service of guiding it to a genetic structure of concept formation that, while it may not meet the requirement of univocity, nonetheless permits the univocity of the end result to be recognized as an impoverishment of the imaginative background and the threads leading back to the Life-world.[35]

So, while this book will not go so far as to follow Haverkamp's claim that *Paradigms* is an unfinished experimental draft that critiques Heidegger, it will suggest instead that *Paradigms* shows us a case study of a larger thesis in Blumenberg's work about meaning production. Therefore, by observing the 'working relationship' or 'auxiliary service' of metaphor in relation to concepts, we can view Blumenberg as representative of the pragmatic function of metaphor. In this way, he can also be seen as implicitly responding to the hermeneutic tensions in the Nietzschean concept of metaphor. Therefore, *Paradigms* is not only a response to Heidegger but rather part of a larger thesis that contributes to problems relating to the production of meaning in post-Nietzschean European thought more generally.

Blumenberg opens *Paradigms* with a hypothetical situation in which Descartes's wish has been fulfilled. Descartes, in his *Meditations*, calls for concepts in philosophical language to be 'clear and distinct'. Blumenberg infers from this that this conceptual clarity would render all metaphors, figurative language, anything that works according to the logic of substitution, obsolete. Blumenberg writes:

> clarity and distinctness [are] the first rule required [for] all matters apprehended in judgment. In its terminal state, philosophical language would be purely and strictly 'conceptual': everything can be defined; therefore, everything must be defined; there is no longer anything logically 'provisional' [...][36]

If we use the metaphor of light for the concept of a life-giving force that overcomes evil as an example, we could imagine a situation under the remit of Descartes's call for conceptual clarity, of a philosopher of religion finding clear and distinct language to define the divine without recourse to the metaphor of light.[37] Yet as we have seen from the history of religion, while conceptual arguments abound, the metaphors continue to change.

Blumenberg points to the failure of Descartes's project as the impetus for why the role of metaphors needs to be re-evaluated. He re-evaluates metaphor by observing its role in the construction of concepts. In various case studies, Blumenberg shows the metaphoric basis of concepts such as the powerful truth, the naked truth, *terra incognita*, the incomplete universe, and the book of nature. This form of re-evaluation reminds us of Nietzsche's understanding of metaphors in 'On Truth and Lying' where Nietzsche writes, 'an edifice of concepts [is] constituted [...] from the metaphors themselves [...] language [...] works on building the edifice of concepts'.[38] Blumenberg says as much in *Paradigms* when he writes: 'metaphors can also [...] be *foundational elements* of philosophical language, "translations" that resist being converted back into authenticity and logicality'.[39] Like the metaphor of light for the divine, the concept seems continually to find itself expressed through new metaphors. The metaphor of light for the divine, the naked truth and the book of nature are all examples of the key term 'absolute metaphor'. We will explore how Blumenberg defines this term more in a moment. However, first a disclaimer is needed.

While this view that 'absolute metaphors' are '*foundational elements* of philosophical language' may have made the name Blumenberg synonymous with metaphor in the German-speaking world, as Petra Gehring has claimed, Blumenberg's view on what a metaphor is, the perennial question after Nietzsche, is not immediately apparent.[40] Despite extensively examining the relationship between metaphor and concepts, Blumenberg spends precious little time defining metaphor itself. When he does define metaphor, we see that his view that metaphors form the substructure of thought is not simply a thesis on how metaphor pragmatically relates to concept formation, but is also a view of the nature of metaphor itself.

Definitions: Metaphor and Kant's Definition of the Symbol

One fairly clear definition of metaphor that Blumenberg provides us with at the beginning of *Paradigms for a Metaphorology* references Kant's *Critique of Judgement*. In this section the reader will note that not only does he place metaphor under the heading of Kant's definition of symbol, but he also relates to the term 'absolute metaphor' and 'pragmatic function'. Blumenberg writes,

> Readers familiar with Kant will at this point recall [section 59] of the 'Critique of the Power of Judgment,' where the procedure of 'transportation of the reflection' is thematized under the heading 'symbol,' even if the expression 'metaphor' does not appear in this context [...] Our 'absolute metaphor' appears here as 'the transportation of the reflection on one object of intuition to another, quite different concept, to which perhaps no intuition can ever directly correspond.' Metaphor is clearly characterized as a model invested with a pragmatic function, from which a 'rule of the reflection' can be gleaned that may then 'be applied' in the use of the idea of reason; it is thus 'a principle not of the theoretical determination of what an object is, but the practical determination of what the idea of it ought to be for us and for the purposive use of it.' In this sense, 'all our cognition of God is merely symbolic' (in the Kantian terminology), an argument intended to skirt the twin perils of anthropomorphism and deism [...][41]

Here we see that metaphor, in Blumenberg's view, is said to have a 'pragmatic function' or a 'practical determination' rather than a 'theoretical determination'. He relates metaphor's 'pragmatic function' to his definition of 'absolute metaphor'. Here 'absolute metaphor' is defined in the same way that the term 'symbol' is in Kant's philosophy.

We can better understand the relationship between an 'absolute metaphor' and its 'pragmatic function' if we look at the traditional distinction between symbol and metaphor. These are closely related literary devices and one might think that the similarity between the two that Blumenberg points out has as much to do with Kant as it does with the similar literary operations performed by the two. This, however, can be misleading. Contrasting it with the *sign* in Saussure's thought, *The Princeton Encyclopedia of Poetry and Poetics* states that:

> *symbol* refers to a more polysemous representation of one thing by another, such as when the sea, e.g., is used to stand for such different feelings as the danger of being overwhelmed (by analogy with drowning) or the excitement and anxiety of making a transition (as in a journey) or the power and fulfilment of strength (as in mighty), and so on.[42]

In this broad sense, the close relationship to metaphor is clear and it is even broadly related to Kant's use of the term in that the indirect representation that Kant discusses is a product of representing one thing by another.

But Kant's terminology is specific to his philosophy and does not necessarily relate to the symbol as it is discussed in literary studies. Kant's use of the term symbol has wider theoretical applications in a number of contexts and cannot simply be limited to 'an aspect of art, of literary theory [...] and of poetry'.[43] It is important to recognise, then, that despite this broad similarity to the way one may think of the symbol in literary studies, Blumenberg is taking something very specific from Kant's philosophy. He is taking the similarity he sees between a logical operation that the symbol performs on the level of cognition and a logical operation that metaphor performs on the level of cognition. Blumenberg's concern about metaphor is more about how it relates to the concept and to epistemological problems than it is about metaphor as a literary device.

To understand Blumenberg's appeal to Kant, we need to look at the passage itself. The quote Blumenberg points to comes from the penultimate chapter of part I of section 59 of the *Critique of Judgement*, entitled 'Beauty as the Symbol of Morality'; it is one of the classic reference points for Kant's definition of the symbol.[44] As we saw in chapter 1, we have seen that for Kant, the *symbol* applies to a certain type of concept. This type of concept can only be thought by reason and cannot be intuited sensibly. Because it cannot be intuited sensibly, Kant views the symbolic use of judgement as indirect, later calling it 'schematism by analogy'.[45] The concept of God would be such a concept, for in Kant's view 'all our knowledge of God is merely symbolic'.[46]

When Blumenberg draws a comparison between the Kantian notions of symbol and his own conception of metaphor, he is claiming that metaphors can be understood as performing this indirect operation of judgement for concepts. As we saw in chapter 1, an example of the type of symbol that Kant is discussing can be seen in the beginning of the Gospel of John where the author describes Christ as a divine light that both animates being and overcomes dark forces:

> All things came into being through him [God], and without him not one thing came into being. What has come into being in him was life, and the life was the light of all people. The light shines in the darkness, and the darkness did not overcome it.[47]

While the Gospel of John is clearly presenting a symbolic representation of Christ as light, the word 'light' is employed as a metaphor in the passage. In the phrase 'The light shines in the darkness', the word 'light' is metaphorically standing in for Christ. It is Blumenberg's argument that the cognitive operation performed by absolute metaphors such as the divine light is akin to the Kantian notion of symbol that we have seen outlined.

However, there is a second aspect of metaphor's relation to concepts which, while complementing the first, is markedly different. This is the 'pragmatic function' of metaphor that Blumenberg mentions. When Blumenberg says in the above quotation that 'metaphors [...] resist being converted back into authenticity and logicality', it certainly does mean that metaphor 'provides one with a basic frame of theoretical expectations', to requote Nicholls, but it also means that metaphor cannot be understood solely in relation to the concept. Blumenberg states this in 'Prospect' when he says, 'The riddle of metaphor cannot be understood solely in relation to difficulties in the formation of the concept.'[48] This is not to say that Blumenberg sees metaphor as illogical, but rather that metaphor, in its 'pragmatic function', does not simply give birth to concepts but works in a fundamentally different way from conceptual logic.

The Indissolubility of Metaphor in Logicality

In chapter 7 of *Paradigms*, Blumenberg writes that metaphors display an, 'Unauflösbarkeit in Logizität'.[49] We could translate this phrase literally as 'metaphors are indissoluble in logicality'. Robert Savage's translation of *Paradigms* reads, 'Metaphor has an indissoluble alogicality'. However, the word choice can imply that metaphor does not have a logic. This does not seem to be Savage's intention, however. Presumably Savage has chosen to use the word 'alogicality' to represent a larger point that Blumenberg is making. Metaphor operates in a different province from conceptual thinking. Even though it is one of the things that helps conceptual thinking to function, it is not confined to the powers of conceptual logic.

In chapter 7 of *Paradigms* Blumenberg points out the similar functions of myth and 'absolute metaphor'. Blumenberg is perhaps best known in the anglophone world for his philosophy of myth laid out, among other places, in his magnum opus, *Work on Myth*, written in 1979. Published nineteen years before *Work on Myth*, *Paradigms* highlights the shared function of metaphor and myth in both rhetoric and cognition by pointing to a scene in Plato's *Gorgias*. In the *Gorgias*, while discussing law and judgment, Socrates appeals to the myth of Rhadamanthus judging the souls of the dead in Hades. When he has exhausted his argumentative ability, Socrates finds that he must resort to *mythos*. Socrates says that he realises that his interlocutor will take the example as a *mythos*, but Socrates himself will take it to be a *logos*. Blumenberg reads this episode in the *Gorgias* as an example of how *mythos* stands in when *logos* reaches the limits of its ability to be precise enough for the given situation. Socrates realises that he cannot find an 'adequate account' or a *logos*, so for Socrates the *mythos* will be a more 'adequate account' than any normal *logos*. Blumenberg writes: 'While Socrates would like to have something that satisfies his logical requirements, for want of an alternative it (myth) will have to do.'[50]

In this chapter of *Paradigms*, Blumenberg draws our attention to the fact that myth and metaphor share a similar function in both rhetoric and cognition. Like myth, Blumenberg suggests, an absolute metaphor stands in for moments in discourse where concepts cease to satisfy. This is where Savage's translation comes in. In this section, Blumenberg writes:

> What has emerged from our reflections under the heading of 'absolute metaphor' has, in its indissoluble alogicality, given us reason to believe that such Cartesianism *avant la lettre* brings an inappropriate norm to the historical findings. In myth, too, questions are kept alive that refuse to yield to theoretical answers without thereby becoming obsolete.[51]

What does indissoluble alogicality mean in relation to metaphor? It means that metaphors are not able to be logically distilled or converted back into logic or broken down into clear conceptual parts. While we can say that they provide the groundwork for concepts and provide one with a framework within which our theoretical expectations are cognised, they are not simply the stepping stone to a higher, distinct platform, but make up part of the platform itself.

So, to speak metaphorically for a moment, we find that metaphor is not instant coffee that can be dissolved in the waters of logic. Perhaps, instead, it's like a nice strong minty tea leaf. It infuses the water with its minty essence but retains its shape and character. Once instant coffee hits water, you cannot pull the granules out, but take a good strong tea leaf and you can still pull it out, bite in to it and taste the mint. It is important to think of metaphor in these terms of solubility. When you can dissolve something in something, that which does the dissolving has power. The law of its natural structure trumps the natural structure of that which is being dissolved. This is not the case with metaphor and the concept. Rather, metaphor is indissoluble in logicality. Metaphor and the concept, then, have an interesting coexistence and we require further texts by Blumenberg to understand it. In 'Prospect', Blumenberg discusses metaphors and concepts in relation to the philosophy of Heidegger, analysing metaphors here under the broader heading of 'Nonconceptuality'. This is where we can perhaps see a more explicit critique of Heidegger, via metaphor, than the one we see in *Paradigms*. Also, understanding how Blumenberg's position on metaphor relates to Heidegger's thesis on language as a device for poetic revelation will move us a step closer towards understanding Blumenberg's claim that metaphor has a 'pragmatic function', orienting the human being by providing historical truths.

Blumenberg and the Legacy of Davos

In chapter 3, we used Davos to frame the distinctiveness of Heidegger's philosophy in the early twentieth century. Blumenberg once called Davos 'an embodiment of the state of philosophy at the time'.[52] As we have seen earlier in this chapter, Haverkamp has argued that it was

> Heidegger's Kant-interpretation [at Davos] that triggered Blumenberg's own *Paradigms for a Metaphorology* as a response to the challenge unsatisfactorily met by Cassirer's *Philosophy of Symbolic Forms* [...] The methodological grounding of this new foundation [a Metaphorology] is a result of the radicalization of Kant's metaphysics, which surfaced in Davos, and Blumenberg's Metaphorology of 1960 is the methodological consequence, drawn from [Heidegger's] *Kant and the Problem of Metaphysics* of 1929.[53]

However, the main text we have that gives us insight into Blumenberg's reflections on Davos, 'Affinitäten und Dissonanzen', was only posthumously published and written well after the publication of *Paradigms*.[54]

Whether or not *Paradigms* was an explicit response to Davos and Heidegger's thought is unimportant. It is apparent in 'Affinitäten und Dissonanzen' that Blumenberg retrospectively reflects on the primacy of the *ground* metaphor, in the sense of a 'transcendental ground' or an 'existential ground' in Heidegger's writing on Kant and in the Davos debate.[55] We obviously walk on the ground, but when the word 'ground', taken literally, is applied by Kant or Heidegger to transcendence or existence, it suddenly becomes figurative. Haverkamp suggests that Blumenberg might encourage a 'belated metaphorologist' to examine such metaphors in Heidegger's thinking of which Heidegger himself seems unaware.[56] However, on the other hand, we see from 'Affinitäten und Dissonanzen' that Heidegger's question of the meaning of Being excited a greater sense of expectation than Cassirer's defence of his *Philosophy of Symbolic Forms*.[57] So it is clear that, retrospectively at least, Blumenberg had a mixed relationship with Heidegger's thinking at Davos and was attentive to the 'metaphoric ground' of Heidegger's own ideas. However, what is important for us is not whether *Paradigms* was an explicit response to Davos, but rather whether it presents an implicit theoretical alternative to Heidegger's philosophy. In the world of metaphor after Nietzsche, Heidegger's philosophy and his limited views on metaphor chart one course of rethinking the grounds for metaphoric meaning. Blumenberg's philosophy provides another, distinct course. What is apparent in *Paradigms* is that metaphors give the human being, not existential, but pragmatic meaning rooted in a historical context.

We can see Heidegger's call for an existential analytic to answer the question of Being as the opposite pole of Descartes's call for clarity and distinctness of conceptual thinking. Yet Heidegger can symbolise another kind of desire to speak directly or literally, without any figurative substitution. As we have seen, we have a glimpse into Blumenberg's feelings about Heidegger in his letter to Erich Rothacker when he writes that 'expositions in the history of concepts quite simply demand the spreading out of "material", otherwise everything becomes as unreal as if one were talking about Being'.[58] If there is any doubt that this line is meant as a criticism of Heidegger's philosophy as it relates to metaphor, Blumenberg explicitly lays it out in in the second half of 'Prospect'. As we have seen, Blumenberg writes at the beginning of 'Prospect' that the 'riddle of metaphor cannot be understood solely in relation to difficulties in the formation of the concept. What is enigmatic is precisely why metaphors are "tolerated" at all.'[59] Blumenberg then goes on in the second half of the essay to engage with Heidegger's concept of the existential analytic and to show why it does not account for the 'toleration' of metaphor.

In the second half of 'Prospect' Blumenberg works out how metaphor might fit into one of the most foundational tenets of Heidegger's philosophy: the existential analytic or metaphysics of *Dasein* that we examined at length in chapter 3. As one of the famous twentieth-century oppositions to metaphysics, the implication of the existential analytic for the concept is that, for Heidegger, a history of concepts was a history of Being's concealment. If the existential analytic is the alternative, can metaphor fit into the existential analytic?

As we have seen, Heidegger does not explicitly write on metaphor as a part of his larger philosophical project. Rather, for Heidegger, a metaphor understood through the metaphysical distinction of figurative/literal stays within the confines of metaphysics.[60] Thus, from the perspective of Heidegger's history of Being, metaphors, as understood by a logic of substitution, do not have a place. They exist within the boundary of the conceptual and are therefore part of the 'history of Being's concealment'. But the riddle is, Blumenberg claims, that metaphors are tolerated. For Heidegger, as we saw in chapter 3 with his appeal to read Hölderlin's metaphors literally, we only encounter 'authentic being' in the language of poetry and myth. As we saw in chapter 3, this is where we encounter our 'throwness'.

But as we also saw in chapter 3, beginning with 'The Letter on Humanism', Heidegger extends this thesis to all language. This makes language itself take on a revelatory function and it follows that all linguistic functions, whether figurative or literal, take on a revelatory function: unless metaphor is to be bound up in a type of metaphysics, language itself must be re-understood as speaking literally about existence and in doing so revealing *Dasein*. Referencing this characterisation of language in 'Prospect', Blumenberg asserts, '*Dasein* was able to become the very type of the symbol for being, or rather the type of the grounding of all symbols.'[61] Blumenberg is making the point that when Heidegger famously uses a quote, such as 'language is the house of Being, in it man dwells', Heidegger has dramatically altered the Western conception of language so that it does not fall into the trap of metaphysics. Language houses Being. It contains existence itself and as such, as Blumenberg says, existence is what grounds all symbols.

As we have seen, the main proponent of extending Heidegger's thesis on language to metaphor is Paul Ricoeur. For Ricoeur, metaphor is a 'lively expression' that 'expresses existence as alive'.[62] For Ricoeur, if metaphor is understood solely as a rhetorical device or in regard to its referential function, we fail to see its ontological function, which can give us truth about existence. It then follows that the traditional idea of substitution that frames metaphor has no place in the existential analytic. Is Blumenberg then defending traditional metaphysics?

Certainly not. He is pointing out that by rushing to characterise the metaphoric act of substitution as metaphysics, Heidegger fails to catch the 'riddling moment' of metaphor. The fact is that metaphor stands, like the tea leaf, stubbornly in the conceptual waters without dissolving. Metaphors are in fact tolerated in the same way that Socrates tolerates the myth in the *Gorgias* because he has no other alternative. While the logic of substitution may be both a term and a logical operation that arises from Western metaphysics, it is by no means confined to this logic when we observe its historical use in the socio-political Life-world. Therefore, while a hermeneutics of metaphor in the vein of Heidegger and Ricoeur may be useful for describing certain moments in the experience of metaphor, there is something about metaphor that such a hermeneutics does not explain.

The historical 'toleration of metaphor' produces a different kind of truth that is neither metaphysics, in the sense of Descartes, nor existential in the sense of Heidegger and Ricoeur, and this is the riddle. Blumenberg refers to it as metaphor's 'historical truth' in *Paradigms* and it is 'a pragmatic truth in a very broad sense'.[63] Considering this critique of both Descartes and Heidegger, we can see that the term 'tolerated' is not meant to be disparaging of metaphor, but rather gives voice to the cultural dimension of metaphor where rhetoric has no choice, like Socrates in the *Gorgias*, but to take recourse to it. This moves us a step closer to understanding what the 'pragmatic function' of metaphor that Blumenberg writes about might be.

Historical Truth and the Creation of Mutual Understanding

We have seen in the last section Blumenberg's rejection of Heidegger's existential analytic as a route to understanding the nature of metaphor. This is a definitive move away from a Heideggerian appropriation of Nietzsche and thus emphasises a different aspect of Nietzsche's philosophy of metaphor. In this section, we will now look at the deeper philosophical thesis about the nature of metaphors that Blumenberg develops from observing the human being's continual recourse to them throughout history.

As we have seen in chapter 3, the view that rhetoric must take refuge in metaphor is distinct from the classical view found in both Aristotle and Cicero where metaphor is employed, as a part of rhetoric, in the service of the orator to persuade the listener of the truth. Blumenberg points this out in the essay 'An Anthropological Approach to the Contemporary Significance of Rhetoric' (1971) where he writes that:

> the most influential doctrine of rhetoric in our tradition [...] that of Cicero [...] starts from the premise that one can possess the truth, and gives the art of speaking the function of beautifying the communication of this truth, making it accessible and impressive [...][64]

We have traced this reversal of the role of metaphor to Nietzsche. As is shown in the above quotation, for Cicero, metaphor is ornamental, whereas for Nietzsche, metaphor is fundamental. While we can observe in Blumenberg's philosophy Nietzsche's thesis on the role of metaphor in the construction of abstract concepts like truth, we can also see the Nietzschean thesis of the stabilisation of meaning via rhetorical consensus. These are the two functions of metaphor for Nietzsche: pragmatic and relativising.

Nietzsche highlights the role of language in creating 'peace treaties' so that human beings can live together in society rather than have a perpetual Hobbesian 'war of all against all'.[65] However, while Nietzsche may have a somewhat bleak outlook about our dependency on metaphor, Blumenberg takes a more pragmatic approach. After emphasising the classical role of metaphor within rhetoric, Blumenberg characterises metaphor and all of language in a similar way to Nietzsche's Hobbesian peace treaty when he writes: 'language, is a set of instruments not for communicating information or truths, but rather, primarily, for the production of mutual understanding, agreement, or toleration, on which the actor depends'.[66] It is this pragmatic dimension of Nietzsche's thesis that we will explore in this section. We will also see how in this pragmatic approach, Blumenberg provides one solution to the crisis of likeness. For Blumenberg, metaphorical meaning is determined by rhetorical consensus and this is always historically relative.

In an unpublished text from the Blumenberg *Nachlass* in the Deutsches Literaturarchiv Marbach, Blumenberg makes this point regarding Nietzsche's own use of metaphor in *Thus Spoke Zarathustra*. It is a typewritten manuscript that dates from 1983, one hundred years after *Thus Spoke Zarathustra* was published. Below is the text in its entirety, first in German, then followed by my own translation:

'Unwahrwerden einer Metapher'[67]

Wie bestimmt kann einer etwas sagen und es mit einer mächtigen Metapher bekräftigen, was kaum jemals dieser Verstärkung zu seinem unbestrittenen Zeitlosigkeitswert bedurft hatte und dennoch Unrecht bekommen?

Nietzsches Rhetorik am Ende des 'Zarathustra', Fragment seiner Höhlenrede an die versammelten Subjekte der Tageswanderung auf der Oberwelt, steigert sich zu einem Satz, der die Forderung nach dem neuen Menschentypus und seiner rechtmäßigen Bedenkenlosigkeit aufs Kürzeste zu bringen hat. Er proklamiert den Verzicht auf alle Einstellungen, die ein 'Für' enthalten, und beschwört rigide Selbstigkeit als Abwendung von der Tugend der kleinen Leute. Deren bloße Negation suggeriert Kraft zum Eigennutz, ohne die es das Gedeihen der Frucht, die Austragung des Werkes nicht geben kann. An die Stelle jenes Nächsten, dem eine Fremdliebe gelten sollte, ist das Nächste in einem unüberbietbaren Sinne der Interiorität getreten. Eben dieses beschwört die Pathosformel: 'Ihr Schaffenden, ihr höheren Menschen! Man ist nur für das eigene Kind schwanger' (WW XIII 368).[68]

So geschrieben im Jahr 1883. Ein Jahrhundert später, in der anbrechenden Ära der Leihmütter und Mietausträgerinnen, ist die Metapher in dieser singulären Wendung schon nicht mehr wahr.

['A Metaphor Becomes Untrue'

How definitively can a person say something and reinforce it with a powerful metaphor, something which would barely ever have needed this reinforcement to become an uncontested eternal value, and yet still turn out to be wrong?

Nietzsche's rhetoric at the end of *Zarathustra*, a fragment of his cave-speech to the assembled subjects of the daytime expeditions into the higher world, culminates in a sentence that is meant to express, in the most concise form, the demand for a new type of human being and its justified unscrupulousness. This sentence proclaims the renunciation of all attitudes that contain a 'for', and invokes rigid self-interestedness as a disavowal of the virtue of the little people. The simple negation of this virtue suggests a power to be used for self-interest, in the absence of which a fruit would not grow and prosper, a work could not be delivered. The place of that neighbour who should be loved as the other, is taken by that which is closest in an unsurpassable sense of interiority. It is precisely this which is invoked in the highly charged formulation: 'You creators, you Higher Men! One is only pregnant with one's own child.'

So it was written in 1883. A century later, in the dawning era of surrogate mothers and the women who rent out their wombs, the metaphor invoked in this singular turn of phrase is no longer true.]

The phrase in question, 'One is only pregnant with one's own child', was true in Nietzsche's time. However, as Blumenberg points out, with the change in the social and technological possibilities, the truth of the metaphor changed as the consensus surrounding its meaning changed. When Blumenberg wrote in 1983, the advancements of modern science and the possibility of artificial insemination and surrogacy had rendered the literal ground of Nietzsche's metaphor untrue. The metaphor of intellectual pregnancy itself goes back to Plato's *Symposium*; as always, Nietzsche is subverting it. In *Zarathustra*, the metaphor of being pregnant with a child is dramatically connected to the philosophical idea that Nietzsche is espousing: namely, self-interest and self-empowerment at the expense of love for one's neighbour. But, while this idea may hold a certain poignancy, the metaphor Nietzsche uses to ground this radical reversal of traditional values loses its truth; or rather, as Blumenberg puts it, it becomes false because the literal ground becomes false.

Here we see clearly, that whether a metaphor is true or false — Blumenberg's title perhaps echoing Nietzsche's 'On Truth and Lying' — depends on the historical meaning determined by rhetorical consensus. So, it is no longer truthlikeness that determines the meaning of metaphor, nor is it simply human perception as we saw in 'On Truth and Lying'. Rather it is the consensus of perception in history that is highlighted by Blumenberg. This key difference from the relativising function of metaphor is crucial. While it is certainly the case that Blumenberg's position partially holds with the relativising position, in that metaphors do not reflect a fixed truthlikeness, we can nevertheless see the suggestion in this short text that a metaphor can indeed become false. Part of the reason it becomes false is because of the historical change in technology. In the case of the above passage on *Zarathustra*, the new technological ability provided by artificial insemination has upset our instant acceptance of Nietzsche's metaphor of being pregnant with one's own child.

With respect to the question of technology, Blumenberg had a markedly different view from that of Heidegger, who viewed technology as something which obstructs an authentic relation to Being.[69] In a 1959 lecture, Blumenberg suggests that if changes in technology become successful, they become taken for granted in the same way that other objects in the Life-world do.[70] Ringing the doorbell, for example, is something we do automatically. The 1959 lecture was later developed into an essay that was published three years after *Paradigms* in 1963.[71] Here Blumenberg writes,

> Ich wähle das primitive Beispiel einer Türklingel. Da gibt es die alten mechanischen Modelle von Zugklingeln oder Drehklingel: betätigt man sie, so hat man noch das unmittelbare Gefühl, den beabsichtigten Effekt in seiner Spezifität zu erzeugen, denn zwischen der tätigen Hand und dem erklingenden Ton besteht ein adäquater Nexus, d.h. wenn ich vor einer solchen Einrichtung stehe, weiß ich nicht nur, was ich tun muss, sondern auch, weshalb ich es tun muss.[72]

> [I choose the primitive example of a doorbell. There are the old mechanical models of door bells which are pulled on or bells with turning handles: when you activate them, you still have the immediate feeling of producing the effect specifically intended, because there is an adequate nexus between the active hand and the ringing sound; that is, when I stand in front of such a mechanism, I know not only what I have to do, but also why I have to do it.]

When Blumenberg writes that 'when I stand in front of such a mechanism, I know not only what I have to do, but also why I have to do it' he is reminding us that we use this technology automatically. Rather than it being an obstruction in the Life-world it is something in the background that blends into the landscape of our automatic, everyday ways of being-in-the-world. Yet we could point out that human beings have existed for hundreds of years without doorbells. It is an historically appropriate part of the Life-world in the same way that today glancing at one's phone to see the time is an action we do without thinking, although, even since Blumenberg's time, it is a radical advance in technology.

The change in technology is but one example of historical change but it reflects Blumenberg's interest in the relationship between technology and Husserl's notion of the Life-world. Accepting something in the Life-world automatically, like the doorbell, has to do with Husserl's concept of the self-evidence of the Life-world. To understand the relationship between metaphor, technology, and the Life-world, we will briefly remind the reader of Husserl's conception of the Life-world to give ourselves context for how Blumenberg's notion of metaphor might relate to it.

Husserl's Concept of the Life-world

One of the keys to understanding Blumenberg's view of rhetorical consensus creating historical or pragmatic truths is found in his appropriation of Edmund Husserl's concept of the Life-world (*Lebenswelt*), from *The Crisis of European Sciences and Transcendental Phenomenology* (1936/54).[73] The *Crisis*, which was based on a handful of lectures given shortly before Husserl's death, was published in two parts, the first in 1936 and then an incomplete third section in 1954 from the *Nachlass*.[74] The concept of a Life-world as a pre-theoretical world that the human theoretical attitude is dependent on was deeply influential for Blumenberg. It was directly appropriated by Blumenberg in his posthumously published *Theorie der Lebenswelt* (2010) and though this is never explicitly stated, it can be seen as a fundamental philosophical influence on Blumenberg's magnum opus *Work on Myth* (1979).[75] Dermot Moran, in his book on the *Crisis*, also suggests that Blumenberg's book *The Genesis of the Copernican World* was influenced by the *Crisis*.[76] But is Husserl's conception of the Life-world relevant to metaphor? Let us briefly look at the key ideas in Husserl's *Crisis*.

In the *Crisis*, written during the period of National Socialism, Husserl seeks to understand the origins of the contemporary problems of irrationalism in philosophy and politics and the hostility towards science in the younger generation. This irrationalism and hostility was seen in the existentialism of Heidegger and Jaspers and in the politics of Nazi Germany.[77] The first section of the *Crisis* is entitled 'The Crisis of the Sciences as an Expression of the Radical Life-Crisis of European Humanity'. Therefore, for Husserl, the crisis extends beyond that of a hostility towards science but is a life-crisis for all European humanity and can only be assessed by a 'teleological historical' method.[78] The teleological part refers to the goal of theory and the historical part refers to the historical rootedness of theory.

Husserl finds the origins of the problem in the notion that Greek theory was not a new theory but a new attitude that the human being adopted. It is a shift, Husserl claims, from a pre-theoretical attitude to a theoretical attitude. Husserl's translator, David Carr, interprets this as follows,

> The very notion or motive of approaching the world 'theoretically' at all is itself a tradition, one whose origin we normally associate with the Greeks. In order to understand Galileo's accomplishment, for example, we must understand not only his inheritance of the 'ready-made' science of geometry but also his

> inheritance of the very idea of science, the task of finding nonrelative truths about the world as such, the task the Greeks defined by distinguishing between 'appearance' and 'reality,' between δόξα and ἐπιστήμη. What we associate with the 'origin of philosophy' in Greece must be seen not as the presentation of a new hypothesis about the nature of the world but as a change in man's recognition of his relation to his surroundings, a change in his style of life which first made questions about the nature of the world 'as such' possible. This amounts to not simply a change of doctrine, or even of method, but a change of attitude.[79]

Following Carr's interpretation here, we can say that Husserl associates this 'change of attitude' with a change from a pre-theoretical attitude. The pre-theoretical is what he calls the Life-world. In the *Crisis* Husserl writes:

> we speak in this connection of the natural primordial attitude, of the attitude of original life, of the first originally natural form of cultures, whether higher or lower, whether developing uninhibitedly or stagnating. All other attitudes are accordingly related back to this natural attitude as reorientations [of it].[80]

This 'attitude of original life' Husserl refers to as Kant's presupposition, in that Kant takes a Life-world for granted in his key philosophical discoveries. Because of this, Kant's theory of the understanding, for example, as something that develops meaningful configurations that are 'intuitively given in the surrounding world', cannot be fully accomplished by Kantian theory. This is because, according to Husserl, these inquiries have 'an unquestioned ground'.[81] Therefore, Husserl posits that understanding the existence of a pre-theoretical attitude is essential for understanding the contemporary crisis of irrationalism.[82]

In the *Crisis*, Husserl describes the Life-world as 'the universe of things' and claims that:

> for those of us who wakingly live in it, [it] is always already there, existing in advance for us, the 'ground' of all praxis whether theoretical or extratheoretical. The world is pregiven to us [...] always and necessarily as the universal field of all actual and possible praxis, as horizon. To live is always to live-in-certainty-of-the-world. Waking life is being awake to the world, being constantly and directly 'conscious' of the world and of oneself as living in the world, actually experiencing and actually effecting the ontic certainty of the world.[83]

There are two related things to take note of in this description. Beyond the general description of the immediacy of our experience of everyday life, Husserl calls it the 'ground' of all praxis whether theoretical or extratheoretical. This is a reminder that the Life-world is where all theories and skills, all praxis arise. It is the ground of praxis. The second thing to note is that when we experience the Life-world, we are experiencing an ontic certainty of the world. Our ontic experience of the world means our actual or physical existence in it. This was one of the ways in which Heidegger described the pre-ontological knowledge of Being in *Being and Time*. For Heidegger, all ontology remained blind from giving an accurate description of our ontic experience of the world.[84] Husserl, on the other hand, sees all theoretical knowledge, which would include ontology, as arising from the same ground that provides our ontic experience of the world.

But what about the way in which we, as human beings, are directed towards this 'universe of things' that is the ground for all praxis? In Husserl's 'Vienna Lecture' (1935), which is one of the texts on which the *Crisis* is based, he gives a description of this:

> Now [the Life-world] can be characterised as a life naively, straightforwardly directed at the world, the world being always in a certain sense consciously present as a universal horizon, without, however, being thematic as such. What is thematic is whatever one is directed toward. Waking life is always a directedness toward this or that [...] toward the private or public, toward what is daily required or intrusively new. All this lies within the world-horizon; but special motives are required when one who is gripped in this Life-world reorients himself and somehow comes to make the world itself thematic, to take up a lasting interest in it.[85]

What Husserl is describing in this 'reorientation' is a change from a pre-theoretical attitude to a theoretical attitude.

When I sit here typing on my laptop, I am directed towards pushing the keys and looking at the screen to make certain the correct letters have appeared. The process is automatic and unthinking. However, when I begin to reflect on the process of typing, when I think that it involves the memorisation of the position of the keys on the keyboard through practice, the ability of muscle reflexes to coordinate with the letters going through my head and the corresponding keys, I am making typing itself thematic. I am no longer simply directed towards typing, in that I am not simply carrying out the task of typing which I know so well. My former state, before I made typing 'thematic', is the pre-theoretical attitude that Husserl describes as being straightforwardly directed at the world. Once I make typing a theme for reflection, I have gone through the reorientation to the theoretical attitude. As we have seen, for Husserl, this pre-theoretical attitude did not go away once the theoretical attitude was born. This is why, as Carr claims in the passage that we have seen above, Husserl attempts to show the theoretical attitude's dependency on the Life-world.[86]

Metaphor and the Life-world

In this book, we will maintain that Blumenberg sees in Husserl's distinction between the theoretical and pre-theoretical attitude, not only an articulation of the theoretical attitude but also the attitudes and beliefs in the Life-world on which the theoretical attitude depends. As we have already seen in the section on metaphor and concepts, in 1971 Blumenberg suggested that metaphors are 'the threads leading back to the Life-world'.[87] This idea is clearly seen in a text entitled 'Selbstverständlichkeit, Selbstaufrichtung, Selbstvergleich' (Self-Evidentness, Self-Erection, Self-Comparison) from the Blumenberg *Nachlass*, where Blumenberg combines the changes and adaptations of the human cultural world with Husserl's notion of the Life-world.[88]

The text comes from a larger collection of essays that Blumenberg wrote about the Life-world, entitled *Theorie der Lebenswelt* (2010). The editor of this collection,

Manfred Sommer, cautions his readers that the collection of essays presented in the book are not about the Life-world as such or even the structure of the Life-world; rather, they are Blumenberg's reflections on the *theory* of the Life-world.[89] We can certainly agree that Blumenberg is preoccupied with what the theory of the Life-world could accomplish. However, in asking what such a theory could accomplish, Blumenberg is also making his own contribution to ideas about the structure of the Life-world. As we will see, Blumenberg views metaphor as a foundational functional tool, along with myth and philosophy, thus providing a fusion of a theory of the structure of the human cultural world with Husserl's account of the Life-world. As noted earlier, Blumenberg wrote his *Habilitation* on Husserl's phenomenology and as Nicholls notes in *Myth and the Human Sciences*, *Lebenswelt* was a term of crucial importance for Blumenberg.[90] Some of the texts from the Blumenberg *Nachlass* published in *Theorie der Lebenswelt* (2010) were written in the lead-up to one of Blumenberg's most significant works, *Work on Myth* (1979).[91]

In 'Selbstverständlichkeit, Selbstaufrichtung, Selbstvergleich', one of the examples that Blumenberg gives of the relationship between metaphor and the Life-world concerns the expression *Augenblicksgott* (God of the moment). The German expression was coined in the nineteenth century to refer to the earliest ideas of God, those before the conceptions of God found in formalised religion and theology.[92] Blumenberg links up the expression *Augenblicksgott* to the function of metaphor in the Life-world when he writes:

> Die Funktion der Metapher ist aber auch gegeben bei den Phänomenen des Schreckens. Zwar wird der Blitz, der die panische Furcht auslöst, im Augenblick selbst zum Gott, zum 'Augenblicksgott'. Aber als eine der vielen Äußerungsformen des Numinosen ist die Dauerhaftigkeit seiner Funktion doch umgekehrt die einer Metapher: Nicht der Blitz ist der Gott, sondern Gott ist in seinen Handlungen so unerwartet und so tödlich wie der Blitz. Es ist klar, dass nach der Erfindung des Blitzableiters so etwas nicht mehr stattfinden kann, dass umgekehrt die technische Zurüstung zum Symbol dafür wird, dass die Welt der Vorurteile über Unbekanntes und Unbezähmbares zu Ende geht. Jede Aufklärung erschöpft das Potential der Namen und Metaphern [...] Es ist klar, dass dieser langfristige Integrationsprozess des Unbekannten, die Aufarbeitung der Angst durch Furcht, der Furcht durch Institutionalisierung der Mächte im Mythos, der Erfassung des Mythos als Metaphorik für das, was man auch begrifflich erfassen zu können glaubt in Gestalt der Philosophie, dass dieser Integrationsprozess die Lebenswelt komplizierter und ausgedehnter macht, dass es in ihr selbst Schwierigkeiten der Orientierung gibt, Konkurrenzen des Naheliegenden mit dem Fernliegenden, also eine Art von Zonenbildung der Aufmerksamkeit, des Interesses, der Intensität der Bekanntheit.[93]

> [But the function of metaphor is also given in the phenomena of terror. To be sure, the lightning that triggers the panic-stricken fear becomes a God, the 'God of the moment'. But as one of the many manifestations of the numinous, the permanence of its function is conversely that of a metaphor: lightning is not God, but God is as unexpected and as deadly in his actions as lightning. It is clear that, after the invention of the lightning conductor, such a thing can no longer take place, that, on the contrary, technological preparedness becomes a symbol of the fact that the world of prejudices about the unknown

and indomitable comes to an end. Every Enlightenment depletes the potential of names and metaphors [...] It is clear that this long-term process of integration of the unknown, the processing of anxiety into fear, the institutionalisation of the powers in myth, the registering in myth, as a metaphorical method, of that which one believes oneself able to understand conceptually in the form of philosophy, that this process of integration makes the Life-world more complicated and extended, that in the Life-world itself there are difficulties of orientation, competitions of the nearby with the distant, a kind of creation of zones of attention, of interest, of the intensity of familiarity.]

The progression Blumenberg identifies as it relates to metaphor is, first, to give a name to something, such as lightning, to keep fear at bay, and second to use that word to describe a conception of God, God as unexpected and deadly. The part of the process that concerns us here is that once humans have technical mastery over the thing that frightened them, in this case the lightning, the metaphor is exhausted. The invention of the lightning rod renders the panic-stricken metaphor for God, the *Augenblicksgott*, useless. As Blumenberg writes, 'every Enlightenment depletes the potential of names and metaphors'. Here Blumenberg has described the function of metaphor generally as aiding human survival, but particular metaphors have particular historical limits. Blumenberg writes that 'this process of integration makes the Life-world more complicated and extended, that in itself there are difficulties of orientation'.[94] Therefore, in this passage, it seems that the metaphor provides initial orientation in the Life-world to the human being and then reaches a historical limit as the Life-world reaches new difficulties of orientation. About this process, Angus Nicholls writes, 'at the most basic level, [the new threats in the Life-world] need to be named, before being integrated into the Life-world by myth, by metaphor, or by philosophical concepts'.[95] As Nicholls points out, metaphor is but one of the ways of naming threats and the opening of Blumenberg's *Work on Myth* famously asserts the decisive role of myth in anthropogenesis.[96]

As we have seen, this text was written in the lead-up to *Work on Myth* and in fact, metaphor also plays a role in the opening of *Work on Myth*. In relation to metaphor's role in keeping the anxieties of early human cognition at bay, Blumenberg writes:

the situations that enforced [the flight of early humans from predators] either had to be dealt with by standing one's ground or had to be avoided by means of *anticipation*. The transition from reacting [...] to the ongoing state of maximum excitement and suspense of the organic system in a state of alarm makes the *creature dependent on means by which to master dangerous situations*, even when they cannot be avoided. The focus of the state of excitement and suspense necessarily becomes less specific as the ambiguity and indefiniteness of the data defining the situation increase. This produces a readiness for an attitude of expectation, *of feeling one's way forward, that refers to the entire horizon*. It has its *functional value* precisely in not depending on determinate [...] actual threats. The generalized excitement and suspense must always be reduced, again, to the assessment of specific factors [...] this occurs primarily, not through experience and knowledge, but rather *through devices like that of the substitution of the familiar for the unfamiliar, of explanations for the inexplicable, of names for the unnameable* [...] what has become identifiable by means of a name is raised out of its unfamiliarity by *means of metaphor and is made accessible, in terms of its significance, by telling stories. Panic and paralysis, as the two extremes of anxiety behaviour, are dissolved by the appearance of calculable magnitudes to deal with and regulated ways of dealing with them [...]*[97]

Rather than explore the relationship between metaphor and myth we will limit ourselves in this book to the functional and pragmatic role of metaphor. In this quotation, Blumenberg emphasises metaphor's role in making the unfamiliar familiar. This is very similar to the role metaphor plays in the discussion above about the *Augenblicksgott* and the Life-world. In the same way that human beings metaphorically pair God and lightning to orient themselves in the Life-world prior to more advanced technology surmounting this need, metaphor, on a cognitive level, makes the unfamiliar familiar and therefore manageable.[98]

Essentially, we are creating an analogy between metaphor and technology, because, as we have seen, for Blumenberg, language is a tool for survival in the Life-world. We have seen, for example, the way in which the doorbell can become part of the 'self-evidence' of the Life-world. We do not reflect on it; we just use it. We have also seen in both the example of the lightning and the example of Nietzsche's metaphor of being pregnant with one's own child that a metaphor can serve a similar purpose. In the case of the lightning, the metaphorical connection with God helps the human being process fear of the lightning. In the case of Nietzsche's metaphor, in Nietzsche's own time, before the technological advance, it would have been self-evident as a true metaphor about the world. In both the case of the Nietzsche metaphor and the lightning example, it is not until a technological change occurs that the metaphor ceases to act 'technologically', or perhaps better put, functionally. And this is precisely what Blumenberg writes when he says: 'the function of the metaphor is also given in the phenomena of terror'.[99]

This is like the argument seen in *Paradigms*. The idea of the history of metaphors as an alternative conceptual history is a case study of this more fundamental philosophical principle on the nature of metaphors. From this background, we can see that metaphors create paradigms and assimilate new information into the pre-theoretical Life-world upon which theory depends. For example, while today we can readily understand the metaphor of a clockwork universe to denote a mechanistic universe, the paradigm had to be created by assimilating the new technology of the clock into the Life-world. Today I glance at a clock when I want to know the time, whether this is my watch or my phone. I do not, however, go outside and consider the position of the sun. The fact that relying on the clock for the time is such an automatic behaviour and that the metaphor of a clockwork universe makes me think not of a clock but of a mechanistic universe shows just how assimilated into the Life-world the technology of a clock is. Yet the metaphor, clockwork universe, produces a theoretical concept far beyond my automatic directedness towards the clock. In Husserl's language, we might say that our familiarity with the clock allows us to use the metaphor of the clockwork to thematise the universe itself.

Seen from this perspective, metaphors are fundamental survival strategies in the unconscious make-up of the Life-world and the theoretical attitude is dependent upon metaphor. One could also say that, on this view, metaphors are essential for human orientation. Seen in the light, as an essential element for orientation in the Life-world, one can see the relevance of metaphor more clearly in the quote from Blumenberg's 'Anthropological Approach' which we referred to in an earlier section: 'language, is a set of instruments not for communicating information or truths, but rather, primarily, for the production of mutual understanding, agreement, or toleration, on which the actor depends'.[100] From this we can infer that metaphor, for Blumenberg, is not simply an archaeology of conceptual history, but rather an essential ground for the production of rhetorical meaning.

It is important to add a critical distinction here. Meaning, in the sense we are using it here, is fundamentally different from the type of existential meaning that Heidegger's philosophy may indicate. Meaning, in the sense of Blumenberg's philosophy, gestures in the direction of a cultural and social semantics. By contrast, meaning in the sense of Heidegger's philosophy has deeply existential overtones that one might associate with purpose or destiny. Therefore, as has already been pointed out, Heidegger's philosophy and Ricoeur's appropriation of it prove extremely useful when one is analysing a religious text or the language of romantic poetry in that it speaks about the meaningful experience that metaphor creates as a mode of revealing Being. Blumenberg's cultural semantics, on the other hand, understands meaning as the 'production of mutual understanding' and as we have seen, this is a survival method that is adaptive. The type of truth that arises from this meaning is pragmatic and historical rather than existential and accounts not for the meaningful experiences of metaphor but for metaphor's pragmatic ability to orient human beings in historical moments. Metaphor for Blumenberg shows a 'functional competence' in the Life-world. In fact, Blumenberg declares that functional competence defines the entire Life-world when he writes, 'Die Lebenswelt ist eine durch ihre Funktionstüchtigkeit definierte Welt' (The Life-world is a world defined by its functional competence).[101]

One of the ways in which Blumenberg derives the argument of human beings using language in a technological or functional capacity is through the distinction between humans and other animals. Animals of course have instincts, but as we have seen, the Life-world demands 'functional competence'.[102] This is an argument taken from the tradition of philosophical anthropology and one that Blumenberg fleshes out in his essay on 'An Anthropological Approach'. It is here where we finally see how Blumenberg's view of the pragmatic function of metaphor links up with his argument concerning the ground of metaphorical meaning being founded in rhetorical consensus.

Metaphorical Meaning as Rhetorical Consensus

In 'An Anthropological Approach' Blumenberg matches up two competing anthropological views of the human being with two corresponding approaches to rhetoric which he draws from philosophical anthropology. One of the founders of philosophical anthropology, Paul Alsberg, thought the discrepancy between human cultural origins and human animal origins was a distinct theoretical problem. In his book *Das Menschheitsrätsel* (1922), which was published in English in 1970 under the title *In Quest of Man*, Alsberg argued that the existence of human culture implied that humans acquired a new method of evolution, which Alsberg called 'body liberation' (in German: *Körperausschaltung* or 'deactivation of the body').This is because there is an 'unbridgeable gulf' between a human being's mode of biological evolution and the later phenomenon of technological civilisation.[103] Alsberg extends 'body liberation' to language when he writes, 'language, then, appears to set Man free from the compulsion and the natural limitations of his sense-organs [...] [cultural adaptations] are essentially extra-bodily, or artificial, means made and used for the ends of body-liberation'.[104] Language as a form of body liberation compensates for the lack of natural adaptations possessed by humans in comparison with non-human animals, such as the pre-historic mastodon. If humans had not had technology and the ability to communicate in a complex manner through language, the mastodon would clearly have been the more formidable animal during human prehistory. But, as Alsberg puts it, language frees the human being from 'the compulsion and the natural limitations of his sense-organs'.

Alsberg's *In Quest of Man* was not as well known as it could have been in Germany because of his Jewish origins and the book burnings of 1933.[105] Blumenberg may have been exposed to Alsberg either through the German sociologist Dieter Claessens or through classic texts in philosophical anthropology by Max Scheler and Helmuth Plessner.[106] Blumenberg referred to Alsberg's ideas as 'the only possible scientific course for an anthropology'.[107]

In the 'Anthropological Approach' essay, Blumenberg draws on this idea, along with the work of other philosophical anthropologists such as Arnold Gehlen, to sketch out different views of the human being. Either the human being is viewed as a poor creature and 'needs rhetoric as the art of appearance to deal with the lack of truth', or the human being is viewed as a rich creature that 'exercises his disposition over the truth that he possesses with the aid of the rhetorical *ornatus* (ornament)'.[108] As we have seen in the quote above, Blumenberg's own position is that rhetoric is something we depend on for understanding. We may be a weak creature, but we have a cultural adaptation, language, which coincides with Alsberg's category of 'body liberation'. Blumenberg quotes Nietzsche early in the essay to reflect his point: 'with rhetoric the Greeks had invented form in itself'.[109] This dependence on rhetoric for the creation of form may have driven Nietzsche to his critique of truth, but Blumenberg sees here the possibility of rhetoric acting as a driving force in the human race's survival.

Along with Nietzsche, Blumenberg takes for granted the idea that purportedly self-evident truths are an unhelpful starting point for understanding what a concept like the good means.[110] But he goes a step further towards stating his theory of rhetorical consensus when he discusses Aristotle. In the 'Anthropological Approach' essay, Blumenberg suggests that Aristotle always has a teleological argument for the function of rhetoric in that the function of rhetoric, for Aristotle, is to communicate the truth. Blumenberg then writes: 'only a skeptical destruction of this teleological support makes the pragmatic substratum of consensus visible again'.¹¹¹ Blumenberg seems to be saying that Aristotle is in tune to rhetorical consensus or *sensus communis*, as a useful starting point. However, Blumenberg is also making the point that in Aristotle the teleology overshadows the pragmatic substratum and suggests that only a sceptical destruction of this teleology reveals this pragmatic substratum. This refers to the pragmatic role played by rhetoric in creating merely provisional or functional truths, which might better be referred to as mere modes of proceeding. Nietzsche is the sceptical destroyer *par excellence*. But Blumenberg goes on to say why Nietzsche's type of scepticism ultimately does not go any further to answering the riddle of metaphor than Heidegger does. Blumenberg writes that: '[scepticism] deprives itself of a favourable opportunity to yield dividends for anthropology'.¹¹² For Blumenberg, these dividends for anthropology arise, as we have seen in the last section, because the human being is dependent on metaphor in order to communicate and create a social consensus of the meaning of our various perceptions and experiences.

In the 'Anthropological Approach' essay Blumenberg writes:

> Man's deficiency in specific dispositions for reactive behaviour vis-à-vis reality — that is, his poverty of instincts — is the starting point for the central anthropological question as to how this creature is able to exist despite his lack of fixed biological dispositions. The answer can be reduced to the formula: by not dealing with this reality directly. The human relation to reality is indirect, circumstantial, delayed, selective, and above all 'metaphorical'.¹¹³

Here we see in much clearer terms why Heidegger's existential analytic does not answer the riddle of metaphor. The indirect relation to reality via the substitution of metaphor answers the question why metaphors are tolerated in a different way from saying that we must reduce metaphors to a literal, existence-revealing moment. Rather, for Blumenberg, the act of metaphoric substitution is a tool that creates 'mutual understanding'. As Blumenberg writes, 'language, is a set of instruments not for communicating information or truths, but rather, primarily, for the production of mutual understanding, agreement, or toleration, on which the actor depends'.¹¹⁴

To remind the reader, 'An Anthropological Approach' was written in 1971. The year after, in 1972, an essay by Blumenberg was published in English entitled 'The Life-world and the Concept of Reality'.¹¹⁵ Here Blumenberg seems to link up the production of mutual understanding with the Life-world by appealing to the concept of intersubjectivity. Here Blumenberg writes:

> Intersubjectivity founds the reality concept, as consolidated to 'objectivity,' of the consensual context of consciousness. But this can be achieved only because in intersubjectivity the consensus of the other subjects with my experience stands under the risk of negation. Every Other is potentially the one who disputes my perception[...]¹¹⁶

We have seen how the human being has a 'metaphorical' relation to reality by using metaphor as a tool in the Life-world. This 'metaphorical' relation produces mutual understanding in the midst of subjective perceptions by creating what Blumenberg refers to here as a 'consensual context of consciousness'. This works, not simply because we need to create a stable meaning to keep the unfamiliar at bay, as we saw in the example of the lightning as an *Augenblicksgott*; rather, Blumenberg seems also to be suggesting that consensus can be reached in the Life-world because mutual consensus is predicated on the possibility of a conflict of interpretations. Therefore, unlike Ricoeur, who grounds the possible conflict of interpretations of metaphor in the poetic revelation of Being, Blumenberg grounds it in the evolving process of mutual consensus. As we have seen, one of the ways in which consensus between both human beings and between metaphor and the Life-world can be negated is by historical and technological change, such as the development of the lighting rod or the development of artificial insemination and the surrogate mother.

This is the significance of the unpublished *Nachlass* text 'Unwahrwerden einer Metapher'. While Nietzsche made a significant metaphorical point in Zarathustra, the mutual understanding of metaphoric meaning is always evolving, as is shown by the case of technology changing, and thus the metaphors we take for granted in the Life-world are not valid once and for all. The 'truth' then in *Zarathustra* is not just once and for all. Rather, because of our 'lack of a fixed biological disposition', we find ourselves in a situation of continual metaphorical substitutions that 'stand under the risk of negation'.

As we have seen, for Blumenberg the human being can orient him- or herself in the Life-world through this metaphorical substitution. The act of metaphorical substitution helps to create provisional rhetorical consensus, and this stabilises meaning. This provides a distinct notion of the nature of metaphor. Like Nietzsche, Blumenberg sees metaphor as a cognitive pattern that has a pragmatic function. But unlike Nietzsche, he sees the possibility of the negation of the meaning of a metaphor as precisely what holds the historical consensus together. While the relativising function of the Nietzschean conception of metaphor threatens to throw the meaning of metaphor into hermeneutic crisis, Blumenberg is more interested in how consensus is formed, and he sees the relativising function of metaphor as essential to this process. The very fact that the meaning of metaphor is simply a human relation means that we need metaphors to set the parameters of a given debate. Therefore, meaning being negated or changing from perception to perception, or with technological changes, is the condition of the need for metaphor in the first place. This is what Blumenberg means in his essay on 'The Life-World and the Concept of Reality' when he writes that, while intersubjectivity founds a given reality concept, it can only be achieved because intersubjectivity necessarily risks negation. Why? Because every other interlocutor can possibly dispute every other perception.[117]

In chapter 5, we will see the final representative strand of metaphor after Nietzsche in the thought of Jacques Derrida. For Derrida, meaning is also constantly in flux. However, rather than seeing metaphor as a provider of orientation, Derrida sees in metaphor a relativising function that extends across all cognition and responds to the hermeneutic crisis after Nietzsche in a way distinct from Blumenberg.

Notes to Chapter 4

1. Hans Blumenberg, *Paradigms for a Metaphorology*, trans. by Robert Savage (Ithaca: Cornell University Press, 2010), p. 14.
2. Henceforth *Paradigms*.
3. Hans Blumenberg, 'Prospect for a Theory of Nonconceptuality', in *Shipwreck with a Spectator: Paradigm of a Metaphor for Existence*, trans. by Steven Rendall (London: MIT Press, 1997), pp. 81–102 (p. 82). Henceforth 'Prospect'.
4. Hans Blumenberg, *Shipwreck with a Spectator: Paradigm of a Metaphor for Existence*, trans. by Steven Rendall (London: MIT Press, 1997), p. 82.
5. Blumenberg, *Paradigms*, pp. 3–4.
6. Friedrich Nietzsche, 'On Truth and Lying in a Non-Moral Sense', in *The Birth of Tragedy and Other Writings*, trans. by Ronald Speirs (Cambridge: Cambridge University Press, 2012), p. 150.
7. Angus Nicholls, *Myth and the Human Sciences: Hans Blumenberg's Theory of Myth* (London: Routledge, 2015), p. 9.
8. Ibid., pp. 11–12.
9. Ibid., p. 13.
10. Ibid., p. 9.
11. Ibid., p. 8.
12. Ibid.
13. Ibid.
14. Ibid., p. 13. The Publication of *Prefiguration: Work on Political Myth* gives a more nuanced picture to Blumenberg's political reflections.
15. Nicholls, *Myth*, p. 15.
16. Ibid., p. 13.
17. Emmanuel Faye, *Heidegger: The Introduction of Nazism into Philosophy*, trans. by Michael B. Smith (New Haven: Yale University Press, 2009), pp. 39–58.
18. Anselm Haverkamp, 'Das Skandalon der Metaphorologie: Prolegomena eines Kommentars', in *Metaphorologie: Zur Praxis von Theorie*, ed. by Anselm Haverkamp and Dirk Mende (Frankfurt am Main: Suhrkamp, 2009), pp. 33–61.
19. Nicholls, *Myth*, p. 14.
20. Ibid. The Senatskommission was discontinued in 1966 but the idea of a conceptual history lived on in the publication of the thirteen-volume *Historisches Wörterbuch der Philosophie* (1971–2007).
21. Robert Savage, 'Translator's Afterword', in Hans Blumenberg, *Paradigms for a Metaphorology*, trans. by Robert Savage (Ithaca: Cornell University Press, 2010), pp. 133–46 (p. 139).
22. Blumenberg, *Paradigms*, p. 17.
23. See translators note number 1 in Heidegger, *Being and Time*, p. 97.
24. Martin Heidegger, *Being and Time*, trans. by John Macquarrie and Edward Robinson (New York: Harper Collins, 2008), pp. 97–98.
25. Anselm Haverkamp, 'Blumenberg in Davos: The Cassirer–Heidegger Controversy Reconsidered', *MLN*, 131.3 (2016), 738–53 (pp. 741, 747); Anselm Haverkamp, 'Editorisches Nachwort', in Hans Blumenberg, *Theorie der Unbegrifflichkeit* (Frankfurt am Main: Suhrkamp, 2007), pp. 115–19 (p. 115). See also Haverkamp, 'Skandalon'.
26. Ibid., p. 35.
27. Savage, 'Translator's Afterword', p. 140.
28. Blumenberg did, in fact, follow up the idea of an examination of the voyage metaphor in 1979 in *Shipwreck with a Spectator*.
29. Savage, 'Translator's Afterword', p. 140.
30. Blumenberg, *Paradigms*, p. 135.
31. Blumenberg, *Shipwreck*, p. 100.
32. Nicholls, *Myth*, p. 143.
33. Savage, 'Translator's Afterword', p. 139. On the theme of metaphor 'directing [our] attention to the roots of concept formation' we could also cite Rüdiger Zill, '"Substrukturen des Denkens": Grenzen und Perspektive einer Metapherngeschichte nach Hans Blumenberg', in

Begriffsgeschichte, Diskursgeschichte, Metapherngeschichte, ed. by Hans Erich Bödeker (Göttingen: Wallstein, 2002), pp. 209–58.
34. Petra Gehring, 'Metapher', in *Blumenberg lesen: Ein Glossar*, ed. by Robert Buch and Daniel Weidner (Berlin: Suhrkamp, 2014), pp. 201–13 (p. 201).
35. Hans Blumenberg, 'Beobachtungen an Metaphern', *Archiv für Begriffsgeschichte*, 15 (1971), 161–214 (p. 163). The translation is taken from Savage, 'Translator's Afterword', p. 138.
36. Blumenberg, *Paradigms*, pp. 1–2.
37. Though it does not presume to begin from Descartes, contemporary analytic philosophy of religion, particularly in a figure like Alvin Plantinga and the methodology he employs in *God and Other Minds*, undertakes this task. See Alvin Plantinga, *God and Other Minds* (London: Cornell University Press, 1967).
38. Nietzsche, 'On Truth and Lying', p. 150.
39. Blumenberg, *Paradigms*, pp. 3–4.
40. Gehring, 'Metapher', p. 201.
41. Blumenberg, *Paradigms*, p. 4.
42. Norman Friedman, 'symbol', *The Princeton Encyclopedia of Poetry and Poetics*, 4th edn (Princeton: Princeton University Press, 2012), pp. 1391–95.
43. Ibid.
44. Howard Caygill, *A Kant Dictionary* (Oxford: Blackwell, 1995), p. 360.
45. Ibid.
46. Immanuel Kant, *Critique of Judgement*, trans. by James Creed Meredith (Oxford: Oxford University Press, 2008), pp. 179–80.
47. John 1: 3–5 NRSV.
48. Blumenberg, *Shipwreck*, p. 82.
49. Hans Blumenberg, *Paradigmen zu einer Metaphorologie* (Frankfurt: Suhrkamp, 1998), p. 112.
50. Blumenberg, *Paradigms*, p. 79.
51. Ibid., p. 78.
52. Hans Blumenberg, 'Affinitäten und Dissonanzen', in *Ein mögliches Selbstverständnis* (Stuttgart: Reclam, 1997), pp. 161–68 (p. 167).
53. Haverkamp, 'Blumenberg', pp. 741, 747.
54. Nicholls, *Myth*, p. 99.
55. Blumenberg, 'Affinitäten', p. 162.
56. Haverkamp, 'Blumenberg', pp. 743–45.
57. Blumenberg, 'Affinitäten', pp. 164–65. Also see Nicholls, *Myth*, pp. 99–103 for an assessment of Blumenberg's view on the significance of Davos.
58. Savage, 'Translator's Afterword', p. 140.
59. Blumenberg, *Shipwreck*, p. 82.
60. Martin Heidegger, *The Principle of Reason*, trans. by Reginald Lilly (Indianapolis: Indiana University Press, 1996), p. 48.
61. Blumenberg, *Shipwreck*, p. 100.
62. Paul Ricoeur, *The Rule of Metaphor*, trans. by Robert Czerny (London: Routledge, 2003), p. 48.
63. Blumenberg, *Paradigms*, p. 14.
64. Hans Blumenberg, 'An Anthropological Approach to the Contemporary Significance of Rhetoric', in *After Philosophy: End or Transformation?*, ed. by Kenneth Baynes, James Bohman and Thomas McCarthy (Cambridge, MA: MIT Press, 1987), p. 430. Henceforth 'An Anthropological Approach'.
65. Nietzsche, 'On Truth and Lying', p. 143.
66. Blumenberg, 'Anthropological Approach', p. 433.
67. Hans Blumenberg, 'Unwahrwerden einer Metapher', Nachlass Hans Blumenberg, Deutsches Literaturarchiv Marbach.
68. 'WW XIII 368' is Blumenberg's abbreviation and seems to refer to an edition of Nietzsche's complete works. While the fragment gives us no clues as to the exact edition of Nietzsche's works that Blumenberg was using, the quotation comes from the fourth and final section of *Thus Spoke Zarathustra* and can found in Friedrich Nietzsche, *Werke in drei Bänden*, ed. by Karl Schlechta, 3 vols (Munich: Hanser, 1954), II, 277–561 (p. 526).

69. Martin Heidegger, 'The Question Concerning Technology', in *Basic Writings* (London: Routledge, 2010), pp. 333–35.
70. It bears noting the way Heidegger uses the term *Zeug* as a characterisation of things that we accept automatically as a part of the environment. Here, Blumenberg is making the case that technology, too, is something we accept automatically, unlike Heidegger's view that it obstructs our relation to Being.
71. Robert Savage suggests that in this essay we can see Blumenberg's fully developed view on the capacity of metaphor to 'come up with practical solutions to problems that cannot [...] be made to yield to rational insight' (Savage, 'Translator's Afterword', p. 145).
72. Hans Blumenberg, 'Lebenswelt und Technisierung unter Aspekten der Phänomenologie', in *Wirklichkeiten in denen wir leben* (Stuttgart: Reclam, 1981), pp. 7–54 (p. 35).
73. Henceforth referred to as *Crisis*.
74. David Carr, 'Translator's Introduction', in Edmund Husserl, *The Crisis of European Sciences and Transcendental Phenomenology* (Evanston: Northwestern University Press, 1970), pp. xv–xliii (pp. xxv–xxvii).
75. For context surrounding the influence of Husserl's thought on *Work on Myth*, see Nicholls, *Myth*, p. 103. For Blumenberg's own appropriation of the concept of the Life-world, see Hans Blumenberg, *Theorie der Lebenswelt*, ed. by Manfred Sommer (Berlin: Suhrkamp, 2010).
76. Dermot Moran, *Husserl's Crisis of European Sciences and Transcendental Phenomenology: An Introduction* (Cambridge: Cambridge University Press, 2012), p. 260.
77. Carr, 'Translator's Introduction', pp. xxv–xxvii.
78. Edmund Husserl, *The Crisis of European Sciences and Transcendental Phenomenology*, trans. by David Carr (Evanston: Northwestern University Press, 1970), p. 3.
79. Carr, 'Translator's Introduction', pp. xxxviii–xxxix.
80. Husserl, *Crisis*, p. 281.
81. Ibid., pp. 103–04.
82. Ibid., p. 104.
83. Ibid., p. 142.
84. Heidegger, *Being and Time*, pp. 31–35.
85. Husserl, *Crisis*, pp. 281–82.
86. Carr, 'Translator's Introduction', p. xl.
87. Blumenberg, 'Beobachtungen', p. 163.
88. Hans Blumenberg, 'Selbstverständlichkeit, Selbstaufrichtung, Selbstvergleich', *Theorie der Lebenswelt*, ed. by Manfred Sommer (Berlin: Suhrkamp, 2010), pp. 135–48, This is the translation given in Nicholls, *Myth*, p. 106.
89. Manfred Sommer, 'Nachwort des Herausgebers', in Hans Blumenberg *Theorie der Lebenswelt*, ed. by Manfred Sommer (Berlin: Suhrkamp, 2010), p. 243.
90. Nicholls, *Myth*, p. 13.
91. Ibid., p. 22.
92. Heike Kunz, 'Moment, God of the', *Religion Past and Present*, <http://dx.doi.org/10.1163/1877-5888_rpp_SIM_01286> [accessed 13 May 2020].
93. Blumenberg, 'Selbstverständlichkeit', pp. 138–39.
94. Ibid., p. 139.
95. Nicholls, *Myth*, pp. 22–23.
96. See Hans Blumenberg, *Work on Myth*, trans. by Robert M. Wallace (London: MIT Press, 1985), pp. 3–6.
97. Ibid., pp. 5–6. Emphasis added.
98. There is an echo here of Max Müller's thesis on metaphor's role in the creation of myth. While Blumenberg does not emphasise the forgetfulness of metaphor as Müller and Nietzsche do, the metaphoric name for a natural phenomenon is similar and is indeed echoed through several of the thinkers, such as Rousseau, whom we saw outlined in chapter 1.
99. Blumenberg, 'Selbstverständlichkeit', pp. 138–39.
100. Blumenberg, 'Anthropological Approach', p. 433.
101. Blumenberg, 'Selbstverständlichkeit', p. 135.

102. Ibid.
103. Paul Alsberg, *In Quest of Man: A Biological Approach to the Problem of Man's Place in Nature* (Oxford: Pergamon Press, 1970), p. 3.
104. Ibid., p. 51.
105. Nicholls, *Myth*, p. 111.
106. Ibid., pp. 111–12.
107. Blumenberg, 'Anthropological Approach', pp. 438–39.
108. Ibid., p. 430.
109. Ibid., p. 431. For the Nietzsche quotation see Friedrich Nietzsche, *Kritische Gesamtausgabe*, ed. by Giorgio Colli and Mazzino Montinari, 9 vols (Berlin and New York: De Gruyter, 1967), VII, 105.
110. Blumenberg, 'Anthropological Approach', p. 432.
111. Ibid., p. 433.
112. Ibid.
113. Ibid., p. 439.
114. Ibid., p. 433.
115. The English translation was the first publication of this text. The German edition was published in 2010 in *Theorie der Lebenswelt*. On the history of this text's publication see, Manfred Sommer, 'Editorische Notiz', in *Theorie der Lebenswelt*, ed. by Manfred Sommer (Berlin: Suhrkamp, 2010), pp. 248–50 (p. 249).
116. Hans Blumenberg, 'The Life-World and the Concept of Reality', in *Life-World and Consciousness: Essays for Aron Gurwitsch*, ed. by Lester E. Embree (Evanston: Northwestern University Press, 1972), pp. 443–44.
117. Ibid.

CHAPTER 5

Jacques Derrida and the Undecidability of Metaphoric Meaning

In the previous chapter, we saw Hans Blumenberg's pragmatic response to the Nietzschean crisis of metaphoric meaning. In this final chapter, we will see our second representative strand of European thinking on metaphor after Nietzsche, the relativising function, illustrated in the philosophy of Jacques Derrida. We have seen how Blumenberg's thinking represents the assertion that the human being as the metaphorical animal orients his or herself with metaphors via the ground of rhetorical consensus. We have also seen that conceptual systems are built through this metaphoric orientation. There is much in Derrida's philosophy that is like Blumenberg. However, Derrida's conclusion about our ability to orient ourselves with metaphor and to read Western conceptual history through metaphors is fundamentally different. For Derrida, metaphoric meaning is caught in an infinite semantic flux; for him, even if we think we are orienting ourselves with metaphor, metaphor is in fact orienting us. This position implies something that we will call a 'new semantics' of metaphor, which Derrida outlines in both 'White Mythology' (1971) and 'The *Retrait* of Metaphor' (1978), and which represents the relativising function of metaphor derived from the Nietzschean conception.

The task that we must set ourselves is to understand why the meaning of metaphor is ultimately undecidable in Derrida's philosophy and how this theoretical undecidability relates to the claim, as represented by Blumenberg, that metaphor provides social and historical orientation for cognition. Derrida asserts that whenever language is used, one must resort to 'some sort of figurative representation'[1] and that this results in both a surplus and a decay of meaning. Because of this surplus and decay of meaning, whether in rhetoric or in hermeneutics, we are ultimately unable to orient our understanding with metaphor.[2] This chapter will argue that while Derrida's assertion of the undecidability of metaphoric meaning opens up enormous hermeneutic possibilities, it also gives rise to a hermeneutic challenge.

Derrida's philosophy of metaphor does not account for metaphor's pragmatic function. Nor does it account for the use of metaphor in ideology. As we have seen earlier, in this book, we are viewing ideology as one of the symptoms of swift social and historical orientation. Thus, this chapter, beyond seeking to provide an overview of Derrida's philosophy of metaphor, also seeks to elucidate the hermeneutic limit of Derrida's philosophy of metaphor. This chapter will conclude that the theoretical undecidability of the meaning of metaphor that Derrida advocates is fundamentally different from the social and historical orientation that metaphor can provide. The very surplus and decay that Derrida outlines in his 'new semantics' is in fact precisely what generates the social and historical meaning with which we orient our understanding. As we have been arguing all along, the tension between metaphor's relativising function and its pragmatic function is inherent in the Nietzschean conception. The hermeneutic questions that Derrida's thought poses provide us with the perfect opportunity to bring this tension to the foreground in post-Nietzschean European philosophy. It also must be noted that we could portray the relativising function of metaphor in Derrida's philosophy less drastically and argue for a certain 'Neopragmatism' inherent in deconstruction, as Anselm Haverkamp has done.[3] However, for the purposes of this book it is useful to draw out the relativising tendencies in Derrida's thought to help us better understand the intellectual-historical development with which we are concerned.

But as we are transitioning from Blumenberg to Derrida, we need to pause and remind ourselves of the general intellectual-historical context of post-war France and the particularities of the French context that shaped the philosophical questions surrounding the post-Nietzschean concept of metaphor. We also need to remind ourselves of Derrida's biography, particularly of how Derrida's own experience, both as a Sephardic Jew in Vichy French Algeria and as an Algerian in post-war Parisian intellectual life, contributed significantly to his thesis of the undecidability of metaphoric meaning. Because our reflections on metaphor after Nietzsche have political implications, it is especially important to outline the political-historical contexts in which our chosen theorists were developing their ideas.

Derrida the French-Algerian Jew and Post-War French Philosophy

Practically at least, Derrida suffered less severely than Blumenberg at the hands of National Socialism. Unlike Blumenberg, Derrida was never interned. Nonetheless, Derrida's childhood in French Algeria during the Second World War was to have a profound effect on his relation to both philosophical questions about meaning as well as his feelings about the French language and French intellectual life. Jacques Derrida (1930–2004) was born in 1930 into a Sephardic Jewish family living in El Biar on the outskirts of Algiers in French Algeria. His was a colourful family, the father the director of a wine shipping business and his mother a passionate poker player. They were not particularly religious, attending synagogue only on major festivals.[4] As Algerian Jews, his family would have suddenly found themselves without French citizenship when Derrida was ten years old in 1940 due to the annulment of the Crémieux decree that had given Jews the opportunity to become French citizens.[5] As the situation intensified, Derrida was directly affected in 1942 when he was expelled from school and increasingly had the insult 'dirty Jew' thrown at him.[6] However, the Allied invasion of North Africa in November 1942 halted the quickly deteriorating situation. The yellow star of David armband was manufactured for Algerian Jews to wear, for example, but its distribution was blocked with the arrival of the Allied forces.[7]

However, this did not mean that things were particularly easy during Derrida's teenage years. While the Allied presence in wartime Algeria did halt worsening conditions, Jews were still persecuted under the Vichy regime. This was because the Vichy leadership was deferred to in the management of local matters, even though the official decrees of Nazi-inspired governments, such as that concerning the armband, were halted.[8] Living in occupied Algeria was also an anxious experience. Derrida recalls the frequent gunfire, bombing raids, and searchlights that caused him to 'tremble uncontrollably'.[9] He continued his schooling during the war in an improvised school set up by Jewish teachers.[10] Reflecting on his childhood, Derrida said that he was 'a sort of child on the margins of Europe, a child of the Mediterranean, who was neither simply French, nor simply African'.[11] He also maintained that 'he never felt fully at home in the French language'. Because the correct usage of French was administered from Paris, Derrida confessed to finding the language a colonial imposition. In this way, he found himself caught between two heritages as a 'Franco-Maghrebian'.[12] We shall see how the undecidability of his identity is reflected in the 'new semantics' of metaphor outlined later in this chapter.

This sense of being caught between two heritages as a child under the Vichy regime was exacerbated by the majority of Derrida's adult life being spent as a part of Parisian intellectual culture from his admission into the École Normale Supérieure in 1952 onwards.[13] Post-war French intellectual life in Paris was fraught with its own conflict between heritages. While there is truth to the common conception that 'Heidegger and structuralism can be said to be responsible [for the changes] in French philosophy during [the post-war period]', the influence of Heidegger was more bound up in the reassessment of phenomenology after the decline of the once dominant Sartrean interpretation of Heidegger.[14] In this context, Derrida could be described as a '"post-existentialist," navigating the phenomenological wilderness', as Edward Baring has so poetically put it.[15]

Jean-Paul Sartre's *Being and Nothingness* (1943) was a highly successful appropriation of Heidegger in which Heidegger's philosophy was omnipresent.[16] Sartre translated Heidegger's key term *Dasein* as 'réalité-humaine' (human-reality), which gave a distinctly humanist interpretation to Heidegger's thought after the war.[17] However, in the same year that *Being and Nothingness* took French culture by storm, communist pamphlets were accusing Sartre, who was a member of the Communist Party himself, of 'being a disciple of the Nazi philosopher Martin Heidegger'.[18] However, this initial resistance seems to have been limited, in part due to the 'all too readable' and 'sensational passages' that circulated in the Parisian cafés.[19] Derrida himself had one of his first encounters with Heidegger's thought while reading *Being and Nothingness* as a student in *hypokhâgne*, the pre-university preparatory course in the French system, and up until 1952, like many in his generation, he considered himself an existentialist.[20]

But by the time Derrida was admitted to the École Normale Supérieure in 1952, the Parisian intellectual landscape was undergoing a sea change. As the editor of the French journal *Les Temps Modernes*, Sartre took it upon himself after the

Nazi occupation had ended to publish a debate on Heidegger's thought, the first instalment appearing in 1946. And while Sartre's celebrity status continued, after his 1946 lecture 'Existentialism is a Humanism', he moved away from in-depth philosophical reflections that were engaged with Heidegger's philosophy.[21]

Heidegger himself attempted to distance himself from Sartre's humanistic interpretation of his work, declaring that 'every humanism remains metaphysical' in 1947's 'Letter on Humanism'.[22] By the time Derrida was admitted to the ENS, groups that formerly considered themselves existentialists, notably Christian and communist groups, had stopped referring to Sartre and his centrality in interpreting Heidegger began to diminish.[23] This led to the re-reading, by what was to become the 1968 generation, of both Heidegger and Husserl. By 1954, when Derrida had completed his dissertation, references to Sartre in Derrida's works had declined. Instead Derrida went back to Heidegger's teacher Husserl, writing his dissertation on Husserl under the title, *The Problem of Genesis in Husserl's Philosophy*.[24] This is important for us because it highlights that a statement like 'Heidegger and structuralism can be said to be responsible [for the changes] in French philosophy during [the post-war period]', is true only because it was an era in which Heidegger was undergoing a reinterpretation in French intellectual life.[25] Another wave of this reinterpretation came in the early 1960s via structuralism.[26]

Structuralism hit a highpoint in French intellectual life in the 1960s.[27] As we have seen in the introduction, for Claude Lévi-Strauss, the mental structures of the 'savage mind' are deepened by *imagines mundi* (world pictures) and, because of this, 'savage thought' can be said to be 'analogical thought'.[28] We have cited that Lévi-Strauss's concern with 'analogical thought' provides a structuralist parallel to our preoccupation with metaphor as fundamental to cognition rather than as incidental to it. Lévi-Strauss's concern with structure of course had evolved from the reception of Ferdinand de Saussure's *Course in General Linguistics*. To remind the reader, Saussure oriented the question of language away from a specific question that was purely 'the business of a handful of specialists', considering only, for example, the history of language, or its phonetic qualities, and argued for the 'importance of linguistics for culture in general'.[29] To achieve the study of a 'general linguistics', Saussure argued that 'the linguist must take the study of linguistic *structure* as his primary concern, and relate all other manifestations of language to it'.[30] As Peter Steiner, Henryk Baran, Conor Klamann and Jonathan Culler have pointed out, in French intellectual life the application of the study of linguistic structure, which came to be known as structuralism, 'began as a revolt against the literary, historical and biographical criticism that dominated the French university orthodoxy'.[31] One of the results of this was the privileging of a synchronic study of language over a diachronic study of language. For structuralism, an implication of synchronic study meant 'treating language as a formal system of interrelated elements functioning at a particular time [that take] precedence over diachronic study'.[32]

We have seen the distinction between synchronic and diachronic studies of language in the introduction, and Derrida's use of structural linguistics to analyse metaphor is part of what distinguishes him from Blumenberg, who, it could be argued, has a more diachronic (which is to say historical) approach. As we have seen, Blumenberg's work on a metaphorology began as a part of a history of concepts. That is not to say, however, that Derrida was uninterested in etymology. On the contrary, it is one of his abiding interests. However, it does remind us that his engagement with structural linguistics was a break from the diachronic approach and was in step with this revolt against the traditions of the French university system.[33] Blumenberg's analysis of metaphor, on the other hand, does not offer an explicit engagement with a linguistic method.

When Derrida was first introduced to structural linguistics is unclear, but we do know that his writing prior to 1964 continued to focus on phenomenology, working with figures like Jean Wahl and Paul Ricoeur while he was a teaching assistant at the Sorbonne after finishing his dissertation. However, in 1964, Derrida took up a role at the ENS, which was what Edward Baring calls 'a structuralist lion's den'.[34] This was only two years before Derrida presented his famous critique of structuralism, 'Structure, Sign and Play in the Discourse of the Human Sciences' at John Hopkins University in 1966 and only three years before the publication of *Of Grammatology* (1967). So, while America's first encounter was with Derrida the 'post-structuralist', it was a relatively recent development for Derrida himself and, to a certain extent, a theoretical world that was still in transition.

An Escape from the History of Metaphysics with a History of Metaphors

A common understanding of Derrida's position on metaphor is that one can understand the history of Western metaphysical thinking through the history of various metaphors. This is a position not so far away from Blumenberg's. In the case of Derrida, this common understanding comes from the initial anglophone reception of an essay entitled 'Freud and the Scene of Writing' (1967). The essay is a reflection on how themes in Freud's psychoanalysis, such as sublimation, relate to writing. In it, Derrida makes his now famous connection between sublimation and the term 'supplement', which also appears in *Of Grammatology* (1967) and 'Plato's Pharmacy' (1972). For Derrida, writing as a supplement of speech is a prime example of the connection he sees between sublimation and supplement. In the essay, there comes a point where he relates the Western conception of writing to the history of metaphysics. In this discussion, the topic of metaphor arises. Derrida writes:

> The history of metaphysics, like the history of the West, is the history of [various] metaphors and metonymies. Its matrix [...] is the determination of being as *presence* in all the senses of this word. It would be possible to show that all the names related to fundamentals, to principles, or to the center have always designated the constant of a presence — *eidos, arché, telos, energeia, ousia* (essence, existence, substance, subject) *aletheia*, transcendentality, consciousness, or conscience, God, man, and so forth.[35]

The original French version of this essay appears in *L'écriture et la différence* (1967), later republished as *Writing and Difference* (1978). But the quotation makes its first appearance in English in Gayatri Chakravorty Spivak's 'Translator's Preface' to *Of*

Grammatology (1976). Spivak reads this fragment as a succinct articulation of Derrida's position on metaphysics. Spivak writes that 'Derrida uses the word "metaphysics" very simply as shorthand for any science of presence'.[36] When Spivak describes the term 'metaphysics' in Derrida's thought as 'shorthand for any science of presence' and then links it to the above quotation, she makes an implicit connection between metaphor and presence. Derrida writes that 'the history of metaphysics [...] is the history of these metaphors and metonymies. Its matrix [...] is the determination of being as *presence* in all the senses of this word.' This passage could then read: 'the matrix of the history of various metaphors is the determination of being as *presence*'. What might this mean? We can of course see the collapse between metaphor and ontology reflected in Nietzsche. It is no surprise then that Spivak goes on to explain Derrida's 'shorthand for any science of presence' in relation to Nietzsche's philosophy of metaphor because, in Spivak's words, 'Derrida's relationship to Nietzsche is so inescapable.'[37]

Spivak's view is that Nietzsche's suspicion of truth, meaning, the concept, the primary signified, and Being is shared by Derrida. Therefore, philosophical discourse is something to be deciphered or interpreted.[38] What is the shared suspicion between Nietzsche and Derrida? It is the value of truth itself, and we have seen Nietzsche outline this suspicion in 'On Truth and Lying'. Spivak is asserting that, like Nietzsche, Derrida believes we can read the history of the philosophical discourses concerning truth through the history of figurative discourses about truth. Spivak continues in the preface to follow Sarah Kofman's reading of Nietzsche in asserting that a figurative discourse that creates truth claims emerges from a fundamental drive that Nietzsche will later call the will to power. The significance of the link between metaphor and the will to power, Spivak claims, is that, 'without Nietzsche the "question" of the text would have never erupted'.[39] Why? Because the will to power is a process of interpretation and the process of interpretation, without a clear truth claim to have recourse to, is to assign a figurative value to the world.[40]

What is Spivak claiming here? She is claiming that Derrida follows Nietzsche in viewing the history of philosophy as a history of interpretation and that philosophy's various interpretations can be read in the history of metaphors. For Spivak, interpretation itself brings meaning into language. Therefore, Spivak is claiming that, for Derrida, this inescapable fact of interpretation that Nietzsche presents us with brings the question of the text to the foreground of Western philosophy. This is vital for Derrida, Spivak claims, because the values and prejudices within philosophy are seen in the history of metaphor and therefore metaphor is a tool that can lay bare the prejudices and values within philosophical concepts. This would be to view Derrida's thinking on metaphor as akin to aspects of Nietzsche's thinking in *Beyond Good and Evil* or *On the Genealogy of Morality*.

What follows from this is the second common perception concerning Derrida and metaphor. This second perception is that if one can 'lay bare' the history of the values and prejudices within the metaphysical tradition, one can overcome or escape metaphysics. Therefore, on this view metaphor would function as a tool in the *destruction* of the metaphysical tradition. This is one way in which Derrida's term 'deconstruction' is read in conjunction with metaphor. Julia Kristeva popularised this conception about Derrida's thinking in an interview on 3 June 1968. Opening with a question about the field of semiology, she asked Derrida about how language could 'serve as the basis for a notation attempting to escape metaphysics'.[41] This characterisation is not limited to Kristeva alone. Spivak herself, in the 'Translator's Preface' to *Of Grammatology*, sets out a number of different ways in which Derrida's philosophy can be seen as a call to abandon the traditional language of metaphysics. In one section she writes: 'Derrida, then, is asking us to change certain habits of mind: the authority of the text is provisional, the origin is a trace; contradicting logic, we must learn to use and erase our language at the same time.'[42] While we can certainly agree with Spivak that reading Derrida demands one to confront one's 'habits of mind', we must point out that the call to 'contradict logic' and 'learn to use and erase our language at the same time' shares Kristeva's presupposition that there could be a 'basis for a notation attempting to escape metaphysics'.[43]

Finally, we could cite Jürgen Habermas's collection of lectures, *Philosophical Discourses of Modernity* (1985). While Kristeva and Spivak seem eager to escape metaphysics, Habermas is critical of this tendency in Derrida's thought. In a lecture on Derrida from the *Philosophical Discourses* he suggests that one of Derrida's concerns is a response to Heidegger's philosophy through linguistics. Habermas notes that Heidegger never formally studied linguistics or language in depth, so part of the power of Derrida's critical relationship with Heidegger comes from applying the linguistics of his time to the problems in Heidegger's thought.[44] In an attempt to unpack why structural linguistics lends itself to a critique of Heidegger, Habermas characterises Derrida's major work, *Of Grammatology*, as something which recommends itself as a guide for the critique of metaphysics because it goes to the roots of phonetic writing, that is, of writing that copies the sound of words; and this is not only coextensive but also equiprimordial with metaphysical thought.[45]

In the end, Habermas reads this critique of the origin of metaphysical thought as a type of anti-foundationalism.[46] However, whether one is eager to escape metaphysical thinking, such as Kristeva and Spivak, or whether one is critical of such an anti-foundational tendency, such as Habermas, we find that an escape from the metaphysical tradition is impossible, according to Derrida. To think that an escape from metaphysics would be possible would also be to understand one of Derrida's most famous concepts, deconstruction, as 'destruction'. But from the earliest appearances of the term 'deconstruction', Derrida makes clear that one should not equate it with 'destruction'.

Deconstruction and Metaphor

While Derrida's philosophy may certainly be 'asking us to change certain habits of mind', Spivak is incorrect in writing that Derrida wants us to 'contradict logic [and] learn to use and erase our language at the same time'.[47] As we shall see, the concepts of use and erasure are quite important in Derrida's philosophy of metaphor; however, the call for *us* to 'use and erase our language at the same time', as it is outlined by Spivak, would be an active *destruction* of metaphysical logic on the part of the philosopher. 'As we have previously stated, 'deconstruction' is not the same as 'destruction'. This is, in fact, the first thesis that emerges in Derrida's lecture series from 1964 to 1965 on Heidegger. When Derrida was appointed to the ENS in Paris in 1964, he was first appointed to the post of *agrégé-répétiteur*, a professor who prepared students for their *agrégation* examination, the highly competitive, week-long exam in the French system for both civil service and public education.[48] Because of this post, Derrida was free to choose his lectures' subject matter.[49] In the first lecture, Derrida takes pains to make his students aware that Heidegger's destruction of the history of ontology is not an annihilation or refutation of the history of ontology. Here we find Derrida's interpretation of Heidegger's move from metaphysics towards the existential analytic, an interpretation that still reads quite radically today. Derrida writes:

> As to this notion of destruction, a few remarks are necessary. Destruction does not mean annihilation, annulment, rejection into the outer darkness of philosophical meaning. It does not even mean critique or contestation or refutation within a theory of the knowledge of Being. The point is not to say that all the thinkers of the tradition were wrong or committed an unfortunate error that would need to be corrected [...] In destroying the history of ontology, Heidegger never refutes. Refutation in the sense in which it can be understood in the sciences or in common parlance has no meaning for thinking [...] the concept of refutation belongs — implicitly — to an anti-historical metaphysics of truth.[50]

What clearly emerges here is that Derrida sees in Heidegger's thought the breakdown of traditional notions, like refutation, within the history of philosophy. As we have seen in chapter 3, Heidegger's destruction of ontology is at the same time a critique of the 'metaphysics of truth'. Therefore, if destruction were simply to mean a philosophical refutation, in the traditional sense, it would play right back into the metaphysics of truth that Heidegger is critiquing. Nietzsche of course springs to mind when we think of a critique of the 'metaphysics of truth'. As we have seen in the last section, scholars like Spivak have pointed to Derrida's Nietzschean connection and suggested that metaphor could be viewed as a tool in such a critique. But it is clear from Derrida's reading of Heidegger here that it is not that straightforward. Derrida thinks Heidegger is up to something other than a simple destruction of metaphysics. This is the first aspect of deconstruction. Deconstruction does not destroy but elucidates the boundaries and limits of traditional philosophical oppositions and terminology. It then poses the question 'what other ideas might be occurring in an author's text?' This question also presents itself to us here: if the destruction of the history of ontology is not a simple refutation of that history, what else might Heidegger be up to?

Derrida walks his students through another form of refutation that they may be familiar with, that of Hegel. To remind the reader, in Hegelian dialectics, refutation is not the proving wrong of a proposition but instead a negative exclusion of a past philosophy in the movement towards synthesis. Derrida asks: is Heidegger's destruction or refutation of the history of ontology more like this? After a complicated exegesis of Hegel and refutation, Derrida concludes that 'the *Destruction* of the history of ontology is not a *refutation* even in this Hegelian sense'.[51] Derrida finally concludes that Heidegger's destruction of the history of ontology is in fact a 'deconstruction'. This is one of the first appearances of this term in Derrida's work.[52] Derrida writes:

> Heideggerian destruction is neither the critique of some error, nor the simply negative exclusion of some past of philosophy. It is a destruction — that is, a deconstruction, a de-structuration, the shaking that is necessary to bring out the structures, the strata, the system of deposits. As Heidegger said in the passage from a moment ago, sedimentations of the ontological tradition — sedimentations that have, according to a certain necessity, always covered over the naked question of being — covered over a nudity that in fact never unveiled itself as such.[53]

As we can see, deconstruction makes its appearance as a descriptive term for Heidegger's destruction of the history of ontology. It is the 'shaking that is necessary to bring out structures, the strata, the system of deposits'.[54] It is true that this brilliantly clear description of Derrida's reading of Heidegger is simply an early formulation of the term 'deconstruction' that will go through later developments. As the editor of these lectures, Thomas Dutoit notes,

> the very term *deconstruction* [...] is several times put aside here in favour of other translations such as 'solicitation' and 'shaking up' which will, with a few exceptions, not be retained to describe Derrida's thinking. It is only much later Derrida will lay claim to the word *deconstruction* and devote many developments to it.[55]

However, while Dutoit is rightly cautious to attribute the characteristics of this early appearance of deconstruction to Derrida's later thought, there is an aspect of this early characterisation that does capture something significant about the way we see deconstruction in operation throughout Derrida's work. What else are Derrida's famous readings of Plato, Rousseau, Nietzsche, Saussure, Marx, and other figures from the history of philosophy, but a 'shaking that is necessary to bring out structures the strata, the system of deposits'? It is characteristic of Derrida's philosophy as a whole, and particularly, as we shall see, of the way he uses metaphors in philosophy, to elucidate the 'sedimentations of the ontological tradition — sedimentations that have, according to a certain necessity, always covered over the naked question of being'.[56] If we extract this description out of Derrida's reading of Heidegger, we can say that the elucidation of the boundaries and limits of traditional concepts reveals to us two things.

On the one hand, it reveals to us the 'sediments' of the metaphysical tradition. Metaphysical reasoning leaves a trace. It leaves a trace of ways of constructing concepts, based on oppositions, that are built into concepts and language. Deconstruction reveals this. On the other hand, deconstruction reveals 'naked questions' that the sediments of the ontological tradition have covered over. From this early glimpse into Derrida's use of the term, we can conclude that deconstruction is the elucidation of the limits of traditional concepts and then the revelation of the metaphysical traces of those concepts, followed by the uncovering of the questions that those metaphysical traces have covered over. Deconstruction, in this early form, is a way of sifting through the history of philosophy to find the ways in which concepts are oriented. As we have seen outlined earlier, Derrida asserts that metaphors and metaphysical concepts are intertwined to such an extent that we cannot abandon one without the other.

So, from this understanding of deconstruction, the tradition that asserts that, with an attention to metaphor, we can see the 'sediments' of the metaphysical tradition and the other questions that those 'sediments' have covered over, is correct. However, the line we are drawing is a clear distinction, if one can say that in relation to Derrida's philosophy, between destruction and elucidation. In this book we are asserting that metaphor elucidates the sediments of the metaphysical tradition in a deconstructive mode of critique; it does not destroy them or provide escape from them.[57] We have gone to such lengths to clarify the relationship between deconstruction and metaphor because we must clarify the difference between metaphor's *function* in Derrida's thought and a *concept* of metaphor in Derrida's thought. In the case of Nietzsche, we have asserted that while Nietzsche certainly does critique propositional truth with metaphor in 'On Truth and Lying' he also fundamentally shifts the Western conception of metaphor. To see how Derrida represents the relativising function of metaphor in Nietzsche's thought, we need to see Derrida's thinking on metaphor as not simply one way of 'performing a deconstruction' or, to use Spivak's words, of 'learning to use and erase our language at the same time'.[58]

If deconstruction is a way of sifting through the history of philosophy to elucidate the ways in which concepts are oriented, metaphor is an inescapable companion on this journey but not a companion that seeks to destroy the history of philosophy. To view metaphor through the lens of what it can *do* for philosophy still addresses the problem of metaphor in terms of function rather than viewing it through the conceptualisation of metaphor itself. In this way, Spivak's idea of learning to use and erase language at the same time is simply the inversion of Cicero's orator, who, as we saw in chapter 1, strives for the most truthlike use of language in order to persuade listeners of the truth. But this is not the case for Derrida. We can ultimately never 'perform a deconstruction' for this would be to impose a dialectic onto the history of philosophy and thus to fall back into the very 'determinability' that Derrida is attempting to move away from with a new conception of metaphor. Therefore, while the common conception that we might have of Derrida and metaphor in the form of Spivak's 'Translator's Preface' to *Of Grammatology* is a helpful entry to discussion, it does not ultimately get us any closer to a new conception of metaphor but stays in the realm of metaphor's function. We also do not get any closer to a new conception of metaphor to say that in Derrida's thought we are escaping metaphysics and entering the realm of poetic revelation. Derrida is not trying to recall to the Western tradition the revelatory power of metaphor that is in some hidden primordial space underneath concepts. This would be similar to the thesis we saw implied in Ricoeur's thought in chapter 4 and Derrida does not read Heidegger in the same way.

In fact, we see that far from being an escape to the realm of poetic revelation or a functional tool to destroy the metaphysical tradition, the undecidability of metaphoric meaning means that it is incapable of 'serving as the basis for a notation attempting to escape metaphysics'.[59] When Kristeva asks about the possibility of an escape from metaphysics, Derrida answers: 'I do not believe, that someday it will be possible simply to escape metaphysics.'[60] To understand the relevance of Derrida's reply for a conception of metaphor, we can view this reply in conjunction with a statement from Geoffrey Bennington in his book *Jacques Derrida* (1991). Bennington admits that it is tempting to place Derrida on one side of a tradition that 'not only demands the right to metaphor but recalls the austere conceptual tradition to *its* own metaphorical truth'. This is because '[Derrida] appears to play metaphor against concept'.[61] However, as Bennington points out, an escape from metaphysics by 'recalling the conceptual tradition to *its* own metaphorical truth'[62] is impossible because 'any attempt to exceed metaphysics which appeals to the concept of metaphor to do so can only fail, because this concept is an essentially metaphysical concept'.[63] The first place we see this clearly laid out in is in Derrida's classic essay on metaphor, 'White Mythology' (1971).

Metaphor is a Metaphysical Concept

The title of Derrida's essay, 'White Mythology', is a reference to metaphysics. Metaphysics is the white mythology in that it is the 'white man's' mythology, and it is both determined by and determines the long history of metaphors that are used in its construction.[64] On the opening page of 'White Mythology', Derrida frames his theme by suggesting that metaphors in philosophical discourse 'engrave themselves' on the text of philosophy. Here we might think of Blumenberg's concept of the absolute metaphor such as light as a metaphor for truth or the book of nature. But Derrida's interest in philosophical language is more general. He writes that, 'metaphor seems to involve the usage of philosophical language in its entirety, nothing less than the usage of so-called natural language *in* philosophical discourse, that is, the usage of natural language *as* philosophical language'.[65] So rather than concern himself with key or absolute metaphors, such as the book of nature, Derrida's concern seems to be the metaphoric basis of *all* philosophical language. He says that he sees this metaphoric basis in the 'usage of natural language *as* philosophical language'. The term natural language is often used to describe the natural evolution of a particular language such as English and therefore, just as we saw Gustav Gerber proposing in chapter 2, Derrida seems to be describing the metaphoric basis of all human language. If this is the case, then philosophy cannot help but use metaphor in its creation of metaphysical conceptions.

But as we move further into 'White Mythology' we quickly see that it is not simply the metaphorical origin of metaphysical concepts that concerns Derrida, but his thesis that metaphor itself is a metaphysical concept, when he writes: 'metaphor remains, in all its essential characteristics, a classical philosopheme, a metaphysical concept'.[66] If this is the case, how would we provide a history of metaphor in philosophy? In response to this question, Derrida states that a 'general metaphorology of philosophy' is doomed to fail.[67] He then goes on to write: 'this question has never been answered with a systematic treatise, doubtless not an insignificant fact'.[68] This would suggest to us that, besides the lack of archival evidence, even if Derrida may have heard of Hans Blumenberg, he certainly was not aware of the publication in 1960 of *Paradigms for a Metaphorology*. However, it is important to note that Derrida's term in the original French, *métaphorologie*, is the same term used in the French translation of *Paradigms for a Metaphorology*.[69] Thus, even if he is unaware of Blumenberg's project, the intellectual concept is similar. In the essay 'Metaphorologie zweiten Grades. Unbegrifflichkeit, Vorformen der Idee', Anselm Haverkamp notes this passage of 'White Mythology', but dismisses Derrida's rejection of a metaphorology as insignificant.[70] However, in this book, we find Derrida's ignorance of Blumenberg's project essential. It highlights the different aspects of Nietzsche's conception of metaphor as represented by each thinker.

To assert the impossibility of a metaphorology in Derrida's thought is a markedly different position from that of Dirk Mende who, as we saw in the introduction, asserts that Derrida's philosophy provides the possibility of performing an analysis of discourse with a metaphorology. Mende writes:

> Derridas und Blumenbergs Metaphorologien, so wie ich sie rekonstruiere, kommen darin überein, dass sie ihre Überlegungen zu einem nachmetaphysischen Metaphernbegriff zu einer Theorie diskursanalytischer Archäologie weiter entwickeln und damit den engeren Rahmen einer Theorie der Metapher übersteigen.
>
> [Derrida's and Blumenberg's metaphorologies, as I am reconstructing them, come to an understanding in that they develop their thinking on a post-metaphysical concept of metaphors into a theory of discourse-analytical archaeology, thus exceeding the narrower framework of a theory of metaphor.][71]

However, Mende's position is untenable when one looks closely at Derrida's description of the impossibility of a 'métaphorologie générale de la philosophie' (general metaphorology of philosophy):

> Instead of venturing into the prolegomena to some future metaphorics, let us rather attempt to recognize in principle the condition for the impossibility of such a project. In its most impoverished, most abstract form, the limit would be the following: metaphor remains, in all its essential characteristics a classical philosopheme, a metaphysical concept. It is therefore enveloped in the field that a general metaphorology of philosophy would seek to dominate. Metaphor has been issued from a network of philosophemes which themselves correspond to tropes or to figures, and these philosophemes are contemporaneous to or in systematic solidarity with these tropes or figures. This stratum of 'tutelary' tropes, the layer of 'primary' philosophemes [...] cannot be dominated. It cannot dominate itself, cannot be dominated by what it itself has engendered, has made to grow on its own soil, supported on its own base. Therefore, it gets 'carried away' each time that one of its products — here, the concept of metaphor —attempts in vain to include under its own law the totality of the field to which the product belongs.[72]

Here we see Derrida come as close to open war with Blumenberg as one who does not name another can. In Derrida's view, a 'métaphorologie générale de la philosophie' (general metaphorology of philosophy) would seek to dominate the field of metaphysics, but this is impossible because metaphor remains a metaphysical concept. Why is it a metaphysical concept? Because the distinctions through which we understand the traditional, Aristotelian conception of metaphor are metaphysical. If we reflect on the fact that metaphor is traditionally understood as a device of figurative language that operates in contrast to literal language, we can see the echoes of metaphysical distinctions such as sensible and supersensible. As Derrida will later write, 'everything, in the theory of metaphor, that is coordinate to this system of distinctions or at least to its principle, seems to belong to the great immobile chain of Aristotelian ontology'.[73] But if we reflect on the fact that, in this essay, Derrida is concerned with the metaphorical basis of all philosophical language, then 'the system of distinctions [that] belong to the great immobile chain of Aristotelian ontology' are in turn metaphorical. The cycle of metaphor to concept continues *ad infinitum*. We see this when Derrida asserts that the concept of metaphor grows out of a network of philosophical concepts that each in turn have their own metaphoric basis.[74]

This is the first moment of a clear point of departure between Blumenberg's and Derrida's conceptions of metaphor. But even though Derrida takes a different position on the possibility of a metaphorology, the emphasis of what a project like a metaphorology might show us is fundamentally different for Blumenberg. For Blumenberg, even if we conceptualise metaphor itself metaphysically, it does not matter whether such a conceptualisation could escape metaphysics or the endless cycle of metaphysics creating metaphorical distinctions and vice versa. Instead, for Blumenberg, the use of metaphor itself shows us something about conceptual thinking that is fundamentally different from metaphysics. Thus, a metaphorology would show us the use of metaphors within the history of concepts. The reason it makes sense to look at the use of metaphors is that they achieve something semantically in history and society that escapes the clutches of theorisation. But even if the emphasis is different, Derrida emphatically rejects the attempt to provide a metaphorology, because such a project would lapse back into the endless cycle described above. The ground from which we could judge the meaning of metaphor gets, as Derrida writes, 'carried away'.[75]

The fact that the ground by which we could judge the meaning of metaphor gets 'carried away' is where we arrive at Derrida's significance for the post-Nietzschean conception. It is also the reason why the common perceptions of Derrida's thesis on metaphor, such as one's ability to read the history of metaphysics through metaphors, can mask this deeper thesis about the undecidability of metaphoric meaning. If we cannot speak about metaphor without using metaphor, then, Derrida asserts that 'there is no access to the *usure* of a linguistic phenomenon without giving it some figurative representation'.[76]

Usure as a Metaphor for Metaphor

The word *usure* is critical for assessing Derrida's 'new semantics' of metaphor. It is one of Derrida's metaphors for metaphor. As Clive Cazeaux reminds us, 'Derrida adopts a more "embodied" or "performative" approach to language, allowing a structuralist thesis on the differential nature of meaning to reveal itself in his writing in the form of word play, association, and the revivification of metaphors'.[77] We see that Derrida does indeed engage in word play when we recall that the literal meaning of *usure* in French is simply wear and tear, but that it also has broader and older meanings including, 'usury, the acquisition of too much interest, and using up, deterioration through usage'.[78] We shall see that this position suggests that, rather than an intentional use and erasure of language, the everyday use of language creates a self-erasure of meaning. Metaphysical conceptions deconstruct themselves as do the meanings of metaphors. This is ultimately why one could not then use metaphor as a tool, as Spivak would like us to, to deconstruct the history of the West. Instead, we see Derrida arguing for a new understanding of the semantics of metaphor.

Therefore, the first part of Derrida's 'new semantics' stands on the Nietzschean-like assumption that all linguistic phenomena are, on some level, metaphoric to the extent that we do not perceive their limits. In this way, Derrida continues the tradition of a cognitive relativism that we first saw in Gustav Gerber's philosophy and then we saw appropriated by Nietzsche. In chapter 2, we saw how metaphor generates a semantic relativism at the very origin of cognition because transference happens, according to Nietzsche, on the level of perception. In holding to this position, Derrida's conclusion is that, if all language is metaphor, then metaphor shows up repeatedly in language *ad infinitum* as 'a progressive erosion, a regular semantic loss, an uninterrupted exhausting of the primitive meaning: an empirical abstraction without extraction from its own native soil'. Because of this, Derrida thinks the term *usure* is an appropriate metaphor for metaphor itself.[79]

To view metaphor simply through its history, a history that Derrida calls 'a regular semantic loss [...] of the primitive meaning', does not account for the unique semantics that occur when a metaphor is used. To understand this, we need to look at the conception of metaphor itself and hence Derrida frames this conception through the metaphor of *usure*. Derrida writes: 'The concept of *usure* belongs not to a narrow historico-theoretical configuration, but more surely to the concept of metaphor itself, and to the long metaphysical sequence that it determines or that determines it.'[80] The first thing we see in this quotation is that to employ *usure* as a metaphor for the concept of metaphor tells us something not just about what metaphor *does*, metaphor's function, but rather about what metaphor *is*, a conception of metaphor. The second thing we see is that in employing *usure* as a conception of metaphor, Derrida is explicitly moving away from a 'historico-theoretical configuration' of metaphor such as we might see in eighteenth-century thinkers like Rousseau and Vico or even in nineteenth-century thinkers like Max Müller.[81] Derrida is not looking to find the metaphorical truth hidden beneath concepts. As Bennington points out in his book *Jacques Derrida*,

> There is, however, a whole tradition which would like to recall philosophy to its forgotten truth in metaphor. It is important not to go wrong here, for Derrida himself has very often been assimilated to this ('artistic') tradition, and this is false [...] This other tradition not only demands the right to metaphor, but recalls the austere conceptual tradition to *its* own metaphorical truth. Thus it is argued that all philosophical concepts have etymological roots in the sensory world [...] if one transcribes a philosophical sentence into its 'true meaning' [...] [the result] makes philosophical discourse look like an oriental myth, unmasks the philosophical imposture which fails to understand that its *logos* is only a *mythos* ('the white mythology') among others, but which arbitrarily and violently attempts to impose as Reason itself. Philosophical discourse, in its apparent seriousness, would then be merely forgotten or worn-out metaphors, a particularly gray and sad fable, mystified in proposing itself as the very truth. One can see how tempting such a reading can be for a critique of philosophy from the human sciences or from literature [...] any attempt to exceed metaphysics which appeals to the concept of metaphor to do so can only fail, because this concept is an essentially metaphysical concept.[82]

But Bennington points out that it is essential to not assimilate Derrida into the tradition that would attempt to 'recall philosophy to its forgotten truth in metaphor.'[83] This reading fails, Bennington maintains, because 'any attempt to exceed metaphysics which appeals to the concept of metaphor to do so can only fail, because this concept is an essentially metaphysical concept'.[84]

Metaphor and Origin

Derrida highlights his break from a 'historico-theoretical configuration' of metaphor by drawing on an example from *The Garden of Epicurus* by the French novelist Anatole France. The Garden of Epicurus is of course a historic garden outside Athens that was owned by Epicurus, used by his followers, became the centre for Epicurean philosophy and was passed to Diogenes upon Epicurus's death. However, throughout the history of Western thought, the Garden of Epicurus has also been used as a symbol for Epicurean philosophy.[85] In his novel of the same name from 1894, France puts a series of essays and meditations into the mouths of various characters, and it is one of these that bears the subtitle 'or the language of metaphysics' from which Derrida picks his example.[86] Derrida suggests that there is an implicit logic in this example, and he wants to use it to reflect on his theme about the *usure* of metaphor in philosophy.[87] The scene is a dialogue between Aristos and Polyphilos. Derrida explains to us that two interlocutors are exchanging views on how, in metaphysical concepts, 'sensory figures are sheltered and used up [...] appearing imperceptible'. Derrida suggests that the two interlocutors feel that 'abstract notions always hide a sensory figure'.[88] Then in their discussion Polyphilos uses a rather startling analogy that Derrida takes as the focal point of his argument:

> Polyphilos: It was just a reverie. I was thinking how the Metaphysicians, when they make a language for themselves, are like [...] knife grinders, who instead of knives and scissors, should put medals and coins to the grindstone to efface the exergue, the value and the head. When they have worked away till nothing

is visible in their crown-pieces, neither King Edward, the Emperor William, nor the Republic, they say: 'These pieces have nothing either English, German or French about them; we have freed them from all limits of time and space; they are not worth five shillings anymore; they are of an inestimable value, and their exchange value is extended indefinitely.' They are right in speaking thus. By this needy knife-grinder's activity words are changed from a physical to a metaphysical acceptation. It is obvious that they lose in the process; what they gain by it is not so immediately apparent.[89]

The passage bears a striking similarity to Nietzsche's 'mobile army of metaphors' passage in 'On Truth and Lying' and while we will return to these similarities in a moment, Derrida is interested in the apparent 'integrity' of the original virtue of the sensory image in this passage. He writes that:

Polyphilos seems anxious to save the integrity of capital, or rather, before the accumulation of capital, to save the natural wealth and original virtue of the sensory image, which is deflowered and deteriorated by the history of the concept. Thereby he supposes — and this is a classical motif, a commonplace of the eighteenth century — that a purity of sensory language could have been in circulation at the origin of language, and that the *etymon* of a primitive sense always remains determinable, however hidden it may be; this etymologism interprets degradation as the passage from the physical to the metaphysical. Thus, he uses a completely philosophical opposition, which also has its own history, and its own metaphorical history, in order to determine what the philosopher might be doing, unwittingly, with metaphors.[90]

Here, in Derrida's reading of Polyphilos's speech, we see the point we have made about the concept of metaphor resting on a metaphysical distinction summed up. For Polyphilos to contrast metaphor with the concept, he must create a philosophical opposition between the physical and metaphysical with metaphor being on the side of the sensory image and the concept being on the side of the metaphysical. Derrida also notes that this recourse to a metaphysical opposition is tied to an assumption about origins.

In this passage, Derrida uses the word *etymon*, which is the name for an original word from which the later words in a given etymological chain are derived. Therefore, the fact that 'Polyphilos seems anxious to save the integrity of capital' is based on the assumption that there is an *etymon*, an originary foundation, that can be saved. This *etymon* would allow for the philosophical opposition between the physical and metaphysical or the sensible and the supersensible in the first place. The origin grounds the metaphysical opposition. This is Derrida's point. It is also his point that to take this 'historico-theoretical' interest in metaphor is to ground the meaning of metaphor in an idea of a historical origin or an *etymon*. We see this implied when Derrida writes:

Metaphor has always been defined as the trope of resemblance between two signs, one of which designates the other. This is the most general characteristic of metaphor, which is what authorizes us to group under this heading all the so-called *symbolical* or *analogical* figures mentioned by Polyphilos (figure, myth, fable, allegory). In this critique of philosophical language, to take an interest in metaphor [...] is therefore also to take a symbolist stand. It is above all to take an interest in the nonsyntactic, nonsystematic pole of language, that is, to take an interest in semantic 'depth,' in the magnetic attraction of the similar [...]⁹¹

Here, when he links up 'semantic depth' with a Polyphilos's critique of philosophical language, Derrida shows us the presupposition of an origin of the meaning of metaphor. It is his lack of faith in this presupposition that above all leads Derrida to critique the possibility of 'recall[ing] philosophy to its forgotten truth in metaphor' or of escaping the history of metaphysics through a reading of the history of metaphor.[92]

However, we should note that Derrida's critique is not of a critique of a diachronic analysis itself. Derrida often employs a diachronic analysis of language in his work and to great effect. In the case of metaphor, when he looks at the evolution of *metaphorá* from ancient to modern Greek, he shows us how the semantic notion of transport has changed from a transport of words to public transportation. He then uses diachronic analysis to create an analogy about the multiple meanings of a metaphor, much like the various stops on a bus route through a city.[93] Because of this, Derrida is clearly not opposed to using diachronic methods, but rather the idea that such methods could ground the meaning of metaphor. Derrida does not replace this ground with anything. As we have seen, whenever we wish to assert a ground from which to judge the meaning of either a concept or a metaphor, we get 'carried away'.[94]

Finally, we must cite the relevance of Polyphilos's speech for the relationship between Derrida and Nietzsche. Derrida draws our attention to the similarities between the two. In fact, he quotes the entire 'what, then, is truth?' passage.[95] However, he then maintains that Nietzsche's analysis, while important, shifts the reader's attention away from a historical or metaphysical preoccupation. For Derrida, this is because Nietzsche focuses on the erasure and decay of concepts but does not acknowledge the metaphysical conception of metaphor.[96] However, Derrida is clearly much closer to Nietzsche's own position than he cares to admit. While it is true that concepts appear as worn-out metaphors in Nietzsche's thought, we have seen in chapter 2 that what distinguishes Nietzsche from both Müller and Kant is the collapse of the distinction between metaphor and reason. This makes our very nature a metaphorical nature and, as we have seen in the influence of Gerber on Nietzsche, the relativising function of metaphor happens on the very level of perception and cognition. This is much closer to Derrida's own position when he writes that 'there is no access to the *usure* of linguistic phenomenon without giving it some sort of figurative representation'.[97] Perhaps the true difference between Nietzsche and Derrida is that Derrida takes the cognitive ubiquity of metaphor to mean that we can neither judge the meaning of metaphor nor orient cognition with it.

Metaphor and a Lack of Orientation

In 'The *Retrait* of Metaphor' (1978), Derrida expands on our lack of ability to orient ourselves with metaphor by using the metaphor of flowing water, perhaps like a wave on the seashore. In *Retrait* Derrida writes:

> metaphor perhaps retires, withdraws from the worldwide scene, and does so at the moment of its most invasive extension, at the instant it overflows every limit [...] Neither metaphoric nor a-metaphoric, this 'figure' consists singularly in changing places and functions [...] [metaphor's] withdrawal would then have the paradoxical form of an indiscreet and overflowing insistence.[98]

What does it mean that metaphor overflows every limit and simply changes places and functions?

The use of Derrida's phrases 'withdrawal' and 'overflowing insistence' reminds us of waves on the shore. One the one hand, just as waves rush onto the land and then recede into the sea, our traditional understanding of metaphor as a literal/figurative split retreats and what was once the firm ground of the beach is sucked out to sea beneath our feet. On the other hand, in the same way that a wave rushes out to sea and pulls with it grains of sand, it also crashes onto the beach again and again, bringing with it bits of sand and all sorts of objects from all over the world. So, while on the one hand Derrida is suggesting to us here that we lose our traditional understanding of metaphoric meaning, on the other hand he is putting forward a theory of metaphoric meaning. Just as the waves returning to the shore bring with them bits of sand and earth and all sorts of artefacts from across the world, so too does the meaning of a metaphor return, or *retrait* to use Derrida's language, again and again bringing a new meaning each time with it. This perhaps mirrors the term *usure* where the use of a metaphor produces both surplus and decay simultaneously.

The final piece to this 'new semantics' is that this ever-present *retrait*, this ever-present surplus and decay of meaning, implies a lack of orientation. In the opening lines of *Retrait*, Derrida writes, '[metaphor] occupies the West, inhabits it or lets itself be inhabited: representing itself there as an enormous library in which we move about without perceiving its limits'.[99] Here we see the very logical conclusion that, if all the language we use is metaphoric and if we understand the world fundamentally through language, then we move about within metaphor rather than using metaphor to describe the world. If all reality is understood metaphorically to the extent that we are *in* metaphor rather than *using* metaphor, this would suggest an ontological value to metaphor akin to what we have seen in Nietzsche and Ricoeur.

Clive Cazeaux provides a helpful distinction about this position in *Metaphor and Continental Philosophy*. Like Derrida, Cazeaux assigns metaphor an ontological value but is quick to clarify precisely what he means by this. Cazeaux writes that:

> assigning metaphor [an] ontological value means I take the view that *everything arises out of metaphor*, but this is not the same as saying 'everything is metaphor'. The latter locates everything within metaphor, has everything belong to metaphor, whereas the former, with its action of 'giving rise' to entities, grants us the room to question what belongs to metaphor.[100]

With this distinction, Cazeaux suggests that a world of ubiquitous metaphorical representation does not necessarily mean that everything 'belongs to metaphor'. Cazeaux seems to be suggesting a position slightly different from Derrida's here, for surely when Derrida writes that 'metaphor occupies the West' and that 'we move about [within metaphor] without perceiving its limits' he means that everything 'belongs to metaphor'.

However, Cazeaux also suggests that his own position is more concerned with ontology than Derrida's. He writes that:

> the main difference between our perspectives would appear to be that Derrida's is textual and thematic, whereas mine is ontological. By 'textual and thematic', I mean that Derrida concentrates upon the tensions and connections that emerge when one focuses upon the paradigmatic, associative properties of words.[101]

Regardless of whether Derrida's position is less ontological than Cazeaux's, Derrida's focus on the 'paradigmatic, associative properties of words' does not, as Cazeaux suggests would be necessary, 'grant us the room to question what belongs to metaphor'. The 'room to question what belongs to metaphor' is absent in Derrida. When Derrida asks the reader at the beginning of *Retrait*, 'what is going on, today, with metaphor? And what gets along without metaphor?', it is rhetorical.[102] For as we have seen in 'White Mythology', when he asks 'is there metaphor in the text of philosophy?', he quickly answers that 'metaphor seems to involve the usage of philosophical language in its entirety, nothing less than the usage of so-called natural language *in* philosophical discourse, that is, the usage of natural language *as* philosophical language'.[103] In short, as we have already seen, not just philosophical language, but all natural language is metaphorical for Derrida, and Derrida takes the all-encompassing nature of metaphor to mean that we do not steer metaphor through the semantic seas. Derrida writes: 'we are not in metaphor like a pilot in his ship'.[104]

With this proclamation, we see Derrida's second departure from Blumenberg. Not only is a metaphorology impossible but we cannot orient ourselves with metaphors. While Blumenberg shows the metaphorical basis of concepts, the lack of a ground for metaphoric meaning is a particularly Derridean motif. But, strangely, Derrida seems to contradict his own logic. On the one hand, he continually points to the impossibility of using language without the recourse to metaphor. All language use, for Derrida, is ultimately figurative, and on the level of cognition we do not see some literal ground or some historical *etymon* when we use a metaphor. The metaphor becomes the literal ground. When Derrida describes metaphor as *usure*, for example, we think of metaphor as *usure*. To contemplate the metaphor of *usure*, we must for a moment suspend our disbelief that it is just a clever metaphor Derrida is using and see the concept of metaphor as *usure* for a moment. The same is true in the classic metaphor 'old age is the evening of life'. To appreciate the metaphor, we must suspend our analysis of the metaphor's literal/figurative structure and appreciate the similarities between old age and evening.

Derrida does show attentiveness to the distinctness of what occurs when one uses figurative language when he makes this point. Blumenberg has a similar attentiveness. However, Blumenberg's concern is with how, through rhetorical consensus, the distinctness of figurative language grounds meaning and orients communities. Metaphor, like myth, is something that works with reason, but resists being translated back into theorisation. By contrast, Derrida does look at the distinctness of figurative language, but then puts it back into a philosophical analysis. While Derrida's critique is powerful for delimiting our understanding of traditional terms such as 'figurative language' and 'metaphysics', he falters here and forces metaphor to remain in theory. It seems he switches back and forth throughout his work. In one moment, he will be very attentive to the actual instances of metaphor and what they can do beyond any conceptualisation, but at other times, when he subjects them to critique, he puts them back into theory. So, while he attempts to deconstruct the metaphysical limit of a traditional theory of metaphor, one that, as we have seen, he says is linked to the idea of origin, at times he reinvokes a theoretical limit, even if it bears the name 'deconstruction'.

This divergence between the two thinkers, however, reflects the cleft in Nietzsche's own thinking on metaphor. On the one hand, Nietzsche speaks of peace treaties produced through metaphors. On the other hand, Nietzsche speaks of an infinite chain of reference based on nothing other than our own perception. From a hermeneutic perspective, this infinite chain of reference we find in Derrida's philosophy opens enormous possibilities for metaphor. If we consider the metaphor 'old age is the evening of life' as we have seen with Nietzsche, the link between old age and evening is not necessarily fixed. For a student in their twenties out late, evening may more truly reflect the youth of life. With Derrida this relativism takes on another layer. The word in Greek for evening would surely have evolved from somewhere and to say with any kind of precision the limits of the concept of evening is ultimately undeterminable. Evening does not have proper etymological origin, nor does it have any kind of clear conceptual boundary by which we can fix an understanding or definition of what evening means. The same is the case with old age. If we describe old age, we may not give the metaphor of evening, but, according to Derrida, all the words in the definition would be figurative and able to be infinitely interpreted. This might prompt us to consider interpretations we had not thought of before. It would also work against a single authority and a stable or fixed declaration of meaning. Oppressive metaphors could easily be cast off, not simply as unethical, but also as semantically incorrect.

However, there is a hermeneutic problem that arises from Derrida's philosophy of metaphor and that is the fact that while his critique may be insightful about the ultimately indeterminate nature of meaning, it does not account for intense and rapid semantic ground that can be established when a metaphor is used. Derrida's critique falls short of recognising the non-theoretical moment of metaphor, the moment when metaphors take hold in history and entire communities are shaped by their meaning. In this aspect Blumenberg is more helpful. This is essentially because the meaning of metaphor is not always as innocent as old age is the evening of life. The political metaphor, for example, presents us with more drastic example of both swift meaning change and deep semantic roots, despite what can be deconstructed away. Political ideology builds its stronghold on the seemingly semantically fixed metaphor. We can question the authority of meaning as well as deconstruct a seemingly straightforward text, in philosophy for example, by looking to its metaphors. But this only accounts for semantics in one way. It does not account for a certain aesthetic phenomenon which is the seemingly semantically fixed metaphor, seen most readily in the discourse of ideology. And it is to this that we will turn in conclusion.

Semantic Change and the Question of Ideology

When Derrida writes 'we are not in metaphor, like a pilot in his ship',[105] what are we to make of this claim? If we reflect on the example we saw in the introduction of Victor Klemperer and his observations of the change in metaphoric meaning due to the use of the metaphor *aufziehen* in the ideology of the Third Reich, we can see the crux of the question that Derrida's philosophy of metaphor poses. This was of course the same example we used to point out a particular type of semantic change that cognitive linguistics could not explain. We have come to the same question when considering Derrida's assertion of the undecidability of metaphoric meaning. When Derrida writes, 'we are not in metaphor, like a pilot in his ship', how does this relate to the historical evidence with which Klemperer presents us?

As we have seen, prior to 1933, the German word *aufziehen*, literally meaning to wind up like one might do with a clock, also had become a playful, but nonetheless pejorative, metaphor used to describe an impressively set up advertising campaign. The implication was that the way a campaign is set up creates an inflated sense of the product's value.[106] But, Klemperer records that in 1933, 'Goebbels stated in the University of Political Science that the NSDAP had 'set up (*aufgezogen*) a massive organisation involving millions of people and bringing together all kinds of activities including folk theatre, popular games, tourism and sport, hiking, singing and all supported financially by the state'.[107] The playfulness is lost and Klemperer provides us with other examples from Nazi rhetoric where *aufziehen* is used in earnest to describe the process of setting up successful organisations or campaigns such as the 1935 Saarland vote where 90 per cent of the region allegedly voted for reunification with Germany. Klemperer reminds us that in this period, all association of the metaphor with advertising was lost.[108]

What are we to make of this historical record of the swift semantic change of a metaphor? While Derrida may write 'we are not in metaphor, like a pilot in his ship', it certainly would seem that Goebbels piloted *aufziehen* successfully, moving it from playful to earnest, mooring it to Nazi ideology.[109] In chapter 3, we concluded that the ground of poetic revelation could not account for the ideological phenomenon as seen in in Goebbels's use of *aufziehen*. However, the hermeneutic tension within Derrida's 'new semantics' of metaphor is fundamentally different from the tensions articulated in chapter 3.

To sum up our argument thus far and remind the reader why Derrida claims the meaning of metaphor is ultimately undecidable, we can first turn to the concept of *usure* that Derrida introduces in 'White Mythology'. For Derrida, our use of language is always *usure*. What does this mean? It means that any time language is used there is always a semantic surplus and a deterioration.[110] These both happen simultaneously in any linguistic event according to Derrida because, in his view, we cannot use language without using metaphor.[111] We have also seen this reflected in the metaphor of the wave that hits the beach in 'The *Retrait* of Metaphor'. While the wave pulls away and 'retreats', it also *retraits*, bringing in new meanings.[112]

The second reason Derrida claims the meaning of metaphor is ultimately undecidable is that while metaphor supports metaphysical conceptions, it is itself a metaphysical conception.[113] Connected with this is the fact that we cannot use language without employing some type of figurative representation. The transference never stops, and a ground is never reached.[114] Finally, for Derrida, there is no historical theorisation of metaphor where a single *etymon* can be pinned down.[115] Because each *usure* of a metaphor generates a new meaning, there is no original meaning and the very usage of language deconstructs any identifiable origin. This view does not banish a historical record as pure fancy, rather it asserts that the historical record does not have claim over the meaning of a metaphor.

All of this can be summed up by saying that due to the surplus and decay present whenever language is used, and due to the inability to use language without recourse to a figurative representation, the meaning of a metaphor is ultimately undecidable, and the human being is left unable to orient him- or herself with metaphor. However, we will conclude that the theoretical undecidability of the meaning of metaphor that Derrida advocates is fundamentally different from the social and historical orientation that metaphor can provide. The key is in Derrida's metaphor of *usure*. Here Derrida contradicts himself, because while he is quick to point out the simultaneous surplus and decay of meaning when a metaphor is used, he also maintains that the human being cannot orient him- or herself with metaphor. Yet in the very moment of surplus, a social and historical meaning is generated. Let us look at this in relation to the Klemperer example.

At first, we see the logic in Derrida's assertions of metaphoric meaning as *usure*. When Goebbels uses *aufziehen* in a new way, a new meaning is generated. We can relate this to the surplus of meaning. We can also see that in this surplus, *aufziehen*'s etymological link is, to a certain extent, washed away and even as a new meaning is generated an originary meaning is washed away. It is perhaps helpful to think about this in terms of Saussure, who, as we have seen, Derrida often drew on in his work. For Saussure, the more general and abstract a term becomes, the more the potential range of its meanings develops.[116] Derrida interprets this phenomenon to mean that, as a result, a single, traceable meaning decays, hence his use of the term *usure*.

In the case of *aufziehen*, we can see it take on this trajectory in the way Klemperer describes it. As *aufziehen* begins to be used pre-1933, to connote a 'winding up' or a 'setting up' of various kinds, one can easily see how the metaphor's relation to advertising comes about. However, one can also see that relationship comes from 'winding up' in a very general sense. To 'wind someone up', as in to tease them or taunt them, is related to the meaning of the metaphor as it relates to advertising, but the 'specific' meaning derived from the wind-up toy or the clock begins to be lost. Therefore, the usage of *aufziehen*, pre-1933, clearly had surplus, the new, pejorative meaning relating to advertising, but also decay, the loss of the specific meaning that the metaphorical borrowed from the literal, mechanical wind-up.

We could also think about the 'decay' of meaning in terms of a metaphor's course toward a 'dead metaphor'. If a Brexiteer and a Remainer were to sit down in a pub late one winter's evening and engage in a passionate debate, and one of the interlocutors began to make vague sweeping statements and bring in the most obscure and random examples, the other might say to him or her, 'I'm sorry, but I really don't *grasp* your point.' We hardly notice that one can't literally *grasp* a point but that it is a dead metaphor. This is of course Lakoff and Johnson's poignant observation in *Metaphors We Live By* about the slew of 'dead metaphors' embedded in everyday speech that relate to larger conceptual categories.

In the case of the 'dead metaphor' *grasp* and in the course of *aufziehen*'s semantic change, we see that the 'face of the coin', the literal meaning that may have grounded the original metaphor through a truthlike relation, is increasingly worn away. Yet, according to Derrida, while the deterioration is occurring, new meanings are being generated and we have seen that reflected in the Klemperer example. While the new meaning of being duped into an inflated sense of value is not a direct, truthlike match to the original meaning of a mechanical wind-up toy, it is nonetheless a new meaning.

So, what are we to make of the semantic change we see in *aufziehen*, in light of Derrida's claim? One interpretation may be to look at the etymology of *aufziehen*, cite both the surplus and decay of meaning, and reply to Goebbels: 'I know you may mean *aufziehen* in earnest, but you clearly haven't read your Derrida. Don't you know that you can't access this new ideological meaning of *aufziehen* without invoking an entire history of surplus and decay of the metaphor's meaning? Even as you use the word now, you are adding to that history.' In other words, we can read both a diachronic analysis of the metaphor's history and a synchronic analysis of the metaphor's current semantic network back against ideology and in doing so claim the ultimate undecidability of the metaphor's meaning. But this is precisely where we encounter our hermeneutic crisis.

Derrida's conclusion is that we cannot stop the movement, moor the ship, or steer it clearly. And while we may smugly say 'hear, hear!' cosied up in the armchairs of our late-night debates, if we simply ontologise the undecidability of meaning and use it as a template for hermeneutics, we run the risk of not providing an account for the way that the meaning of *aufziehen* and similar metaphors certainly did orient the ideology to such an extent that the next phase of 'surplus and decay' was created by it. Klemperer notes that the metaphor began to be used in everyday speech in Germany. He first noticed it used in a biography of a publisher to describe 'the setting up' of an organisation for the training of students. The context, Klemperer notes, was completely unrelated to the war or party rhetoric.[117] While we may ascribe this to the very surplus and decay that Derrida spoke of, we also must admit that there was a very real social and historical orientation via the metaphor that led to the change in meaning. Socially, at least, we see that the surplus and decay of meaning generates power and orientation.

Therefore, we must conclude that theoretical undecidability and social and historical orientation are two different, though related, phenomena. This orientation even extends to hermeneutics. In our example, we not only see that Nazi rhetoric enacted the change of the metaphor's meaning; for Klemperer, the ability to orient the meaning of *aufziehen* within its historical chain was what allowed him to observe the change in meaning in the first place. It seems that hermeneutics needs a certain amount of heuristic decidability to observe semantic change, before then concluding that meaning is ultimately undecidable. While we have seen Derrida begin to gesture in this direction, we see him stop short of pronouncing whether the hermeneutical interpreter is able to decide the meaning of that translation. While of, course, as we have maintained, this 'new semantics' opens extraordinary hermeneutic possibilities, it meets its limit in its ability to account for the social and historical orientation that metaphor provides in the context of ideology. What is perhaps most helpful in Derrida is the recognition that in the usage of language there is always a dual semantic moment, a surplus and decay or a 'trait' and *re-trait*. But when the traits wash onto the shore or pull away from it, this does not simply remind us of the ultimately relative function of metaphor; this pull itself generates a social and hermeneutic power for orientation. This is where the two sides of Nietzsche's conception of metaphor come together.

Notes to Chapter 5

1. Jacques Derrida, 'White Mythology: Metaphor in the Text of Philosophy', in *Margins of Philosophy*, trans. by Alan Bass (Chicago: University of Chicago Press, 1984), pp. 207–71 (p. 209).
2. Jacques Derrida, 'The *Retrait* of Metaphor', in *Psyche: Inventions of the Other*, trans. by Peggy Kamuf (Stanford: Stanford University Press, 2007), pp. 48–80 (p. 49).
3. See Anselm Haverkamp, 'Deconstruction is/as Neopragmatism? Preliminary Remarks on Deconstruction in America', in *Deconstruction Is/In America: A New Sense of the Political*, ed. by Anselm Haverkamp (New York: NYU Press, 1995).
4. Benoit Peeters, *Derrida: A Biography*, trans. by Andrew Brown (Cambridge: Polity Press, 2013), pp. 3–5.
5. Robert Satloff, *Among the Righteous: Lost Stories from the Holocaust's Long Reach into Arab Lands* (New York: Public Affairs, 2006), pp. 30–31.
6. Peeters, *Derrida*, p. 9.
7. Satloff, *Among the Righteous*, p. 37.
8. Ibid., pp. 37–38.
9. Peeters, *Derrida*, p. 10.
10. Ibid.
11. Edward Baring, *The Young Derrida and French Philosophy, 1945–1968* (Cambridge: Cambridge University Press, 2011), pp. 15–16.
12. Ibid., p. 16.
13. Ibid., p. 48.
14. Christopher Johnson, *System and Writing in the Philosophy of Jacques Derrida* (Cambridge: Cambridge University Press, 1993), p. 1.
15. Baring, *Young Derrida*, p. 48.
16. Dominique Janicaud, *Heidegger in France*, trans. by François Raffoul and David Pettigrew (Indianapolis: Indiana University Press, 2015), p. 37.

17. Jacques Derrida, 'Les fins de l'homme', in *Marges de la philosophie* (Paris: Minuit, 1972), pp. 129–64 (p. 136); Jacques Derrida, 'The Ends of Man', in *Margins of Philosophy*, trans. by Alan Bass (Chicago: The University of Chicago Press, 1984), pp. 109–36 (p. 115).
18. Janicaud, *Heidegger*, p. 36.
19. Ibid., pp. 35–36.
20. Ibid., p. 337; Baring, *Young Derrida*, p. 48.
21. Janicaud, *Heidegger*, pp. 63, 66.
22. Martin Heidegger, 'Letter on Humanism', in *Basic Writings*, trans. by Frank A. Capuzzi and J. Glenn Gray (London: Routledge, 2010), pp. 214–65 (pp. 225–26). As was the case at Davos with the term 'anthropology', humanism was also an insufficient label to reflect *Dasein*. In the same way that Heidegger viewed anthropology as 'too regional' a description of human existence, humanism was a metaphysical concept that also was insufficient to analyse *Dasein*, as was Sartre's term 'réalité-humaine'.
23. Baring, *Young Derrida*, p. 104.
24. Ibid., pp. 82, 113. Derrida was completely absorbed in the technical language of Husserl's phenomenology in this period. So much so that Derrida's teacher, Louis Althusser, commented that 'Derrida was too dominated by his master.'
25. Johnson, *System and Writing*, p. 1.
26. Baring, *Young Derrida*, pp. 48, 183.
27. Peter Steiner, Henryk Baran, Conor Klamann and Jonathan Culler, 'Structuralism', in *The Princeton Encyclopedia of Poetry and Poetics*, 4th edn (Princeton: Princeton University Press, 2012), pp. 1361–66.
28. Claude Lévi-Strauss, *The Savage Mind*, trans. by George Weidenfeld (London: The University of Chicago Press, 1966), p. 263.
29. Ferdinand de Saussure, *Course in General Linguistics*, trans. by Roy Harris (London: Bloomsbury, 2013), p. 8, §§21–22.
30. Ibid., pp. 10 — 11, §25.
31. Steiner and others, 'Structuralism'.
32. Ibid.
33. Ibid.
34. Baring, *Young Derrida*, p. 183.
35. Jacques Derrida, *Writing and Difference*, trans. by Alan Bass (Chicago: University of Chicago Press, 1978), pp. 279–80.
36. Gayatri Chakravorty Spivak, 'Translator's Preface', in Jacques Derrida, *Of Grammatology*, trans. by Gayatri Chakravorty Spivak (London: Johns Hopkins University Press, 1976), pp. ix–lxxxvii (p. xxi).
37. Ibid.
38. Ibid., p. xl. The language in this quotation is somewhat awkward. Spivak imbeds several fragmentary quotations from Derrida's own writing with her own interpretation and does not always make clear where her own position ends and Derrida's begins. Therefore, I have chosen to paraphrase the quotation. Upon careful reading, it can be discerned that the quotations of Derrida in this passage are taken from an essay that appears later in Jacques Derrida, *Margins of Philosophy*, trans. by Alan Bass (Chicago: University of Chicago Press, 1982), p. 305.
39. Spivak, 'Translator's Preface', p. xlii.
40. Ibid. Again, Spivak combines various quotations from Derrida, as well as Nietzsche and Phillippe Lacoue-Labarthe in this section. See the notes in Derrida, *Of Grammatology*, p. 372, for Spivak's list of quotations. This list has not been reproduced here because Spivak does not always make it clear where one quotation begins and the next ends. Therefore, a paraphrase is the easiest to read. What is most important to bear in mind is that this is Spivak's reading of these various thinkers, the overarching focus being the similarities between Derrida's and Nietzsche's positions on the close relationship between metaphor and truth claims.
41. Jacques Derrida, *Positions*, trans. by Alan Bass (London: Continuum, 2002), p. 17.
42. Spivak, 'Translator's Preface', p. xxxvi.
43. Derrida, *Positions*, p. 17.

44. Jürgen Habermas, *Philosophical Discourses of Modernity*, trans. by Frederick G. Lawrence (Cambridge, MA: MIT Press, 1990), pp. 162 — 64.
45. Ibid., p. 163.
46. Ibid., p. 164.
47. Spivak, 'Translator's Preface', p. xxxvi.
48. Thomas Dutoit, 'Editor's Note', in Jacques Derrida, *Heidegger: The Question of Being and History*, trans. by Geoffrey Bennington, ed. by Thomas Dutoit (Chicago: University of Chicago Press, 2016), pp. xv-xix) p. xv.
49. Ibid.
50. Jacques Derrida, *Heidegger: The Question of Being and History*, trans. by Geoffrey Bennington (Chicago: University of Chicago Press, 2016), p. 2.
51. Derrida, *Heidegger*, p. 6.
52. Dutoit, 'Editor's Note', p. xix.
53. Derrida, *Heidegger*, p. 16.
54. Ibid., p. 16.
55. Dutoit, 'Editor's Note', p. xix.
56. Derrida, *Heidegger*, p. 16.
57. For a further elucidation of the term 'deconstruction' as it relates to structural linguistics, see Jacques Derrida, *Of Grammatology*, trans. by Gayatri Chakravorty Spivak (London: Johns Hopkins University Press, 1976), pp. 10 — 11.
58. Spivak, 'Translator's Preface', p. xxxvi.
59. Derrida, *Positions*, p. 17.
60. Ibid.
61. Geoffrey Bennington and Jacques Derrida, *Jacques Derrida*, trans. by Geoffrey Bennington (Chicago: University of Chicago Press, 1993), pp. 119, 121.
62. Ibid., p. 121.
63. Ibid., pp. 125 — 26.
64. Derrida, 'White Mythology', p. 213.
65. Ibid., p. 209.
66. Ibid., p. 219.
67. Ibid.
68. Ibid.
69. Jacques Derrida, 'La Mythologie Blanche', in *Marges de la Philosophie* (Paris: Minuit, 1972), pp. 274-324 (p. 261). See Hans Blumenberg, *Paradigmes pour une métaphorologie*, trans. by Didier Gammelin (Paris: Vrin, 2006).
70. Anselm Haverkamp, 'Metaphorologie zweiten Grades: Unbegrifflichkeit, Vorformen der Idee', in *Metaphorologie zur Praxis von Theorie*, ed. by Anselm Haverkamp and Dirk Mende (Frankfurt am Main: Suhrkamp, 2009), pp. 237-55 (p. 237).
71. Dirk Mende, *Metapher — zwischen Metaphysik und Archäologie: Schelling, Heidegger, Derrida, Blumenberg* (Munich: Wilhelm Fink Verlag, 2013), p. 166.
72. Derrida, 'White Mythology', p. 219.
73. Ibid., p. 236.
74. Ibid., p. 219.
75. Ibid.
76. Ibid., p. 209.
77. Clive Cazeaux, *Metaphor and Continental Philosophy* (New York: Routledge, 2007), p. 177.
78. Derrida, 'White Mythology', p. 209. See translators note number two for an additional explanation of the various meanings of the term *usure* in French.
79. Ibid., p. 215.
80. Ibid., pp. 215 — 16.
81. Wallace Martin, 'Metaphor', in *The Princeton Encyclopedia of Poetry and Poetics*, 4th edn (Princeton: Princeton University Press, 2012), pp. 863-70.
82. Bennington and Derrida, *Jacques Derrida*, pp. 121-22, 125-26.
83. Ibid., p. 121.

84. Ibid., pp. 125–26.
85. Anatole France, 'The Garden of Epicurus', Internet Encyclopedia of Philosophy, <http://www.iep.utm.edu/garden/> [accessed 8 September 2017].
86. Anatole France, 'The Garden of Epicurus', Bartleby.com, <http://www.bartleby.com/library/readersdigest/816.html> [accessed 8 September 2017].
87. Derrida, 'White Mythology', p. 210.
88. Ibid.
89. Anatole France, *The Garden of Epicurus*, trans. by Alfred Allinson (New York: Dodd, Mean, 1923), pp. 194–95.
90. Derrida, 'White Mythology', pp. 210–11.
91. Ibid., p. 215.
92. Bennington and Derrida, *Jacques Derrida*, p. 119.
93. Derrida, 'Retrait', p. 49.
94. Derrida, 'White Mythology', p. 219.
95. Ibid., p. 217.
96. Ibid.
97. Ibid., p. 209.
98. Derrida, 'Retrait', pp. 49–50.
99. Ibid., p. 48.
100. Cazeaux, *Metaphor*, p. 12.
101. Ibid., p. 193.
102. Derrida, 'Retrait', p. 48.
103. Derrida, 'White Mythology', p. 209.
104. Derrida, 'Retrait', p. 49.
105. Ibid.
106. Victor Klemperer, *The Language of the Third Reich: LTI-Lingua Tertii Imperii, a Philologist's Notebook*, trans. by Martin Brady (London: Bloomsbury, 2013), p. 47.
107. Ibid., p. 48.
108. Ibid.
109. Derrida, 'Retrait', p. 49.
110. Derrida, 'White Mythology', p. 209.
111. Ibid.
112. Derrida, 'Retrait', pp. 49–50.
113. Derrida, 'White Mythology', p. 219.
114. Ibid.
115. Ibid., pp. 210–11.
116. Saussure, *Course*, §4.
117. Klemperer, *Language*, p. 48.

CONCLUSION

We began this book by posing an interpretive question about metaphor. If, as Nietzsche maintains, all semantic gestures are metaphoric, from where can we judge the meaning of metaphor? To answer this question, we judged it essential to understand which presuppositions underpinned the concept of metaphor. Throughout our intellectual-historical journey a critical distinction became apparent: the concept of metaphor is fundamentally different from the function of metaphor. We have also seen that many of the interpretive conflicts that arise when assessing the meaning of metaphor, whether in the texts of the humanities or in current political discourse, can be seen to come from a theoretical articulation of a metaphor that focuses on metaphor's function without properly assessing the change to the concept itself. This predicament has led to both an intellectual-historical conclusion and a philosophical conclusion. In this final section, we will briefly revisit how the concept of metaphor has shifted and how changes to the meaning of metaphor need to be considered, not just in terms of linguistic and cultural relativism, but in terms of historical and ideological change. We will assert that it is the issue of semantic change that underlines the hermeneutic limits of both the European philosophical conception of metaphor and cognitive linguistics. But first, we will remind ourselves of why the new conception of metaphor that emerges in European philosophy highlights the problem of semantic change.

An Intellectual-Historical Conclusion

Through our intellectual-historical reconstruction of the European philosophical concept of metaphor we have seen how the concept of what a metaphor is has shifted. As concepts like truth, reason, and the very boundary between the literal and the figurative underwent a larger transition in European philosophy, we saw that these were the foundations of the concept of metaphor itself. As a result, these larger transitions did not simply alert us to previously unrecognised ways in which metaphor functions in thought and discourse. Rather, these transitions alerted us to changes in what the concept of metaphor itself meant. This new conception of metaphor can be seen as a 'Janus head' where both a pragmatic function and a relativistic function coexist. This dual function can be best understood by the three 'collapses' that we observed in Nietzsche's philosophy of metaphor: the collapse of truth, the collapse of reason and the collapse of the literal. In these three, we find the heart of the problem of semantic change.

The first collapse was that of truth. The Aristotelian model of truthlikeness held the pragmatic and relative poles of metaphor apart. The truthlike, mimetic function of metaphor, provided a measure to determine metaphor's pragmatic function, that is, how metaphor aided judgement. The *lexis* section of the *Poetics* where metaphor is defined, may not be an elaborated philosophy of metaphor but it does, technically at least, elaborate how metaphors make sense in language and this presupposes Aristotle's measure of truthlikeness that we have seen outlined in chapter 1.[1] This measure of truthlikeness also provides a reference which unifies any kind of suggestion of relativism. Ancient Athens, which housed Aristotle's Lyceum, was by no means a culturally isolated place. But Aristotle's measure of a good metaphor, as we have seen, rested on a discernment of similarities, not between cultural forms but between metaphor and *phusis* (nature).[2] The Nietzschean conception of metaphor is born out of the collapse of this measure between metaphor and truthlikeness. In Nietzsche's thought, the relativising function of metaphor, in which all semantic gestures are metaphoric, appears to be the same as the pragmatic function of metaphor where metaphoric meaning swiftly takes hold and pragmatically orients cognition. These do not feed off a shared truthlike measure, but off each other. What is meant by the creation or judgement of meaning in such a context?

This brings us to the second and third collapses: the collapse of reason and the collapse of the literal. We have seen how, for Nietzsche, meaning is figurative from the beginning of the understanding's interpretation of the world. He takes his cue from Gustav Gerber who wrote that 'all words are *Lautbilder* (phonetic images) and are, from the beginning, tropes with respect to their meaning'.[3] The idea that all words are tropes from their cognitive beginnings produces a cognitive relativism in Nietzsche's thought. It is also what fundamentally distinguishes him from Kant. Unlike Kant's philosophy, where figurative thought is a supplement that reason can draw on, in Nietzsche's philosophy metaphor is something that pervades all of reason.[4] As Nietzsche writes, '[the art of dissimulation] is so much the rule and the law that there is virtually nothing which defies understanding so much as the fact that an honest and pure drive towards truth should ever have emerged in them'.[5] Therefore, for Nietzsche, in the understanding's interpretation of the world, a separation between reason and metaphor and the figurative and metaphor no longer exists. From this is born a conception of metaphor that is split between a pragmatic function and a relativistic function.

What then, does relativism and semantic change mean in such a context? Our history highlighted that while different aspects of European philosophy accounted for aspects of this new conception of metaphor, the changes to metaphor as a whole were often not fully realised or understood. Like an audience member who storms out after only seeing the first half of the play, the lack of fully assessing the change to the concept of metaphor as a whole has sparked several hermeneutic conflicts. This relates to our philosophical conclusion.

A Philosophical Conclusion

Our intellectual-historical reconstruction has helped to illuminate that one of the philosophical challenges at the heart of the contemporary conception of metaphor is an account of semantic change. While there can be no single ground to the hermeneutic crisis that arises from the Nietzschean conception of metaphor, we have seen that the type of meaning that alerts us to the reality of relativism is not just a meaning shift between cultures, languages and symbolics. Yet we have seen that many of the presuppositions that underpin the idea of semantic change in twentieth-century European philosophy privilege change between linguistic and cultural symbolics as their measure. This has a limit. Relative meanings, as we see them operating in metaphor, are also historical, ideological and, ultimately, cognitive.[6]

The sheer breadth of semantic change accounted for by the new conception of metaphor in European philosophy tells us two things. First, it tells us that in the broadest sense, semantic change operates where language transforms into a social context. There is something mutual about how the understanding interprets change to meaning. When discussing metaphor's semantic ground, one must distinguish between a theoretical undecidability and the production of social and historical meaning. The second thing a broader notion of semantic change tells us is that alongside ideological and historical change there is also a basic cognitive relativism operating. The new conception of metaphor in European philosophy alerts us to this.

The broad idea of semantic change is also what links together some of the philosophical issues with more hermeneutical approaches to metaphor that we have seen in European philosophy and more cognitive approaches to metaphor that we saw in the introduction. Some of the limitations to interpreting change in European philosophy are mirrored in cognitive linguistics. As we have seen in the introduction, the synchronic methodology of cognitive linguistics and its semantic grounds of embodiment means that, while the empirical findings of this approach are rich and vital, the ability to interpret the changes to the meaning of metaphor are limited. This is not to say that change is not considered. As we have seen in the introduction, Zoltán Kövecses in his book *Metaphor in Culture: Universality and Variation* writes that 'we can get cases in which social-cultural experiences override embodiment'.[7] However, the 'variation' that Kövecses is primarily concerned with here is variation between cultures, languages, and ultimately between symbolics. The struggle in a European philosophy of metaphor to account for semantic change within a shared symbolic, whether that be long historical changes or swift ideological changes, seems to be shared by cognitive linguistics.

In addition to this, cognitive linguistics shares another hermeneutic problem with European philosophy and that is the problem of a semantic ground to interpret the meaning of metaphor. In European philosophy, we have seen how semantic questions about metaphor can be far too oriented by Nietzsche's critique of the metaphysical foundations of metaphor. In the Aristotelian paradigm of metaphor, truthlikeness provided the ground for metaphoric meaning. Nietzsche's critique of the foundations of this paradigm seems to split the meaning of metaphor between a pragmatic pole and a relative pole. Subsequently, whether the focus is on the loss of the proper as a ground to meaning, as in Sarah Kofman's *Nietzsche and Metaphor*, on a more fundamental ontological ground to meaning, as in the case of Heidegger and Ricoeur, or the inability to determine meaning, as in the case of Derrida, a focus on the problem of a semantic ground can present a lopsided view of metaphor. In cognitive linguistics' attempt to ground the problem of metaphor in embodiment, there is still a latent aspect in its conceptual structure which, however unintentionally, still suggests that the question of truth matters. In other words, while Lakoff and Johnson state that their approach 'rejects any objective or absolute truth', the need for a ground of metaphoric meaning suggests the need for a universal or ahistorical measure.[8] Such a measure is what Aristotle's paradigm of truthlikeness gave to metaphor. While Lakoff and Johnson may not be concerned with the quest for truth, they are still influenced by the larger model in Western thought that links ground and meaning. As we have seen, their attempt to account for this has in turn limited their ability to account for semantic change.

Therefore, whether in the European philosophical account of metaphor or in cognitive linguistics' approach to metaphor, the question of semantic change is a pressing, contemporary focus. It demands a reassessment of the link between metaphor and cognition from both more hermeneutical approaches and more cognitive ones. One way this can be done is by a cognitive account of metaphor, engaging with a European philosophical conception of the Life-world, a pre-theoretical world on which the human theoretical attitude is dependent. In chapter 4, we have seen how Hans Blumenberg saw in Edmund Husserl's concept of the Life-world a model for how metaphor orients cognition's experience of the world prior to an integration of these experiences by a theoretical attitude.[9]

In some ways Blumenberg's account seems to mirror cognitive linguistics' basic claim that 'our ordinary conceptual system, in terms of which we both think and act, is fundamentally metaphorical in nature'.[10] The difference of course is cognitive linguistics' empirical methodology, which aims to show the embodied nature of metaphor. In addition to this, some contemporary accounts of consciousness in both philosophy of mind and cognitive science see the concept of the Life-world and the tradition of phenomenology from which it originates as a failed project.[11] However, we are not arguing for an acceptance of phenomenology's description of consciousness, the abandonment of cognitive linguistics empirical methodology, or the existence of an actual Life-world. Rather, it is in Blumenberg's description of how metaphor orients cognition's experience of the world prior to theoretical integration that we see one way in which a cognitive account of metaphor could better account for semantic change.

Through his diachronic approach that observes how metaphor integrates itself into theoretical attitudes over time, Blumenberg uses the concept of the Life-world to show a historicity of how metaphors orient cognition. In his example of how the meaning of the metaphorical description of God as lightning becomes exhausted once humans begin to have technological mastery over lightning, Blumenberg provides a description of the historicity of semantic changes.[12] If it is true, as Lakoff and Johnson assert, that 'our ordinary conceptual system, in terms of which we both think and act, is fundamentally metaphorical in nature', then descriptions, such as Blumenberg's, of how the meaning of metaphors evolve are not just an antiquated hobby that collects the history of words.[13] Rather they are a clue to how the meaning of metaphor shifts while orienting our 'ordinary conceptual systems'. Because of this, by engaging with aspects of the concept of the Life-world, a cognitive account of metaphor may be able to give a more robust account of the historicity of cognition.

This leads to a second way in which both European philosophy and cognitive linguistics could reassess the link between metaphor and cognition. One contemporary philosopher who writes specifically about a 'historicity of the brain' is Catherine Malabou, who seeks to give a philosophical account of neuroplasticity in *What Should We Do with Our Brain* (2008).[14] In viewing the neuroscientific concept of plasticity as a description of the brain's history, Malabou argues for an understanding of identity that has the capacity to 'adapt itself, to include modifications, to receive shocks, and to create anew'.[15] By defining our changing identities as a part of the brain's history, one of the implications we can take from Malabou's argument is that modern cognitive science does indeed have available to it an empirical methodology that can provide a historicity of cognition.

Malabou's attentiveness to identity formation provides a clear link to the metaphorical foundation of ordinary concepts set out by Lakoff and Johnson. The ordinary conceptual systems that they assert are metaphorical in nature are quite often identity forming. In their classic ARGUMENT IS WAR example, Lakoff and Johnson identify a host of expressions in the English language that use the language of warfare to describe the concept of argumentation. Some of these include, 'your claims are *indefensible*, he *attacked every weak point* in my argument', and, 'he *shot down* all of my arguments'. As Lakoff and Johnson themselves point out, 'we don't just talk about arguments in terms of war. We can actually win or lose arguments. We see the person we are arguing with as an opponent.'[16] Because of this, we can see that one of the implications for the creation of social and cultural meaning in the cognitive linguistics approach, is that metaphors are foundational in both our own identities and how we identify those around us. Therefore, whether it is through an exploration of neuroplasticity or the concept of the Life-world, it is evident that both European philosophical and cognitive approaches to metaphor must provide an account of the historicity of cognition so that one may better understand semantic change within one's own symbolic.

Finally, this leads us to our second gap in an account of how semantic change operates in metaphor: the swift changes to meaning that come in the form of ideology. What does it mean to say that ideology represents a type of semantic change? Because the meanings of metaphors are rapidly shifting today in the West, we must clarify exactly how ideology and semantic change relate. In both the introduction and chapter 5, we saw Victor Klemperer's account of the evolution of the metaphor *aufziehen* throughout the Second World War. Klemperer points out that among its many meanings, *aufziehen* was used as a metaphor before the war to comment on how advertising creates an excessive or inflated sense of value. One clear moment in its swift evolution was on 30 June 1933 when 'Goebbels stated in the University of Political Science that the NSDAP had 'set up (*aufgezogen*) a massive organization involving millions of people and bringing together all kinds of activities including folk theatre, popular games, tourism and sport, hiking, singing and all supported financially by the state'.[17] Klemperer notes that in Goebbels's usage, there is no hint of the pejorative meaning of an excess of value. Then, in 1935, in a context totally unrelated to Nazi rhetoric, *aufziehen* is used convey the meaning of setting up an organisation for the training of students.[18] This is one example of how the meaning of a metaphor, when used in the rhetoric of political ideology, can swiftly change. In this case, the new form of *aufziehen*, as it was first used by Goebbels, went on to be used in contexts completely unrelated to political ideology. This is an example of how the meaning of a specific metaphor can change when it is used in political ideology. However, metaphors can also swiftly change the meaning of key concepts.

At a political meeting in Lyon in 2010, the future French presidential candidate Marine Le Pen metaphorically compared Muslims' praying in the streets of France to the Nazi occupation when she said:

> for those who really like to talk about World War Two, if we're talking about occupation, we could talk about that (street prayers), because that is clearly an occupation of the territory [...] there are no tanks, there are no soldiers, but it is an occupation anyhow, and it weighs on people.

This statement led to a court case in 2015 where she was tried for inciting hatred, but she was cleared of the charges.[19] Le Pen herself clearly states that it is not a literal occupation she is referencing when she says, 'there are no tanks, there are no soldiers, but it is an occupation anyhow'. Yet here, the change to meaning is not in her use of the word occupation as a metaphor, but rather in how she relates occupation to religious freedom. Article Nine of the European Convention on Human Rights states that 'everyone has the right to freedom of thought, conscience and religion' and European legislation has traditionally guaranteed equal treatment of people of different religions.[20] To suggest that the public presence of a religion is akin to wartime occupation by a totalitarian regime is a radical shift in how the concept of freedom is understood in Europe and Le Pen leverages this meaning shift through her use of metaphor. In both our examples, when we say that ideology represents a type of swift semantic change, we are saying that metaphor can swiftly reorient cognition. The way in which our experiences of the Life-world are integrated into a theoretical attitude, such as a long-standing concept in European thought like religious freedom, can swiftly shift, and metaphor is the driver of that change. Whether one personally thinks the new meaning of a metaphor is false is beside the point. In a post-Nietzschean philosophical landscape, it is the phenomenon of such change being able to happen that we must explain. This is different to an analysis of how metaphor functions in a particular ideological discourse.

When a linguist such as Andreas Musolff looks at the role of the metaphorically embedded imagery of a 'body-parasite' in the discourse scenario of National Socialist Germany, for example, one of the key focuses of such an analysis is the discourse scenario itself.[21] However vital a study like Musolff's is in understanding the function of the body-parasite metaphor in a particular discourse scenario, it does not necessarily address the question of how it is possible for metaphor swiftly to reorient cognition. As we have seen throughout this book, semantic change is often viewed as a change between languages, cultures and symbolics. To ask about the type of change that occurs in ideology is often asking about a different type of change as it tends to ask about a change within the same symbolic. In Le Pen's occupation metaphor, she is a European redefining what religious freedom means for other Europeans. The bind we find ourselves in is how to give an account for this type of change if we accept, with both Nietzsche and cognitive linguistics, the metaphorical basis of all thought. In chapter 3, we have seen the problems with looking for a fundamental ontological ground to the meaning of ideological metaphors. And while, as we have seen in chapter 5, we could assert with Derrida that the meanings of ideological metaphors are ultimately undecidable, this does not account for the fact that cognition is swiftly reoriented by metaphor. The rhetoric of figures like Marine Le Pen does generate large followings, as the 2017 French presidential election shows. Finally, while the cognitive approach to metaphor may tell us how ideological metaphors and their network of associated concepts function, this explanation is not an adequate account of ideologies' swift semantic change.[22] So both ideological and historical shifts of meaning are examples of why a renewed account of semantic change is at the heart of the hermeneutic challenges facing both a European philosophical account and a cognitive account of metaphor.

Metaphor is a Peace Treaty

We cannot provide a single answer to these problems. However, as we turn towards a close, Nietzsche's conception of metaphor as a type of peace treaty that provides provisional truths for cognition may provide a useful point of reflection. Nietzsche's understanding that metaphor can both create 'peace treaties' and yet that the ground for these peace treaties is ultimately relative suggests to us that it is the creation of the peace treaty that is the vehicle for semantic change in the first place. This is another way of stating the perceived conflict between the pragmatic and relative functions of metaphor. Their mutual dependence flows from the cognitive relativism that Nietzsche inherited from Gustav Gerber, who wrote that 'all words are *Lautbilder* (phonetic images) and are, from the beginning, tropes with respect to their meaning'.[23] The relativistic nature of metaphor can seem to dominate, however, when Gerber also calls language a process of 'unceasing translation and of unending displacements'.[24] At times, this relativistic nature of metaphor can also seem to dominate in Nietzsche's thought when he equates metaphor with dissimulation and writes that, '[the art of dissimulation] is so much the rule and the law that there is virtually nothing which defies understanding so much as the fact that an honest and pure drive towards truth should ever have emerged in them'.[25]

However, we are not bound by Nietzsche's obsession with the loss of the proper. Beyond this, we can also see another side of Nietzsche. He highlights the pragmatic nature of metaphor when he writes:

> the intellect shows its greatest strengths in dissimulation, since this is the means to preserve those weaker, less robust individuals who, by nature, are denied horns or the sharp fangs of a beast of prey with which to wage the struggle for existence.[26]

The strange reality that human beings find themselves born into this 'art of dissimulation' and yet use that very art as a survival tool is perhaps what leads Nietzsche to highlight the role of language in creating 'peace treaties' so that human beings can live together in society rather than have a perpetual Hobbesian 'war of all against all'.[27] The concept of metaphor in European philosophy that emerges from Nietzsche's thought does not, and should not, place the question of metaphor into the framework of modern cognitive science. It is a specific moment in the history of Western thought. However, it does provide an insight that may extend beyond that specific moment.

From our study of metaphor in European philosophy we may conclude that metaphor acts as a type of peace treaty for cognition, inasmuch as it provides provisional yet ultimately relative truths. On the one hand, because of the figurative foundation of all concepts, one aspect of metaphor is that it is directly responsible for the unceasing attack on a fixed meaning that our consciousness encounters in the Life-world. Yet, on the other hand, another aspect of metaphor is its ability to call a cease fire and allow the mind to navigate through the battlefield of consciousness. We only have to reflect on the nature of conflict to recognise it is those who are fighting who have to sign the peace treaty. While this does not give us a definitive answer to how semantic change works in relation to metaphor, it does provide a much more generous framework within which to understand how meaning changes. Semantic conflict has already happened at the ground or origin of cognition. Because of this, to assess any kind of semantic questions about metaphor solely in relation to a ground for the production of meaning will never give a balanced answer to the question of semantic change. Therefore, perhaps one lesson we can take from the history of the concept of metaphor in European philosophy is that it is not a question of *where* we can find a vantage point to judge the meaning of metaphor. We find ourselves already judging, using and shifting a metaphor's meaning. Perhaps a question we need to ask of metaphor in the future is *how* it continually shifts its meaning. If truth really is a mobile army of metaphors, we need to ask how the army moves, not where the army comes from.[28]

Notes to the Conclusion

1. Aristotle, *Poetics*, 1457b; Aristotle, *Poetics*, 1459a; Aristotle, *Rhetoric*, 1355a14, 1356b10–1357b16.
2. Aristotle, *Poetics*, 1459a; Aristotle, *Poetics*, 1448b.
3. Gustav Gerber, *Die Sprache als Kunst*, 2 vols (Bromberg: Mittler'sche Buchhandlung H. Heyfelder, 1871), I, 333.
4. Immanuel Kant, *Critique of Judgement*, trans. by James Creed Meredith (Oxford: Oxford University Press, 2008), p. 179, §59; p. 352, §248.

5. Friedrich Nietzsche, 'On Truth and Lying in a Non-Moral Sense', in *The Birth of Tragedy and Other Writings*, trans. by Ronald Speirs (Cambridge: Cambridge University Press, 2012), pp. 139–53 (p. 142).
6. For more on the limitations of uncritically affirming a relativistic reading of Nietzsche see Bull, Malcolm, *Anti-Nietzsche* (London: Verso, 2011).
7. Zoltán Kövecses, *Metaphor in Culture: Universality and Variation* (Cambridge: Cambridge University Press, 2007), pp. 286, pp. 290–92.
8. George Lakoff and Mark Johnson, *Metaphors We Live By* (Chicago: University of Chicago Press, 1980), p. x.
9. Hans Blumenberg, 'Beobachtungen an Metaphern', *Archiv für Begriffsgeschichte*, 15 (1971), 161–214 (p. 163).
10. Lakoff and Johnson, *Metaphors*, p. 3.
11. In particular, see Daniel C. Dennett, *Consciousness Explained* (New York: Penguin, 1993).
12. Hans Blumenberg, 'Selbstverständlichkeit, Selbstaufrichtung, Selbstvergleich', in *Theorie der Lebenswelt*, ed. by Manfred Sommer (Berlin: Suhrkamp, 2010), pp. 138–39.
13. Lakoff and Johnson, *Metaphors*, p. 3.
14. Catherine Malabou, *What Should We Do with Our Brain?* (New York: Fordham University Press, 2008), pp.1–2.
15. Malabou, *What Should We Do*, p. 7.
16. Lakoff and Johnson, *Metaphors*, p. 4.
17. Victor Klemperer, *The Language of the Third Reich: LTI-Lingua Tertii Imperii, a Philologist's Notebook*, trans. by Martin Brady (London: Bloomsbury, 2013), p. 48.
18. Ibid.
19. Alexandra Sims, 'Marine Le Pen cleared of inciting hatred after comparing Muslim prayers in the street to the Nazi occupation', *Independent*, 15 December 2015, <https://www.independent.co.uk/news/world/europe/marine-le-pen-cleared-of-inciting-hatred-after-comparing-muslim-prayers-in-the-street-to-nazi-a6774126.html> [accessed 12 May 2020].
20. Council of Europe and European Court of Human Rights, 'Guide on Article 9 of the European Convention of Human Rights', *Case-Law Guides*, 31 December 2019, <https://www.echr.coe.int/Documents/Guide_Art_9_ENG.pdf> [accessed 12 May 2020].
21. Andreas Musolff, *Metaphor, Nation and the Holocaust: The Concept of the Body Politic* (London: Routledge, 2010), pp. 43–68.
22. It bears noting that one particularly useful essay for further study in this field is Andreas Musolff's 'Metaphor and Persuasion in Politics' (2017). While much of Musolff's work focuses on the function of metaphor in relation to ideology, this article focuses on the 'multi-functionality of metaphor as a central feature of persuasive power'. It could be argued that in seeing the concept of metaphor as multi-functional, Musolff moves the conversation of cognitive linguistics a step closer to re-evaluating the concept of metaphor itself along with the concept of semantic change. In this article Musolff considers a multi-functional concept of metaphor in relation to the persuasive power of political rhetoric. See Andreas Musolff, 'Metaphor and Persuasion in Politics', in *The Routledge Handbook of Metaphor and Language*, ed. by Elena Semino and Zsófia Demjén (London: Routledge, 2017), pp. 309–22.
23. Gerber, *Die Sprache als Kunst*, I, 333.
24. Ibid., p. 362.
25. Friedrich Nietzsche, 'On Truth and Lying in a Non-Moral Sense', in *The Birth of Tragedy and Other Writings*, trans. by Ronald Speirs (Cambridge: Cambridge University Press, 2012), pp. 139–53 (p. 142).
26. Ibid., p. 146.
27. Ibid., p. 143.
28. Ibid., p. 146.

BIBLIOGRAPHY

ADELAIDE, GEORGINA, ed., *The Life and Letters of The Right Honourable Friedrich Max Müller* (London: Longmans, Green, & Co., 1903)
AITCHISON, JEAN M. ['J.M.A.'], 'Diachronic and Synchronic', in *Concise Oxford Companion to the English Language*, ed. by Tom McArthur (Oxford: Oxford University Press, 1998 Oxford Reference Online,), p. 288, <https://www.oxfordreference.com/view/10.1093/acref/9780192800619.001.0001/acref-9780192800619-e-352?rskey=7iv7oV&result=357> [accessed 19 June 2020]
ALLISON, DAVID B., *The New Nietzsche: Contemporary Styles of Interpretation* (London: MIT Press, 1985)
ALSBERG, PAUL, *In Quest of Man: A Biological Approach to the Problem of Man's Place in Nature* (Oxford: Pergamon Press, 1970)
ANSELL-PEARSON, KEITH J., *How to Read Nietzsche* (London: Granta Books, 2005)
—— 'The Question of F. A. Lange's Influence on Nietzsche: A Critique of Recent Research from the Standpoint of the Dionysian', *Nietzsche-Studien*, 17 (1988), 539–54
'antinomy, n.', OED Online. June 2017. Oxford University Press. <http://www.oed.com> [accessed 13 May 2020]
AQUINAS, THOMAS, *Summa Theologiae*, trans. by The Dominican Council (Cambridge: Cambridge University Press, 2006)
—— *Super Boethium De Trinitate*, trans. by Rose E. Brennan (London: B. Herder, 1946)
ARISTOTLE, *De interpretatione*, trans. by H. P. Cooke and Hugh Tredennick, Loeb Classical Library (Cambridge, MA: Harvard University Press, 1938)
—— *Metaphysics*, trans. by Hugh Tredennick, Loeb Classical Library (Cambridge, MA: Harvard University Press, 1989)
—— *Nicomachean Ethics*, trans. by H. Rackham, Loeb Classical Library (Cambridge, MA: Harvard University Press, 1934)
—— *On the Soul*, trans. by W. S. Hett, Loeb Classical Library (Cambridge, MA: Harvard University Press, 1957)
—— *Poetics*, trans. by W. H. Fyfe, Loeb Classical Library (Cambridge, MA: Harvard University Press, 1932)
—— *Politics*, trans. by H. Rackham, Loeb Classical Library (Cambridge, MA: Harvard University Press, 1944)
—— *Rhetoric*, trans. by J. H. Freese, Loeb Classical Library (Cambridge, MA: Harvard University Press, 1926)
—— *Topica*, trans. by E. S. Forster, Loeb Classical Library (Cambridge, MA: Harvard University Press, 1989)
ARSENEAULT, M., 'Metaphor: Philosophical Theories', in *Encyclopedia of Language and Linguistics*, ed. by Keith Brown, 2nd edn (Oxford: Elsevier, 2006), pp. 40–43
BADIOU, ALAIN, 'Philosophy and Art', in *Infinite Thought: Truth and the Return of Philosophy*, trans. by Oliver Feltham and Justin Clemens (London: Bloomsbury, 2014), pp. 75–89
BARING, EDWARD, *The Young Derrida and French Philosophy, 1945–1968* (Cambridge: Cambridge University Press, 2011)

BARNES, JONATHAN, 'Rhetoric and Poetics', in *The Cambridge Companion to Aristotle*, ed. by Jonathan Barnes (Cambridge: Cambridge University Press, 1995), pp. 259–86

BEHLER, ERNST, 'Nietzsche's Conception of Irony', in *Nietzsche, Philosophy and the Arts*, ed. by Salim Kemal, Ivan Gaskell and Daniel W. Conway (Cambridge: Cambridge University Press, 2002), pp. 13–35

—— 'Nietzsche's Study of Greek Rhetoric', *Research in Phenomenology*, 25 (1995), 3–26

BEISER, FREDERICK C., *The Genesis of Neo-Kantianism 1796–1880* (Oxford: Oxford University Press, 2014)

BENNINGTON, GEOFFREY and JACQUES DERRIDA, *Jacques Derrida*, trans. by Geoffrey Bennington (Chicago: University of Chicago Press, 1993)

BERNS, LAURENCE, 'Rational Animal — Political Animal: Nature and Convention in Human Speech and Politics', *The Review of Politics*, 38.2 (1976), 177–89

BLACKBOURN, DAVID, *History of Germany 1780–1918: The Long Nineteenth Century* (Oxford: Blackwell, 2003).

BLUMENBERG, HANS, 'Affinitäten und Dissonanzen', in *Ein mögliches Selbstverständnis* (Stuttgart: Reclam, 1997), pp. 161–68

—— 'An Anthropological Approach to the Contemporary Significance of Rhetoric', in *After Philosophy: End or Transformation?*, ed. by Kenneth Baynes, James Bohman and Thomas McCarthy (Cambridge, MA: MIT Press, 1987), pp. 429–58

—— 'Beobachtungen an Metaphern', *Archiv für Begriffsgeschichte*, 15 (1971), 161–214

—— 'Lebenswelt und Technisierung unter Aspekten der Phänomenologie', in *Wirklichkeiten in denen wir leben* (Stuttgart: Reclam, 1981), pp. 7–54

—— 'The Life-world and the Concept of Reality', in *Life-World and Consciousness: Essays for Aron Gurwitsch*, ed. by Lester E. Embree (Evanston: Northwestern University Press, 1972), pp. 443–44

—— *Paradigms for a Metaphorology*, trans. by Robert Savage (Ithaca: Cornell University Press, 2010)

—— *Paradigmen zu einer Metaphorologie* (Frankfurt: Suhrkamp, 1998)—— *Paradigmes pour une métaphorologie*, trans. by Didier Gammelin (Paris: Vrin, 2006)

—— 'Prospect for a Theory of Nonconceptuality' in *Shipwreck with a Spectator: Paradigm of a Metaphor for Existence*, trans. by Steven Rendall (London: MIT Press, 1997), pp. 81–102

—— 'Selbstverständlichkeit, Selbstaufrichtung, Selbstvergleich', in *Theorie der Lebenswelt*, ed. by Manfred Sommer (Berlin: Suhrkamp, 2010), pp. 135–48

—— *Shipwreck with a Spectator: Paradigm of a Metaphor for Existence*, trans. by Steven Rendall (London: MIT Press, 1997)

—— *Theorie der Lebenswelt*, ed. by Manfred Sommer (Berlin: Suhrkamp, 2010)

—— 'Unwahrwerden einer Metapher', Nachlass Hans Blumenberg, Deutsches Literaturarchiv Marbach

—— *Work on Myth*, trans. by Robert M. Wallace (London: MIT Press, 1985)

BULL, MALCOLM, *Anti-Nietzsche* (London: Verso, 2011)

BYCHKOV, OLEG V. and ANNE SHEPPARD, 'Introduction', in *Greek and Roman Aesthetics*, ed. by Oleg V. Bychkov and Anne Sheppard (Cambridge: Cambridge University Press, 2010), pp. xi–xxx

CARR, DAVID, 'Translator's Introduction', in Edmund Husserl, *The Crisis of European Sciences and Transcendental Phenomenology* trans. by David Carr (Evanston: Northwestern University Press, 1970), pp. xv–xliii

CASSIRER, ERNST, *The Philosophy of Symbolic Forms*, trans. by Ralph Manheim, 3 vols (London: Yale University Press, 1953)

CAYGILL, HOWARD, *A Kant Dictionary* (Oxford: Blackwell, 1995)

CAZEAUX, CLIVE, *Metaphor and Continental Philosophy* (New York: Routledge, 2007)

CICERO, *On Invention*, trans. by H. M. Hubbell, Loeb Classical Library (Cambridge, MA and London: Loeb, 1949)
CHILTON, PAUL, 'Metaphors in Political Discourse', in *Encyclopedia of Language and Linguistics*, ed. by Keith Brown, 2nd edn (Oxford: Elsevier, 2006), pp. 63–65
COSTELLOE, TIMOTHY, 'Giambattista Vico', in *The Stanford Encyclopedia of Philosophy*, ed. by Edward N. Zalta (Summer 2016 Edition), <https://plato.stanford.edu/archives/sum2016/entries/vico/>
COULSON, SEANA, 'Metaphor and Conceptual Blending', in *Encyclopedia of Language and Linguistics*, ed. by Keith Brown, 2nd edn (Oxford: Elsevier, 2006), pp. 32–39
COUNCIL OF EUROPE and EUROPEAN COURT OF HUMAN RIGHTS, 'Guide on Article 9 of the European Convention of Human Rights', *Case-Law Guides*, 31 December 2019, <https://www.echr.coe.int/Documents/Guide_Art_9_ENG.pdf> [accessed 12 May 2020]
DE BRAUW, MICHAEL, 'The Parts of the Speech', in *A Companion to Greek Rhetoric*, ed. by Ian Worthington (Oxford: Blackwell, 2007), pp. 187–202
DE MAN, PAUL, *Allegories of Reading* (New Haven: Yale University Press, 1979)
—— 'Theory of Metaphor in Rousseau's *Second Discourse*', *Studies in Romanticism*, 12.2 (1973), 475–98
DENNETT, DANIEL C., *Consciousness Explained* (New York: Penguin, 1993)
DERRIDA, JACQUES, 'The Ends of Man', in *Margins of Philosophy*, trans. by Alan Bass (Chicago: University of Chicago Press, 1984), pp. 109–36
—— *Heidegger: The Question of Being and History*, trans. by Geoffrey Bennington, ed. by Thomas Dutoit (Chicago: University of Chicago Press, 2016)
—— 'Les fins de l'homme', in *Marges de la philosophie* (Paris: Minuit, 1972), pp. 129–64
—— *Margins of Philosophy*, trans. by Alan Bass (Chicago: University of Chicago Press, 1982)
—— 'La mythologie blanche', in *Marges de la Philosophie* (Paris: Minuit, 1972), pp. 247–324
—— *Of Grammatology*, trans. by Gayatri Chakravorty Spivak (London: Johns Hopkins University Press, 1976)
—— *Positions*, trans. by Alan Bass (London: Continuum, 2002)
—— 'The *Retrait* of Metaphor', in *Psyche: Inventions of the Other*, trans. by Peggy Kamuf (Stanford: Stanford University Press, 2007), pp. 48–80
—— 'White Mythology', in *Margins of Philosophy*, trans. by Alan Bass (Chicago: University of Chicago Press, 1984), pp. 207–71
—— *Writing and Difference*, trans. by Alan Bass (Chicago: University of Chicago Press, 1978)
DAVIDSON, DONALD, 'What Metaphors Mean', *Critical Inquiry*, 5.1 (1978), 31–47Denis Diderot, 'Lettre sur sourds et les muets I', *Œuvres complètes*, II (Paris: J. L. J. Brière, 1821), pp. 9–80
DIRVEN, RENÉ, HANS-GEORG WOLF and FRANK POLZENHAGEN, 'Cognitive Linguistics, Ideology, and Critical Discourse Analysis', in *The Oxford Handbook of Cognitive Linguistics*, ed. by Dirk Geeraerts and Hubert Cuyckens (Oxford: Oxford University Press, 2007), pp. 1222–40
DIVASSON, LOURDES and ISABEL K. LEÓN, 'Metaphors in English, French, and Spanish Medical Written Discourse', in *Encyclopedia of Language and Linguistics*, ed. by Keith Brown, 2nd edn (Oxford: Elsevier, 2006), pp. 58–63
DUTOIT, THOMAS, 'Editor's Note', in Jacques Derrida, *Heidegger: The Question of Being and History*, trans. by Geoffrey Bennington, ed. by Thomas Dutoit (Chicago: University of Chicago Press, 2016), pp. xv–xix
EUCLID, *Euclid's Elements*, trans. by Thomas L. Heath (Ann Arbor: Green Lion Press, 2007)
FAYE, EMMANUEL, *Heidegger: The Introduction of Nazism into Philosophy*, trans. by Michael B. Smith (New Haven: Yale University Press, 2009)
FINK, EUGEN, *Nietzsche's Philosophy*, trans. by Goetz Richter (London: Bloomsbury, 2013)

FRIEDMAN, NORMAN, 'symbol', *The Princeton Encyclopedia of Poetry and Poetics*, 4th edn (Princeton: Princeton University Press, 2012), pp. 1391–95
FRANCE, ANATOLE, *The Garden of Epicurus*, trans. by Alfred Allinson (New York: Dodd, Mean, 1923)
—— 'The Garden of Epicurus', by Anatole France, *Bartleby.com*, <http://www.bartleby.com/library/readersdigest/816.html> [accessed 13 May 2020]
—— 'The Garden of Epicurus', *Internet Encyclopedia of Philosophy*, <http://www.iep.utm.edu/garden/> [accessed 13 May 2020]
FULBROOK, MARY, *A History of Germany 1918–2014: The Divided Nation* (Chichester: Wiley, 2014)
GADAMER, HANS-GEORG, *Truth and Method*, trans. by Joel Weinsheimer and Donald G. Marshall (London: Continuum, 2004)
GAGARIN, MICHAEL, 'Background and Origins: Oratory and Rhetoric before the Sophists', in *A Companion to Greek Rhetoric*, ed. by Ian Worthington (Oxford: Blackwell, 2007), pp. 27–36
GARDNER, SEBASTIAN, *Kant and the Critique of Pure Reason* (New York: Routledge, 1999)
GEHRING, PETRA, 'Metapher', in *Blumenberg lesen: Ein Glossar*, ed. by Robert Buch and Daniel Weidner (Berlin: Suhrkamp, 2014), pp. 201–13
GERBER, GUSTAV, *Die Sprache als Kunst*, 2 vols (Bromberg: Mittler'sche Buchhandlung H. Heyfelder, 1871)
GIBBS JR., RAYMOND W., 'Metaphor: Psychological Aspects', in *Encyclopedia of Language and Linguistics*, ed. by Keith Brown, 2nd edn (Oxford: Elsevier, 2006), pp. 43–50
—— *The Poetics of Mind: Figurative Thought, Language and Understanding* (Cambridge: Cambridge University Press, 1994)
GORDON, PETER ELI, *Continental Divide* (Cambridge, MA: Harvard University Press, 2010)
GREISCH, JEAN, 'Les mots et les roses: la métaphore chez Martin Heidegger', *Revue des sciences théologiques et philosophiques*, 57.3 (1973), 443–56
GRIMM, JACOB UND WILHELM, 'Schlange', *Deutsches Wörterbuch*, IX (Leipzig: Hirzel, 1899)
HABERMAS, JÜRGEN, *Hermeneutik und Ideologiekritik*, ed. by Jürgen Habermas and Karl-Otto Apel (Frankfurt: Suhrkamp, 1971)
—— 'The Liberating Power of Symbols', in *The Liberating Power of Symbols: Philosophical Essays*, trans. by Peter Dews (Cambridge: Polity Press, 2001), pp. 1–29
—— *Philosophical Discourses of Modernity*, trans. by Frederick G. Lawrence (Cambridge, MA: MIT Press, 1990)
HALLIWELL, STEPHEN, *Aristotle's Poetics* (Chicago: University of Chicago Press, 1998)
HAVERKAMP, ANSELM, 'Blumenberg in Davos: The Cassirer–Heidegger Controversy Reconsidered', *MLN*, 131.3 (2016), 738–53
—— 'Deconstruction is/as Neopragmatism? Preliminary Remarks on Deconstruction in America', in *Deconstruction Is/In America: A New Sense of the Political*, ed. by Anselm Haverkamp (New York: NYU Press, 1995)
—— 'Editorisches Nachwort', in Hans Blumenberg, *Theorie der Unbegrifflichkeit*, ed. by Anselm Haverkamp (Frankfurt am Main: Suhrkamp, 2007), pp. 115–19
—— *Leaves of Mourning: Hölderlin's Late Work: With an Essay on Keats and Melancholy*, trans. by Vernon Chadwick (Albany: State University of New York Press, 1996)
—— 'Metaphorologie zweiten Grades: Unbegrifflichkeit, Vorformen der Idee', in *Metaphorologie zur Praxis von Theorie*, ed. by Anselm Haverkamp and Dirk Mende (Frankfurt am Main: Suhrkamp, 2009), pp. 237–55
—— 'Das Skandalon der Metaphorologie: Prolegomena eines Kommentars', in *Metaphorologie: Zur Praxis von Theorie*, ed. by Anselm Haverkamp and Dirk Mende (Frankfurt am Main: Suhrkamp, 2009), pp. 33–61

HEIDEGGER, MARTIN, *Being and Time*, trans. by John Macquarrie and Edward Robinson (New York: Harper Collins, 2008)
—— *Kant and the Problem of Metaphysics*, trans. by Richard Taft (Bloomington: Indiana University Press, 1997)
—— 'Letter on Humanism', in *Basic Writings*, trans. by Frank A. Capuzzi and J. Glenn Gray (London: Routledge, 2010), pp. 214–65
—— *Nietzsche*, trans. by David Farrell Krell (New York: Harper Collins, 1991)
—— *The Principle of Reason*, trans. by Reginald Lilly (Indianapolis: Indiana University Press, 1996)
—— 'The Question Concerning Technology', in *Basic Writings* (London: Routledge, 2010), pp. 308–41
—— *Unterwegs zur Sprache* (Tübingen: Neske, 1979)
HOBBES, THOMAS, *Leviathan*, ed. by Richard Tuck (Cambridge: Cambridge University Press, 1996)
HUBBELL, H. M., 'Introduction', in Cicero, *On Invention; The Best Kind of Orator; Topics*, trans. by H. M. Hubbell (Cambridge: Loeb, 1949), pp. vii–xivEdmund Husserl, *The Crisis of European Sciences and Transcendental Phenomenology*, trans. by David Carr (Evanston: Northwestern University Press, 1970)
ISOCRATES, *Evagoras*, trans. by George Norlin, 3 vols (Cambridge, MA: Harvard University Press, 1980)
JAKOBSON, ROMAN, 'Two Aspects of Language and Two Types of Aphasic Disturbances', in *On Language*, ed. by Linda R. Waugh and Monique Monville-Burston (Cambridge, MA: Harvard University Press, 1995), pp. 115–33
JANAWAY, CHRISTOPHER, 'The Real Essence of Human Beings: Schopenhauer and the Unconscious Will', in *Thinking the Unconscious: Nineteenth Century German Thought*, ed. by Angus Nicholls and Martin Liebscher (Cambridge: Cambridge University Press, Cambridge Books Online, 2010), <http://dx.doi.org/10.1017/CBO9780511712272> [accessed 13 May 2020]
JANICAUD, DOMINIQUE, *Heidegger in France*, trans. by François Raffoul and David Pettigrew (Indianapolis: Indiana University Press, 2015)
JOHNSON, CHRISTOPHER, *System and Writing in the Philosophy of Jacques Derrida* (Cambridge: Cambridge University Press, 1993)
JOHNSON, MARK, 'The Philosophical Significance of Image Schemas', in *From Perception to Meaning: Image Schemas in Cognitive Linguistics*, ed. by Beate Hampe (Berlin: De Gruyter, 2005), pp. 15–33
KANT, IMMANUEL, *An Answer to the Question: What is Enlightenment?*, trans. by H. B. Nisbet (London: Penguin, 2009)
—— *Critique of Judgement*, trans. by James Creed Meredith (Oxford: Oxford University Press, 2008)
—— *Critique of Pure Reason*, trans. by Marcus Weigelt (London: Penguin, 2007)
—— *Prolegomena to Any Future Metaphysics that will be able to come forward as Science*, trans. by Gary Hatfield (Cambridge: Cambridge University Press, 2004)
—— *Werke in sechs Bänden: Schriften zur Metaphysik und Logik*, 6 vols (Darmstadt: Wissenschaftliche Buchgesellschaft, 1998)
KEARNEY, RICHARD, *On Paul Ricoeur: The Owl of Minerva* (London: Routledge, 2004)
KIRKHAM, RICHARD, 'Truth, Correspondence Theory of', in *The Shorter Routledge Encyclopedia of Philosophy*, ed. by Edward Craig (London: Routledge, 2005), p. 1027
KLEMPERER, VICTOR, *The Language of the Third Reich: LTI-Lingua Tertii Imperii, a Philologist's Notebook*, trans. by Martin Brady (London: Bloomsbury, 2013)
KOFMAN, SARAH, *Nietzsche and Metaphor*, trans. by Duncan Large (London: Athlone Press, 1993)

KÖVECSES, ZOLTÁN, *Metaphor: A Practical Introduction* (Oxford: Oxford University Press, 2002)
—— *Metaphor in Culture: Universality and Variation* (Cambridge: Cambridge University Press, 2007)
KUNZ, HEIKE, 'Moment, God of the', *Religion Past and Present*, <http://dx.doi.org/10.1163/1877-5888_rpp_SIM_01286> [accessed 13 May 2020]
LAKOFF, GEORGE and MARK JOHNSON, *Metaphors We Live By* (Chicago: University of Chicago Press, 1980)
—— *Philosophy in the Flesh* (New York: Basic Books, 1999)
LAKOFF, GEORGE and MARK TURNER, *More than Cool Reason: A Field Guide to Poetic Metaphor* (London: The University of Chicago Press, 1989)
LAKOFF, GEORGE, *Moral Politics: How Liberals and Conservatives Think* (Chicago: University of Chicago Press, 2002).
LARGE, DUNCAN. 'Introduction', in Sarah Kofman *Nietzsche and Metaphor*, trans. by Duncan Large (London: Athlone Press, 1993), pp. vii–xl
—— 'Kofman's Nietzsche', in *Interpreting Nietzsche: Reception and Influence*, ed. by Ashley Woodward (London: Continuum, 2011), pp. 116–30
LAXNESS, HALDOR, *The Fish Can Sing*, trans. by Magnus Magnusson (London: Harvill Press, 2000)
LÉVI-STRAUSS, CLAUDE, *The Savage Mind*, trans. by George Weidenfeld (London: University of Chicago Press, 1966)
LIPTON, DAVID R, *Ernst Cassirer: The Dilemma of a Liberal Intellectual in Germany, 1914–1933* (London: University of Toronto Press, 1978)
LOCKE, JOHN, *An Essay Concerning Human Understanding*, 27th edn (London: T. Tegg & Son, 1836)
LONGINUS, *On the Sublime*, trans. by W. Hamilton Fyfe, Loeb Classical Library (Cambridge, MA: Harvard University Press, 1995)
MALABOU, CATHERINE, *What Should We Do with Our Brain?* (New York: Fordham University Press, 2008)
MARTIN, WALLACE, 'Metaphor', in *The Princeton Encyclopedia of Poetry and Poetics*, 4th edn (Princeton: Princeton University Press, 2012), pp. 863–70
MARTINICH, A. P., 'Metaphor', in *Routledge Encyclopedia of Philosophy*, v, ed. by Edward Craig (London: Routledge, 1998), p. 6
MARX, KARL, 'Theses on Feuerbach', in *Marx/Engels Selected Works*, I, trans. by W. Lough (Moscow: Progress Publishers, 1969), <https://www.marxists.org/archive/marx/works/1845/theses/theses.pdf> [accessed 13 May 2020]
MEIJERS, ANTHONIE, 'Gustav Gerber und Friedrich Nietzsche: Zum historischen Hintergrund der sprachphilosophischen Auffassungen des frühen Nietzsche', *Nietzsche-Studien*, 17 (1988), 369–90
MEIJERS, ANTHONIE and MARTIN STINGELIN, 'Konkordanz zu den wörtlichen Abschriften und Übernahmen von Beispielen und Zitaten aus Gustav Gerber: Die Sprache als Kunst (Bromberg 1871) in Nietzsches Rhetorik-Vorlesung und in "Über Wahrheit und Lüge im aussermoralischen Sinne"', *Nietzsche-Studien*, 17 (1988), 350–68
MENDE, DIRK, *Metapher — zwischen Metaphysik und Archäologie: Schelling, Heidegger, Derrida, Blumenberg* (Munich: Wilhelm Fink Verlag, 2013)
'Metapher', *Historisches Wörterbuch der Philosophie*, ed. by Ritter, Gründer, v (Basel: Schwabe, 1980)
'μεταφορά', in Henry George Liddell and Robert Scott, *A Greek-English Lexicon*. (Oxford: Clarendon Press, 1940), <http://www.perseus.tufts.edu/hopper/text?doc=Perseus:text:1999.04.0057:entry=metafora/> [accessed 13 May 2020]

'metaphor, n.', OED Online. June 2017. Oxford University Press. <http://www.oed.com/> [accessed 13 May 2020]

MORAN, DERMOT, *Husserl's Crisis of European Sciences and Transcendental Phenomenology: An Introduction* (Cambridge: Cambridge University Press, 2012)

MOORE, GREGORY, *Nietzsche, Biology and Metaphor* (Cambridge: Cambridge University Press, 2002)

MÜLLER, FRIEDRICH MAX, *Comparative Mythology: An Essay* (London: Routledge, 1909)

—— *Lectures on the Science of Language*, 2 vols (London: Longmans, Green, & Co., 1880)

MUSOLFF, ANDREAS, 'Friedrich Max Müller's Cultural Concept of Metaphor', *Publications of the English Goethe Society*, 85.2-3 (2016), 125-34

—— *Metaphor, Nation and the Holocaust: The Concept of the Body Politic* (London: Routledge, 2010)

—— 'Metaphor and Persuasion in Politics', in *The Routledge Handbook of Metaphor and Language*, ed. by Elena Semino and Zsófia Demjén (London: Routledge, 2017), pp. 309-22

—— *Metaphor and Political Discourse: Analogical Reasoning in Debates about Europe* (New York: Palgrave Macmillan, 2004)

—— *Political Metaphor Analysis* (London: Bloomsbury Academic, 2016)

NICHOLLS, ANGUS, *Myth and the Human Sciences: Hans Blumenberg's Theory of Myth* (London: Routledge, 2015)

NIETZSCHE, FRIEDRICH, *Beyond Good and Evil*, trans. by R. J. Hollingdale (London: Penguin, 2003)

—— *Human, All Too Human*, trans. by Marion Faber and Stephen Lehmann (London: Penguin, 2004)

—— *Kritische Gesamtausgabe*, ed. by Giorgio Colli and Mazzino Montinari, 9 vols (Berlin and New York: De Gruyter, 1967)

—— *Nietzsche Briefwechsel*, in *Kritische Gesamtausgabe*, ed. by Giorgio Colli and Mazzino Montinari, 9 vols (Berlin; New York: De Gruyter, 1975)

—— 'On Truth and Lying in a Non-Moral Sense', in *The Birth of Tragedy and Other Writings*, trans. by Ronald Speirs (Cambridge: Cambridge University Press, 2012), pp. 139-53

—— *Über Wahrheit und Lüge im aussermoralischen Sinne* (Stuttgart: Reclams Universal Bibliothek, 2015)

PEETERS, BENOIT, *Derrida: A Biography*, trans. by Andrew Brown (Cambridge: Polity Press, 2013)

PLANTINGA, ALVIN, *God and Other Minds* (London: Cornell University Press, 1967).

QUINTILIAN, *Institutio Oratoria*, trans. by Harold Edgeworth Butler, Loeb Classical Library (Cambridge, MA: Harvard University Press, 1922)

RACE, WILLIAM H, 'Rhetoric and Lyric Poetry', in *A Companion to Greek Rhetoric*, ed. by Ian Worthington (Oxford: Blackwell, 2007), pp. 509-25

RAMUS, PETER, *Arguments in Rhetoric against Quintilian: Translation and Text of Peter Ramus's 'Rhetoricae distinctiones in Quintilianum'*, trans. by Carole Newlands (Carbondale: Southern Illinois University Press, 1986)

RICHARDS, I. A., *The Philosophy of Rhetoric* (Oxford: Oxford University Press, 2001)

RICOEUR, PAUL, 'Hermeneutics and the Critique of Ideology', in *From Text to Action: Essays in Hermeneutics*, II, trans. by John B. Thompson (London: Continuum, 2008), pp. 263-99

—— *The Rule of Metaphor*, trans. by Robert Czerny (London: Routledge, 2003)—— 'The Task of Hermeneutics', in *From Text to Action: Essays in Hermeneutics*, II, trans. by John B. Thompson (London: Continuum, 2008), pp. 51-71

—— *Time and Narrative*, trans. by Kathleen McLaughlin and David Pellauer, 3 vols (Chicago: University of Chicago Press, 1984)

RORTY, RICHARD, 'The Contingency of Selfhood', *London Review of Books*, 8 (1986), 11–15
ROSE, DAVID, 'Metaphor, Grammatical', in *Encyclopedia of Language and Linguistics*, ed. by Keith Brown, 2nd edn (Oxford: Elsevier, 2006), pp. 66–73
ROUSSEAU, JEAN-JACQUES, *Essay on the Origin of Languages*, in *The Collected Writings of Rousseau*, vii, trans. and ed. by John T. Scott, 14 vols (Hanover, NH: University Press of New England, 1998), pp. 289–332
RYAN, SEAN, 'Heidegger's Nietzsche', in *Interpreting Nietzsche*, ed. by Ashley Woodward (London: Continuum, 2011), pp. 5–19
SAFRANSKI, RÜDIGER, *Nietzsche: A Philosophical Biography*, trans. by Shelley Frisch (London: Granta Books, 2002)
SATLOFF, ROBERT, *Among the Righteous: Lost Stories from the Holocaust's Long Reach into Arab Lands* (New York: Public Affairs, 2006)
SAUSSURE, FERDINAND DE, *Course in General Linguistics*, trans. by Roy Harris (London: Bloomsbury, 2013)
SAVAGE, ROBERT, 'Afterword', in Hans Blumenberg, *Paradigms for a Metaphorology*, trans. by Robert Savage (Ithaca: Cornell University Press, 2010), pp. 133–46
SCHOPENHAUER, ARTHUR, *Die Welt als Wille und Vorstellung*, Schopenhauer Sämtliche Werke (Stuttgart and Frankfurt am Main: J. G. Cotta'sche Buchhandlung Nachfolger, 1960)
—— *The World as Will and Representation*, trans. by R. B. Haldane and J. Kemp (London: Kegan Paul, Trench, Trübner & Co., 1909)
SCHRIFT, ALAN D., *Nietzsche and the Question of Interpretation: Between Hermeneutics and Deconstruction* (New York: Routledge, 1990)
SEMINO, ELENA, *Metaphor in Discourse* (Cambridge: Cambridge University Press, 2008)
SILESIUS, ANGELUS, *Cherubinischer Wandersmann*, in *Sämtliche poetische Werke*, I, ed. by Hans Ludwig Held (Munich: Hanser, 1952), pp. 7–218
SIMS, ALEXANDRA, 'Marine Le Pen cleared of inciting hatred after comparing Muslim prayers in the street to the Nazi occupation', *Independent*, 15 December 2015, <https://www.independent.co.uk/news/world/europe/marine-le-pen-cleared-of-inciting-hatred-after-comparing-muslim-prayers-in-the-street-to-nazi-a6774126.html> [accessed 12 May 2020]Sommer, Manfred, 'Editorische Notiz', in *Theorie der Lebenswelt*, ed. by Manfred Sommer (Berlin: Suhrkamp, 2010), pp. 248–50
—— 'Nachwort des Herausgebers', in Hans Blumenberg, *Theorie der Lebenswelt*, ed. by Manfred Sommer (Berlin: Suhrkamp, 2010), pp. 243–47
SPIVAK, GAYATRI CHAKRAVORTY, 'Translator's Preface', in Jacques Derrida, *Of Grammatology*, trans. by Gayatri Chakravorty Spivak (London: Johns Hopkins University Press, 1976), pp. ix–lxxxvii
STACK, GEORGE, *Lange and Nietzsche* (Berlin: De Gruyter, 1983)
STEEN, GERARD, 'Metaphor: Stylistic Approaches', in *Encyclopedia of Language and Linguistics*, ed. by Keith Brown, 2nd edn (Oxford: Elsevier, 2006), pp. 51–57
—— *Understanding Metaphor in Literature: An Empirical Approach* (New York: Longman, 1994)
STEINER, PETER, HENRYK BARAN, CONOR KLAMANN and JONATHAN CULLER, 'structuralism', in *The Princeton Encyclopedia of Poetry and Poetics*, 4th edn (Princeton: Princeton University Press, 2012), pp. 1361–66
UNDERHILL, JAMES W., *Creating Worldviews: Metaphor, Ideology and Language* (Edinburgh: Edinburgh University Press, 2011)
VAN DEN BOSCH, LOURENS P., *Friedrich Max Mueller: A Life Devoted to the Humanities* (Leiden: Brill, 2002)
VICO, GIAMBATTISTA, *The New Science*, trans. by Thomas Goddard Bergin and Max Harold Fisch (London: Cornell University Press, 1984)

WINTERS, MARGARET E., HELI TISSARI, and KATHRYN ALLAN, eds, *Historical Cognitive Linguistics* (Berlin: De Gruyter, 2010)

ZAVATTA, BENEDETTA, 'Nietzsche and Linguistics', in *Nietzsche on Consciousness and the Embodied Mind*, ed. by Manuel Dries (Berlin: De Gruyter, 2016), pp. 265–89

ZILL, RÜDIGER, '"Substrukturen des Denkens": Grenzen und Perspektive einer Metapherngeschichte nach Hans Blumenberg', in *Begriffsgeschichte, Diskursgeschichte, Metapherngeschichte*, ed. by Hans Erich Bödeker (Göttingen: Wallstein, 2002), pp. 209–58

INDEX

absolute metaphor *see* metaphor
Adorno, Theodor W. 22, 124, 126, 128
Allison, David B. 61
Alsberg, Paul 146–47
   body liberation 147
Anglophone reception
   of Blumenberg 5, 123, 124, 127, 133
   of Derrida ix, 159
   of Nietzsche 61, 62
Ansell-Pearson, Keith J. 85 n. 78
anthropology 5, 10, 65, 89, 97, 105–06, 148, 179 n. 22
   Kant's fourth question 89–93, 97
   philosophical anthropology 66, 90, 92, 93, 97, 146, 147
   structural anthropology 9
anthropomorphism 4, 46, 65–67, 78, 81, 131
anti-Semitism 125, 126
a priori 50–53, 73, 74, 95, 120 n. 78
Aquinas, Thomas 11, 38, 42–43, 46, 47, 77
archaeology *see* concept: history of; metaphor, history of
Aristotle 1–3, 6, 10, 11, 16, 17, 31–43, 47, 48, 52, 68, 76, 77, 108, 109, 137, 147, 148, 184, 186
   Metaphysics 38, 77
   Nicomachean Ethics 38–39
   Poetics 32–33, 34–37, 52, 108, 184
   Rhetoric 32, 35, 37, 38, 40, 77, 108
   see also metaphor: Aristotelian paradigm of

Badiou, Alain 112–13
Baring, Edward 157, 159
Barnes, Jonathan 35
Behler, Ernst 60, 68–70, 75
Being 160
   authentic 124, 130, 132, 135, 139
   concealment of 129, 135
   manifestation of 104, 110
   question of 5, 12, 88, 90, 97–117
   see also Heidegger, Martin; metaphysics
Bennington, Geoffrey 165, 168, 169
the Bible 97, 116
Black, Max 8–9, 11
Blumenberg, Hans 1, 5, 12–14, 26, 27, 40, 46, 48, 54, 62, 66, 88, 90, 123–49, 155, 156, 158, 159, 165–67, 173, 174, 186, 187
   experience of National Socialism 126
   see also Anglophone reception

body liberation *see* Alsberg, Paul

Carr, David 140–41, 142
Cassirer, Ernst 66, 87–101, 104, 107, 118 n. 29, 119 n. 44, 120 n. 71, 134, 135
Caygill, Howard 48, 49, 52, 53
Cazeaux, Clive ix, 5, 10–12, 18, 19, 48–52, 93, 101, 107, 118 n. 1, 168, 172–73
change *see* semantics: change
Cicero xi, 32, 40, 41, 44, 77, 137, 164
Claessens, Dieter 147
cognition 4–9, 12, 18–20, 24, 26, 31, 42, 45, 46, 48, 53, 60, 62, 67, 68, 71, 73, 76, 79, 80, 87, 102, 104, 110, 131–33, 144, 149, 155, 158, 168, 171, 173, 184, 186–90
   cognitive orientation 7, 24, 149
cognitive linguistics *see* linguistics: cognitive
Cohen, Hermann 92–94
Coleridge, Samuel Taylor 111
communication 93, 115
   discourse 1, 2, 14, 23, 71, 107–10, 117, 133, 160, 166, 169
   ideological 23–25, 175, 188
   scenarios 23, 24, 189
   speech 2, 6, 32–35, 38, 39, 42, 44, 69, 104, 112, 159, 177
communism 157–58
concept:
   concept formation 9, 17, 19, 23, 68, 124, 129–32, 135, 137
   history of 20, 68, 123, 124, 126, 129, 130, 135, 159, 160, 167
   see also history
consciousness 99, 105, 114, 115, 148, 186, 190
consensus
   mutual rhetorical consensus 146–49
   sensus communis 148
convention 67–82
culture 6, 7, 8, 9, 22, 33, 34, 45, 63, 64, 83, 91, 94, 95, 125, 141, 147, 157, 158, 185, 189
   cultural relativism 7, 21–22, 69, 183
   cultural variation 21, 23
   cultural world 9, 142–43
Curtius, Georg 64, 65

Dasein see existence
Davidson, Donald 8, 9
Davos 5, 87–106, 120 n. 71, 127, 134, 135

deconstruction *see* Derrida, Jacques
Deleuze, Gilles 15
De Man, Paul 45, 60, 61
Derrida, Jacques ix, 5, 6, 8, 12, 13–14, 22, 26, 27, 48, 54, 61, 62, 66, 88, 102, 149, 155–78, 186, 189
  deconstruction 12, 60, 156, 161–64, 174
  experience in Vichy French Algeria 156–57
  retrait 102, 155, 172, 173, 176, 178
  supplement 5, 159
  the text 160–61, 165, 173
  the trace 163–64
  trait 178
  usure 167, 168–69, 171–73, 176
  see also Anglophone reception
Descartes, René 11, 129, 130, 135, 136
diachrony 8, 20, 23, 26, 158–59, 171, 177, 186
  etymology 7, 71, 159, 169, 170, 174, 177
  etymon 170, 173, 174
Diderot, Denis 44, 45, 46, 48, 68
Ding-an-sich 74, 75, 76, 80
  see also Kant
Diogenes 169
Dionysian 16, 35
Dirven, René 17
disease of language *see* metaphor
Dräger, Heinrich 125
Dutoit, Thomas 163

embodiment 18–21, 25, 134, 185–86
  embodied realism 16, 18
Empedocles 1, 3, 35, 36, 37, 78
empirical 17–19, 25, 49, 50, 52, 53, 54, 74, 76, 81, 129, 168, 185, 186, 187
the Enlightenment 32, 40, 43–50, 68, 82, 144
Epicurus 1, 32, 48, 169
epistemology 10, 11, 49–51, 66, 73, 116
  epistemic 19
etymology *see* diachrony
etymon see diachrony
Euclid 52
Europe 32, 40, 90, 140, 157, 188
  European civilisation 45, 93, 147
  post-war *see* post-war: Europe
evolution:
  anthropogenesis and the role of metaphor 144
  biological 19–20, 147
  conceptual 3, 19, 31, 41
  Darwin, Charles 67
  historical 20, 110, 112
  of language *see* language
  of metaphoric meaning *see* metaphor
existence 66–67, 98–101, 107–12, 134, 136, 141, 148
  Dasein 97–101, 109, 112, 115, 135, 157
  Daseingrund 128–29
  existential analytic 5, 89, 98–103, 106, 107, 112, 135–37, 148, 162

existentialism 140
  see also Heidegger, Martin
experience 4, 10–11, 18, 19–21, 39, 48–54, 69, 73, 74, 78, 87, 94, 96, 98, 101, 105, 109, 111, 114–15, 117, 136, 141, 144, 146, 148, 156, 157, 186

false 39, 139, 188
  untrue 138
the figurative 12, 44, 48, 59, 61, 64, 68, 79, 83, 103, 183–84, 190
  literary tropes 53–54, 74, 132
    analogy 1, 11, 34–36, 48–49, 51, 52–55, 68, 81, 97, 99, 132, 145, 169–70, 171
    metonymy 4, 9, 31, 41, 45, 78, 159
    symbolism 9, 53–54, 74, 132
  logic of:
    substitution 9, 42, 46, 103, 104, 130, 135, 135, 144, 148, 149
    transference 1–2, 3, 9, 17, 20, 32–34, 36–37, 40, 63, 70, 78, 168, 176
    transposition 10, 102
finite 98, 100, 101, 103, 114
  finitude 92–93, 95, 96, 97–98, 100, 102, 104, 113–14
Fink, Eugen 62, 77
Foucault, Michel 15, 61
France 14–15, 44, 60, 93, 102, 156–59, 162, 188–89
  language 9, 15, 108, 156–57, 159, 166, 168
  Paris 15, 77, 156, 157, 162
  post-war *see* post-war: France
  Vichy French Algeria 156–57
France, Anatole 169
Fulbrook, Mary 91

Gadamer, Hans-Georg 4, 88, 114–15, 117, 124, 128
Gagarin, Michael 33
Gardner, Sebastian 47, 50
Gehlen, Arnold 147
Gehring, Petra ix, 129, 130
genealogy *see* metaphor: history of; history of concepts
Gerber, Gustav xi, 45, 46, 64, 65, 68
  Lautbilder 69–70, 71, 78, 184, 189
Germany 23, 64, 65, 91, 119 n. 44, 124–26, 140, 147, 175
  language 13, 23, 24, 25, 69, 71, 72, 74, 79–80, 100, 127, 143, 147, 175, 177
  philology ix, 4, 46, 59, 63–65, 68, 70, 72–73, 75, 84 n. 25
  post-war *see* post-war: Germany
  National Socialist 23, 91, 125, 126, 140, 156, 189
    see also Nazi; Third Reich
  in nineteenth century 63–65, 93, 143
  Weimar republic 91, 126
Gibbs, Raymond W. Jr 17
God (Christian) 42–43, 47, 53–54
  Augenblicksgott 143–45, 149

idea of 54, 76
  representation of 52, 132
  see also gods (Greek); gods (Roman); Janus
gods (Greek) 33–34, 58 n. 119, 66
gods (Roman) 45–46, 66
  see also Janus
Goebbels, Joseph 24–25, 175, 176, 177, 188
Goethe, Johann Wolfgang von 71, 73, 75
Gordon, Peter Eli 90–91
Greisch, Jean 102
ground:
  of cognition 102, 190
  existential 128-29, 134
  literal see the literal
  of meaning 4, 5, 7, 12, 21, 31, 32, 35, 61, 69, 72, 88,
    104, 106, 107, 109, 110, 123–24, 135, 146, 167,
    170, 171, 173, 174, 185–86, 190
    see also semantics
  metaphoric 135
  ontological 116, 186, 189
  of praxis 141-42
  of rhetorical consensus 155
  of symbols 136
  transcendental 134
  see also metaphysics

Habermas, Jürgen 22, 114–15, 124, 161
Halliwell, Stephen 37
Haverkamp, Anselm 88, 103, 126, 127–28, 129, 134,
  156, 166
Heidegger, Martin 4, 5, 12–14, 15, 51, 87–118, 123,
  126, 127–29, 134–36, 137, 139, 140, 141, 146, 148,
  157–58, 161–63, 164, 186
Hegel, Georg Wilhelm Friedrich 162–63
Henry VIII 31, 47
Herder, Johann Gottfried 45, 46
hermeneutics 4, 6, 9, 18, 88, 97, 105–06, 113–18, 126,
  136, 155, 177–78
  biblical hermeneutics 97, 99, 116
  distanciation 109, 116–17
  hermeneutic limit 6, 18, 25, 26, 113, 155, 183
  interpretation 4, 7, 8–9, 15, 17, 51, 59, 61, 62–63,
    82–83, 93, 94, 95, 97, 106, 112–13, 115–17,
    120 n. 81, 126, 127, 129, 134, 157–58, 160, 162,
    174, 177
  conflict of 110, 116–17, 149
  philosophical hermeneutics 4, 114
Heselhaus, Clemens 126
Hesiod 33
history, intellectual 2, 32, 107, 119 n. 44, 123, 124
  see also concept: history of; metaphor, history of
Hobbes, Thomas 44, 46, 47, 48, 68, 81, 137, 190
Hölderlin, Friedrich 102–03, 104, 111–12, 135
Homer 33, 34, 37, 116, 127
Horkheimer, Max 126
human sciences 105–06, 117

Husserl, Edmund 92, 105, 125, 140–43, 145, 158, 186
hypotyposis see the understanding

identity see metaphysics
ideology 6–7, 8, 22–24, 25, 26, 29 n. 29, 83, 98, 112,
  113–18, 123, 155, 175, 177, 178, 183, 185, 187–89
  hate speech 6, 112
  political 2, 6, 13, 22–23, 26, 175, 188
imagination 40, 51, 52, 54, 58 n. 109, 92, 94–96, 98,
  101, 104, 108, 109, 111
  exhibitio derivative 52, 95
  exhibitio originaria 52, 95
instinct 39, 45, 82, 146, 148
the intellect 67, 68, 79, 81, 82, 190
intellectual history see history
interpretation see hermeneutics
intuition 51, 53, 62, 83, 95, 128, 131, 132, 141
irrationalism 38, 39, 67, 140, 141
Isocrates 1, 32, 34

Jakobson, Roman 8–9
Janus (Roman god) 3, 60, 87, 123, 183
Jaspers, Karl 140
Jauss, Hans Robert 126
Johnson, Mark 1, 2, 11, 17–20, 21, 25, 51, 177, 186, 187
Judaism 23, 125, 126, 147, 156–57
judgement 38, 44, 47, 49–51, 53–54, 62, 77, 89, 94–95,
  104, 132, 184
  the ability to judge 39, 47, 55, 117
  a practical vs a theoretical determination 26–27
  schematism 51–54, 58 n. 109, 95, 101, 104, 132

Kant, Immanuel 2, 4, 11–12, 32, 41, 46, 47–55, 59, 68,
  72–76, 89–90, 92–98, 101, 104, 127, 131–32, 134,
  141, 171, 184
Kearney, Richard 106
Keats, John 110–11, 115
Klemperer, Victor 23–25, 26, 113, 175, 176–78, 187–88
knowledge 9, 43–44, 46–48, 50, 53–54, 62, 70, 73, 76,
  82, 93–94, 97–101, 106, 112, 132, 141, 162
Kofman, Sarah 3, 7, 12, 14–16, 60–61, 62–63, 68, 82,
  90, 104, 160, 186
Kövecses, Zoltán 20–22, 25, 185
Kristeva, Julia 161, 165

Lacoue-Labarthe, Philippe 61
Lakoff, George 1, 2, 11, 16–20, 21, 25, 177, 186, 187
Lange, Friedrich Albert 72
language:
  evolution of over time 165, 171
  natural 165, 173
  phonetics 64, 69–70, 158, 161, 184, 189
  social dimension 7, 17, 24, 69, 81, 83, 146, 148,
    155–56, 176, 177–78, 185, 187
  syntax 33, 171
  as a tool for survival 145

Large, Duncan 15, 16, 63
Lautbilder see Gerber, Gustav
Laxness, Haldor 99
Le Pen, Marine 188, 189
Lévi-Strauss, Claude 9–10, 18, 158
Levinas, Emmanuel 91
lexis 34, 35, 37, 71, 108, 184
Liebmann, Otto 93
Life-world 123, 128, 129, 136, 139–46, 148–49, 186–88, 190
  framework of expectations 129, 132, 133
  horizon 123, 141, 142, 144
  pre-theoretical 140–42
likeness 2, 3, 6, 19, 31, 36, 37–41, 43, 46–47, 59, 63, 69, 72, 76–83, 112, 137
  resemblance 78, 110–11, 170
  similarity 3, 36, 40, 48, 52–54, 68, 131, 132, 170
  see also mimesis
linguistics 2, 3, 7, 8, 9, 10, 16–22, 23, 25–26, 32, 36, 64, 68, 105, 107, 158–59, 161, 175, 183, 185–87, 189
  cognitive 2, 3, 7, 8, 16–22, 25–26, 36, 68, 175, 183, 185–87, 189, 191 n. 22
  comparative 64
  linguisticality 114
  structural *see* structuralism
the literal 2, 36, 44, 59, 64, 71, 103, 129, 183, 184
  literal ground 138–39, 173
literature 9, 16–17, 20, 31, 80, 131–32, 169
Locke, John 44, 45, 46, 47, 48, 68
logic 9, 38, 47–48, 50, 52, 55, 68, 93, 103–04, 130, 132, 133, 135–36, 161–62, 169, 173, 176
  logicality 124, 130, 132, 133–34
logos 35, 36, 39, 52, 133, 169
Longinus, Cassius 33
Löwith, Karl 126
Lyceum 184

Macquarrie, John 100
Malabou, Catherine 187
Mann, Thomas 90–91, 125
Martin, Wallace 46
Marx, Karl 113, 163
meaning 1–8, 11–13, 16–22, 24–27, 31–33, 36–37, 40, 43, 45, 47, 58 n. 109, 59, 61, 62, 69–70, 72, 74, 78–79, 81, 82, 83, 87, 88–89, 93, 96, 97, 98, 100, 103, 104, 106–07, 109, 110, 112, 117, 123–24, 128–29, 134–35, 137, 138–39, 146, 148, 149, 155, 156, 160, 162, 165, 167, 168, 169, 170–71, 172–78, 183–90
  creation of 8, 12–13, 87, 103, 107, 109, 110, 112, 117
  see also semantics
Meijers, Anthonie 69, 70, 71
Mende, Dirk 13–14, 166
Merleau-Ponty, Maurice 11, 18, 19
metaphor:
  absolute 5, 14, 126, 130–33, 165

  Aristotelian paradigm of 1–17, 25, 31–55, 59, 72, 76, 88, 137, 167, 185, 186
  and biology 19–20, 63, 147–49
  concept of 2–3, 6, 8, 9, 14, 16–18, 23–27, 32, 41, 42, 52, 59, 61, 73, 75, 78, 83, 87–91, 102, 103, 112, 124, 129, 156, 164–70, 173, 183, 184, 190, 191 n. 22
  dead 177
  as a disease of language 65–67, 79, 80
    see also Müller, Max
  everyday 6, 16, 19, 22, 24–25
  evolution of over time 3, 20, 110, 187–88
  forgotten 66, 169, 171
  as a foundational element 1, 89, 102, 110, 124, 130, 135, 143, 187
  in the Graeco-Roman world 1–3, 6, 10, 11, 16, 17, 31–46, 47, 48, 52, 68, 76, 77, 108, 109, 116, 127, 133, 137, 138, 147, 148, 159, 163, 184, 186
  as a *Halbzeug* 127–28
  history of 2, 41–42, 62, 124, 145, 159–60, 165, 171
  as indissoluble in logicality 133–34
  inventive 11, 48, 49
  and literature 9, 16–17, 20, 31, 80, 131–32, 169
  of light for truth 6, 83
  of light for the divine 6, 83, 130
  metaphorical animal 16, 61, 68, 80, 90, 98, 103, 155
  metaphorology 5, 13–14, 126–29, 134, 159, 166–67, 173
  metaphysical concept of 14, 166
  mobile army 4, 59, 78, 79, 83, 102, 170, 190
    see also Nietzsche
  network of 167, 177, 189
  as ornament in rhetoric 37, 137, 147
  as a peace treaty 81–82, 137, 174, 189–90
  in philosophical discourse 13, 59, 165, 169
  poetic 6, 16
  political 2, 6, 23, 174
  as providing auxiliary service to cognition 129
  as providing social and historical orientation 27, 144, 146, 155–56, 176–78
  referential function 109–10, 136
  religious 54, 130
  riddle of 123–24, 132, 135–36, 148
  as a sum of human relations 4, 72, 78, 79, 127
  toleration of 124, 135–36, 148
metaphysics 3, 8, 11, 13, 14, 32, 35, 37, 38–40, 47–55, 66, 72, 73, 75–77, 82, 88, 89, 91, 93, 94, 97–104, 109–10, 113, 114, 116, 123–24, 129, 134–36, 159–71, 174, 176, 185
  actuality 110, 111
  destruction of 162
  essence 3, 15, 43, 47, 61, 159
  identity 42, 48–49, 68, 76, 99, 187
  loss of the proper 3, 7, 12, 15–16, 61, 62, 63, 82, 186, 190
  metaphysical concept of metaphor *see* metaphor

ontology 5, 10–11, 89, 90, 92, 97, 98, 99, 100, 101, 105–11, 114, 116–17, 127–28, 141, 160, 162–63, 167, 172–73, 186, 189
potentiality 108, 112
presence 159–60
see also Being
mimesis 3, 38, 39–40, 108, 109, 110
imitation 39, 108
see also likeness
modernism 91
Moore, Gregory 62, 63
Moran, Dermot 140
Müller, Friedrich Max 45, 46, 64, 65–68, 69, 70, 71, 79, 80–82, 152 n. 98, 168, 171
Musolff, Andreas ix, 17, 23, 24, 25, 56 n. 64, 66–67, 188–89, 191 n. 22
mutual understanding 83, 87–89, 93, 95, 96, 98, 107, 112–13, 117, 137, 146, 148–49
mysticism 54, 100, 112
mythos 133, 143, 169
myth 9, 65–66, 90, 92, 94, 124, 133, 135, 136, 143–45, 169, 173, 174
myth and metaphor 90, 133, 145, 152 n. 98
mythology 9, 46, 65–66, 68, 70, 80, 165, 169

Nancy, Jean-Luc 61
narrative 40, 107, 108, 112–13
see also mythos
nature:
natural phenomena 65–67
phusis 108, 184
Nazi 23–25, 113, 140, 157–58, 175, 178, 188
rhetoric *see also* ideology
see also Germany: National Socialist; Third Reich
neo-Kantian 85 n. 53, 92–94
see also Cohen, Hermann
neuroscience 187
nerve stimulation 71
neurological 19
neuroplasticity 187
Nietzsche, Friedrich ix, 3–8, 11–16, 18–19, 24–26, 31–32, 35–36, 41–42, 45–49, 51, 55, 59–83, 87–94, 98, 101–04, 107, 110, 112–13, 115, 117, 123–24, 129–30, 135, 137–39, 145, 147–49, 155–56, 160, 162–64, 166, 167, 168, 170, 171, 172, 174, 178, 183–86, 188–90
deception 67, 79–81, 82
dissimulation 67, 68, 79, 81, 82, 90, 184, 189–90
forgetfulness 65, 66, 67, 81, 82, 83, 152 n. 98
a mobile army 4, 59, 78, 79, 83, 102, 170, 190
the new Nietzsche 14–15, 60–61
post-Nietzschean 4–8, 11, 12, 14, 18, 25, 26, 48–49, 68, 83, 87–90, 98, 101, 123, 129, 156, 167, 188
will to power 15, 60–61, 104, 160
see also Anglophone reception
Nicholls, Angus ix, 90, 124–26, 129, 132, 143, 144

Norton, Thomas 31

objective 12, 53, 73, 91, 92–93, 95, 96–101, 104, 148
ontology:
fundamental 89, 98–99, 101, 105–06, 107, 109, 110, 117, 127, 128, 186, 189
see metaphysics
origin 4, 6, 8, 19, 27, 44, 52, 66, 68, 70–72, 74, 76, 77, 78, 87, 94, 115, 117, 140–41, 147, 161, 165, 168, 169–71, 174, 176, 190
of meaning *see* semantics
see also metaphysics

paradigm 2, 4, 5, 31–32, 35–37, 39, 41, 43, 44, 47, 49, 55, 59, 64, 72, 87, 92, 93, 110, 115, 145, 173, 185–86
perception 19, 37, 39, 48, 63, 65, 68–74, 76, 79, 81, 82, 83, 117, 139, 148–49, 160, 168, 171, 174
phenomenology 92, 125, 143, 157, 159, 186
philology *see* Germany: philology
philosophy
analytic 9, 10
continental 10
as a critical gesture 113–15, 151 n. 37
European 2–27, 41, 42, 59, 83, 87–88, 91–92, 105, 118 n. 1, 156, 183–90
as an interpretive gesture 114
of language 60, 112
philosophical language 44, 124, 130, 165, 167, 170–71, 173
post-Kantian 2, 11, 59, 72
of religion 151 n. 37
scholastic philosophy *see also* Aquinas, Thomas
Plato 34, 38, 47, 48, 77, 133, 138, 159, 163
Plessner, Helmuth 147
poetry 1, 3, 4, 6, 9, 13, 16, 20, 31, 34, 35, 37, 40, 45, 46, 78, 80, 89, 102, 103, 104, 107–13, 116, 117, 131, 135, 146
the poetic 33, 34, 35, 41, 52, 107, 109, 110
poetic revelation *see* revelation
romantic 13, 46, 89, 110–12, 117, 146
the political
political discourse 17, 183
political metaphor *see* metaphor: political
Polzenhagen, Frank 17
post-war:
Europe 61, 105
France 14–15, 60, 120 n. 81, 156–59
Germany 124–26
pragmatic 4–7, 10–13, 25–26, 59, 62, 63, 64, 68, 79, 81–83, 88–89, 112, 113, 118, 123, 124, 131–32
pragmatic function of metaphor 4, 5, 10–13, 25–26, 59, 64, 68, 79, 81–83, 88–89, 112, 113, 118, 123, 129, 131–32, 134, 136, 146, 149, 155–56, 183–84
prejudice *see* the understanding; *see also* Gadamer, Hans-Georg

primordial 109–12, 116, 117, 141, 164
Pythagoras 52

Quintilian, Marcus Fabius 41, 42, 43, 44, 46

Ramus, Peter 41, 43, 45, 46
reality 6–8, 12, 24, 38, 53, 62, 77, 100, 104, 108, 114, 120 n. 81, 141, 148–49, 157, 172, 185, 190
reason 11–12, 16, 17, 20, 24, 37, 38, 39, 43–55, 59, 62, 64, 67–68, 71–72, 73, 74, 76, 83, 89, 92, 94–95, 96, 102, 104, 131, 133, 139, 169, 171, 174, 183–84
  rationality 16, 38–39, 61, 67–68, 72
  rational animal 16, 35, 38–39, 61, 67, 80, 82
reference *see* semantics
relative 4, 6, 7, 12, 18, 59, 69, 71, 79, 83, 87, 112, 113, 137, 178, 183, 185–86, 189, 190
  relative function of metaphor 64, 69, 79, 112, 178
relativism 6, 7, 18, 21–22, 25, 60–62, 68–69, 117, 168, 174, 183–85, 189
religion 54, 60, 89, 130, 143, 151 n. 37, 188
representation 3, 15, 39, 52, 54, 72–76, 82, 95, 131–32, 155, 167, 171, 173, 176
  Vorstellung 72–74
  image 15, 20, 51, 53, 58 n. 109, 69–71, 76, 79, 92, 95–96, 101, 170
  phonetic image 69–70, 184, 189
revelation 108, 109, 112, 117, 164
  poetic 87, 88, 103–04, 109–13, 116, 123, 134, 149, 164–65, 175
rhetoric 1, 3, 4, 5, 20, 23, 32–35, 37–38, 40–41, 60–63, 76, 78, 107, 108, 113, 133, 136–37, 146–49, 155, 175, 177–78, 188, 189
  persuasion 23, 31, 35–36, 38, 40
  rhetorical consensus *see* consensus
  rhetorician 32, 41
  rhetorical schools 32, 34
Ricoeur, Paul xi, 4, 5, 11, 12–13, 18, 32, 40, 66, 87–89, 101–02, 104, 105–18, 123, 136, 146, 149, 159, 164, 172, 186
Ritschl, F. W. 64, 65
Ritter, Henning 125
Robinson, Edward 100
Rorty, Richard 4, 62, 66
Rothacker, Erich 126, 128, 135
Rousseau, Jean-Jacques 44–45, 46, 70, 152 n. 98, 163, 168

Safranski, Rüdiger 64, 72
Sartre, Jean-Paul 120 n. 81, 121 n. 122, 157–58
Saussure, Ferdinand de 22, 131, 158, 163, 176
Savage, Robert 127–29, 133, 152 n. 71
Scheler, Max 90, 147
Schelling, Friedrich Wilhelm Joseph von 13–14, 46
schematism *see* judgement
Schopenhauer, Arthur 59, 72–76

Schrift, Alan D. 61
science 18–19, 64, 69, 81–82, 90, 92–94, 97, 105–06, 120 n. 78, 138, 140, 160, 162, 186, 187, 190
semantics 25, 27, 83, 146, 155–57, 168, 172, 178
  change 2, 7–8, 22–26, 175–78, 184–90
  of metaphor 27, 32, 117, 155, 157, 168, 172
  origin of meaning 117
  reference 174
  semantic shifts *see* semantics: change
  surplus and decay of meaning 155–56, 172, 176–77, 178, 155–56, 172, 176–78
  undecidability 22, 26, 155–78, 185
semiology 161
sign 131, 171
Semino, Elena 17
sensible 12, 53, 55, 58 n. 119, 102, 167, 170
  non-sensible 102
  sensory 19–20, 169–70
  supersensible 12, 53, 55, 58 n. 119, 167, 170
Shelley, Percy Bysshe 46
Sherry, Richard 31
Silesius, Angelus 111–12
Socrates 38, 133, 136
Sommer, Manfred 143
Spivak, Gayatri Chakravorty 159–62, 164, 168
Steen, Gerard 17
Stingelin, Martin 69, 70, 71
structuralism 157–59, 168
  structural linguistics 9, 158–59, 161
style 37, 62–63
  stylistic analysis 15, 61
subjective 20, 74, 93, 148
substitution *see* the figurative: logic of
synchrony 8, 20, 21, 158, 177, 185

technology 138–40, 143, 145–47, 149, 186
teleology 140, 147–48
terminus a quo 90, 95, 96, 100, 101, 106
terminus ad quem 90, 95, 96, 97, 100
theology 44, 53, 64, 112, 125, 143
theoretical expectations, frame of 129, 132, 133
Third Reich 23, 175
  see also Germany: National Socialist
the trace *see* Derrida, Jacques
transference *see* the figurative: logic of
  translation xi, 4, 5, 15, 25, 31, 32, 36, 40, 70, 74, 80, 100, 107, 108, 120 n. 81, 124, 127, 130, 133, 157, 163, 174, 178, 189
tropes, literary *see* the figurative
truth ix, 3–4, 15, 24, 38–41, 44, 45, 46–47, 49, 59–83, 89, 94, 98, 102, 103, 104, 109–13, 115–17, 123–24, 130, 134, 136, 137–40, 146, 147, 160, 162, 164, 165, 168–69, 177, 183–86, 189–90
  correspondence theory 38, 40, 64, 76–79
  divine 43, 47

historical 123–24, 134, 136, 137–40
metaphoric basis of 4, 31, 59, 79, 102, 124, 165, 168–69, 171, 185, 190
metaphors for 66, 83, 111, 130, 165
propositional 15, 59, 61, 164
truthlikeness 3–4, 19, 22, 31, 37, 39, 40, 43, 47, 55, 59, 72, 76–78, 81, 82, 87, 111, 113, 115, 117, 123, 124, 139, 164, 177, 183–86
verisimilitude 40, 77
Turner, Mark 16

Underhill, James W. 22–25
the understanding 51, 53–54, 95, 96, 101, 115–17, 141, 184, 185
hypotyposis 53–54
intuition 51, 53, 62, 83, 95, 131
prejudice 75, 114–16, 160
pure 51

universal 21, 38, 73, 98, 114, 186
usage 60, 69, 100, 124, 165, 168, 173, 176–78, 188
of language 176–78

Van Den Bosch, Lourens P. 65
Vico, Giambattista 45–46, 70, 107

Wahl, Jean 15, 159, 168
Weimar *see* Germany
will to power *see* Nietzsche
Wolf, Hans-Georg 17
world pictures 9, 158
world-view 22–24, 97

Zavatta, Benedetta 65, 66
Zill, Rüdiger 150–51 n. 33

www.ingramcontent.com/pod-product-compliance
Lightning Source LLC
Chambersburg PA
CBHW050453110426
42743CB00017B/3347